# Hebrew Scripture
# in Patristic Biblical Theory

# Supplements
## to
# Vigiliae Christianae

### Texts and Studies of
### Early Christian Life and Language

*Editors*

J. den Boeft – B.D. Ehrman – J. van Oort
D.T. Runia – C. Scholten – J.C.M. van Winden

VOLUME 114

*The titles published in this series are listed at brill.nl/vcs*

# Hebrew Scripture
# in Patristic Biblical Theory

## Canon, Language, Text

*By*

Edmon L. Gallagher

BRILL

LEIDEN · BOSTON
2012

Library of Congress Cataloging-in-Publication Data

Gallagher, Edmon L.
  Hebrew scripture in patristic bibilical theory : canon, language, text / by Edmon L. Gallagher.
     p. cm. – (Supplements to Vigiliae Christianae, 0920-623X ; v. 114)
  Includes bibliographical references and index.
  ISBN 978-90-04-22633-3 (alk. paper) – ISBN 978-90-04-22802-3 (e-book)
  1. Christian literature, Early–History and criticism. 2. Bible–Criticism, interpretation,
etc.–History–Early church, ca. 30-600. 3. Bible. N.T.–Relation to the Old Testament. 4. Theology,
Doctrinal–History–Early church, ca. 30-600. 5. Fathers of the church–History. I. Title.

BR67.G34 2012
   221.109'015–dc23

BS
500
. G35
2012

2012001749

This publication has been typeset in the multilingual "Brill" typeface. With over 5,100 characters
covering Latin, IPA, Greek, and Cyrillic, this typeface is especially suitable for use in the
humanities. For more information, please see www.brill.nl/brill-typeface.

ISSN 0920-623X
ISBN 978 90 04 22633 3 (hardback)
ISBN 978 90 04 22802 3 (e-book)

This book is printed on acid-free paper.

Printed by Printforce, the Netherlands

# CONTENTS

# PREFACE

The research for this work began in the autumn of 2006, just after I had taken up an appointment as an instructor in Old Testament at Heritage Christian University (Florence, Alabama). It was at that time that I read Julius Africanus' *Letter to Origen,* and Origen's lengthy reply, which gave me the initial idea to research the way that Hebrew scripture featured in arguments about the Bible among the Church Fathers of the second to fifth centuries. I had earlier (Fall 2003) read sections of Origen's *Letter to Africanus* during a course on the Septuagint (LXX) under Adam Kamesar during my second year of study at Hebrew Union College (Cincinnati), so I had a basic familiarity with the correspondence. But only in 2006 did I read the full text of both letters and thereby realize how important the Hebrew Bible was for both Africanus and Origen.

My six years at Heritage Christian University have been rewarding in many ways. For a small religious school focused mostly on undergraduate education, it has been unusually conducive to research and writing. I appreciate my academic dean, William R. Bagents, for limiting my course load while I completed this research project. My colleagues in biblical studies, Jeremy W. Barrier and Nathan B. Daily, have constantly stimulated (better, provoked!) my thinking on a number of issues, for which I am grateful. The conversations and debates have improved my scholarship. My students have also taught me how to present my views in an effective manner and to get to the point. The Overton Memorial Library has served my scholarship admirably; the librarian Jamie Cox does an amazing job of keeping up with publications on a limited budget. Finally, Ashley Hudson, our faculty secretary, performed some tedious proofreading tasks in an outstanding manner, for which I thank her.

In 2010, I submitted a version of this work to the faculty of the graduate program at Hebrew Union College as a doctoral thesis. I owe the greatest debt to my advisor, Prof. Adam Kamesar, for his guidance and example of scholarship. Prof. Richard Sarason, second reader for the dissertation, provided helpful critique at many points, for which I am grateful. I also thank Prof. David Aaron (HUC), Dr. Michael Graves (Wheaton), and Dr. Adam McCollum (Hill Museum & Manuscript Library) for reading some or all of the dissertation and offering comments. Some portions of the dissertation have been expanded and are being published elsewhere; what is here presented has been revised, sometimes slightly, sometimes substantially. I am very grateful to the editorial board of the Supplements to Vigiliae Christianae for accepting this work into their series and for improving it through their helpful editorial suggestions.

My family has constantly supported me in my research, though none of them is really very interested in what Origen or Jerome or Augustine thinks about the Hebrew Bible. Neither am I overly interested in pharmacy, the profession that both of my parents and my sister (and her husband) all share. But truly I can say that no set of parents ever encouraged their son's interests more than mine; words on paper can hardly do justice to the appreciation I feel for them. Two of my children were born during the time that I was working on this project, and my oldest was already two years old when I turned to it. They have blessed me in countless ways; needless to say, increased speed in research and writing has not been one of them. More than all, I thank my wife, who has brought joy to my life beyond measure. To her I dedicate this book.

### Note on Citations, Abbreviations, Editions, Translations

I have used the abbreviations and citation method outlined in *The SBL Handbook of Style for Ancient Near Eastern, Biblical, and Early Christian Studies* (ed. P.H. Alexander, et al.; Peabody, Mass., 1999). The footnotes present an abbreviated referencing system, while full publication information in SBL style is found in the bibliography. I have tried to follow it for abbreviations of journals and reference works, as well as ancient works covered by it. The recent volumes of ancient Jewish inscriptions are not included in the SBL Handbook; they are herein abbreviated according to scholarly custom thus:

*IJudO*   *Inscriptiones Judaicae Orientis*, 3 vols. (Tübingen: Mohr [Siebeck], 2004).
          Vol: 1: *Eastern Europe*, ed. D. Noy, A. Panayotov, and H. Bloedhorn.
          Vol. 2: *Kleinasien*, ed. W. Ameling.
          Vol. 3: *Syria and Cyprus*, ed. D. Noy and H. Bloedhorn.
*JIGRE*   *Jewish Inscriptions of Graeco-Roman Egypt*, ed. W. Horbury and D. Noy
          (Cambridge: Cambridge University Press, 1992).
*JIWE*    *Jewish Inscriptions of Western Europe*, 2 vols., ed. D. Noy (Cambridge: Cambridge University Press, 1993–1995).

I have checked all citations of Greek literature through the *Thesaurus linguae graecae*, and all citations of Latin literature through the *Library of Latin Texts* (Brepols). Usually I have not considered it necessary to give a specific reference to a modern edition of these works, though sometimes I have given such a reference for one reason or another. Those editions are listed in the bibliography below under the editor's name, except for the LCL edition of Philo, listed under his name. When the most recent edition of a patristic work has been that of Migne (PG or PL), I have always provided the exact reference in the text based on volume and column numbers.

For editions of rabbinic texts, one may consult H.L. Strack and G. Stemberger, *Introduction to the Talmud and Midrash* (trans. M. Bockmuehl; Minneapolis: Fortress, 1991). Much of the main literature has now been translated into English by Jacob Neusner and his associates.

Most of the translations offered in the text are my own; these do not aim at beauty but simply at helping the reader understand the thought of the ancient writer. I have almost always included both the original text and a translation. I have tried to follow the orthography and punctuation of the various editions used to access the Greek and Latin authors, even when it might make for inconsistencies within this book (e.g., Latin 'u' or 'v'; both appear). Occasionally, the need arose to transliterate Hebrew words, for which I employed a simplified system.

# CHAPTER ONE

## INTRODUCTION

Toward the middle of the third century CE, Julius Africanus sent a letter to Origen, chiding the great scholar for employing the Story of Susanna in debate with another Christian.[1] Though the two Greek versions of Daniel used by Christians at the time both included Susanna, Africanus points to several problems with the story, including its absence from the Jewish version of Daniel and the presence of Greek puns in the story, which proves that it is not a translation from Hebrew.[2] For these reasons, according to Africanus, Christians should reject the story as a genuine part of Daniel; indeed, they should consider it spurious (κίβδηλος) and a recent fabrication (νεωτερικὸς καὶ πεπλασμένος; § 2).[3] Origen responds with a detailed refutation of each of Africanus' points, especially the suggestions that the Christian OT should mimic the Jewish Bible and that the Story of Susanna could not have been written in Hebrew. The sophisticated argumentation of these two early Christian biblical critics has impressed their modern counterparts: Walther Reichardt hailed Africanus' letter as a model of philological research, while Gilles Dorival declared Origen's letter to have few rivals in the history of biblical studies.[4]

---

[1] The most recent edition of the correspondence is N. de Lange (ed.), *Origène, La Lettre à Africanus sur l'histoire de Suzanne*, in *Origène, Philocalie, 1–20: Sur les Écritures*, SC 302 (ed. M. Harl; Paris, 1983), 469–578; on the date of the correspondence, see pp. 498–501. For a biographical sketch of Africanus, see *Iulius Africanus Chronographiae: The Extant Fragments*, GCS NF 15 (ed. M. Wallraff; trans. W. Adler; Berlin, 2007), xiii–xvii; W. Adler, "Sextus Julius Africanus and the Roman Near East in the Third Century," *JTS* 55 (2004): 520–550.

[2] On the relationship between LXX-Daniel, which concludes with Susanna, and Theodotion-Daniel, which begins with Susanna, see [R.]T. McLay, *The OG and Th Versions of Daniel* (Atlanta, 1996). See also now C. Leisering, *Susanna und der Sündenfall der Ältesten* (Berlin, 2008). The arguments of Africanus receive extensive treatment in chapters 2 and 3 below.

[3] For the paragraph divisions of the letters of Africanus and Origen, I rely solely on those found in de Lange's edition, cited above in n. 1. These, being smaller, are much more convenient than the older divisions.

[4] See W. Reichardt, *Die Briefe des Sextus Juilius Africanus an Aristides und Origenes*, TU 34/3 (Leipzig, 1909), 63: "Das Muster einer philologisch-kritischen Untersuchung möchte man den knappen und doch so inhaltreichen Brief des Africanus an Origenes nennen." Compare the similar evaluation of Africanus' letter by R.M. Grant, "Historical Criticism in the

This correspondence provides a fascinating glimpse at how some ancient Christians gauged the importance of Hebrew scripture for the Church. Origen and Africanus, along with virtually all Greek-speaking (and Latin-speaking) Christians of their day, used the various Greek translations of the Hebrew Bible that collectively were known as the Septuagint. Moreover, they shared with their contemporary Christians the sense that the Septuagint was the authoritative form of the OT for the Church, either by virtue of its inspiration or simply by tradition. However, Origen and Africanus also recognized that the status of the Septuagint as a translation meant that it was in an important sense unoriginal and that the Hebrew form of their scriptures demanded some attention. For Origen, this acknowledgment bore fruit particularly (but not exclusively) in his massive multi-columned Bible known as the *Hexapla*, which enabled ready comparison between the traditional Greek Bible of the Church and the traditional Hebrew Bible of the Synagogue. For Africanus, we have seen that his letter to Origen expresses concern that the traditional Greek text of Daniel should conform largely to the Hebrew text extant among Jews.

In light of this appreciation for Hebrew scripture in the work of Origen and Africanus, the present study explores how pervasive such a concern was in patristic literature more broadly. That is, here we are interested in uncovering some of the ways that Hebrew scripture featured in patristic biblical theory. This wording is deliberate. On the one hand, we will investigate, not the practice of exegesis, but the way the Fathers conceptualized their OT. The many excellent studies of patristic exegesis have disclosed important details regarding how the Fathers went about the business of interpreting their scripture. That is not the focus of this study; it is hoped, however, that some of the conclusions reached here will contribute toward the further illumination of patristic biblical interpretation. Rather, we concentrate here on patristic biblical theory, that is, the way the Fathers thought about their Bible. On the other hand, the term 'Hebrew scripture' indicates both that our study concerns that part of the Christian Bible that is shared with Jews (= OT) and that our particular focus is on its original language. More specifically, we wish to examine how the Fathers thought about the original language of their OT and what consequences this had for the OT itself.

The following four chapters divide easily into three sections, corresponding to the three words in the subtitle of this monograph. First, we turn our

---

Ancient Church," *JR* 25 (1945): 183–196 (190, 191–192). Dorival's comment on Origen's letter is found in "Origène, témoin des textes de l'Ancien Testament," in J.-M. Auwers and A. Wénin (eds.), *Lectures et relectures de la Bible* (Leuven, 1999), 351–366 (357).

attention to the canon of the OT. Chapter Two seeks to bring some clarity to the options available in early Christianity with regard to the criteria of canonicity; Chapter Three advances an original proposal for interpreting the patristic discussion of canon as in some ways a reflection on the status of scripture as originally composed in Hebrew. Next, the brief Chapter Four treats patristic conceptions of the nature of the Hebrew language, an under-explored topic, especially in comparison to the corresponding discussion of Jewish views now capturing scholarly attention. Finally, the long concluding chapter considers patristic textual scholarship and the role of Hebrew scripture in adjudicating among the various textual forms of scripture available to the Fathers. The general result of the entire study finds that Hebrew scripture featured much more prominently in the Christian imagination than hitherto realized.

This is not to deny that Greek scripture played a more direct role than the Hebrew text in the reception of the Bible among the Fathers. Studies addressing the impact of the Septuagint on Early Judaism and Christianity have emphasized its often crucial role in ancient biblical interpretation, as well as in matters pertaining to the text and canon of the OT.[5] Not infrequently Jewish authors such as Philo and Christian authors generally treated the Greek translation as if it were the original text; they developed elaborate models for understanding the nature of the translation, models which served to justify their use of it. By declaring the LXX inspired by God as a translation, these Jewish and Christian authors permitted themselves to ignore the Hebrew text in practice.

Nevertheless, these same Jewish and Christian authors admitted that the LXX, though inspired, was in fact a translation, so that before the Greek text became scripture, the Hebrew text pre-existed it. In some cases, this had important bearing on exegesis, especially for rather technical matters such as etymologies, or the correct form of numbers in the Bible (cf. Augustine, *Civ.* 15.10–14). Though very few Christians put forth the effort to learn Hebrew to any great extent, a larger number did seek out information about the Hebrew text and its interpretation which could aid their own exegesis.[6]

---

[5] On the place of the LXX in Christianity, see, e.g., G. Dorival, M. Harl, O. Munnich, *La Bible grecque des Septante* (Paris, 1988), 289–334; C. Mondésert (ed.), *Le monde grec ancien et la Bible* (Paris, 1984); M. Hengel, *The Septuagint as Christian Scripture* (Grand Rapids, 2002). For the LXX in Philo, see A. Kamesar, "Biblical Interpretation in Philo," in Kamesar (ed.), *The Cambridge Companion to Philo* (Cambridge, 2009), 65–91; and for its place in Judaism more broadly, see T. Rajak, *Translation and Survival* (Oxford, 2009).

[6] See references below, ch. 5.

Besides these matters of exegesis, which have been studied by a number of scholars, how else might Hebrew scripture have played a role in the way the Fathers thought about the Bible? Origen and Africanus seem to have thought that Hebrew scripture had important implications for the correct OT text and canon. Was this view shared by other Christians? Did any of the Fathers think of Hebrew as a holy language in a way similar to the contemporary Rabbis? These questions direct the present study. Without seeking to be exhaustive, we will explore some of the ways that acknowledgment of the original language of the OT shaped the biblical theory of some Fathers.

## THE CANON OF SCRIPTURE

We will begin by studying the OT canon, a topic of perennial interest for scholars, but especially so in the last several decades. Because this topic has generated frequent controversies, not least over the definition of terms, some prefatory remarks about the nature of our study may benefit the reader. We have already seen some of the ways Africanus and Origen endeavored to demarcate Jewish writings that they considered sacred from others which were not. These two early Christian scholars confronted a variety of Jewish literature that offered theological potential but could also present heterodox teachings. What is more, they lived at a time when the distinction between these two possibilities was not so clearly delineated as it would become. While many Christians may not have reflected on this difficulty, their correspondence reveals that Origen and Africanus approached the problem after careful deliberation and with judicious arguments.

By the time Origen and Africanus exchanged letters, the shape of the Jewish Bible had found widespread agreement. The process by which this agreement came about has long ignited scholarly interest and is now receiving renewed attention.[7] Several recent studies have sought to track the development of the Hebrew scriptures and their reception as authoritative during

[7] For a recent overview of the history of the debate in modern times, see G. Dorival, "La formation du canon biblique de l'Ancien Testament," in E. Norelli (ed.), *Recueils normatifs et canons dans l'Antiquité* (Prahins, 2004), 83–112. As examples of the variety of approaches currently pursued, see the essays in L.M. McDonald and J.A. Sanders (eds.), *The Canon Debate* (Peabody, Mass., 2002); J.-M. Auwers and H.J. de Jonge (eds.), *The Biblical Canons*, BETL 163 (Leuven, 2003); C.A. Evans and E. Tov (eds.), *Exploring the Origins of the Bible* (Grand Rapids, 2008).

the formative stages of composition and collection.[8] Some scholars have pointed to the era of the Maccabean uprising and the establishment of the Hasmonean dynasty as the time when there emerged a scriptural collection that closely resembles the Jewish Bible as the Rabbis would later define it.[9] Others have sought to minimize the level of stabilization in the Jewish canon at this early date, instead emphasizing its fluid boundaries until it was definitively settled during the first couple centuries of the common era.[10] However one wishes to conceive of the early stages in what is often termed the 'canonical process' of Hebrew scripture, few of these fascinating issues will receive treatment here.

---

[8] Recent works that rely heavily on external data, such as cross-cultural comparisons and archaeology, to explain the emergence of the biblical canon include P.R. Davies, *Scribes and Schools* (Louisville, 1998); W.M. Schniedewind, *How the Bible Became a Book* (Cambridge, 2004); D.M. Carr, *Writing on the Tablet of the Heart* (Oxford, 2005); K. van der Toorn, *Scribal Culture and the Making of the Hebrew Bible* (Cambridge, Mass., 2007). Other scholars have focused more on internal evidence for the 'canonical process,' i.e., indications within the biblical text for an intentional shaping of the material resulting in the present, canonical form of the books, or even resulting in the canon as a whole; for an introduction, see C.G. Bartholomew, et al. (eds.), *Canon and Biblical Interpretation* (Grand Rapids, 2006); S.B. Chapman, *The Law and the Prophets* (Tübingen, 2000), who begins with a lengthy survey of previous scholarship (1–70).

[9] This Maccabean dating for the emergence of the (at least, incipient) Jewish canon is argued by Davies, *Scribes*, 169–182; A. van der Kooij, "Canonization of Ancient Hebrew Books and Hasmonean Politics," in Auwers and de Jonge, *Biblical Canons*, 27–38; Carr, *Writing*, 253–272; van der Toorn, *Scribal Culture*, 233–264. These works allow for the canon still to be 'open' until the rabbinic period (though see below for cautions against this type of phrasing). Scholars who see a sharply defined canon in the second century BCE include R. Beckwith, *The Old Testament Canon of the New Testament Church* (Grand Rapids, 1985); S.Z. Leiman, *The Canonization of Hebrew Scripture* (Hamden, Conn., 1976); D.N. Freedman, "Canon of the OT," in K.R. Crim (ed.), *IDBSup* (Nashville, 1976), 130–136; E.E. Ellis, *The Old Testament in Early Christianity* (Tübingen, 1991), 1–6. For an (unconvincing) argument that the *text* of the MT was stabilized as a result of the success of the Maccabean revolt, see S. Kreuzer, "From 'Old Greek' to the Recensions: Who and What Caused the Change of the Hebrew Reference Text of the Septuagint," in W. Kraus and R.G. Wooden (eds.), *Septuagint Research* (Atlanta, 2006), 225–237.

[10] Cf. A.C. Sundberg, *The Old Testament of the Early Church* (Cambridge, Mass., 1964), 113–128; D. Barthélemy, "L'État de la Bible juive depuis le début de notre ère jusqu'à la deuxième révolte contre Rome (131–135)," in J.-D. Kaestli and O. Wermelinger (eds.), *Le Canon de l'Ancien Testament: Sa formation et son histoire* (Geneva, 1984), 9–45; J.A. Sanders, "Canon: Hebrew Bible," in D.N. Freedman (ed.), *Anchor Bible Dictionary* (New York, 1992), 1.837–852 (843); E. Ulrich, "The Canonical Process, Textual Criticism, and Latter Stages in the Composition of the Bible," in M. Fishbane and E. Tov (eds.), *Sha'arei Talmon* (Winona Lake, Ind., 1992), 267–291, repr. in Ulrich, *The Dead Sea Scrolls and the Origins of the Bible* (Grand Rapids, 1999), 51–78; L.M. McDonald, *The Biblical Canon* (Peabody, Mass., 2007), 186–189.

The reason for mostly bypassing this discussion is that the ancient sources relevant to the period permit little insight into the reasons favoring one document's authoritative status over that of another. Philip Davies begins his book on the topic with the unassailable assertion, "The first thing to be said on the subject of canonizing the Hebrew scriptures, then, is that there is too little data."[11] The present study begins at a point when there is more data, in the form of statements of principle similar to those of Africanus and Origen already noted; but, this decision to begin with such statements of principle necessarily entails that our investigation will start more-or-less at the end, when the shape of the Hebrew Bible was practically a settled issue.

The time period covered by our study also allows us actually to use the term 'canon' to describe our subject. John Barton has shown that incompatible theories of canonization generally derive from incompatible definitions of the term 'canon' more than any disagreement on what actually took place historically. If one defines 'canon' as a (potentially open-ended) collection of authoritative documents, one will date canonization early; if one defines 'canon' as a definitively closed list of authoritative documents, one will date it late. In this way, "the term 'canon'," in Barton's words, "has merely darkened counsel."[12] Eugene Ulrich advises against using the term 'canon' in this context for anything other than "a closed list of books that have been considered, debated, sifted, and accepted."[13] The present study will be concerned with the period when this had taken place in Judaism and was well under way in Christianity. Our goal will be to illuminate the grounds of the "considering, debating, sifting, and accepting," and one way of proceeding will be to examine the several lists of OT books transmitted to us. Since these individual lists, though each differing in some ways, were intended to 'catalogue' (cf. Eusebius, *Hist. eccl.* 4.26.12) the complete and authoritative collection of OT books, at least as accepted by the authors who transmitted them, we will be justified in speaking of the 'canon' even on a very strict definition of the term.

---

[11] Davies, *Scribes*, 1; see also B.S. Childs, *Introduction to the Old Testament as Scripture* (Philadelphia, 1979), 67, who summarizes his discussion with the statement: "the Jewish canon was formed through a complex historical process which is largely inaccessible to critical reconstruction."

[12] J. Barton, *Holy Writings, Sacred Text* (Louisville, 1997), 1–34; the quotation is from p. 15.

[13] E. Ulrich, "The Notion and Definition of Canon," in McDonald and Sanders, *Canon Debate*, 21–35; quotation from p. 34. For a recent challenge to this way of defining the biblical canon, see S.B. Chapman, "The Canon Debate: What It Is and Why It Matters," *Journal of Theological Interpretation* 4 (2010): 273–294.

Barton's work also highlights another issue important in the present context. His own book attempts in part to investigate the texts actually used as scripture, regardless of which documents a particular author would list as scripture. Indeed, according to Barton, "lists bear no exact relation to what may be called the 'effective' canon of most Christian writers."[14] One discovers this 'effective' canon in scriptural citations, which reveal a threefold classification among books used frequently, used some, or used hardly at all.

> But if we ask how these writers described their attitude to the texts they used, we are much more likely to find an either/or mentality [i.e. a twofold classification], because in each case a writer would need to take up a definite position.[15]

The 'effective' canon in early Christianity is an important and stimulating issue, but it is not the topic of our investigation. We will be concerned, rather, with the 'either/or mentality' and the reasons behind each author's 'definite position.' We are interested here in the arguments favoring certain books instead of others, the theoretical positions as to the types of documents a canon should comprise.

Most of all, we will be concerned with the criteria used to separate one document from another in terms of the OT canon in patristic literature. The situation in Judaism will provide some background, but, as noted above, Jewish writers do not begin to state their principles of canonicity until very late in the 'canonical process.' Indeed, the earliest such statement comes from Josephus (*C. Ap.* 1.37–43) in the very passage in which he says that the 22-book Jewish canon had been settled for a long age. By correlating his statements with others in Jewish literature we could infer a considerable history to the criterion first voiced by him (one of antiquity, to be discussed in the next chapter), but this line is not pursued in the present study. Rather the Jewish position serves only to set the stage for our lengthy examination of Christian views. However, we will find that the Jewish Bible, though not the Jewish criteria of canonicity, exerted a significant influence on the ways Christians defined their OT.

Very early, some Christian writers determined that the major principle of OT canonicity was the acceptance of a particular book into the Jewish canon. The first record of any Christian's giving thought to the proper collection of OT books involves the writer Melito of Sardis in seeking out

---

[14] Barton, *Holy Writings*, 32.
[15] Barton, *Holy Writings*, 22.

and transmitting what is essentially the Jewish Bible (cf. Eusebius, *Hist. eccl.* 4.26.12–14). We have already seen that Africanus criticizes Origen for using as authentic scripture something not to be found among the Jews. Chapter Two will elaborate on these points and uncover other evidence for what we will designate the 'synagogal criterion' of OT canonicity.

On the other hand, Origen's response to Africanus presents an alternative viewpoint on the relationship between the Christian OT and the Jewish Bible. Origen holds that the Church is in no way bound by Jewish decisions of canonicity. While study of their writings is most informative and exegetically enlightening, the Jews have no authority to decide what Christians should deem as scripture. Our examination of his position in Chapter Two will demonstrate that he was an early exponent of the 'ecclesiastical criterion' of OT canonicity, which posited that the Church's Bible should encompass those books that it finds useful, especially in a liturgical context. In practical terms, this criterion leads to the acceptance of the entire Jewish canon, plus a small collection of literature considered non-canonical in the Synagogue. The conflicting principles of the 'synagogal criterion' and the 'ecclesiastical criterion' shape the debate about the contours of the Christian OT into the fifth century, when we find Jerome and Augustine on opposite sides of the issue.

The influence of the Jewish Bible on Christian canonical theory has not gone unnoticed by scholars, but the distinct lines between the positions we have just described are sometimes blurred.[16] The analysis presented here advances the discussion by framing the issue in terms of considered criteria that were themselves the object of debate. Jerome and Augustine differed on the extent of the OT canon, not because one or both of them failed to perceive the defining criteria of the canon, but because they disagreed precisely on what those criteria should be.[17] Moreover, we will attempt in this discussion to clarify the oft-debated canonical views associated with Origen, Jerome, and others.

---

[16] E g., see O. Wermelinger, "Le canon des latins au temps de Jérôme et d'Augustin," in Kaestli and Wermelinger, *Canon de l'Ancien Testament*, 153–196, who speaks of the same two perspectives we have just noted, but immediately says, "Ces deux perspectives ne sont pas contradictoires" (195).

[17] The opposite viewpoint may be illustrated from J. Barton's characterization of Jerome's position as one based on a misplaced allegiance to the Hebrew tradition, so that his call for a 'return' to the Hebrew canon arose from a misunderstanding of the nature of the canon; see "Canons of the Old Testament," in J. Day (ed.), *Text in Context* (Oxford, 2000), 200–222 (207–208). Also, Ellis, *Old Testament*, 19, discusses the disagreements over the OT canon in the late fourth century under the rubric 'custom versus judgment,' as if those Fathers following 'custom' were doing so unreflectively.

Chapter Three will build on this foundation by establishing the existence of a third criterion of OT canonicity employed in the ancient Church, one that has not previously received its share of attention. Looking back once again at the correspondence between Origen and Africanus, we realize that both authors singled out the original language of composition of Susanna as potentially decisive for its canonical status. In response to Africanus' assertion that Susanna should be rejected because it was not written in Hebrew, Origen demands to see the evidence for the story's original language. He proceeds to build a case for Hebrew as the language of composition because otherwise, as he himself says, the document could not be accepted into the canon.

These rather explicit and bold statements affirming the 'Hebrew criterion' of canonicity have not elicited much comment from scholars, probably because of the overriding emphasis on the 'effective' canon, as Barton called it. However, the correspondence displays clearly that no matter what literature Africanus and Origen found valuable, a document had to meet certain criteria to form an acknowledged part of their OT. The way both Africanus and Origen assume that the Hebrew criterion is legitimate and widely acknowledged compels us to search out further evidence for it in patristic literature. The investigation proves fruitful. Hebrew's prominent position in the consciousness of Christians with regard to the origins of their OT finds expression in at least two common motifs. First, the lofty status of the Septuagint necessitates that the OT should comprise only Greek translations of the Hebrew Bible. Second, the ubiquity of the number 22 as encompassing the books of the OT connects these books directly to the Hebrew alphabet. The ferocity with which Christians maintained these traditions, especially the first, suggests that they held the idea of Hebrew scripture in no little esteem.

## THE LANGUAGE OF SCRIPTURE

Being alerted to the theoretical importance of Hebrew scripture in early Christian conceptions of the OT canon, we next pursue the question as to what these Christians thought about the Hebrew language itself. If they considered composition in the Hebrew language to be a necessary criterion for canonicity in their OT, does this attitude reflect any peculiar conceptions about the nature of that language? Or, given the recent scholarly attention to ancient Jewish ideologies of Hebrew, might we find in Christianity similar notions, i.e., that Hebrew is in some way a 'sacred language'? In short, how did the language of Hebrew scripture feature in patristic biblical theory? The fourth chapter focuses on these questions.

The status of Hebrew in ancient Judaism has increasingly attracted scholarly attention. The first half of Chapter Four, then, surveys the results of this work on Hebrew as the 'holy language' (לשון הקדש) of Judaism. This includes a survey of the oft-studied issue of the languages used by Jews in Palestine and outside their homeland from the Persian period to Late Antiquity. Following this, the chapter highlights the more recent scholarship on the status of the Hebrew language in the minds of these Jews, whether they used it regularly or not. Attention focuses on evidence to be gleaned from the Dead Sea Scrolls, inscriptions, coins, and documentary texts, all from the centuries surrounding the turn of the era. The conclusion of this section attempts briefly to delineate some of the particular aspects of the language ideology of the Rabbis.

Scholars have examined Christian ideas about the Hebrew language less intensely than the corresponding Jewish notions. The second half of Chapter Four demonstrates that Christians adopted several features of Jewish ideologies of Hebrew. In fact, the Hebrew criterion itself was a reflection of the general Christian concept of the Hebrew language. Patristic authors routinely classify Hebrew as the primordial language from which all other languages derive, but they also associate Hebrew uniquely with Abraham and his descendants. The diversity of Christian opinion regarding the origins and nature of the Hebrew language caution against painting with too broad a brush; but, usually any patristic discussion of human language needed to deal with the language of scripture. Since the OT features not just Hebrew but also Aramaic, conceptions regarding this latter language also merit consideration in the present context. We will find that Aramaic played virtually no role in patristic biblical theory, but once again Hebrew held a prominent position.

## THE TEXT OF SCRIPTURE

The final chapter focuses on how Hebrew scripture features in the textual theory of the Fathers. The discovery of the Dead Sea Scrolls has stimulated a radical re-evaluation of the development of the text of the Hebrew Bible. The concrete evidence of textual plurality among Hebrew manuscripts before the rabbinic period has contributed toward the formulation of new theories regarding the status of Hebrew textual forms at the turn of the era. Hebrew scrolls like 4QJer[b], which closely matches the LXX Jeremiah even where it deviates from the MT, have renewed scholarly interest in the LXX as a faithful witness to a Hebrew text (if not *the* Hebrew text). For some scholars, these two new pieces of evidence—Hebrew textual plurality and the LXX as a faithful translation—work together to vindicate patristic reliance on the LXX as the Church's Bible. Nevertheless, the role that Hebrew scripture played in the textual theory of the Fathers has not received attention in these discussions of the Fathers use of the LXX.

As a matter of course, patristic authors base their exegesis on the received Greek text, even arguing for the inspiration of this translation in its own right. Once again, we find that this view was inherited from Judaism, especially the *Letter of Aristeas* and Philo, the latter being the first author explicitly to declare the Seventy translators inspired. Moreover, despite the attempts of some scholars to pit Philo's 'pro-LXX' views against what might be designated a 'pro-Hebrew party,' we will see that this involves a misreading of Philo's position as well as that of his 'opponents.' For, Philo conceived of the 'miracle of the LXX' in terms that reveal his own profound understanding that the Hebrew text was correct and authoritative.

The Church Fathers largely echo Philo's sentiments, although their disputes with Jews over the accurate biblical text obliged them to nuance the position somewhat. Scholars have often seen in patristic comments on the OT text an emphasis on the LXX to the exclusion of the Hebrew text. While this analysis accurately reflects Christian practice, a true appreciation for the role of Hebrew in the textual theory of the Fathers requires a closer study of their statements on the relationship between the LXX and its Hebrew *Vorlage*. Chapter Five attempts to sketch in broad outline how the Greek and Latin Fathers incorporated the idea of 'the original Hebrew text' into their textual theory. We will pause to consider at length some Fathers whose positions have proven to be problematic in this regard, such as Origen and Epiphanius. The chapter as a whole will suggest that the Hebrew text remained important and authoritative in theory even for those who ignored it in practice.

As we saw at the beginning of this introduction, Origen and Africanus disagreed on the suitability of Susanna for the Christian OT, but they both agreed that the Hebrew language constituted a valid and decisive criterion in the debate. The goal of this study is to understand the reasons for this agreement by exploring other indications for the importance of Hebrew scripture in Christian biblical theory. The results show that even as the OT became more Christianized through translation and exegesis, the Fathers endeavored to preserve a connection with the origins of the Bible as Hebrew scripture.

# CHAPTER TWO

# THE OLD TESTAMENT CANON IN PATRISTIC BIBLICAL THEORY

As we saw in the Introduction, Origen and Julius Africanus both acknowledge Hebrew scripture to be an important criterion in considering the proper contents of the OT. The full presentation of this view, however, must wait for the next chapter. The present chapter must set the stage for that discussion by identifying other criteria for canonicity discussed in our ancient sources. This is necessary for two reasons: first, we need to be able to distinguish what we will call in Chapter Three 'the Hebrew criterion' from another often confused with it ('the synagogal criterion'); and second, the views of Origen, Africanus, and others merit careful study in the context of these other criteria in order to properly analyze them. Therefore, here we will examine the criteria most often articulated by ancient Christians as they sought to determine the extent of the Old Testament canon. We will briefly begin with Jewish evidence for comparative purposes.

The discussion will focus on the principles consciously employed and debated by the ancients. As we mentioned in the Introduction, this entails that our survey of material will necessarily begin very late in the formation of the Hebrew Bible, at a point when many books were already considered sacred and, indeed, canonical, as a matter of course.[1] The debates about canonicity transmitted to us from Jewish and Christian sources deal almost exclusively with books that we could consider at the 'fringe' of the Bible, especially the wisdom books such as Proverbs, Ecclesiastes, Song of Songs, Wisdom of Solomon, and the Wisdom of Ben Sira. It was in dealing with these books that the ancients attempted to develop principles by which the canonicity of a book could be determined. This chapter will categorize the major criteria articulated by Jews and Christians.

---

[1] For attempts to re-imagine the formative period of the Hebrew Bible, see the recent studies by K. van der Toorn, *Scribal Culture and the Making of the Hebrew Bible* (Cambridge, Mass., 2007); and D.M. Carr, *The Formation of the Hebrew Bible* (Oxford, 2011).

## The Date Criterion

### *Judaism*

Rabbinic literature preserves few comments relating to what may be called 'canonical decisions.' Roger Beckwith's investigation into the relevant passages shows that while biblical books should be pious (as opposed to certain interpretations of the Song of Songs and Ecclesiastes) and harmonious internally and with the rest of the Bible (as opposed to possible readings of Ezekiel, Esther, Proverbs, and Ecclesiastes), these principles were too broad and subjective to play a vital role in determining the canon. In fact, rabbinic testimony gives no definite indication that any book was excluded from the canon based on these reasons, while the books that were discussed in connection with these issues all enjoyed esteem too great to be diminished by alleged contradictions or charges of secularity.[2] In light of these facts, Sid Leiman has sought out the actual criteria that figured in the canonical theory of ancient Jews ("the rabbis, or their immediate predecessors"), and has proposed four.[3] The last three of these principles entailed the exclusion of any document that was not written in Hebrew, that contradicted "*central halakic teachings*," or that was unduly venerated by sectarian groups (e.g. Ben Sira).[4] However, while ancient Jews probably took each of these points into account, the last two of these principles engender the same criticism as those outlined by Beckwith (broad and subjective), with the additional problem that for none of these three ideas can Leiman cite ancient testimony in support. It seems that the Rabbis did not reflect on these principles

---

[2] R. Beckwith, *The Old Testament Canon of the New Testament Church* (Grand Rapids, 1985), 283–291. Beckwith cites all the relevant passages from Mishnah, Tosefta, and the Talmudim, which deal with storing books away or questioning whether they defile the hands. For discussions of the meanings of these expressions, see Beckwith, op. cit., 278–283; S. Zeitlin, "An Historical Study of the Canonization of the Hebrew Scriptures," *PAAJR* 3 (1931–1932): 121–158; repr. in S.Z. Leiman (ed.), *The Canon and Masorah of the Hebrew Bible* (New York, 1974), 164–201 (164–171, 178–184); S.Z. Leiman, *The Canonization of Hebrew Scripture* (Hamden, Conn., 1976), 72–86, 102–120; J. Barton, *Holy Writings, Sacred Text* (Louisville, 1997), 108–121; T.H. Lim, "The Defilement of the Hands as a Principle Determining the Holiness of Scriptures," *JTS* 61 (2010): 501–515.

[3] S.Z. Leiman, "Inspiration and Canonicity: Reflections on the Formation of the Biblical Canon," in E.P. Sanders (ed.), *Jewish and Christian Self-Definition*, vol. 2: *Aspects of Judaism in the Graeco-Roman Period* (Philadelphia, 1981), 56–63. The quotation is from p. 61.

[4] Leiman, "Inspiration," 61–63; Leiman's emphasis. One may compare the article by Zeitlin, "Historical Study," which concludes with an attempt at explaining why certain books (Jubilees, Ben Sira, Tobit, Susanna, Judith) were excluded from the canon (184–199). Zeitlin is forced to resort to conjecture for all but the Book of Ben Sira, for which he cites *t. Yad.* 2.13, which justifies the exclusion of Ben Sira on the basis of the date criterion.

so much as assume them. Rather, the first principle Leiman lists appears to be the only one that ancient Jews consciously and explicitly employed for the purposes of defining their biblical canon—the 'date criterion.'

Some Jewish authors indicate that the date of a work was the single most important factor in determining its canonicity. Josephus is the most prominent of these authors, and his discussion in *Contra Apionem* 1.37–43 is well-known.[5] There, Josephus says that Jewish records post-dating Artaxerxes were not considered of equal weight with the earlier writings, and he connects this *terminus* with the cessation of "the exact succession of the prophets" (§ 41). As others have noted, Josephus does not say that prophecy is what had ceased, but merely the exact succession of prophets.[6] Indeed, Josephus asserts that certain Jews after Artaxerxes did have the gift of prophecy, such as John Hyrcanus (*B.J.* 1.68) and Josephus himself (*B.J.* 3.399–408; 4.625). In light of this, some recent discussion has downplayed the significance of the view that prophecy ended and emphasized that prophecy did continue, at least in some form.[7] However, this re-interpretation has not gone unchallenged, and Shaye Cohen has recently written that "[b]y the second century BCE, classical prophecy had ceased," thus making room for "apocalypse."[8] Moreover, scholars have noted that Josephus typically reserves the title προφήτης for the biblical prophets, using μάντις for more recent inspired persons.[9]

---

[5] See especially S. Mason, "Josephus and His Twenty-Two Book Canon," in L.M. McDonald and J.A. Sanders (eds.), *The Canon Debate* (Peabody, Mass., 2002), 110–127, which is a revision of the author's essay, "Josephus on Canon and Scripture," in M. Saebø (ed.), *Hebrew Bible/Old Testament: The History of Its Interpretation* I.1 (Göttingen, 1996), 217–235; also see the commentary by J.M.G. Barclay, *Against Apion*, vol. 10 of *Flavius Josephus: Translation and Commentary*, ed. S. Mason (Leiden, 2007), 28–31; and R. Gray, *Prophetic Figures in Late Second Temple Jewish Palestine: The Evidence from Josephus* (Oxford, 1993), who situates this passage within the larger tradition of the cessation of prophecy.

[6] E.g. D.E. Aune, *Prophecy in Early Christianity and the Ancient Mediterranean World* (Grand Rapids, 1983), 106; F.E. Greenspahn, "Why Prophecy Ceased," *JBL* 108 (1989): 37–49 (40); though, against this reading of Josephus, see Beckwith, *Old Testament*, 371–372. Barclay, *Against Apion*, 30–31 n. 169 presents a brief but balanced survey of evidence.

[7] See the works cited in G.L. Green, "'As for Prophecies, They Will Come to an End': 2 Peter, Paul and Plutarch on 'The Obsolescence of Oracles'," *JSNT* 82 (2001): 107–122 (107–108 n. 2).

[8] S.J.D. Cohen, *From the Maccabees to the Mishnah*[2] (Louisville, 2006), 187. Additionally, contrast Greenspahn, "Prophecy," who affirms the continuation of prophecy, with B.D. Sommer, "Did Prophecy Cease? Evaluating a Reevaluation," *JBL* 115 (1996): 31–47, who criticizes Greenspahn and asserts that "the view that Jews in the Second Temple period viewed prophecy as having ceased" is preferable to the alternative (32). Beckwith, *Old Testament*, 369–376, also advocates the view set forth by Sommer.

[9] See D.E. Aune, "The Use of ΠΡΟΦΗΤΗΣ in Josephus," *JBL* 101 (1982): 419–421, and the

Thus, it is reasonable to connect Josephus' claims in *C. Ap.* 1.41 to the tradition attested elsewhere that the type of prophecy known in the Bible had come to an end early in the Second Temple Period. This doctrine is clearly attested in some rabbinic passages, e.g., *t. Sotah* 13.3: "When the latter prophets died, that is, Haggai, Zechariah, and Malachi, then the Holy Spirit came to an end in Israel."[10] The passage continues by saying that the 'heavenly voice' (*bat qol*) is still available, but the current generation is unworthy of the 'Holy Spirit.' Another passage lists prophecy as one of the five aspects of the First Temple missing from the Second Temple (*b. Yoma* 21b), and elsewhere it is declared that the book of Ben Sira does not defile the hands because of the time period in which it was written (*t. Yad.* 2.13).[11] Though Samuel Sandmel denied that this view was operative outside rabbinic circles, it does seem implicit in three passages in 1 Maccabees (4:46; 9:27; 14:41), which speak of the absence of prophets.[12] Moreover, the same chronology is implied in the tradition of Ezra's rewriting the 24 books following the exile, a tradition first attested in 4 Ezra 14 at the end of the first century CE. These statements, together with the evidence from rabbinic literature, show that, in the words of John Barton, "prophecy was widely believed to be a thing of the past."[13]

---

literature cited there. While Aune himself tries to overturn this evidence, his examples are few and dubious. See also the discussion in Sommer, "Prophecy," 40. Josephus' practice in this regard may be comparable to that of Philo; cf. Philo's description of himself at *Cher.* 27, and see D.M. Hay, "Philo's View of Himself as an Exegete: Inspired, but not Authoritative," *SPhA* 3 (1991): 40–52.

[10] Translation by J. Neusner, *The Tosefta*, 2 vols. (Peabody, Mass., 2002), 1.885. For the equation of 'Holy Spirit' with the 'spirit of prophecy,' see Str-B 2.126–127; P. Schäfer, *Die Vorstellung vom heiligen Geist in der rabbinischen Literatur* (Munich, 1972), 14–17, 21–26. For other rabbinic references to the end of prophecy, see R. Meyer, προφήτης, *TDNT* 6.812–819; Aune, *Prophecy*, 374 n. 1; Beckwith, *Old Testament*, 369–376; and D.M. Carr, "Canonization in the Context of Community: An Outline of the Formation of the Tanakh and the Christian Bible," in R.D. Weis and D.M. Carr (eds.), *A Gift of God in Due Season* (Sheffield, 1996), 22–64 (51 n. 78). Add to the references cited in these sources *b. B. Bathra* 12a–b.

[11] For a different view of this passage, see G. Veltri, *Libraries, Translations, and 'Canonic' Texts* (Leiden, 2006), 212–213, who takes the statement excluding particular books not chronologically but as "a modal indication on the special matter of how to write the texts."

[12] For discussion, see Meyer, *TDNT* 6.815–816; Aune, *Prophecy*, 104–105; and J. Barton, *Oracles of God* (Oxford, 1986; repr., Oxford, 2007), 107–108. Sandmel's view is given in *Judaism and Christian Beginnings* (New York, 1978), 174.

[13] Barton, *Oracles*, 116. Barton characterizes this statement as a "rough generalization" and admits that there are exceptions. See also the provocative suggestion by van der Toorn, *Scribal Culture*, 252–264, that the notion of a 'canonical era' or 'prophetic era' was a creation of scribes in the third century BCE which inevitably led to the closing of the canon as inclusive only of those books thought to be composed during the 'canonical era.' D.M. Carr, *Writing*

The cessation of prophecy would naturally imply the cessation of the production of scripture, for all canonical books were written by the spirit of prophecy and could be considered prophetic. This applies to those books of the Jewish canon included among the Writings just as much as to those in the Prophets. There is much evidence that Daniel was considered a prophet.[14] David was also a prophet, as was Solomon, and, of course, Moses was the chief of the prophets (Num. 12:6–8; Deut. 34:10–12).[15] Since these prophets were responsible for writing scripture (cf. *b. B. Bathra* 14b–15a), scripture could no longer be produced once prophecy ended, just as Josephus said that the canon could not be expanded once "the exact succession of the prophets" ceased (*C. Ap.* 1.41). In this way, we see that Josephus' date criterion for canonicity is linked to the view that prophecy had ceased around the time of Artaxerxes. We may thus infer, even without explicit testimony, that his chronological limit for inspired literature also had other Jewish adherents.

## Christianity

Did Christians share this view? Greenspahn cites several patristic sources for the idea that prophecy was taken away from the Jews.[16] Most of these passages locate the end of prophecy in the early Christian period, without disclosing whether the authors think of Christian prophets as continuing an unbroken string of prophecy since ancient times, or as reviving the

---

*on the Tablet of the Heart* (Oxford, 2005), 263, suggests that the chronological limit of the 'canonical era' relates to the anti-Hellenism promoted (to some degree) by the Hasmoneans. See now the full study of this issue by L. Stephen Cook, *On the Question of the "Cessation of Prophecy" in Ancient Judaism* (Tübingen, 2011). This work came to my attention too late for me to take advantage of its insights, but apparently Cook argues that ancient Jews did commonly hold the view that 'classical prophecy' had ceased, even if modern scholars do not have to agree with them.

[14] Cf. 4Q174 1–3 II, 3–4; Matt. 24:15; Josephus, *A.J.* 9.267–269; 10.249, 266–267; *b. Meg.* 15a. However, see L. Jacobs, *Structure and Form in the Babylonian Talmud* (Cambridge, 1991), 40–41, who insists that the rabbinic view attributes to Daniel not the spirit of prophecy but "the lesser degree of inspiration known as the 'holy spirit' (*ruaḥ ha-kodesh*), typical of the *Ketuvim.*"

[15] For David, cf. 11QPs^a XXVII. 3–11; Acts 2:25–31; Josephus, *A.J.* 8.109–110; *b. Sotah* 48b; for Solomon, cf. *Sifre Deut.* 1:1; *b. Sotah* 48b. Note that the tradition recorded in *b. B. Bathra* 14b–15a ascribes to Moses the authorship of the Book of Job, in addition to the Pentateuch. For the possibility that Sir. 49:9 classifies Job as a prophet, see A. Goshen-Gottstein, "Ben Sira's Praise of the Fathers: A Canon-Conscious Reading," in R. Egger-Wenzel (ed.), *Ben Sira's God*, BZAW (Berlin, 2002), 235–267 (242). For further references and analysis, see Barton, *Oracles*, 35–37, 39–41; van der Toorn, *Scribal Culture*, 280 n. 24.

[16] Greenspahn, "Prophecy," 42 and nn. 28–30.

ancient form of prophecy.[17] Some Christian authors are more explicit, but the evidence is contradictory. In one passage, Justin says that the Jews never lacked a prophet until Christ came (*Dial.* 52). On the other hand, Lactantius seems to imply that there was a gap between the last prophets and Christ: after asserting that the Israelites resisted the prophetic message, Lactantius writes, *itaque desiit prophetas mittere ad eos. Sed illum filium suum primogenitum* [...] *delabi iussit e caelo* ("therefore he ceased to send them prophets. But he commanded his own son to descend from heaven"; *Inst.* 4.11.7). Augustine does explicitly affirm that there were no prophets between Ezra and the advent of Christ, at which time various prophets appeared, as narrated in the NT (*Civ.* 17.24; 18.45). However, he does not connect this with the closing of the canon, and he later says that the books of the Maccabees, which he knows to have been composed during the 'gap,' are considered canonical not by the Jews but by the Church (*Civ.* 18.36). Obviously his notion of the cessation of prophecy did not lead him to accept the date criterion of canonicity, and Augustine elsewhere says that the only chronological criterion is that the OT documents predate the birth of Jesus.[18] There is no clear patristic understanding that prophecy ceased (or paused) at the time of Artaxerxes, and none of these Christian passages connects the removal of the Holy Spirit from Judaism with the closure of the canon. Even Eusebius, who incorporates Josephus' canon list into his *Historia Ecclesiastica* (3.10.1–5), makes no comment on the date criterion.

On the other hand, the date criterion may be implicit in the widespread tradition that Ezra rewrote the scriptures by inspiration following their destruction by the Babylonians.[19] As noted earlier, 4 Ezra 14:37–48 (ca. 100 CE) provides our earliest extant version of this story. The Rabbis attest

---

[17] Justin, *Dial.* 87; Tertullian, *Adv. Jud.* 13; Origen, *Cels.* 7.8; Athanasius, *Inc.* 40. Origen may know the Jewish tradition, as he writes: Τὸ γὰρ ἅγιον πνεῦμα ὡμολόγηται ἐκείνους [sc. τοὺς Ἰουδαίους] καταλελοιπέναι (*Cels.* 7.8). The use of ὡμολόγηται here could refer to the Jewish 'admission' that they no longer had access to the Holy Spirit.

[18] Cf. the introduction to *Speculum* 22, which is quoted below, p. 53.

[19] See, e.g., Irenaeus, *Haer.* 3.21.2; Clement of Alexandria, *Strom.* 1.22; Tertullian, *Cult. fem.* 1.3; Theodoret, *Comm. Ps.*, prol. 7; Jerome, *Helv.* 7. Further references are given in H.E. Ryle, *The Canon of the Old Testament* (London, 1899), 250–261. Also see J.-D. Kaestli, "Le récit de IV Esdras 14 et sa valeur pour l'histoire du canon de l'Ancien Testament," in Kaestli and O. Wermelinger (eds.), *Le Canon de l'Ancien Testament* (Geneva, 1984), 71–97; and, for the history of the tradition and its influence on the development of modern Pentateuchal criticism, N. Malcom, *Aspects of Hobbes* (Oxford, 2002), 383–431 (for antiquity specifically, 398–401). For the canonical implications of this tradition, see G.W. Anderson, "Canonical and Non-Canonical," in P.R. Ackroyd and C.F. Evans (eds.), *The Cambridge History of the Bible*, vol. 1 (Cambridge, 1970), 113–159 (115–116).

some elements of the tradition,[20] and it is found in pagan polemic against Christians.[21] Typically, patristic authors follow 4 Ezra in attributing to Ezra the restoration of all the scriptures,[22] rather than just the Pentateuch (as do the Rabbis), and so the Christian form of the tradition implies that the OT was complete by Ezra's time. The Fathers do not seem to have always perceived this implication.[23]

## The Synagogal Criterion

It did not take long for Christians to recognize that the Jewish canon did not encompass all the books that Christians considered helpful or edifying. The earliest indications for this recognition are found in Melito of Sardis (ca. 170) and Tertullian (ca. 200).[24] These two early witnesses also attest the two

---

[20] Compare the traditions of Ezra's establishing the Torah and of his re-writing the Torah in 'Assyrian' characters. For references, see L. Ginzberg, *Legends of the Jews*, 7 vols. (Philadelphia, 1909–1938; repr. Philadelphia, 1998), 4.355–356, and the corresponding notes at 6.443–444. The rabbinic passages do not say that Ezra was inspired to perform these tasks.

[21] See the collection of G. Rinaldi, *Biblia Gentium* (Rome, 1989) for the fragments of Julian the Apostate (frg. 189, p. 308) and the anonymous pagan opponent of Macarius of Magnesia (frg. 505, pp. 544–545). The pagan addressed by Macarius in his *Apocritica* (or *Monogenes*) has usually been identified with Porphyry, though other nominations are numerous. For a survey of opinions, see Rinaldi, op. cit., 151–154; and A. Kofsky, *Eusebius of Caesarea Against Paganism* (Leiden, 2000), 19–22. The most recent editor of Macarius argues for his indirect reliance on Porphyry; see R. Goulet, *Macarios de Magnésie: Le Monogénès*, 2 vols. (Paris, 2003), 1.112–149; as well as idem, "Porphyre et Macaire de Magnésie," *StPatr* 15 = TU 128 (1984), 448–452; repr. in *Études sur les Vies de philosophes de l'Antiquité tardive* (Paris, 2001), 295–299; and idem, "Hypothèses récentes sur le traité de Porphyre Contre les chrétiens," in M. Narcy and É. Rebillard (eds.), *Hellénisme et christianisme* (Villeneuve d' Ascq, 2004), 61–109. For a recent alternative view, see E.D. Digeser, "Porphyry, Julian, or Hierocles? The Anonymous Hellene in Makarios Magnēs' Apokritikos," *JTS* 53 (2002): 466–502, who argues for Hierocles. For the fragment of Julian, which has been preserved in the *Contra Julianum* by Cyril of Alexandria (book 5; PG 76.757a), see R. Goulet, "Porphyre et la datation de Moïse," *RHR* 4 (1977): 137–164 (155); repr. in Goulet, *Études*, 245–266 (258); and E. Stein, *Alttestamentliche Bibelkritik in der späthellenistischen Literatur* (Lwow, 1935), 43.

[22] Kaestli questions how far we may say that the Fathers were dependant specifically on 4 Ezra 14 for their version of the legend ("Récit," 72–83).

[23] Some late Fathers did draw out this implication. See the quotations of Leontius and Bede in Ryle, *Canon*, 256.

[24] *Contra* Éric Junod, "La formation et la composition de l'Ancien Testament dans l'Église grecque des quatre premiers siècles," in Kaestli and Wermelinger, *Canon*, 105–134, who cites Justin as the earliest evidence for this perception, based on the lack of citations in Justin's writings from books absent from the Jewish canon. Junod interprets this as apologetic acquiescence on Justin's part (110–111). However, Justin's scriptural citations could also reflect his own convictions about the content of the OT; cf. R. Hennings, *Der Briefwechsel zwischen Augustinus und Hieronymus* (Leiden, 1994), 147–149. Justin himself gives no explanation, and,

different responses which would become paradigmatic for the later period. One position followed Jewish precedent rather closely in determining the canon; the other position accepted a variety of other writings based on their use in the Church.[25] The first position may be called the 'synagogal criterion,' as it represents a Christian attempt to follow the synagogue in matters of the biblical canon. The second position, which we will call the 'ecclesiastical criterion,' will be discussed below.

Tertullian is the earliest Christian author who makes his criterion for canonicity explicit. In his treatise *De cultu feminarum*, Tertullian comments on the value of 1 Enoch as a source for the cohabitation of angels with women (1.3). He is aware that the Jews do not accept 1 Enoch as scripture, which has led some Christians to doubt the document's worth.[26] Tertullian even provides a supposition for why the Jews have rejected it: Enoch lived before the flood, and so anything he wrote would have presumably perished in the deluge.[27] Tertullian himself rejects all this reasoning.

> *Sed cum Enoch eadem scriptura etiam de Domino praedicarit, a nobis quidem nihil omnino reiciendum est, quod pertineat ad nos. Et legimus omnem scripturam aedificationi habilem diuinitus inspirari.*

> But since Enoch in the same scripture preached also concerning the Lord, what pertains to us is most definitely not to be rejected by us. And we read, "all scripture suitable for edification is divinely inspired."

---

in fact, never raises issues of canon (though he does raise textual concerns). On this issue, see O. Skarsaune, "The Question of Old Testament Canon and Text in the Early Greek Church," in Saebø, *Hebrew Bible/Old Testament*, 443–450 (445–446).

[25] Previous scholars have recognized that these were the two basic positions in the Church. See, e.g., the discussions in J. Ruwet, "Duo Textus Origenis de Canone Antiqui Testamenti," *Bib* 2 (1921): 57–60; C. Larcher, *Études sur le livre de la Sagesse* (Paris, 1969), 44–46, 61–63; O. Wermelinger, "Le canon des latins au temps de Jérôme et d'Augustin," in Kaestli and Wermelinger, *Canon*, 153–196 (194–195); Beckwith, *Old Testament*, 2; E.E. Ellis, *The Old Testament in Early Christianity* (Tübingen, 1991), 6–36.

[26] On Tertullian's attitude toward Enoch throughout his career, see J.C. VanderKam, "1 Enoch, Enochic Motifs, and Enoch in Early Christian Literature," in VanderKam and W. Adler (eds.), *The Jewish Apocalyptic Heritage in Early Christianity*, CRINT 3.4 (Minneapolis, 1996), 33–101 (47–54).

[27] Though Tertullian dismisses the argument (by means of the tradition that Ezra rewrote all scripture pre-dating him), it does perhaps reflect a further dimension of the Jewish chronological criterion for canonicity: the document must be before Artaxerxes, as we have seen, but it also must come after the flood. Jewish sources also advocated a *terminus post quem* for the canon: nothing before Moses was canonical. Cf. Josephus, *C. Ap.* 1.37–43; *b. B. Bathra* 14b; and see Anderson, "Canonical," 115–116; M. Hengel, *The Septuagint as Christian Scripture* (Grand Rapids, 2002), 72–73; H.-P. Rüger, "Apokryphen," *TRE* 3 (1978), 289–316 (290, 291).

The Vulgate of 2 Timothy 3:16 reads *omnis scriptura diuinitus inspirata et utilis* ("all scripture is divinely inspired and suitable [...]"). Tertullian relies here on a rather loose paraphrase of the verse.[28] The standard derived therefrom is rather broad, and it is unclear how Tertullian actually implemented it. Both the criterion and the rendering of 2 Timothy seem specially designed for his argument here. Despite this idiosyncratic formulation, we can include Tertullian broadly with those who adhere to the 'ecclesiastical' criterion, to be discussed below.

Tertullian does testify to another test of canonicity, one that he himself disallows. He says that some Christians reject 1 Enoch because the Jews also do. This 'synagogal criterion' seems to have been particularly influential; as Junod has written, "En définitive, l'influence du judaïsme sur la formation et le délimitation de l'A.T. chrétien dans l'Église grecque semble avoir été très profonde."[29] Nevertheless, Christians typically avoid affirming explicitly that their OT should be limited to the books accepted by Jews. This causes no surprise, given the frequent accusations of 'Judaizing' lobbed at those who relied too heavily on Jewish information or modes of thinking.[30] Tertullian himself already illustrates this tactic, and we may wonder how his opponents would have portrayed their own position. It is doubtful that they would have assented to Tertullian's characterization, even if it were correct in practical terms.

The synagogal criterion exerted its influence, then, not always in the direct statements of its adherents, but often implicitly, especially in the numerous canonical lists transmitted in patristic literature. The earliest of these still extant is that of Melito of Sardis (*apud* Eusebius, *Hist. eccl.* 4.26.12–14), who reports how he obtained an accurate list for his brother Onesimus:

> ἀνελθὼν οὖν εἰς τὴν ἀνατολὴν καὶ ἕως τοῦ τόπου γενόμενος ἔνθα ἐκηρύχθη καὶ ἐπράχθη, καὶ ἀκριβῶς μαθὼν τὰ τῆς παλαιᾶς διαθήκης βιβλία, ὑποτάξας ἔπεμψά σοι.

---

[28] No other Latin writer offers the same reading for this verse. See the evidence compiled by H.J. Frede, *Ad Thessalonicenses, Timotheum*, Vetus Latina 25/1, fasc. 10 (Freiburg, 1982), 780–783. This is the only quotation of this verse in Tertullian.

[29] Junod, "Formation," 133.

[30] Two recent studies on charges of 'Judaizing' in early Christianity are M. Graves, "'Judaizing' Christian Interpretations of the Prophets as Seen by Saint Jerome," *VC* 61 (2007): 142–156; and C. Shepardson, "Paschal Politics: Deploying the Temple's Destruction against Fourth-Century Judaizers," *VC* 62 (2008): 233–260.

Accordingly when I came to the east and reached the place where these things were preached and done, and learnt accurately the books of the Old Testament, I set down the facts and sent them to you.[31]

There follows a list of twenty-five separate titles, provided that the mention of Σολομῶνος Παροιμίαι ἡ καὶ Σοφία refers to one book—"the Proverbs of Solomon, i.e., his Wisdom"—rather than to the deuterocanonical Wisdom of Solomon. The first option receives support both from the information provided by Eusebius earlier that 'Wisdom' was a common alternative title for the Book of Proverbs (*Hist. eccl.* 4.22.9), and from Rufinus' translation of Melito's canonical list, who renders the phrase *Salomonis Proverbia quae et Sapientia* ("Proverbs of Solomon, which is also Wisdom"; *Hist.* 4.26.14).[32] Thus, Melito's list matches the parameters of the Jewish canon, save for the absence of Esther and its unusual sequence.[33] Melito fails to tell us whom he

---

[31] Translation by K. Lake, *Eusebius: The Ecclesiastical History*, vol. 1, LCL (Cambridge, Mass., 1926), 393.

[32] Cf. A.C. Sundberg, *The Old Testament of the Early Church* (Cambridge, Mass., 1964), 133–134 n. 10. For the opposite view, that Melito refers to the Wisdom of Solomon, see Hennings, *Briefwechsel*, 151; and Lake, *Eusebius: Eccl. Hist.*, LCL, 933, whose translation reads: "the Proverbs of Solomon and his Wisdom." Larcher thinks Melito cites the Wisdom of Solomon in his Passover Homily (*Études*, 38 n. 2; so also Hennings, *Briefwechsel*, 151), but Hengel thinks the similarities "can be explained equally well through the terminology of Judaeo-Hellenistic passover preaching Melito employs" (*Septuagint*, 120; see also 61 n. 11). L.H. Cohick seems to support the position of Hengel; see *The Peri Pascha Attributed to Melito of Sardis* (Providence, R.I., 2000), 95–99.

[33] As for the odd sequence of Melito's books, the most striking example is the placement of Numbers before Leviticus (also in the Mommsen Catalogue), on which see Leiman, *Canonization*, 165 n. 264. Melito's unique arrangement is the more curious since he specifies that he sought to satisfy his brother's request for accurate information on the number and order (ἐπειδὴ ... καὶ μαθεῖν τὴν τῶν παλαιῶν βιβλίων ἐβουλήθης ἀκρίβειαν πόσα τὸν ἀριθμὸν καὶ ὁποῖα τὴν τάξιν εἶεν, ἐσπούδασα τὸ τοιοῦτο πρᾶξαι). Regarding the absence of Esther, see Ellis, *Old Testament*, 11 n. 34, who entertains the possibility that the omission was accidental, but concludes that "it is possible if not probable that the book was not recognized as Scripture by Melito's informants." See also Hennings, *Briefwechsel*, 151 n. 85, who suggests that Esther's omission from some Christian lists (Melito, Athanasius, Gregory of Nazianzus, and Amphilochius of Iconium) was due to either Jewish hesitancy about the book, or its pro-Jewish content. Amphilochius appends a note to his list explaining that some add Esther. Athanasius and Gregory both explicitly count 22 books, reckoning Ruth separately from Judges in order to compensate for the omission of Esther. Neither Melito nor Amphilochius states the number of books. J. Ruwet thinks the omission of Esther in Melito's list was due to Jewish influence, the omission in Gregory and Amphilochius was due to Melito's influence (all from the same region), and the omission of Esther in Athanasius was due to Jewish influence; see "Le canon alexandrine des Écritures. Saint Athanase," *Bib* 33 (1952): 1–29 (15–20). For the omission of Esther in Jewish and Christian sources, see H.-P. Rüger, "Le Siracide: un livre à la frontière du canon," in Kaestli and Wermelinger, *Canon*, 47–69 (53). Esther was still being omitted in the ninth century by Nicephorus, who made Baruch one of the 22 books

asked for this information, leaving scholars to guess whether he sought out Palestinian Jews or Palestinian Christians.[34] Regardless, most scholars have been willing to attribute the list ultimately to Jewish sources.[35]

Did Melito intend to acquire the Jewish canon? He does not say so, yet clearly he thought he would get an authentic list from the place where all things biblical "were proclaimed and occurred." It seems safe to say that Onesimus had been pressing Melito for this information (Melito writes to Onesimus, πολλάκις ἠξίωσας) due to the prominence of certain recent pseudepigrapha purporting to be prophecies of Christ.[36] An authentic list of OT books would then include only those writings that were legitimate prophecies, and one way (the only way?) of guaranteeing their legitimacy would be by their preservation within the synagogue.[37] It is likely that

---

to make up for Esther's absence; see Th. Zahn, *Geschichte des neutestamentlichen Kanons*, 2 vols. (Erlangen, 1888–1892), 2.295–301. As for the apparent omission of other books from Melito's list, L.M. McDonald asserts (*The Biblical Canon* (Peabody, Mass., 2007), 201), that Nehemiah is absent, but the title 'Esdras,' referring no doubt to the Greek 1 Esdras, would have encompassed (some material from) Nehemiah; likewise, Lamentations was included under the title 'Jeremiah,' as Hennings recognizes (*Briefwechsel*, 151 n. 86).

[34] Identifying Melito's informants with Jews has been the general assumption, and is sometimes supported by counting Melito's books as 22. See, e.g., P. Katz, "The Old Testament Canon in Palestine and Alexandria," *ZNW* 47 (1956): 191–217; repr. in Leiman, *Canon and Masorah*, 72–98 (77–78); Sundberg, *Old Testament*, 133–134; N.R.M. de Lange, *Origen and the Jews* (Cambridge, 1976), 50; Hengel, *Septuagint*, 61. Others have preferred to see Melito asking Christians about the OT. So Beckwith, *Old Testament*, 184–185, who emphasizes Melito's non-Jewish number 25, and asks why he would come to Palestine to consult Jews when there was a large community of Jews in his own city. J. Ruwet also thinks this option more likely, without giving reasons; see "Canon alexandrin," 16. G. Dorival, "L'apport des Pères de l'Église à la question de la clôture du canon de l'Ancien Testament," in J.-M. Auwers and H.J. de Jonge (eds.), *The Biblical Canons*, BETL 163 (Leuven, 2003), 81–110, considers Melito's informants to be Jewish Christians (88 n. 6).

[35] Hennings writes: "Es ist unverkennbar, daß Melito sich dabei an der hebräischen Bibel orientiert" (*Briefwechsel* 151). So also Ellis, *Old Testament*, 11. Even Beckwith attributes the similarities between Melito's list and the Jewish canon to the "exceptional knowledge of Jewish tradition" possessed by the Palestinian church consulted by Melito (*Old Testament*, 185).

[36] For the controversies raging over the Christian use of pseudepigrapha around the time of (or a little later than) Melito, see W. Adler, "The Pseudepigrapha in the Early Church," in McDonald and Sanders, *Canon Debate*, 211–228. On the other hand, D. Barthélemy thinks that Onesimus' request was prompted by Jewish-Christian controversy; see "Origène et le texte de l'Ancien Testament," in J. Fontaine and C. Kannengiesser (eds.), *Epektasis* (Paris, 1972), 247–261; repr. in Barthélemy, *Études d'histoire du texte de l'Ancien Testament* (Göttingen, 1978), 203–217 (206).

[37] Two and a half centuries later, Augustine would say of Enoch and other such pseudepigraphic writings (*Civ.* 15.23): *non frustra non sunt in eo canone Scripturarum, qui seruabatur in templo Hebraei populi succedentium diligentia sacerdotum*. He further remarks

upon coming to the east, presumably on some official business, he would
have questioned the local Christians rather than Jews, but the more intimate acquaintance of eastern Christians with Jewish traditions would have
assured him of obtaining what he considered an authentic canon. His attitude toward Judaism, evidenced by his Passover sermon, makes it unlikely
that Melito would have expressly advocated the synagogal criterion, but his
view probably amounted to the same thing.[38] At least we can say that Melito
commences the practice of composing canon lists for the OT that almost
exactly reproduce the Jewish list of books.[39]

Subsequent to Melito, nearly all the early Greek commentators on the
canon, and some of the Latin ones, limit the OT to 22 books, and many
of these writers invest this number with significance due to the Hebrew
alphabet's totaling 22 letters.[40] The first author who certainly connects the
Hebrew alphabet to the extent of the OT canon is Origen, though already
Josephus counted the Jewish sacred books as 22, and he says that this
number for the canon had been widely accepted for a long time (*C. Ap.* 1.37–
43).[41]

---

concerning the writings attributed to Enoch specifically: *nec utrum haec essent, quae ille scrip-
sisset, poterat inueniri, non talibus proferentibus, qui ea per seriem successionis reperirentur
rite seruasse.*

[38] For analysis of the anti-Jewish rhetoric in Melito's *Peri Pascha*, see E. Werner, "Melito
of Sardis, the First Poet of Deicide," *HUCA* 37 (1966): 191–210; A.T. Kraabel, "Melito the
Bishop and the Synagogue at Sardis: Text and Context," in D.G. Mitten, et al. (eds.), *Studies
Presented to George M.A. Hanfmann* (Cambridge, MA, 1971), 72–85; repr. in J.A. Overman
and R.S. MacLennan (eds.), *Diaspora Jews and Judaism* (Atlanta, 1992), 197–208; Cohick, *Peri
Pascha*, 52–87, though Cohick is not convinced that the *Peri Pascha* was written by Melito of
Sardis (31–51).

[39] Hennings, *Briefwechsel*, 152, calls Melito's list "der erste Beleg für die Auffasung [*sic*],
daß der hebräische Kanon auch für Christen verbindlich ist." This evaluation does not
ignore the distinction in text-form, Greek versus Hebrew, of the books included in the
Jewish and Christian canons, but merely relates to the list of documents included. Ruwet
("Canon alexandrin," 19) judges that Melito has influenced especially Gregory of Nazianzus
and Amphilochius of Iconium, due to their all residing in Asia Minor.

[40] See the survey of "Griechische Kanontradition" in Hennings, *Briefwechsel*, 146–183, and
especially his discussion of the significance of Origen's linking the alphabet and the canon,
pp. 158–161. On the mystical theology associated with the alphabet, see de Lange, *Origen*, 175–
176 n. 24; D.H. Aaron, "Judaism's Holy Language," in J. Neusner (ed.), *Approaches to Ancient
Judaism, New Series*, vol. 16 (Atlanta, 1999), 49–107 (49–50, 100–105); Ginzberg, *Legends*, 1.5–
8, and the corresponding notes at 5.5–6. Christian authors who mention the relationship
between the OT canon and the Hebrew alphabet include Origen, Athanasius, Epiphanius,
Gregory of Nazianzus, Hilary, and Jerome. For references, see below.

[41] If R.H. Charles is correct, the connection between the alphabet and the sacred books
would be attested already in the Book of Jubilees. Though the extant versions of that book
lack any mention of the alphabet or the canon, Charles detected a lacuna at Jub. 2:23 and,

Twelve OT canon lists from the Greek Church of the first four centuries have survived.[42] Most of these lists mention the number 22—Origen (*Sel. Ps.* 1; apud Eusebius, *Hist. eccl.* 6.25.1–2), Cyril of Jerusalem (*Catach.* 4.33–36), Athanasius (*Ep. fest.* 39),[43] Epiphanius (three lists: *Pan.* 8.6.1–4; *Mens.* 4; 22–23),[44] Gregory of Nazianzus (*Carmen* 1.12), and the Council of Laodicea, canon 59.[45] The other lists, while not citing the number 22, nevertheless include only the books of the Jewish canon (regardless of additional Greek elements in those books)—Melito (*Eklogai*; apud Eusebius, *Hist. eccl.* 4.26.12–14), the *Bryennios List* (in *Hierosolymitanus 54*),[46] Amphilochius

---

on the basis of later Greek citations of Jubilees, he restored the text to include mention of 22 sacred books and 22 Hebrew letters (*The Book of Jubilees or the Little Genesis* (London, 1902), 17–18). James VanderKam points to the sole Qumran fragment preserving this portion of Jubilees (4QJub^a) as testifying against Charles' view and stresses that no extant texts of Jubilees contain any reference to the canon in this passage; see J.C. VanderKam, *From Revelation to Canon* (Leiden, 2000), 18–19; also see VanderKam's edition, with Jozef Milik, of the Qumran fragment 4QJub^a in H. Attridge, et al. (eds.), *Qumran Cave 4, VIII: Parabiblical Texts, Part 1*, DJD 13 (Oxford, 1994), 19–22; and VanderKam's critical edition of the Ethiopic text, English translation, and introduction, *The Book of Jubilees*, 2 vols. (Leuven, 1989), 1.13–14; and idem, "Genesis 1 in Jubilees 2," *DSD* 1 (1994): 300–321 (315–316). Beckwith, *Old Testament*, 235–240, adopts a variant of Charles' position, according to which the Greek translator of Jubilees (first century BCE, p. 236) inserted the reference to the 22 letters and 22 books. Carr, *Writing*, 249–251, seems to accept Beckwith's position, but he later describes it as based on "tenuous argumentation" (270). Recently, M. Segal has rejected Charles' emendation based on contextual reasons (*The Book of Jubilees* (Leiden, 2007), 258 n. 4). But see also C. Bandt, *Der Traktat "Vom Mysterium der Buchstaben"*, TU 162 (Berlin, 2007), 74–76, who argues that the Jub. 12:26 "besteht meines Erachtens darin, daß für die Autoren des *Jub.* der Zusammenhang zwischen den 22 Schöpfungswerken und den 22 hebräischen Buchstaben bereits auf der Hand lag" (76).

[42] According to Junod, "Formation," 107–108 n. 7. Junod gives the text of these lists (usually in French) in the appendix to his article (135–151).

[43] For a recent study of the letter with full English translation of its entire contents, including a recently discovered fragment, see D. Brakke, "A New Fragment of Athanasius's 39th *Festal Letter*: Heresy, Apocrypha, and the Canon," *HTR* 103 (2010): 47–66.

[44] In each of his three lists, Epiphanius mentions also the number 27, which is simply a different way of counting the 22 books, in accordance with the five doubled letters of the Hebrew alphabet which bring the number of Hebrew letters to 27. Jerome also mentions the number 27 and the five doubled letters/books (*Prol. gal.* 15–19).

[45] The text of the Council of Laodicea is given in P.-P. Joannou, *Discipline générale antique*, 2 vols., Fonti codificazione canonica orientale 9 (Grottaferrata (Rome), 1961–1964), 1/2.154–155. The canon list from this Council is a later appendage to the text, but the citation of the number 22 in canon 59 is original; see Zahn, *Geschichte*, 2.197–202.

[46] The *Bryennios List* was studied by J.-P. Audet, "A Hebrew-Aramaic List of Books of the Old Testament in Greek Transcription," *JTS* 1 (1950): 135–154; repr. in Leiman, *Canon and Masorah*, 52–71. The early date (first or second century) assigned to the source of the *Bryennios List* by Audet has been accepted by, among others, Katz, "Old Testament," 85–89; and F.M. Cross, *From Epic to Canon* (Baltimore, 1998), who considers this dating "sound

of Iconium (*Iambi ad Seleucum* 261–289), and the Apostolic Canons (Canon 85).[47]

As for Latin lists, several expand the OT canon beyond the 22 books: the Mommsen Catalogue (= the Cheltenham List, from North Africa ca. 359), those of the North African Councils at the end of the fourth century (Hippo in 393 and Carthage in 397),[48] Augustine's list (*Doctr. chr.* 2.13), and the list of Pope Innocent I (*Ep. ad Exsuperium Tolosanum* 7, ca. 405). Each of these sources (except, perhaps, the Mommsen Catalogue) transmits a list including the same six books rejected by the Jews: Wisdom of Solomon, Sirach, Tobit, Judith, and 1 and 2 Maccabees. While the Mommsen Catalogue does list the latter four books, it is uncertain whether its title 'Salomonis' includes Wisdom and Sirach, though the given stichometry makes this probable.[49] On the other hand, some Latin Fathers continue to limit their lists of canonical books to the number 22: Hilary of Poitiers (*Instr. Ps.* 15), Rufinus (*Symb.* 34–36), and Jerome (*Prologus galeatus*), all of whom were directly influenced by the Greek tradition. Hilary and Jerome both mention the number 22, though they both also mention the alternative reckoning of 24. Rufinus does not give a number, but he does make it clear that he is aiming for the number 22 by counting Ruth with Judges (*Judicum simul cum Ruth*) and by explicitly following 'the Hebrews' in counting the books of Reigns (Samuel and Kings) as two (*quos Hebraei duos numerant*).[50]

---

and even overly cautious" (222 n. 8). Although, Beckwith, *Old Testament*, 188–190, thinks this dating too early, his reasons are dubious.

[47] For the text of the Apostolic Canons, see Joannou, *Discipline*, 1/2.51–52. Other manuscript readings do include some of the deuterocanonical books: the edition by F.X. Funk (*Didascalia et Constitutiones Apostolorum*, 2 vols. (Paderborn, 1905), 1.590–592) includes Ἰουδὶθ ἕν, Μαχχαβαίων τρία, while F. Lauchert (*Die Kanones der wichtigsten altkirchlichen Concilien nebst den Apostolischen Kanones* (1896; repr. Frankfurt, 1961), 12–13) prints Μαχαβαϊκῶν τρία and relegates Ἰουδεὶθ ἕν to the note on p. 191.

[48] The scriptural canon promulgated at Hippo is preserved as canon 36 in the *Breviarium Hipponense* and was reaffirmed at Carthage in 397; for the text, see C. Munier (ed.), *Concilia Africae a. 345–525*, CCSL 149 (Turnhout, 1974), 43; idem, "La tradition manuscrite de l'Abrégé d'Hippone et le Canon des Écritures des églises africaines," *Sacris Erudiri* 21 (1972–1973): 43–55. For the relationship between the lists from the North African Councils and Augustine's list, see A.-M. La Bonnardière, *Biblia Augustiniana, A.T.* (vol. 4): *Le Livre de la Sagesse* (Paris, 1970), 44–57; idem, "The Canon of Sacred Scripture," in P. Bright (ed.), *Augustine and the Bible* (Notre Dame, Ind., 1999), 26–41 (30–32); M. Moreau, I. Bochet, and G. Madec, *La doctrine chrétienne*, Bibliothèque augustinienne, Oeuvres de saint Augustin 11/2 (Paris, 1997), 512–514. For the motivations leading to the determination of the canon by the North African Councils, see pp. 507–510 of this last work.

[49] Zahn, *Geschichte*, 2.151.

[50] The Latin lists are analyzed by Otto Wermelinger and included in the appendix to his

The ubiquity of the 22-book canon list within early Christianity may descend from Josephus, whose influence among the Fathers was great, or from Origen, whose influence was greater still.[51] In either case, those who adhered to this number would be cognizant of transmitting the Jewish canon, for Josephus was a Jew, and Origen makes plain in the preface to his list that he is presenting "the twenty-two books according to the Hebrews" (αἱ εἴκοσι δύο βίβλοι καθ᾽ Ἑβραίους). Indeed, some other Fathers explain that they are imparting the Jewish canon.[52] Thus, Ellis has good reason to state that on the issue of the OT canon the Church "remained in conscious and intentional accord with the Jewish community."[53]

Nevertheless, scholars have often stressed that early Christians quote freely from works outside the 22 canonical books, sometimes using this as an excuse to accuse the Fathers of inconsistency on this issue.[54] However, exclusion from the canon does not entail exclusion from use. In fact, the two basic positions in the Church with regard to Jewish religious literature outside the Jewish canon were either to include a selection within the canon or to exclude it from the canon but to allow for its use among Christians. The latter position was quite common, and it is not difficult to locate Fathers who advocated a 22-book canon while citing books not numbered within the twenty-two.[55] Eventually, this resulted in the establishment of a threefold categorization of religious literature—canonical, ecclesiastical,

---

article ("Le canon des Latins," 153–196, appendix 197–210). Wermelinger omits Hilary's list, which is included and discussed by Hennings, *Briefwechsel*, 184–186.

[51] On the Christian reception of Josephus, see H. Schreckenberg, *Die Flavius-Josephus-Tradition in Antike und Mittelalter* (Leiden, 1972); idem, "The Works of Josephus and the Early Christian Church," in L.H. Feldman and G. Hata (eds.), *Josephus, Judaism, and Christianity* (Detroit, 1987), 315–324; idem, "Josephus in Early Christian Literature and Medieval Christian Art," in H. Schreckenberg and K. Schubert, *Jewish Historiography and Iconography in Early and Medieval Christianity*, CRINT 3.2 (Minneapolis, 1992), 1–138; M.E. Hardwick, *Josephus as an Historical Source in Patristic Literature through Eusebius*, BJS 128 (Atlanta, 1989); for the influence of Josephus' *C. Ap.* specifically in early Christian literature, see Hardwick's summary on pp. 114–116, 119–121. For the influence of Origen, note the statement by M. Wiles, *The Divine Apostle* (Cambridge, 1967), 6: "Origen stands out in splendid isolation at the fountain head of the tradition of Greek exegesis."

[52] Cf. Athanasius, *Ep. fest.* 39; Epiphanius, *Mens.* 22–23; Jerome, *Prol. gal.*

[53] Ellis, *Old Testament*, 6; cf. Hengel, *Septuagint*, 29: "Because Christians addressed the problem of the Old Testament 'canon' later than Jews, they were, on this point, never really completely independent of the synagogue."

[54] See, e.g., Sundberg, *Old Testament*, 129–169; Junod, "Formation."

[55] See Sundberg, *Old Testament*, 138–142 for Athanasius; 142, 147 for Gregory of Nazianzus and Cyril of Jerusalem; for Hilary of Poitiers, see H.H. Howorth, "The Influence of St. Jerome on the Canon of the Western Church. II," *JTS* 11 (1909–1910): 321–347 (323–325). The most striking example is Jerome, on whom see below.

and apocryphal—as attested explicitly by Athanasius (*Ep. fest.* 39) and Rufinus (*Symb.* 36).[56] The apocrypha were to be avoided altogether, but the other two classes were to be used by the Church, and scholars have, in fact, found little distinction between the way the Fathers used the canonical books and those termed ecclesiastical.[57]

It is true that Athanasius is the first writer on record expressly to categorize religious literature in this threefold schema, but he attributes his categories to his predecessors (βιβλία [...] τετυπωμένα [...] παρὰ τῶν πατέρων), and scholars have been able to locate some antecedents.[58] Epiphanius may serve as an example of a Father who does not mention these specific categories of scripture while seeming to adopt the classification system. For instance, immediately after giving a 22-book canon list which he attributes to Jewish sources, Epiphanius says of Sirach and the Wisdom of Solomon: καὶ αὗται χρήσιμοι μέν εἰσι καὶ ὠφέλιμοι, ἀλλ᾽ εἰς ἀριθμὸν τῶν ῥητῶν οὐκ ἀναφέρονται ("Now these books are useful and profitable, but they are not brought into the number of those mentioned"; *Mens.* 4.122–123).[59] This seems to be an acknowledgment of a middle category. It may be that these categories even have Jewish origins, as some scholars have asserted,[60] though it is not clear how extensively Jews used the documents that came to be included in the 'ecclesiastical' category.[61] At any rate, for our purposes it is important to

---

[56] The middle category bears the label 'ecclesiastical' in Rufinus (*Symb.* 36), while Athanasius (*Ep. fest.* 39) uses the term ἀναγινωσκόμενα, or ἕτερα βιβλία ... οὐ κανονιζόμενα. Note, against Hengel (*Septuagint*, 64), that ἀναγινωσκόμενα does not mean 'read publicly' for Athanasius, since he expressly limits the reading to catechumens.

[57] See the helpful summary in Junod, "Formation," 130–132. For Athanasius in particular see the two articles by J. Leemans, "Athanasius and the Book of Wisdom," *ETL* 73 (1997): 349–369; "Canon and Quotation: Athanasius' Use of Jesus Sirach," in Auwers and de Jonge, *Biblical Canons*, 265–277. However, Hengel (*Septuagint*, 66–70, esp. 67 n. 23) points out that the deuterocanonical books are used comparatively less frequently among patristic authors.

[58] Ruwet (citing *Hom. Num.* 27.1) and Ellis (citing *Comm. ser. Matt.* 28) both trace the three categories back to Origen. See J. Ruwet, "Les 'Antilegomena' dans les œuvres d'Origène: les antilegomena de l'Ancien Testament," *Bib* 24 (1943): 18–58 (21–42); and Ellis, *Old Testament*, 17–18. Ellis (op. cit.) argues for seeing an ecclesiastical category implicit also in Josephus and the Rabbis (17–18), as well as Cyril of Jerusalem (20–21), Epiphanius (22 n. 69; 23), and Augustine (29).

[59] I cite the critical Greek text of Elia D. Moutsoula, "Τὸ 'Περὶ μέτρων καὶ σταθμῶν' ἔργον Ἐπιφανίου τοῦ Σαλαμῖνος," *Theologia* 44 (1973): 157–200. The line numbers refer to this edition.

[60] Junod, "Formation," 132, 133; Ellis, *Old Testament*, 17–18; G. Dorival in Dorival, M. Harl, and O. Munnich, *La Bible grecque des Septante* (Paris, 1988), 324; idem, "Pères," 107–108; idem, "Has the Category of 'Deuterocanonical Books' a Jewish Origin?" in G.G. Xeravits and J. Zsengellér (eds.), *The Books of the Maccabees* (Leiden, 2007), 1–10.

[61] Both Rufinus (*Symb.* 36) and Athanasius (*Ep. fest.* 39) include in the OT ecclesiastical books Tobit, Judith, Wisdom, and Sirach. Athanasius adds Esther, which did not feature in

note that this way of viewing non-canonical but useful literature alleviates some of the tension between the canon lists and the scriptural citations. We may assume that the canon lists authentically represent the canonical theory of their authors, and that the Fathers generally saw no problem in citing books falling outside canonical limits.[62] Our discussion will treat these lists as reflecting what their authors thought should be the OT canon for the Church.

We have seen that the canon lists seem to reflect a rather widespread Christian adherence to the synagogal criterion of canonicity, even though

---

his listing of the 22 canonical books. For Rufinus, Esther is canonical, but he also includes the Books of the Maccabees as ecclesiastical. (Both Athanasius and Rufinus include the Shepherd of Hermas and the Didache (or 'Two Ways' in Rufinus) as the two NT ecclesiastical books.) As for Jewish use of these same books, the Rabbis certainly did highly value Sirach, even while explicitly denying it scriptural status (t. Yad. 2.13: "does not defile the hands"); see the discussion in Leiman, Canonization, 92–102; Veltri, Libraries, 190  222. Jerome reports that he had seen a Hebrew copy of 1 Maccabees (Prol. gal. 55–56), and Origen also seems to hint at its continuing use in Judaism (i.e., he reports the Hebrew name for 1 Maccabees at the conclusion of his canon list). But, the Books of Maccabees were not included in the ecclesiastical category of Athanasius (see Junod, "Formation," 127 n. 50; Hengel, Septuagint, 73, this latter explaining the omission as due to the Maccabees falling outside the chronological limits of the canon). Jerome asserts that the Jews of his day do read Tobit and Judith (see the prefaces to his translations of those books), although Origen had earlier said that the Jews did not possess these two books even among their Hebrew apocrypha (Ep. Afr. 13). Possibly some Jews in the Western Diaspora, and even some Rabbis, would have made use of the Wisdom of Solomon, as argued by W. Horbury, "The Christian Use and the Jewish Origins of the Wisdom of Solomon," in J. Day, R.P. Gordon, and H.G.M. Williamson (eds.), Wisdom in Ancient Israel (Cambridge, 1995), 182–196 (185–186). It may be that Christians followed a Diaspora Jewish practice of using these books, as suggested by R. Katzoff and reported in A. Edrei and D. Mendels, "A Split Jewish Diaspora: Its Dramatic Consequences II," JSP 17 (2008): 163–187 (183).

[62] For a similar point regarding Josephus, see Mason, "Josephus and His Twenty-Two Book Canon," 126–127. The best patristic example for possible inconsistency is perhaps Cyril of Jerusalem, who forbids all use of the 'apocrypha,' while stressing the exclusive use of the 22 books that are read in the churches (Catach. 4.36–39). Yet, Cyril himself uses and cites Wisdom and Sirach (Catach. 9.2; 6.4, respectively; see Hennings, Briefwechsel, 163 n. 142 for statistics of Cyril's citations of the deuterocanonicals). Cyril's canon list was written for catechumens, and so he may have intended his prohibition to apply to them alone, as those who are unable to properly separate the wheat from the chaff. This would then be equivalent to Origen's attitude regarding the 'apocrypha' (i.e., pseudepigrapha; cf. Comm. ser. Matt. 28; and see the comments by J. Ruwet, "Les apocryphes dans les œuvres d'Origène, II," Bib 25 (1944): 311–334 (311–312)). In that case, Cyril's view would represent a novel theory regarding the proper position of the ecclesiastical books in the Church, since Athanasius and Rufinus both assigned the deuterocanonicals the role of elementary pedagogy, while Origen seems to do the same in his Hom. Num. 27.1 (preserved only in Rufinus' Latin translation). Junod thinks that Cyril's position developed in conscious opposition to that of Origen and Athanasius ("Formation," 129–130). See also Ellis, Old Testament, 19–21, who thinks Cyril adopts Athanasius' threefold schema.

we have few explicit statements from the Fathers that Christians should follow the Jews in this matter. Three Christian authors may give more explicit evidence for the synagogal criterion, and to these we now turn. We will deal first with the positions of Julius Africanus and Origen as revealed in their correspondence; then we will examine Origen's statements outside this correspondence; finally, we will investigate briefly Jerome's canonical views.

### The Correspondence between Julius Africanus and Origen

We have no list of canonical books from Julius Africanus. Nevertheless, his letter to Origen against the authenticity of Susanna preserves certain statements of principle relevant to the present discussion. Africanus intends his letter to demonstrate that Susanna is no genuine part of the Book of Daniel: τὸ μέρος τοῦτο βιβλίου κίβδηλον ὄν ("this part of the book is spurious"; §2).[63] He assembles seven arguments in support of this aim.[64]

1. The form of prophetic inspiration is inconsistent with that of the genuine parts of Daniel (§3)
2. Daniel's cross examination of the two villains is silly (§4)
3. The Greek play on words is proof that there is no Hebrew original (§5)
4. Historical inaccuracies preclude the sixth-century prophet from having composed Susanna (§6)
5. The story is absent from the Jewish version of Daniel (§7)
6. Contrary to the nature of true prophecy, Daniel quotes scripture in the story (§8)
7. The style of the story diverges from the rest of Daniel (§9)

One should note carefully that Africanus' third argument concerns the language in which Susanna was composed, while the fifth argument concerns the Jewish reception (rather, rejection) of Susanna. Africanus draws no explicit connection between these two points; in fact, he does not even juxtapose them, but inserts a historical argument in the middle. I stress this here because students of this correspondence have sometimes combined

---

[63] The paragraph divisions follow those in the most recent edition of the correspondence: N. de Lange (ed.), *Origène, La Lettre à Africanus sur l'histoire de Suzanne*, in *Origène, Philocalie, 1–20: Sur les Écritures*, SC 302 (ed. M. Harl; Paris, 1983), 469–578.

[64] For analysis of the seven arguments, see R.M. Grant, "Historical Criticism in the Ancient Church," *JR* 25 (1945): 183–196 (191–192); de Lange, *Lettre*, 478–479; and G. Dorival, "Origène, témoin des textes de l'Ancien Testament," in J.-M. Auwers and A. Wénin (eds.), *Lectures et relectures de la Bible* (Leuven, 1999), 351–366 (354–356).

these two arguments and Origen's response to them, as we will see. The third argument regarding the language of composition will feature prominently in our discussion in the next chapter. Here, we are concerned with the fifth argument.

According to Africanus, the absence of Susanna in the Jewish version of Daniel, more than anything else, condemns the story as inauthentic.

> Πρὸ δὲ τούτων ἁπάντων ἤδε ἡ περικοπὴ σὺν ἄλλαις δύο ταῖς ἐπὶ τῷ τέλει τῷ παρὰ τῶν Ἰουδαίων εἰλημμένῳ Δανιὴλ οὐκ ἐμφέρεται.        (§ 7)

> Before all these things, this pericope along with two others at the end [= Bel and the Dragon] does not circulate in the [version of] Daniel received from the Jews.

Unfortunately, Africanus keeps his comments rather terse, leaving his readers to wonder why he considered this particular argument so powerful, how exactly he conceived of the relationship between the Christian OT and the Jewish Bible, and what implications this statement has for other books of the Bible. At first sight, Africanus appears explicitly to affirm the synagogal criterion, but two points should give us pause before reaching this conclusion.

First, just before his statement in § 7, Africanus employs the Book of Tobit (without citing it by name) as a historical witness to the experience of exile (§ 6).[65] Now, we know that this does not necessarily imply that Africanus attributed scriptural status to Tobit, but it might; indeed, Origen himself remarks with pleasure on the apparent inconsistency in his correspondent's citing Tobit while arguing against Susanna (§ 19). Of course, Africanus may be relying on the distinction outlined earlier between canonical books and ecclesiastical books, or, at least, an embryonic form of such a classification. Yet, since we cannot be sure which books Africanus himself regarded as canonical, we should probably interpret his statement at § 7 so as to leave the matter open.

The second caution leads to a similar conclusion. Africanus may understand the absence of Susanna from the Jewish version of Daniel to be a matter bearing on the correct textual form of the Book of Daniel rather than a matter of the canonicity of a book. In other words, Susanna may constitute here not an independent document but merely (a spurious) part of the Book of Daniel. The beginning of Origen's reply (§ 3–9) lends support to this view, since he details many differences between the Jewish and Christian textual

---

[65] See de Lange, *Lettre*, 519 n. 2.

forms of various books deemed canonical by both groups, but he does not at this point delve into what we would consider canonical disputes, that is, arguing over which books belong to the Bible.[66] On the other hand, this correspondence involves not just a routine matter of textual criticism, such as Origen might treat in one of his commentaries, but rather a substantial narrative, which could itself be regarded as a separate work. When in the next chapter we examine more closely Origen's comments in the second section of his letter (§ 10–15), we will see that he compares the situation of the Susanna narrative to that of the *Ascension of Isaiah* and, later, even that of Tobit and Judith (§ 19). Origen, at least, could envision Susanna as a work on its own terms. But, again, Africanus gives us too little information to determine whether he thought similarly.

Our general lack of knowledge regarding Africanus' canonical theory should restrain the interpretation we place on his comment at § 7. Rather than believing that the Christian OT should equal the Jewish Bible in terms of canon (in accordance with the synagogal criterion), Africanus may have limited his fifth argument to the textual sphere generally, or even specifically to the case of Susanna's relationship to the Book of Daniel. In other words, Africanus may have been asserting that Susanna's absence from the Jewish version of Daniel decisively proves that the story is not intrinsic to the book. We recall that Origen's employment of material from Susanna in a particular debate provided the initial impetus for Africanus to write his letter.[67] He intended to caution Origen against citing evidence from this narrative, since it is 'spurious' (κίβδηλος) and a 'recent fabrication' (νεωτερικὸς καὶ πεπλασμένος; § 2). He obviously does not hold the same view of Tobit, despite its absence from the Jewish Bible.[68] This implies that if Africanus would have classified Tobit in a sort of 'ecclesiastical' category (*à la* Athanasius and Rufinus), he would not have done the same for Susanna. But, once again, we simply do not have the evidence to say whether Africanus would have considered Tobit, on the one hand, canonical or, on the other hand, non-canonical but useful. He does not say at § 7 that the Christian OT should reproduce the Jewish canon.[69] All we can certainly

---

[66] See Beckwith, *Old Testament*, 394; Ellis, *Old Testament*, 16–17.

[67] Cf. § 2 of Africanus' letter, and see the introduction (ch. 1) above.

[68] The same may be said of 1 Maccabees, which Africanus used in his *Chronicle* (see Hengel, *Septuagint*, 119 n. 57).

[69] *Contra* W. Adler, "'What the Hebrews Say': Translation, Authority, and the Story of Susanna and the Elders," in F.W. Knobloch (ed.), *Biblical Translation in Context* (Bethesda, MD, 2002), 19–39, who says that Africanus' letter is "holding up the Hebrew Bible as the

deduce from this comment is that, for Africanus, the Jewish version of Daniel demonstrates that Susanna is neither canonical nor useful.

Nevertheless, Origen was convinced that Africanus did in fact believe that the Christian OT should equal in all its particulars the Jewish Bible. Indeed, the great scholar from Caesarea spends the first half of his reply refuting Africanus' dependence on the Jewish Bible. He details the differences between the OT as it had been received by the Church and the scriptures as they existed 'among the Hebrews.' Africanus had pointed out that Susanna and Bel and the Dragon were absent from the Jewish Bible; Origen informs him that the differences between the Jewish and Christian scriptures extend to many more passages than Africanus realized: large sections of Esther (§ 5), Job (§ 6), Jeremiah, and Exodus (§ 7) diverge widely between Christian and Jewish copies. Thus, Origen strongly rejects the idea that the Christian should entreat Jews for accurate copies of the scriptures, and to make it clear that one should not dismiss Christian tradition lightly he quotes Prov. 22:28—"Do not remove the ancient landmark that your ancestors set up" (§ 8). Tertullian would certainly agree.

At least, this is how Gilles Dorival understands Origen's opening offensive.[70] Nicholas de Lange holds a different view of this section. The contrasting positions of Dorival and de Lange revolve around the question regarding which of Africanus' arguments Origen refutes first. De Lange maintains that Origen first responds to the statement made by Africanus at § 5 to the effect that the Christian Bible should be limited to that for which there is a Hebrew *Vorlage*, i.e., Africanus' third argument.[71] In this view, Origen's survey of the disagreements between the Hebrew and the Greek (§ 3–9) is intended to indicate the seriousness of requiring the Church's Bible to match the Hebrew. Following this, argues de Lange, Origen focuses on Susanna but is still treating the question of a Hebrew original (§ 10–15). The letter closes with a point-by-point refutation of Africanus' arguments, except that Origen does not return to Africanus' fifth argument concerning Susanna's absence from the Jewish Bible "dont il a parlé longuement dans sa première partie."[72]

---

canonical standard," which should exclude Tobit (27). Adler thus judges Africanus to be "inconsistent" (27 n. 23). This is not quite correct, though we will see that Origen makes the same mistake.

[70] Dorival, "Origène," 354–355.

[71] N.R.M. de Lange, "The *Letter to Africanus*: Origen's Recantation?" *StPatr* 16.2 = TU 129 (1985), 242–247 (243); he makes the same point in the introduction to his edition of the letters, *Lettre*, 479.

[72] De Lange, *Lettre*, 480. A similar view is offered in P. Nautin, *Origène* (Paris, 1977), 345.

There is a clear contradiction in de Lange's position. He himself provides a numbered list of the seven arguments of Africanus, and says that Origen first attacks the principle that the Greek Bible should be derived from the Hebrew (argument three).[73] De Lange later says that, in the final section of his response, the reason Origen omits the fifth point about Susanna's absence from the Jewish Bible is because he had dealt with it in the first section. So, de Lange confounds Africanus' third and fifth arguments, as if a document's composition in Hebrew (argument three) and its presence in the Jewish Bible (argument five) were two ways of saying the same thing.[74] Certainly, they are related concepts, but they are not equivalent. Africanus clearly separates these issues—after all, he makes two distinct arguments, without any explicit connection between them. He and Origen both know that the Jews do not accept all Hebrew literature as canonical; indeed, Origen dedicates a large section of his letter (§10–15) to explaining why the Rabbis reject some original Hebrew compositions. Therefore, we must interpret Origen's opening section as an attempt to dismantle Africanus' fifth argument under the assumption that his correspondent advocated a Christian OT that matches exactly the Jewish canon.

Three other lines of evidence confirm our interpretation of Origen as beginning his response with Africanus' fifth argument. First, according to his custom,[75] Origen quotes at the beginning of his letter the particular argument from Africanus that he is about to refute:

Ἴσθι τοίνυν πρὸς ταῦτα ὅτι χρὴ ἡμᾶς πράττειν οὐ περὶ τῶν κατὰ Σουσάνναν μόνον, ἐν μὲν τῷ καθ' Ἕλληνας ἑλληνικῷ φερομένων ἐν πάσῃ ἐκκλησίᾳ Χριστοῦ, παρὰ δὲ Ἑβραίοις μὴ κειμένων, οὐδὲ περὶ τῶν, ὡς ἔφασκες, ἄλλων δύο περικοπῶν τῶν ἐπὶ τέλει τοῦ βιβλίου, περί τε τῶν κατὰ τὸν Βὴλ καὶ τὸν δράκοντα ἀναγεγραμμένων, οὐδ' αὐτῶν ἐν τῷ Δανιὴλ τῶν Ἑβραίων γεγραμμένων, ἀλλὰ καὶ περὶ ἄλλων μυρίων ἃ κατὰ τὴν μετριότητα ἡμῶν τοῖς ἑβραϊκοῖς συγκρίναντες ἀντιγράφοις τὰ ἡμέτερα πολλαχοῦ εὕρομεν. (§3)

Know, therefore, with respect to these things that it is necessary for us to treat not only Susanna, which circulates in every church of Christ in Greek according to the Greeks but is not present among the Hebrews, nor those, as you say, two other pericopae at the end of the book, those entitled 'About Bel and the Dragon,' these also not being written in the Daniel of the Hebrews,

---

[73] De Lange, *Lettre*, 478–479.

[74] See also Adler, "Hebrews," 24–25, who likewise combines the two concepts. He first says that Africanus' point about the puns [argument three] was "most damning." Later, he says of Africanus' fifth argument concerning the omission of Susanna from the Jewish Bible, "[a]nd once again, he plays his trump card [...]."

[75] Cf. *Ep. Afr.* §10.7–9 (to be discussed below); §16; §17.3–11; §19.1–11; §20.1–2; §21.1–7; §22.

but also myriad others which we have found everywhere after making a comparison between the Hebrew copies and ours, in accordance with our abilities.

When Origen explicitly cites Africanus' comment about the 'two other pericopae at the end of the book,' clearly he refers to §7 of Africanus' letter, where this comment is found and where Africanus advanced his fifth argument, concerning the Jewish rejection of Susanna.[76] This section of Origen's letter, therefore, must constitute a reply to Africanus' fifth argument.

The final section of Origen's letter (§16–22) provides a second indication leading to this conclusion. Here, he proceeds point-by-point through all of Africanus' objections to the authenticity of Susanna, but he leaves unmentioned Africanus' fifth argument. As de Lange has correctly seen, this can only be because he had spent so long discussing and refuting the point earlier.[77]

Third, the analysis presented here gives due weight to the transition apparent at the beginning of §10 of Origen's letter. There, Origen writes:

Ταῦτα μὲν οὖν εἰρήσθω πρὸς τὸ μὴ φέρεσθαι παρ' Ἑβραίοις τὰ περὶ Σουσάννας· ἴδωμεν δὲ καὶ ἃ προσφέρεις τῷ λόγῳ ἐγκλήματα. Καὶ πρῶτόν γε ἀρξώμεθα ἀπὸ τοῦ δυνηθέντος ἂν δυσωπῆσαι πρὸς τὸ μὴ παραδέξασθαι τὴν ἱστορίαν· ὅπερ ἐστὶ τὸ περὶ τὴν παρωνυμίαν πρίνου μὲν πρὸς πρίσιν, σχίνου δὲ πρὸς σχίσιν.

Let these things be said with regard to Susanna's not circulating among the Hebrews. Now, let us see what accusations you bring against the narrative. And let us begin first from the point that would be able to shame us into not accepting the story, which is the play on words between *prinos* and *prisis*, *schinos* and *schisis*.

In the first clause above, Origen reviews what he has been talking about, viz., that the Hebrews do not accept Susanna. He has now completed his discussion of this topic and will turn to the argument from the puns. Because de Lange interprets the first section of Origen's letter as a refutation of the argument from the puns, he must encompass all of §3–15 in a discussion of the original language of scripture and treat the transition apparent at §10 as merely one of general (the Bible) to specific (Susanna).[78] This fails to do justice to Origen's language, who is rather proceeding from one argument (number five) to the next (number three). In essence, Origen is saying, "I have dealt with your synagogal criterion, now for your Hebrew criterion."

---

[76] De Lange ("Origen's Recantation?" 243 n. 7) fails to recognize Origen's quotation of Africanus' fifth argument and instead looks in vain for a quotation of Africanus' third argument.

[77] De Lange, *Lettre*, 480.

[78] De Lange, *Lettre*, 479–480.

Thus, the text sufficiently demonstrates that Origen treats first Africanus' fifth argument regarding the omission of Susanna from the Jewish version of Daniel, and not his third argument (original language of Susanna). Origen interprets this argument as if Africanus advocated a Christian OT in complete accord with the Jewish Bible, an idea Origen finds objectionable. Africanus may, in fact, have advocated such a position, but his comments at §7 of his letter, and those preserved elsewhere in his works, fail to confirm this. Thus, Africanus may not hold to a synagogal criterion for canonicity, though his comments are close enough to an affirmation of such that Origen rebuts the idea at length.

Why does Origen feel compelled to begin his letter with this fierce repudiation of the idea that the Christian OT should correspond to the Jewish Bible? De Lange is likely correct to see in Origen's 'aggressive and defensive' tone in §8 of his letter a hint that he had been attacked as maintaining such a principle,[79] and he sees in Africanus' statements the opportunity to clear his name. Though de Lange is probably also correct in saying that Origen does not tell the whole story in this section regarding the purpose behind the *Hexapla*, the evidence does not favor the view that he was thus being disingenuous and actually adhered to the synagogal criterion.[80] While, on the one hand, Origen emphasizes in *Ep. Afr.* 8 the apologetic purposes behind his great compendium of biblical texts, which would facilitate effective confrontations with Jews, and, on the other hand, he emphasizes scholarly text-critical motivations in *Comm. Matt.* 15.14, where he evinces a concern to 'heal' the biblical text, Adam Kamesar has shown that Origen's exegetical practice confirms that both accounts (*Ep. Afr.* 8 and *Comm. Matt.* 15.14) genuinely reflect Origen's intentions.[81] Indeed, Origen's exegetical practice also demonstrates that often he uses the hexaplaric texts neither for apologetics nor for textual-criticism, but simply for exegesis, exploiting the divergent biblical texts to expand the interpretive possibilities for a given passage.[82] The complex interaction of these motivations does not

---

[79] De Lange, "Origen's Recantation?" 244. He seems to be following Nautin who writes, "Cette phrase [at the end of §8] fait visiblement allusion à des critiques qui lui ont été adressées sur ce point alors qu'il était un prédicateur célèbre" (*Origène*, 345). Neither author conveys whether the criticism involved textual or canonical issues.

[80] This is de Lange's main point in his essay, "Origen's Recantation?" (see esp. p. 245). See also Nautin, *Origène*, 346.

[81] A. Kamesar, *Jerome, Greek Scholarship and the Hebrew Bible* (Oxford, 1993), 10–17.

[82] This is the chief emphasis in T.M. Law, "Origen's Parallel Bible: Textual Criticism, Apologetics, or Exegesis?" *JTS* 59 (2008): 1–21. On the purpose behind the *Hexapla*, see also S.P. Brock, "Origen's Aims as a Textual Critic of the Old Testament," *StPatr* 10 = TU 107

permit us to privilege one over the other; rather, we should take Origen's statements at their face value.[83] When he says in *Ep. Afr.* 3–9 that the Christian OT need not correspond to the Jewish Bible, we have no grounds to suggest that he believed otherwise.

So, while the correspondence between Africanus and Origen does not, after all, present any unambiguous support for the synagogal criterion, the criticisms against Origen perceptible in his defensive tone do provide further evidence that this criterion was influential in early Christianity. In other words, Origen's readiness to disassociate himself from the synagogal criterion shows that it was viable enough to be attacked.

### *Origen outside His Correspondence with Africanus*

#### *Origen's Canon List*

There are some other indications that Origen himself did indeed adhere to the synagogal criterion, and these indications form part of the basis for de Lange's accusation noted earlier that Origen is disingenuous in his response to Africanus. First, we must return briefly to the passage that most obviously relates to the current discussion—Origen's canon list preserved by Eusebius (*Hist. eccl.* 6.25.1–2). Eusebius introduces the list by quoting Origen as follows:

> οὐκ ἀγνοητέον δ᾽ εἶναι τὰς ἐνδιαθήκους βίβλους, ὡς Ἑβραῖοι παραδιδόασιν, δύο καὶ εἴκοσι, ὅσος ἀριθμὸς τῶν παρ᾽ αὐτοῖς στοιχείων ἐστίν.

> But it should be known that there are twenty-two canonical books, accord-ing to the Hebrew tradition; the same as the number of the letters of their alphabet.[84]

Immediately before transcribing the canon list, Eusebius again quotes Ori-gen to the effect that this list transmits "the twenty-two books according to the Hebrews."[85] These comments are variously taken as introducing Ori-gen's own OT canon, or as Origen's way of distancing himself from this

---

(1970), 215–218; J. Wright, "Origen in the Scholar's Den: A Rationale for the Hexapla," in C. Kannengiesser and W.L. Petersen (eds.), *Origen of Alexandria* (Notre Dame, Ind., 1988), 48–62; and J.L.P. Schaper, "The Origin and Purpose of the Fifth Column of the Hexapla," in A. Salvesen (ed.), *Origen's Hexapla and Fragments* (Tübingen, 1998), 3–15.

[83] Cf. Kamesar, *Jerome*, 21.

[84] Translation by J.E.L. Oulton, *Eusebius: The Ecclesiastical History*, vol. 2, LCL (Cambridge, Mass., 1932), 73. On the adjective ἐνδιάθηκος, translated by Oulton as "canonical," see Harl, *Philocalie*, 265–266 n. 3; Hennings, *Briefwechsel*, 157 n. 112.

[85] For a convenient presentation of Origen's canon list, see Table IV in Sundberg, *Old Testament*, 136.

particular canon and ascribing it to the Hebrews alone.[86] It is true that those who followed Origen, including Eusebius himself, seem to have understood this list as representing their master's own canon.[87] Moreover, as we have already seen, Origen's list here did contribute toward the general acceptance, especially in the east, of the narrower 22-book canon. Yet, the statements introducing the canon clearly associate it with the Hebrews, and give no indication that the Church should follow their practice. That Origen should make a special effort to inform the Church of the exact boundaries of the Jewish canon fits well with his emphasis evident elsewhere that Christians must be informed of where their Bible differs from that of the Jews before entering into debate with them.[88] Given Origen's acceptance of other books outside this list as divine records (cf., e.g., *Ep. Afr.* 19), it seems likely that those scholars are correct who see this list as merely a report of the Jewish canon, not as encouraging the Church to follow suit.

### Origen on the Wisdom of Solomon

The second passage we need to consider is found in Origen's commentary on the Song of Songs, preserved only in the translation made by Rufinus.[89] At the end of the prologue, Origen discusses how many songs Solomon wrote. He limits them to merely the Song of Songs itself, and gives his reason as follows:

> [...] *cum neque ecclesia Dei ulla extrinsecus Solomonis cantica legenda susceperit neque apud hebraeos, a quibus eloquia Dei ad nos videntur esse translata, aliquid praeter hos tres libellos Solomonis, qui et apud nos sunt, amplius habeatur in canone.*

> ... since neither the Church of God has accepted any further songs of Solomon to be read, nor is anything more contained in the canon among the Hebrews, from whom the oracles of God were evidently transferred to us, beyond these three books of Solomon, which we also have.[90]

---

[86] Those who think Origen is advocating this canon for the Church include Hennings, *Briefwechsel*, 157–158; Ellis, *Old Testament*, 13–19; A.E. Steinmann, *The Oracles of God* (St. Louis, 1999), 155. Those who say Origen is merely presenting the Jewish canon include Barthélemy, "Origène," 207; Harl, *Philocalie*, 266; J.N.B. Carleton Paget, "The Christian Exegesis of the Old Testament in the Alexandrian Tradition," in Saebø, *Hebrew Bible/Old Testament*, 478–542 (503); Hengel, *Septuagint*, 63; McDonald, *Biblical Canon*, 201–202. Ruwet, "Duo Textus," 59, traces this latter interpretation of Origen's canon back to R. Cornely in 1894.

[87] Ruwet, "Duo Textus," 59; Harl, *Philocalie*, 265–266; Ellis, *Old Testament*, 17.

[88] Cf. *Ep. Afr.* 8; see Sundberg, *Old Testament*, 135–137.

[89] J. Quasten dated Origen's *Comm. Cant.* to ca. 240, and Rufinus' translation to 410 (*Patrology*, vol. 2 (1950; repr. Westminster, Md., 1994), 50).

[90] For a different translation, see R.P. Lawson, *Origen: The Song of Songs, Commentary and Homilies*, ACW 26 (Westminster, Md., 1957), 55.

Two aspects of this passage bear on our investigation. A little later (p. 46) we will look at the clause "from whom the oracles of God were evidently transferred to us," which would seem to be a clear admission of the synagogal criterion. Before treating those words we should note that this passage does not mention the Wisdom of Solomon as one of Solomon's books accepted by the Church, with the possible implication that the Church should follow the synagogue in rejecting the book.

However, it is exactly the absence of the Wisdom of Solomon in this passage that has led some scholars to doubt the fidelity of Rufinus to his *Vorlage* here. Rufinus is quite candid in his admission that he often translates in a free manner, sometimes altering even the sense of the original if he deems this to have been corrupted in transmission. His criteria for judging whether the text has been corrupted would hardly win the approval of modern textual critics. For Rufinus, the text of Origen is subject to emendation (1) if the passage contradicts received orthodoxy or (2) if it disagrees with what Origen has said elsewhere.[91] Though de Lange considers the possibility that Rufinus altered the text quoted above "hard to imagine,"[92] others have regarded it as very plausible, or even virtually certain. For instance, Hanson, in the midst of his cautions about trusting Rufinus as a translator, introduces this passage and says that it cannot be an exact translation because Origen never used the word κανών as Rufinus does here (*in canone*).[93] That reasoning must be conceded, but, of course, it does not show that the thought does not derive from Origen. Ruwet has demonstrated that even without the technical term 'canon,' Origen still recognized the concept of 'canonical books,' typically indicated by the term ἐνδιάθηκος.[94] In fact, in the passage cited above, in which Origen introduces the canon list "according to the Hebrews," he labels these books the ἐνδιάθηκοι βίβλοι (Eusebius, *Hist. eccl.*

---

[91] See Rufinus' preface to his translation of Origen's *Princ.*, as well as his preface to Origen's *Comm. Rom.* A recent overview of information, with bibliography, concerning Rufinus as a translator is given by M. Humphries, "Rufinus' Eusebius: Translation, Continuation, and Edition in the Latin *Ecclesiastical History*," *JECS* 16 (2008): 143–164. Humphries describes a recent trend toward a more positive evaluation of Rufinus (150), for which see especially E.C. Brooks, "The Translation Techniques of Rufinus of Aquileia (343–411)," *StPatr* 17.1 (1982), 357–364. A very negative appraisal of Rufinus is found in R.P.C. Hanson, *Origen's Doctrine of Tradition* (London, 1954), 40–47. Lawson, *Origen: The Song of Songs*, 4–6, 317–318 n. 65, judges Rufinus' fidelity to Origen's *Comm. Cant.* rather positively.

[92] De Lange, "Origen's Recantation?" 247.

[93] Hanson, *Doctrine*, 45–46.

[94] Ruwet, "Antilegomena de l'Ancien Testament," 26; see also de Lange, *Origen*, 52; cf. Origen, *Or.* 14.4. Cf. G.W.H. Lampe (ed.), *A Patristic Greek Lexicon* (Oxford, 1961), 468 s.v. ἐνδιάθηκος: "*covenantal*, hence of scriptures *canonical*."

6.25.1), which Rufinus translates as *libri in canone veteris testamenti*. Thus, the use of the word 'canon' in our passage from the *Comm. Cant.* does not suggest that Rufinus altered the wording beyond recognition. But Hanson suspects tampering from Rufinus more particularly because of the statement that the Church receives only three books of Solomon.[95] He argues that this view is more indicative of Rufinus, whom we know to have thus restricted the canonical Solomonic books, than Origen, who cites the Wisdom of Solomon quite freely, even in this same commentary.[96]

To determine whether Origen would have said that Christians accept three or four Books of Solomon, we must consider another passage earlier in the prologue:

> *Et tentemus primum de eo requirere quid illud sit, quod cum tria volumina ecclesiae Dei a Solomone scripta susceperint, primus ex ipsis Proverbiorum liber positus sit, secundus is qui Ecclesiastes appellatur, tertio vero in loco Cantici canticorum volumen habeatur.*

> And let us first investigate the reason why, when the churches of God have adopted three books from Solomon's pen, the Book of Proverbs has been put first, that which is called Ecclesiastes second, while the Song of Songs is found in the third place.[97]

The passage continues in a quite lengthy discussion of the significance of the three Solomonic books in the traditional Christian order, which corresponds with the ideal exposure to the three branches of philosophy—Ethics, Physics, and Enoptics, according to Origen's formulation here.[98]

---

[95] Hanson, *Doctrine*, 45–46. A. Merk, "Origenes und der Kanon des Alten Testaments," *Bib* 6 (1925): 200–205, accepts Rufinus' translation as faithful (he does not even question it) and attempts to harmonize the statements here with Origen's use of Wisdom by positing that Origen here referred to 'songs' only, and he did not deem Wisdom to be a song (203). Hanson, *Doctrine*, 46 and n. 1, thinks this interpretation unlikely, but possible. However, Merk's suggestion will not work. The passage does not say that the Church accepts three of Solomon's songs. Rather, the Church accepts only one of Solomon's songs (i.e., the Song of Songs), and only three of Solomon's books. The passage excludes either that Solomon composed Wisdom, or that the Church accepts it, or both. Lawson (*Song*, 318 n. 65) also mentions Merk's suggestion as a potential explanation before ruling it out as "quite impossible."

[96] On Origen's seeming acceptance of Wisdom, see Ruwet, "Antilegomena de l'Ancien Testament," 23–31; Larcher, *Études*, 43–46. Some of Origen's more striking quotations of Wisdom in his *Comm. Cant.* are collected in Hanson, *Doctrine*, 45. For Rufinus' placement of Wisdom in his 'ecclesiastical' category, cf. his *Symb.* 36, and see Larcher, *Études*, 55–57, who fails to mention any Rufinian citation of Wisdom.

[97] Translation by Lawson, *Origen: The Song of Songs*, 39.

[98] Origen does say that a fourth branch is sometimes added, *viz.*, logic, which in most other schemes finds a place among the three branches instead of Origen's Enoptics. Jerome

Now, it is difficult to imagine that Rufinus added this entire discussion, and he cannot have omitted reference to the Wisdom of Solomon, because the total of four books would not find a correspondence with Greek learning. Aside from these obvious points, we may also note that Rufinus does not elsewhere scruple to include Origen's citations of Wisdom.[99] Furthermore, there is the evidence from Basil of Caesarea and his brother, Gregory of Nyssa, both of whom treat the three Books of Solomon in a way similar to Origen here, no doubt drawing on this passage or something similar in one of Origen's lost works. Indeed, Basil uses Origen's terminology for the first two books (ἦθος, φυσιολογία), while he associates Song of Songs with τελείωσις τῶν ψυχῶν ("the perfection of souls"), which is perhaps an interpretation of Origen's 'Enoptics.'[100] Thus, this earlier passage in Origen's *Comm. Cant.* authenticates the thoughts of the later passage as genuinely from Origen, since both of them assert that the Church accepts only three Books of Solomon. These two passages imply, then, either that Wisdom is not canonical, or that Solomon did not write it.

Several passages in Origen's works indicate that he did receive Wisdom as a divine book, useful in the Church, and indeed canonical. In *Comm. Cant.* 3, he gives an extended treatment of Wis. 7:17–21. Elsewhere, he does not hesitate to label the author of Wisdom a prophet, and he interprets certain passages as predictions of the Passion (*Hom. Exod.* 6.1; *Hom. Jer.* 2.1). In the *Comm. Jo.* 28.15(122), Origen introduces a quotation of Wis. 1:5 with the phrase εἰ δέ τις προσίεται ("if anyone accepts it"). This probably indicates that though he recognizes that the Church is divided on this issue, Origen himself does 'accept' the testimony of Wisdom.

---

(*Epist.* 30.1) uses the more traditional classification to link Proverbs to Ethics, Ecclesiastes to Physics, and Song of Songs to Logic. On the early history of the division of philosophy into three parts, an idea traceable to Xenocrates, see G. Reale, *A History of Ancient Philosophy, III: The Systems of the Hellenistic Age*, trans. J.R. Catan (Albany, 1985), 73–74. For Origen's categories and the use to which he puts them, see H. de Lubac, *Medieval Exegesis*, 2 vols. (1959; trans. Mark Sebanc; Grand Rapids, 1998), 1.148–149, and the corresponding notes on pp. 368–369; A. Louth, *The Origins of the Christian Mystical Tradition*² (Oxford, 2007), 56–58. M.J. Edwards lists the closest parallel to Origen as Theon of Smyrna, who includes the category *epopteia* ("Precursors of Origen's Hermeneutic Theory," *StPatr* 29 (1996), 232–237 (236)).

[99]   See Larcher, *Études*, 43–44 n. 6.

[100]   Basil, *Hom.* 12.1, PG 31.388a–b. For Gregory's presentation of these ideas, cf. his first homily on the Song of Songs in the edition of H. Langerbeck (ed.), *In Canticum Canticorum*, GNO 6 (Leiden, 1960), 17–19. On Gregory's reliance on Origen in his *Hom. Cant.*, see R.A. Norris, "The Soul Takes Flight: Gregory of Nyssa and the Song of Songs," *AThR* 80 (1998): 517–532 (523).

Finally, in an early work preserved only in Rufinus' Latin translation, Origen includes the following discussion on the proper definition of the word ὕλη (*materia*).

> *Et primo quidem sciendum est quod nomen ipsum materiae pro ea substantia quae subesse corporibus dicitur, positum in Scripturis canonicis nusquam usque ad praesens invenimus; illud enim quod dicit Esaias* [10:17], *"Et comedet sicut faenum ὕλην," id est materiam, dicens de eis, qui in suppliciis constituti sunt, materiam posuit pro peccatis. Sed et sicubi in alio loco scriptum forte materiae nomen est, nusquam, ut ego arbitror, hoc, de quo nunc quaerimus, significare invenietur, nisi tantummodo in Sapientia quae dicitur Salomonis, qui utique liber non ab omnibus in auctoritate habetur.*[101]

> And first of all it should be known that we have never found the word 'matter' used in the canonical scriptures for that substance which is said to underlie bodies. For that which Isaiah [10:17] says, "And he will consume hay (ὕλη)," i.e., 'matter,' speaking about those who were appointed for punishment, the word 'matter' stands for 'sins.' But also if anywhere in another place the word 'matter' is perhaps written, it will never, I think, be found to signify that concerning which we are seeking, unless only in Wisdom, which is called 'of Solomon,' which book is certainly not held in authority by all.

Ruwet argues persuasively that these thoughts originate with Origen and not with Rufinus, but he also thinks that Origen here implies that Wisdom is not one of the *Scripturae canonicae* because of the phrase *in alio loco* ("in another place") in reference to Wisdom.[102] However, the phrase *in alio loco* seems to contrast Wisdom with Isaiah, rather than with the canonical scriptures, and so this would imply that Wisdom, just as much as Isaiah, was in the canon.[103] Origen does acknowledge that not all of his readers will consider Wisdom to be authoritative, as he does in *Comm. Jo.* 28.15(122). But, Origen himself trusts what he finds in Wisdom and considers it *Scriptura canonica* (γραφὴ ἐνδιάθηκος?).

Since these passages suggest that Origen did accept Wisdom as scripture, then the two sections from the prologue to *Comm. Cant.* examined earlier, wherein he limits the canonical books of Solomon to Proverbs, Ecclesiastes, and Song of Songs, indicate not that he rejected Wisdom but that he did not attribute it to Solomon. The recognition that Solomon did not compose Wisdom would not be unique in patristic literature. When Augustine

---

[101] *Princ.* 4.4.6(33). The passage continues with a citation of Wis. 11:17 (Vul.: 11:18).

[102] Ruwet, "Antilegomena de l'Ancien Testament," 23–29, whose view is accepted by Horbury, "Christian Use," 188.

[103] See Larcher, *Études*, 43–44, who seems to understand the passage as I do.

presented his list of canonical books, he included the three universally accepted books of Solomon, and followed this by pointing out that Sirach and Wisdom are attributed to Solomon for stylistic reasons, but were both probably written by Jesus son of Sirach (*Doctr. chr.* 2.13; cf. *Civ.* 17.20; *Praed.* 26–29). Later, Augustine admitted that attributing Wisdom to Jesus son of Sirach had been a mistake, but offered no alternative suggestion for the author (*Retract.* 2.30.2). The Muratorian Fragment assigns the authorship of Wisdom either to Solomon's friends or to Philo.[104] This depends on whether the extant Latin *et sapientia ab amicis Salomonis in honorem ipsius scripta* ("and Wisdom, written by the friends of Solomon in his honor") is an accurate rendering of the Greek original, or whether S.P. Tregelles was correct in suggesting that the Latin translator misread his *Vorlage*, which would have contained καὶ ἡ Σοφία Σαλομῶνος ὑπὸ Φίλωνος εἰς τὴν τιμὴν αὐτοῦ γεγραμμένη ("and the Wisdom of Solomon, written by Philo in his honor"). This theory assumes that the translator confused ὑπὸ Φίλωνος with ὑπὸ φίλων.[105] Jerome is also aware that Solomon could not have composed the Book of Wisdom, for *ipse stilus graecam eloquentiam redolet* ("the very style is redolent of Greek eloquence"; *Praef. lib. Sal.* 17–18). He reports that many older writers (*nonnulli scriptorum veterum*) attributed the book to Philo, and in this statement he may have relied on material preserved in the Muratorian Fragment.[106] Eusebius of Caesarea refers to the author of Wisdom as ὁ τὴν

---

[104] The dating of the fragment is in dispute. The traditional second-century date has recently been defended by J. Verheyden, "The Canon Muratori: A Matter of Dispute," in Auwers and de Jonge, *Biblical Canons*, 487–556. A fourth-century date, accepted by many scholars now, is especially associated with A.C. Sundberg, "Canon Muratori: A Fourth Century List," *HTR* 66 (1973), 1–41; and G.M. Hahneman, *The Muratorian Fragment and the Development of the Canon* (Oxford, 1992).

[105] S.P. Tregelles, *Canon Muratorianus* (Oxford, 1867), 53; for the text of the fragment, see folio iia, lines 7–9, which Tregelles transcribes on p. 20. See also Larcher, *Études*, 40–41, who approves the retroversion and cites previous scholars in agreement. Hahneman (*Fragment*, 6–7) gives the Latin text of the fragment and accepts Tregelles' suggestion (13–14). However, W. Horbury has cast doubt on the suggestion of Tregelles ("The Wisdom of Solomon in the Muratorian Fragment," *JTS* 45 (1994): 149–159 (149–152)), and his proposal that we accept the extant Latin as an accurate translation finds agreement in J.R. Davila, *The Provenance of the Pseudepigrapha* (Leiden, 2005), 221.

[106] See Tregelles, *Canon*, 53. Tregelles believed that Jerome's dependence on the fragment was probable whether the fragment originally read ὑπὸ Φίλωνος or ὑπὸ φίλων; see p. 55 and note. The fourth-century dating of the Fragment does not rule out Jerome's dependence; even Hahneman believes that "Jerome may have seen the Fragment or derived his information from it" (*Fragment*, 201). It may be that the attribution to Philo is also reflected in Basil's *Epist.* 190.3, on which see A. Kamesar, "San Basilio, Filone, e la tradizione ebraica," *Henoch* 17 (1995): 129–140; Horbury, "Christian Use," 190 n. 36.

πανάρετον σοφίαν εἰς αὐτοῦ [sc. Σολομῶντος] πρόσωπον ἀναθείς ("the one who ascribed to his [Solomon's] person all-virtuous wisdom"; *Praep. ev.* 11.7.5), a circumlocution that avoids attributing the work directly to Solomon. Furthermore, Larcher notes the hesitancy with which the Cappadocians and Antiochenes speak about the author of the book, never attributing it to Solomon.[107] Thus, while some Christians apparently did not question the Solomonic authorship of the Book of Wisdom,[108] *non autem*, as Augustine remarks, *esse ipsius non dubitant doctiores* ("the more learned do not doubt that it is not his"; *Civ.* 17.20).

Origen himself does not outright say that Solomon did not author the Book of Wisdom, and he does sometimes cite Wisdom as from Solomon.[109] These instances could without difficulty be attributed to a failure of memory on Origen's part regarding which 'wisdom' book he was citing; he also cites Sirach as from Solomon (*Hom. Jes. Nav.* 11.2, citing Sir. 2:1), though he knows certainly the correct name of its author (*Cels.* 6.7; cf. *Comm. Jo.* 6.183).[110] Origen's citations of Wisdom as from Solomon also may exhibit mere customary expression in a context not requiring precision of language. In any case, Origen is more careful elsewhere to describe the book as ἡ Σοφία ἡ ἐπιγεγραμμένη Σολομῶντος ("Wisdom inscribed 'of Solomon'"), which implies some ambiguity as to the actual authorship.[111] In fact, by this phrase Origen probably intended merely to distinguish this ἡ Σοφία from that other one by Jesus son of Sirach, which he also cites by the unqualified title ἡ Σοφία,

---

[107] Larcher (*Études*, 51–54) collects their citations of Wisdom. He says that especially Basil and Gregory of Nyssa, along with John Chrysostom, "paraissent éprouver un certain malaise au sujet de l'auteur du livre. Ils citent volontiers ce dernier comme Écriture, mais ils hésitent à y voir l'œuvre de Salomon" (53). Larcher later says that Theodoret of Cyrus also "évite le nom de Salomon" (54).

[108] Larcher has assembled the evidence in his *Études*: for Clement of Alexandria and Ps.-Hippolytus, see 39–40; for Tertullian and Cyprian, see 41–42; for Cyril of Jerusalem, see 47 n. 5; for Hilary and Ambrose, see 54–55. Larcher does not cite any other ancient writer as explicitly attributing a statement from the book to Solomon. Horbury, "Christian Use," 189–190, surveys Christian views on the authorship of Wisdom and finds a great deal of diversity.

[109] *Hom. Lev.* 12.4.1; *Comm. Rom.* 7.4.10. These passages would have been better support for Hahneman's claim (*Fragment*, 201) that Origen cited Wisdom "frequently as a work of Solomon." Instead, Hahneman cited *Cels.* 5.29, which does not attribute the work to Solomon, or, at least, not without a great deal of ambiguity.

[110] For a similar explanation regarding some of Jerome's citations of the deuterocanonical wisdom literature, see L. Schade, *Die Inspirationslehre des heiligen Hieronymus* (Freiburg, 1910), 194, 195–198, 201.

[111] *Hom. Jer.* 8.1.3. A slightly different but equivalent formulation is found in *Cels.* 5.29; *Comm. Jo.* 20.26; *Princ.* 1.2.5; *Comm. Cant.* prologue.

as do other writers.[112] 'Wisdom of Solomon' was the only title that clearly expressed which book was intended, and it is the logical title since Solomon is the persona assumed by the author of the book. The problem of a title distinguishing Wisdom of Solomon from Sirach was removed only when Sirach received the title 'Ecclesiasticus.'[113] This allowed Augustine to refer to Wisdom of Solomon simply by *Sapientia* without further elaboration (*Praed.* 27; *Doctr. chr.* 2.13).

All of this indicates that while Origen did not think Solomon wrote the Book of Wisdom, he did consider it to be scripture. His attitude toward the book was not determined by the Jewish rejection of it. Whether he would put Wisdom in a category apart from the 'certainly canonical' and into a category that Rufinus would call ecclesiastical, as Ruwet has argued,[114] is a moot point; we will argue below that Origen accepted the canonicity of the ecclesiastical books, in any case. The Wisdom of Solomon was in the canon, but Solomon did not write it.[115]

Origen does attest that not all Christians shared his positive evaluation of Wisdom. He does not say that their negative stance toward the book derived from the Jewish opinion of the work, but this influence is very probable.[116] The questions surrounding the book's authorship may also have

---

[112] For Origen, cf. *Hom. Jer.* 6.2.2; *Comm. Rom.* 7.17.5; *Hom. Jes. Nav.* 15.6. Cf. also Clement of Alexandria, *Paed.* 1.8, 9.

[113] D. de Bruyne argued that this title arose in the Latin tradition likely as a result of an early translation from a Greek text that lacked the grandson's prologue ("Le prologue, le titre et la finale de l'Ecclésiastique," *ZAW* 47 (1929): 257–263). De Bruyne thus attributes the title to the original Latin translator. J.N.D. Kelly lists Cyprian (*Test.* 3.110–113) as the first to use this title; see *Rufinus: A Commentary on the Apostle's Creed*, ACW 20 (New York, 1954), 139 n. 232. However, de Bruyne's insistence (260–261) that Rufinus incorrectly attributed the origin of the title 'Ecclesiasticus' to its pre-eminent position among the ecclesiastical books is based on a misreading of Rufinus. De Bruyne's suggestion that the Latin title for Sirach is based on the model of Ecclesiastes has more to commend it, though it is unclear how it is supported by Jerome's report of a Hebrew manuscript containing Sirach (under the name *Parabolae*), Ecclesiastes, and Song of Songs (262; cf. Jerome, *Praef. lib. Sal.* 14–17). On recent research into the VL of Sirach, see A.J. Forte, "The Old Latin Version of Sirach: Editio Critica and Textual Problems," in J.-S. Rey and J. Joosten (eds.), *The Texts and Versions of the Book of Ben Sira* (Leiden, 2011), 199–214; and, in the same volume, Th. Legrand, "La version latine de Ben Sira: état de la question, essai de classement thématique des 'additions'," 215–234.

[114] Ruwet, "Antilegomena de l'Ancien Testament," 29–31.

[115] *Contra* Sundberg (*Old Testament*, 138), who thinks that though Origen did not limit his canon to that of the Jews, he did not admit Wisdom. Sundberg's evidence is that Wisdom was not accepted in all the churches. That could equally be said of any of the deuterocanonicals, or even some of the protocanonicals (e.g. Esther), and cannot serve as a criterion for Origen's own canon.

[116] Larcher, *Études*, 44.

induced some to hold it in suspicion. Indeed, these two factors could have arisen together. Certain Christians (the *doctior*, as Augustine calls them) may have become aware of the authorship problems under guidance from the Jews, or possibly they applied their own critical faculty, as did Jerome.[117] Origen himself was fully aware of the authorship problems and of the Jewish rejection of the book, but these facts did not deter him from frequently citing it and accepting its canonicity. His attitude toward Wisdom, then, does not prove that he adhered to the synagogal criterion; quite the reverse is the case.

### The Jews and the Oracles of God

We may now examine the other phrase of interest in the passage quoted earlier from the end of the prologue to Origen's *Comm. Cant.* There, Origen says of the Jews, "from whom the oracles of God were evidently transferred to us." De Lange used this phrase as evidence that Origen did abide by the synagogal criterion, thus showing his rejection of that standard in his *Ep. Afr.* to be disingenuous.[118] However, we have seen from other passages that Origen himself does not abide by the synagogal criterion. We have also seen that it is unlikely that Rufinus altered the phrasing here in any significant way. Therefore, the necessary conclusion is that Origen's phrase simply states the obvious fact that the OT is a collection of Jewish documents. Origen does not intend to address which books are in or out of the Jewish canon. The context concerns the proper name of the Song of Songs, and whether this Song might be one of many from Solomon's pen. In fact, says Origen, there are no others anywhere, among Christians or Jews.

### Origen and Enoch

One final piece of evidence for Origen's acceptance of the smaller Jewish canon concerns his attitude toward the books going under the name Enoch.[119] Origen references 1 Enoch in four of his extant works. The earliest

---

[117] Jerome, *Praef. lib. Sal.* 17–18, rejects Wisdom as pseudonymous based on its Greek style. Larcher (*Études*, 53) thinks that literary criticism may have played a part in doubts held by other Fathers over the authorship of Wisdom.

[118] De Lange, "Origen's Recantation?" 247.

[119] For discussion of which passages in 1 Enoch Origen quotes, see VanderKam, "1 Enoch," 54–59. On the parts of 1 Enoch known to Origen, see G.W.E. Nickelsburg, *1 Enoch 1*, Hermeneia (Minneapolis, 2001), 92, who lists "the Book of the Watchers [chs. 1–36], the Book of the Luminaries [chs. 72–82], and probably the Book of Parables [chs. 37–71]." That Origen thought of these as separate books is indicated by his comments in *Hom. Num.* 28.2 and *Cels.* 5.54.

of these contains a reference to the *Enoch liber* (*Princ.* 1.3.3) and some citations of it (*Princ.* 4.4.8(35); all preserved in Rufinus' Latin) without any apparent hesitation. Increased caution accompanies his move to Caesarea. In the sixth book of his *Comm. Jo.*, Origen introduces a quotation with the concession, ὡς ἐν τῷ Ἐνὼχ γέγραπται, εἴ τῳ φίλον παραδέχεσθαι ὡς ἅγιον τὸ βιβλίον ("as it is written in Enoch, if one wants to accept this book as sacred Scripture"; 6.25(217)).[120] Later still, he confesses in the *Hom. Num.* 28.2 his reluctance to draw evidence from Enoch because it is rejected by the Jews:

> *Sed quia libelli ipsi* [sc. *qui appellantur Enoc*] *non videntur apud Hebraeos in auctoritate haberi, interim nunc ea, quae ibi nominantur, ad exemplum vocare differamus, sed ex his, quae habemus in manibus, de quibus dubitari non potest, rerum prosequamur indaginem.*

> But because those books [which are called 'Enoch'] are evidently not considered authoritative among the Hebrews, for now let us delay calling to example those things that are named there, but rather from these which we have in hand, concerning which there is no possibility of doubt, let us pursue the investigation of the matters.

Finally, he criticizes Celsus for his ignorance that the churches do not accept the Book of Enoch: ἐν ταῖς ἐκκλησίαις οὐ πάνυ φέρεται ὡς θεῖα τὰ ἐπιγεγραμμένα τοῦ Ἐνὼχ βιβλία ("in the churches the books inscribed 'Of Enoch' do not at all circulate as divine"; *Cels.* 5.54). And in the same context, Origen describes a statement from Enoch as πρᾶγμα οὔτε λεγόμενον οὔτ' ἀκουόμενον ἐν ταῖς ἐκκλησίαις τοῦ θεοῦ ("a thing neither read nor heard in the churches of God"; *Cels.* 5.55).

These statements could indicate an evolution in Origen's opinion of the books of Enoch,[121] and one might attribute this evolution to Origen's growing awareness of the (lack of) reception of Enoch in Jewish circles. However, Origen's statements may point toward only increased caution in using the Enochic materials rather than a declining estimation of them. In fact, Origen's position regarding Enoch very well may have remained consistent throughout his career if we interpret the statements cited above in terms

---

[120] The translation is by R.E. Heine in FOC 80 (1989). VanderKam ("1 Enoch," 56) seems to think that the sixth book of Origen's *Comm. Jo.*, was written while he was still in Alexandria, but the opening section of the sixth book (*Comm. Jo.* 6.1(8, 11)) makes it clear that Origen has by now moved to Caesarea, a fact recognized already by Eusebius (*Hist. eccl.* 6.24). Aside from this, VanderKam (60) does recognize that Origen's statements about 1 Enoch reflect more caution upon his move north.

[121] See, e.g., Ruwet, "Antilegomena de l'Ancien Testament," 48–50; Hanson, *Doctrine*, 136; VanderKam, "1 Enoch," 54–59.

of his cautious use of 'apocrypha' (i.e., pseudepigrapha) as articulated in
*Ep. Afr.* 13–15 and *Comm. ser. Matt.* 28.[122] In these two latter passages, Origen explains that the apocrypha, properly used, can provide information valuable to the exegesis of biblical texts. He does not advocate the canonicity of these apocrypha, and he does recognize heretical elements in them, so that they prove useful only to mature Christians. Nevertheless, they can be regarded as 'sacred' in some sense (cf. *Comm. Jo.* 6.25(217), quoted earlier), along the lines expressed in 4 Ezra 14, where 70 inspired books stand alongside the 24 canonical books. In regard to the general attitude toward scripture in early Judaism and early Christianity, Richard Bauckham has written:

> The collection [of Hebrew Scriptures] was virtually closed. This did not prevent anyone recognizing other books as also inspired, but the status of such other, noncanonical books was not agreed.[123]

Such a view probably underlies Origen's early citations of Enoch in *Princ.* 1.3.3 and 4.35. Maintaining this tempered approval of the book, Origen nevertheless grew more hesitant to cite Enoch without qualification after his move north. The citations in *Comm. Jo.* 6.25(217) and *Hom. Num.* 28.2 seem to indicate that Origen himself still found the Enochic works useful even as he increasingly recognized that others did not. It is probably no coincidence that this recognition occurred in Palestine, where the influence of Jews on the Church in general was more prominent. While some groups of Palestinian Jews at an earlier time deemed the Enochic literature valuable, this seems to have been no longer the case by the time Origen wrote, and Palestinian Christian use of it before Origen is limited to the Epistle of Jude.[124] This implies that the books of Enoch did not enjoy great esteem among Christians generally in Palestine by the time of Origen, perhaps due in part to their low estimation among Palestinian Jews.

From this vantage point, Origen's later statements about Enoch may reveal only his rhetorical strategy in dealing with material rejected by many. In *Cels.* 5.54–55, Origen exploits effectively the non-canonical status of

---

[122] On Origen's use of OT pseudepigrapha, see Ruwet, "Les apocryphes, II"; Hanson, *Doctrine*, 134–136; on Origen's *Comm. ser. Matt.* 28, see Ruwet, *art. cit.*, 311–312; Hanson, op. cit., 142–143. On Origen's use of the term 'apocrypha' for what now goes under the name 'pseudepigrapha,' see Adler, "Pseudepigrapha," 212–215.

[123] R. Bauckham, *Jude and the Relatives of Jesus in the Early Church* (Edinburgh, 1990), 230.

[124] See the survey in VanderKam, "1 Enoch," 33–60. In regard to Jude's citation of Enoch, see Bauckham, *Jude*, 225–233, who explains Jude 14 in a fashion very similar to the approach to Origen taken here. On the Jewish use, see p. 233.

Enoch to score polemical points.[125] This heightened rhetoric should not be taken as normative for Origen's own views, and it does not show that he accepted the synagogal criterion. Although *Hom. Num.* 28.2 ties Origen's reluctance to cite Enoch to the Jewish reception of the work, even here the Jewish view does not settle the matter for Origen. Rather, his statement about the Jewish rejection of Enoch appears to be merely a concession for his audience—he anticipates an objection to his use of Enoch and obviates it. Nickelsburg evaluates Origen's "ambivalence" toward the text exhibited in his *Hom. Num.* as involving "an inclination to cite it and a recognition that it may not carry the authority necessary to make his point."[126] Origen's *De oratione* 14.4, also written during his Caesarean period, may provide a parallel case. Here, Origen cites the Prayer of the Three Young Men and a passage from Tobit before saying that the absence of these texts from the Jewish Bible prompts him to add another citation from a work that the Jews do consider canonical. Origen obviously found the two deuterocanonical texts helpful, or else he would not have cited them at all. Indeed, as he reveals in his *Ep. Afr.* (§ 4, 19), Origen considered them to be part of the Christian Bible. The fact that he finds it beneficial in *Or.* 14.4 to supplement these citations with another from a passage in the Jewish canon means that the deuterocanonical books will not carry sufficient weight with all of his readers. This is because some of his readers deem the Jewish biblical canon authoritative in the Church, not because Origen does so. Similarly, the Jewish views on Enoch had led many Christians (though probably not Origen) to consider the book worthless, and so Origen does not rely on it to make his argument in *Hom. Num.* 28.2. He himself, however, thought the Enochic materials to be useful apocrypha.

*Conclusion*
We are thus left without any explicit advocacy that the Church should follow the Jews in canonical matters, though we have just seen that Origen makes certain concessions toward such a view, which he believes some among his audience will hold. Moreover, there does seem to be a strong presumption toward the synagogal criterion in the numerous canonical lists transmitted by the Fathers, excepting only Origen's. But now the position of Jerome must be considered.

---

[125] See Nickelsburg, *1 Enoch 1*, 92.
[126] Nickelsburg, *1 Enoch 1*, 91.

## *Jerome*

Jerome is well-known as the chief exponent of the *Hebraica veritas*, but this phrase typically refers to textual matters and so properly belongs to our discussion in Chapter Five. While Megan Hale Williams argues that Jerome can encompass canonical issues within the concept of the *Hebraica veritas*, the one example she provides concerns the order of the Twelve Minor Prophets rather than the issue of which books belong within the Bible, and so it does not exactly fit into our investigation.[127] Nevertheless, the phrase *Hebraica veritas* certainly points in the direction of the Jews as in some way the proprietors of biblical learning, at least for the OT.[128] As we will see later, Jerome considered the *Hebraica veritas* to be authentically Christian because, as he argued, the writers of the New Testament relied on the Hebrew text for their quotations from the OT.[129] By this argument, Jerome sought to obviate any charge of judaizing; to his mind, the Jewish text was actually the Christian text.

When Jerome lists the OT books in his 'Helmeted Preface' (*Prologus galeatus*, henceforth *Prol. gal.*) to his translations from the Hebrew Bible, he once again seeks to establish the Jewish position as normative for the Church.[130] As for the actual contents of the biblical canon, Jerome probably considered himself firmly within ecclesiastical custom, since the books he includes match nearly identically those in the lists of his Greek and Latin predecessors, which we examined earlier. The arrangement of books Jerome

---

[127] M.H. Williams, *The Monk and the Book* (Chicago, 2006), 91 and n. 71. The passages she cites include *Praef. xii proph.* (lines 1–2); *Comm. Joel.* prol.; *Comm. Mal.* prol., but the first of these does not actually contain the phrase *Hebraica veritas*. The correct order of the Minor Prophets bears exegetical consequences since Jerome transmits the tradition that prophets without date formulas in their superscriptions worked under the same kings as the previous prophet in canonical sequence (*Praef. xii proph.*, lines 8–10). On a similar tradition regarding the 'orphan' psalms, transmitted by Origen and other Fathers, as well as the Rabbis, see de Lange, *Origen*, 55.

[128] See the wider discussion by Williams, *Monk*, 81–95.

[129] For the importance of this argument for Jerome's assessment of the Hebrew text, see C. Markschies, "Hieronymus und die *'Hebraica Veritas'*: Ein Beitrag zur Archaologie des protestantischen Schriftverständnisses?" in M. Hengel and A.M. Schwemer (eds.), *Die Septuaginta* (Tübingen, 1994), 131–181: "Die Autorität des Neuen Testamentes autorisiert zugleich die hebräische Bibel; da aber die neutestamentlichen Autoren aus dem masoretischen Text zitieren, ist dieser als autoritative Bibel des Alten Testamentes zu bevorzugen" (147).

[130] Besides the *Prol. gal.*, see *Epist.* 53.8 and 107.12 for the two other listings by Jerome of biblical books. All of these lists date to the last decade of the fourth century. For the slight and, for our purposes, insignificant variations among them, see J. Braverman, *Jerome's Commentary on Daniel* (Washington, D.C., 1978), 48–49. On *Epist.* 53, see M.E. Schild, *Abendländische Bibelvorreden bis zur Lutherbibel* (Heidelberg, 1970), 42–48.

follows in the *Prol. gal.* closely coheres to the standard Jewish arrangement of Law, Prophets, and Writings, and in this Jerome's list distinguishes itself from the other Christian lists, even those that claim to reflect Jewish precedent in terms of order.[131] Thus, Jerome probably thought of his list as innovative within a Christian context not in terms of the identity of the canonical books he lists, but instead in terms of the tripartite division of the OT, as well as his definitive exclusion of all other books as 'apocrypha.' Both of these aspects aim to align the Christian OT more closely with the Jewish Bible.

As for the latter point, the exclusion of the 'apocrypha,' Jerome flatly declares after his listing of the Jewish canonical books: *quicquid extra hos est, inter apocrifa sepondendum* ("whatever is outside these [books] should be consigned to the apocrypha"; lines 53–54). He continues by listing specific books that thus fall into the category of 'apocrypha':

> *Igitur Sapientia, quae vulgo Salomonis inscribitur, et Iesu filii Sirach liber et Iudith et Tobias et Pastor non sunt in canone. Macchabeorum primum librum hebraicum repperi, secundus graecus est, quod et ex ipsa φρασιν probari potest.*[132]                (lines 54–57)

> Therefore Wisdom, which is commonly inscribed 'of Solomon,' and the Book of Jesus son of Sirach, and Judith, and Tobit, and the Shepherd are not in the canon. I have found the first book of Maccabees in Hebrew, but the second is Greek, which can be proven even from the style itself.

Though Jerome elsewhere takes a softer stance against these particular books (cf. esp. *Praef. lib. Sal.* 19–21) and draws citations from them throughout his career, he consistently excludes them from the canon.[133] Schild says that this class of books stands outside the canon "weil sie nicht ursprünglich in hebräischer Sprache geschrieben ist."[134] Clearly, this is not the case.

---

[131] However, for a possible alternative Jewish order reflected in these other lists, see Katz, "Old Testament."

[132] On the inclusion of the Shepherd of Hermas in this list, see Horbury, "Wisdom of Solomon," 152–156, who shows that a common practice entailed grouping *antilegomena* together, whether they properly belong to the *antilegomena* of the OT or NT. Compare the lists of Athanasius (*Ep. fest.* 39) and Rufinus (*Symb.* 34–36), which follow this practice. Admittedly, however, this explanation does not quite solve the problem in reference to Jerome; see further discussion below. On the absence of Baruch from this list, see Schade, *Inspirationslehre*, 173–175.

[133] For further discussion of Jerome's attitude toward what he calls here 'apocrypha,' including an evaluation of the common view that he once included these books in his canon, see E.L. Gallagher, "The Old Testament 'Apocrypha' in Jerome's Canonical Theory," *JECS* 20 (*forthcoming*, 2012).

[134] Schild, *Bibelvorreden*, 27.

Jerome says in this very passage that 1 Maccabees was written in Hebrew, and elsewhere he says the same thing about Sirach (*Praef. lib. Sal.* 14). While it is true that he allowed only Hebrew documents into the canon, the major operative principle for Jerome was the synagogal criterion. As Williams has written, "It was the authority of the Jews, not the Hebrew language alone, that served as Jerome's criterion of canonicity."[135]

A few years later, in the preface to his translation of Ezra, he again made this principle plain. There, he writes: *quae non habentur apud illos* [sc. *Hebraeos*] *nec de viginti quattuor senibus sunt, procul abicienda* ("what things are not contained among the Hebrews and are not from the twenty-four elders, let them be cast away"; *Praef. Ezr.* 20–21). The mention of 'twenty-four elders' relies on the analogy between the 24 elders of John's Apocalypse (4:4) in the New Testament and the 24 books of the OT (cf. *Praef. Dan.* 47–48; *Comm. Ezech.* 43:13–17). It thus involves a Christian interpretation of the OT canon, as opposed to the reckoning of 22 books, which predominates in patristic literature and works on analogy with the number of letters in the Hebrew alphabet, thus seemingly more Jewish in orientation. However, Jerome presents both numbering schemes, 22 and 24, in his *Prol. gal.*, explaining them as alternatives current among the Jews. While the number 22 dominates his discussion early in the preface, and requires him to count Ruth with Judges and Lamentations with Jeremiah as part of the Prophets, he later informs his readers that some Jews enumerate individually Ruth and Lamentations and place them among the Hagiographa (*Prol. gal.* 44–51), thus arriving at the number 24.[136] This is, of course, the number more widely known in Jewish circles, being attested first in 4 Ezra 14:45 (cf. *Gos. Thom.* 52) and later assumed in the Talmudic discussion (*b. B. Bathra*

---

[135] Williams, *Monk*, 91; see also Wermelinger, "Le canon des Latins," 188.

[136] In the same passage he again links the 24 books to the 24 elders of the Apocalypse. We see this analogy also in the *Commentary on the Apocalypse* by Victorinus of Pettau (commenting on Rev. 4:4; CSEL 49, ed. J. Haussleiter, 50.2–6, 54.8–10, 55.3–6) and in the Mommsen Catalogue, which concludes its OT list with the statement: *sed ut in apocalypsis Johannis dictum est "vidi XXIIII seniores mittentes coronas suas ante thronum,"* maiores nostri probant hos libros esse canonicos et hoc dixisse seniores. These words are quite curious following a list of 27 books, including 1 and 2 Maccabees, Tobit, and Judith, but not Ezra; the subsequent list of NT books does include 24 items, and it is possible that the analogy between the 24 elders and the 24 books is meant to apply (also) to the NT. See P.-M. Bogaert, "Aux origines de la fixation du canon: Scriptoria, listes et titres. Le *Vaticanus* et la stichométrie de Mommsen," in Auwers and de Jonge, *Biblical Canons*, 153–176 (168–169). The text is in Zahn, *Geschichte*, 2.144, and his discussion of the number 24 is at 2.148–150. In modern times, the analogy between the 24 elders and the 24 books has been tentatively endorsed by Beckwith, *Old Testament*, 262.

14b).[137] Though Jerome uses a Christian image to 'sanctify' the number 24, he relies on Jewish tradition to establish it as correct. Just as he advocated the Hebrew text as the correct textual base for the Christian OT, so also Jerome advocated the Jewish canon for the Church.

## THE ECCLESIASTICAL CRITERION

Opposed to the synagogal criterion we find some Christian authors advocating an 'ecclesiastical criterion': a document's canonicity is guaranteed by its use in the Church, regardless of what Jews do with it. We have seen that this position was first articulated by Tertullian, but its most ardent patristic defenders were Origen and Augustine. The latter clearly rejects the synagogal criterion and opposes to it a book's Christian reception as determinative for canonicity:

> sed non sunt omittendi et hi [sc. libri] quos quidem ante saluatoris aduentum constat esse conscriptos, sed eos non receptos a Iudaeis recepit tamen eiusdem saluatoris ecclesia.[138]

> But also those books should not be omitted which are agreed to have been written before the advent of the Savior, because even though they are not accepted by the Jews, yet the Church of that same Savior has accepted them.

As Augustine indicates in this passage, the principle of Church usage expanded the Jewish canon to include Second Temple documents post-dating the Jewish chronological termination for inspiration.

---

[137] Aside from the references in the previous note, the number 24 appears in at least two other early Christian sources. Hilary of Poitiers (*Instr. Ps.* 15) reports that as an alternative to the traditional 22-book numbering, which accords with the Hebrew alphabet, some (he does not specify whether Jews or Christians) add Tobit and Judith to arrive at 24 books, in accordance with the Greek alphabet. Twenty-four is also the number given in Ps-Tertullian, *Carmen adv. Marcionem* 4.198–199, again (as in Victorinus, the Mommsen Catalogue, and Jerome) linked to the 24 elders of the Apocalypse. The date of this work is in dispute; for a recent argument for a rather early date (third century), see S. Moll, *The Arch-Heretic Marcion* (Tübingen, 2010), 21–24.

[138] This statement forms part of the preface to *Speculum* 22, in which chapter Augustine discusses the Book of Wisdom. Cf. also *Retract.* 2.20 (Wisdom); *Civ.* 17.20 (Wisdom and Sirach); 18.26 (Judith); 18.36 (Maccabees). J.N. Lightstone strangely calls on Augustine as a witness to a wider Jewish canon in the fourth-century Western Diaspora, on the assumption that Augustine understood that the Christian OT was "supposed to be no more or less than the Jew's scriptures"; see "The Rabbis' Bible: The Canon of the Hebrew Bible and the Early Rabbinic Guild," in McDonald and Sanders, *Canon Debate*, 163–184 (171–172). Augustine himself explicitly denies the principle articulated by Lightstone, so he certainly does not derive his canon from a contemporary Jewish one.

In affirming the canonicity of the two 'Solomonic' books not written by Solomon, Augustine says of Wisdom and Sirach: *eos tamen in auctoritatem maxime occidentalis antiquitus recepit ecclesia* ("the Church especially in the West has accepted them as authoritative from antiquity"; *Civ.* 17.20). A survey of patristic comments on the liturgical use of what Rufinus called the ecclesiastical books bears out Augustine's geographical distinction. Eastern sources restrict the liturgical use of documents to the books of the Jewish canon. Cyril of Jerusalem (*Catach.* 4.36–38) emphatically asserts that only the 22 books accepted by the Jews find a place in Christian liturgy, and he advises catechumens to maintain this standard in their private reading. Athanasius (*Ep. fest.* 39) assigns the ecclesiastical books the role of elementary instruction in the faith, as do the Apostolic Canons (canon 85); this position seems to discount their use in the liturgy. The Council of Laodicea is more explicit; in the same context in which it limits the OT canon to 22 books, it says:

Ὅτι οὐ δεῖ ἰδιωτικοὺς ψαλμοὺς λέγεσθαι ἐν τῇ ἐκκλησίᾳ οὐδὲ ἀκανόνιστα βιβλία ἀναγινώσκεσθαι, ἀλλὰ μόνα τὰ κανονικὰ τῆς καινῆς καὶ παλαιᾶς διαθήκης.

(canon 59)

That psalms composed by individuals must not to be recited in church nor should noncanonical books be read, but only the canonical books of the New and Old Testament.

However, the matter stood differently among Latin writers: Jerome, Rufinus, and Augustine all affirm that the ecclesiastical books are used in the corporate worship of the Church.[139]

The sticking point regards how this Christian use should be interpreted. Jerome and Rufinus leave no doubt as to their position: Christians may use these books not received by the Jews, but they are not canonical. In practical terms, these books may find a place in the public worship of the Church, but they cannot establish dogma. As Jerome says, *non ad auctoritatem ecclesiasticorum dogmatum confirmandam* ("not for authoritative confirmation of ecclesiastical dogmas"; *Praef. lib. Sal.* 21); or, again, Rufinus: *non tamen proferri ad auctoritatem ex his fidei confirmandem* ("but not to be brought forward from these for the authoritative confirmation of the faith"; *Symb.* 36). We could say, then, that Jerome and Rufinus explicitly reject the

---

[139] Jerome, *Praef. lib. Sal.* 19–21; Rufinus, *Symb.* 36; Augustine, *Praed.* 27 (concerning Wisdom of Solomon, specifically). On the occasions for the liturgical use of the ecclesiastical books, see La Bonnardière, "Canon," 35.

ecclesiastical criterion—Christian use is no guarantee of canonicity.[140] Jerome's *Praef. Jud.* leaves no doubt that this book stands outside his canon of scripture, nor that the wise Christian will read and learn from Judith's example.[141] Likewise, in the preface to his *Comm. Jon.*, he introduces a citation of Tobit with the words, *liber quoque Tobiae, licet non habeatur in canone, tamen quia usurpatur ab ecclesiasticis uiris* [...] ("and the Book of Tobit, although it is not contained in the canon, still because it is used by ecclesiastical men ..."). These books are 'ecclesiastical,' or, as Athanasius says, 'to be read' by the Church, but they are not in the canon.

Augustine and the North African Councils take the opposite line. The *Breviarium Hipponense*, which preserves the acts of the Council of Hippo of 393, begins its list of canonical books with the statement: *ut praeter scripturas canonicas nihil in ecclesia legatur sub nomine divinarum scripturarum* ("that beyond the canonical scriptures nothing should be read in Church under the name of the divine scriptures"; canon 36).[142] Therefore, if the Church reads a 'scriptural' book, it is a canonical book. Similarly, Augustine responds to the objection of some that the Book of Wisdom is not canonical by arguing that its employment in the liturgy implies its divine authority.

> [...] non debuit repudiari sententia libri Sapientiae, qui meruit in Ecclesia Christi de gradu lectorum Ecclesiae Christi tam longa annositate recitari, et ab omnibus Christianis, ab episcopis usque ad extremos laicos fideles, poenitentes, catechumenos, cum veneratione divinae auctoritatis audiri.[143]
>
> *(Praed.* 14(27); PL 44.980)

> The judgment of the Book of Wisdom ought not to be repudiated, which has earned the right to be recited in the Church of Christ from the position of the readers of the Church of Christ for such a long age, and to be heard by all Christians, from bishops all the way to the most common believers, penitents, and catechumens, with the veneration belonging to divine authority.

---

[140] Contrast this with the assessment of Rufinus' criterion offered by Wermelinger ("Le canon des Latins," 164): "Un livre est canonique s'il est l'objet d'une tradition vivante, s'il est lu dans l'Église." Rufinus makes exceedingly clear that this is not true—the ecclesiastical books, he says, are read in church but are not canonical.

[141] For a brief commentary on Jerome's prefaces to Judith and Tobit, see P.-M. Bogaert, *Judith*, Vetus Latina 7/2, fasc. 1 (Freiburg, 2001), 30–32.

[142] This canon from the Council of Hippo was reaffirmed a few years later at the Council of Carthage (397), to which we owe its preservation. See the discussion in Zahn, *Geschichte*, 2.246–253; cf. Heinrich Denzinger and Peter Hünermann, *Enchiridion symbolorum definitionum et declarationum de rebus fidei et morum*[39] (Freiburg, 2001), §186.

[143] For the use of the Book of Wisdom in the African liturgy, see La Bonnardière, *Livre de la Sagesse*, 59–83.

In the words of Wermelinger, "C'est l'usage liturgique qui leur confère une force dogmatique et un caractère canonique."[144]

However, for Augustine, the liturgical use of scripture is not the only guarantee of its canonicity. In fact, the passage in which he lists the canonical books does not mention their public reading but rather emphasizes their 'acceptance' by the catholic Church.

> *Tenebit* [sc. *divinarum Scripturarum solertissimus indagator*] *igitur hunc modum in Scripturis canonicis, ut eas, quae ab omnibus accipiuntur Ecclesiis catholicis, praeponat eis, quas quidam non accipiunt; in eis uero, quae non accipiuntur ab omnibus, praeponat eas, quas plures grauioresque accipiunt, eis, quas pauciores minorisque auctoritatis Ecclesiae tenent.*          (*Doctr. chr.* 2.12)

> [The most skilled researcher of the divine scriptures] will therefore maintain this rule for the canonical scriptures, that he should prefer those which are accepted by all catholic churches over the others which some do not accept; but among those which are not accepted by all, he should prefer those which the more numerous and more important churches accept, over those which the churches that are fewer and of less authority maintain.

No doubt, Augustine assumed that these books would be used in the liturgy, and Rufinus and Jerome both report that Latin churches so used all of the books in Augustine's canon, but the ecclesiastical criterion does not have to be based on public reading. Here, Augustine's standard is "time-hallowed Church usage,"[145] however broadly that might be conceived.

---

[144] Wermelinger, "Le canon des Latins," 195. C.J. Costello points out that not all books read liturgically were considered canonical: "The reading of the Acts of the Martyrs on their anniversaries was expressly permitted [by the African Synods; cf. again *Breviarium Hipponense* 36]. Moreover it is not unusual to find St. Augustine himself reading in church from the writings of Cyprian, and from ecclesiastical records, particularly in his many controversies" (*St. Augustine's Doctrine on the Inspiration and Canonicity of Scripture* (Washington, D.C., 1930), 68). Clearly, these non-canonical works would not be read *sub nomine divinarum scripturarum*, in the words of the *Breviarium* (canon 36), so there would be no implication that they were *scripturae canonicae*. Rabbinic Judaism may offer a parallel to the idea that liturgical use implies canonicity: the prohibition against reading 'outside books' (ספרים החיצונים) may concern reading in the public assembly rather than private reading; cf. *m. San.* 10.1, and see Veltri, *Libraries*, 17.

[145] The expression comes from A.D.R. Polman, *The Word of God According to St. Augustine* (1955; ET Grand Rapids, 1961), 190. See also Ellis: "Augustine preferred to rely on the traditional usage of the churches and on patristic citations to establish the limits of the canon" (*Old Testament*, 30). Costello formulates Augustine's criteria this way: a book is canonical "first of all, because it has been received and read by the Church as a divine book, and secondly, because it has been used as divine by the Church from apostolic times" (*St. Augustine's Doctrine*, 77–86; quotation from p. 78, regarding specifically the Book of Wisdom). Or, according to F.D. Taylor: "Thus, apostolic origin or approval of books and their uninterrupted

This latter view of Augustine will contribute to an understanding of what Origen means in his *Ep. Afr.* 19, where he says, χρῶνται τῷ Τωβίᾳ αἱ ἐκκλησίαι ("the churches use Tobit"). We saw earlier that Origen argues strongly against the synagogal criterion in his *Ep. Afr.*, and his other statements sometimes interpreted as exhibiting his true acceptance of the Jewish canon do not actually contradict what he affirms in that letter. His reply to Africanus draws a firm distinction between what is received among the Jews and what is received among the churches, and he stresses the impropriety of following Jewish opinion concerning the makeup of the Bible (§ 2–9). Near the end of this section, he writes the following.

> Ὥρα τοίνυν, εἰ μὴ λανθάνῃ ἡμᾶς τὰ τοιαῦτα, ἀθετεῖν τὰ ἐν ταῖς ἐκκλησίαις φερό-μενα ἀντίγραφα, καὶ νομοθετῆσαι τῇ ἀδελφότητι ἀποθέσθαι μὲν τὰς παρ' αὐτοῖς φερομένας ἱερὰς βίβλους, κολακεύειν δὲ Ἰουδαίους καὶ πείθειν ἵνα μεταδῶσιν ἡμῖν τῶν καθαρῶν καὶ μηδὲν πλάσμα ἐχόντων; Ἆρα δὲ καὶ ἡ Πρόνοια, ἐν ἁγίαις γραφαῖς δεδωκυῖα πάσαις ταῖς Χριστοῦ Ἐκκλησίαις οἰκοδομήν, οὐκ ἐφρόντισε τῶν τιμῆς ἀγορασθέντων [...].[146]

> So then, if such things do not escape our notice, is it now the time to athetize the copies in circulation in the churches and to legislate to the brotherhood to put away the holy books in circulation among them, and to flatter the Jews and persuade them to share with us the copies that are pure and have no fabrication? Did not even Providence, who has given a foundation in the holy scriptures to all the Churches of Christ, give thought to those bought with a price ....

Though contextually this passage concerns textual distinctions between Jewish and Christian manuscripts, Origen here establishes the general principle that what is received in the churches (τὰ ἐν ταῖς ἐκκλησίαις φερόμενα ἀντίγραφα) is given by Providence.[147]

These comments from the first section of the letter should control the interpretation of Origen's statement later that "the churches use Tobit." In other words, if what is received among the churches is given by Providence,

---

transmission and use in the Churches constituted Augustine's fundamental criteria for canonicity" ("Augustine of Hippo's Notion and Use of the Apocrypha" (diss.; University of Notre Dame, 1978), p. 81).

[146] *Ep. Afr.* § 8. The last three words are paraphrased from Paul's first letter to the Corinthians 6:20; 7:23.

[147] For the expression αἱ φερόμεναι ἐν ταῖς ἐκκλησίαις τοῦ θεοῦ γραφαί as Origen's designation of canonical documents, see Hanson, *Doctrine*, 138, who cites *Cels.* 6.20; 6.26; *Comm. Jo.* 19.152; *Ep. Afr.* 2. Larcher (*Études*, 45) says of the appearance of this phrase in the *Comm. Jo.* 1.14 that "c'est pour affirmer qu'il faut faire confiance à l'Église du Christ, seule dépositaire des Écritures authentiques."

then Providence has given Tobit to the Church, since the churches use it. Thus, given the context of the letter, Ellis errs in saying that Origen's remark "is hardly an affirmation of the canonicity of Tobit, and may indicate the opposite."[148] This judgment by Ellis seems to be based merely on the immediate context of Origen's statement:

Περὶ οὗ (sc. τοῦ Τωβία) ἡμᾶς ἐχρῆν ἐγνωκέναι ὅτι Ἑβραῖοι τῷ Τωβίᾳ οὐ χρῶνται, οὐδὲ τῇ Ἰουδίθ· οὐδὲ γὰρ ἔχουσιν αὐτὰ κἄν ἐν ἀποκρύφοις ἑβραϊστί, ὡς ἀπ᾽ αὐτῶν μαθόντες ἐγνώκαμεν. Ἀλλ᾽ ἐπεὶ χρῶνται τῷ Τωβίᾳ αἱ ἐκκλησίαι [...].

(Ep. Afr. 19)

Concerning which [i.e., the Book of Tobit] we should recognize that the Hebrews do not use Tobit or Judith, for they do not have them even in the apocrypha in Hebrew, as we know having learned it from them. But since the churches do use Tobit ....[149]

Here, Origen twice uses χράομαι, once regarding the Jews and once the Christians. The second clause about the Jewish attitude toward Tobit gives a specific example of their non-use, as is apparent by the γάρ—they make no use of Tobit at all, not even as an apocryphal (i.e., 'hidden') book. Ellis seems to interpret χρῶνται τῷ Τωβίᾳ αἱ ἐκκλησίαι as if Origen meant "the churches do use Tobit as an apocryphal book." This reading might be possible if we were to ignore the rest of the letter, in which Origen makes it clear that God has provided the Bible for the Church in the appropriate form. But with this wider context in view, we should interpret Origen's affirmation that "the churches use Tobit" to signify that Tobit constitutes part of the Providentially-ordained Bible.[150]

However, it does not seem that the Church's use of Tobit would have extended to the liturgy. This should cause no difficulty, since Jews and Christians have rarely endeavored to incorporate all canonical books within the liturgy. We have already seen that the liturgical use of the ecclesiastical

---

[148] Ellis, *Old Testament*, 17 n. 53.

[149] Origen completes this sentence with several citations from the Book of Tobit.

[150] For a similar conclusion, see D. Barthélemy, "La place de la Septante dans l'église," in *Aux grands carrefours de la révélation et de l'exégèse de l'Ancien Testament* (Paris, 1967), 13–28; repr. in the author's *Études*, 111–126 (114–115). Ellis argues that Origen is the first author to articulate the existence of a secondary class of scripture, the ecclesiastical books, which are non-canonical but used by the Church (*Old Testament* 17–18). Dorival also presents this view of Origen in Dorival, Harl, and Munnich, *Bible grecque*, 323. However, Origen's ecclesiastical criterion means that books used by the Church are canonical. See de Lange, *Lettre*, 563 n. 2: "Origène lui-même semble accepter *Tobie* et *Judith* comme des livres canoniques (p. ex. *Hom. Num.* 27, 1, *GCS* 7, p. 256)." It is unclear how de Lange would harmonize this statement with his later article ("Origen's Recantation?") which sets out to show that Origen adhered strictly to the Jewish canon.

books was sharply divided between the Greek and Latin churches, as Augustine recognized. There is little evidence that Greek churches read publicly from OT books outside the Jewish canon. No Greek writer of the first four centuries dedicated a commentary to an ecclesiastical book, the earliest such commentary being that of Ambrose of Milan on Tobit.[151] In regard to this commentary, Junod has noted: "On a là un exemple de la différence d'attitude des écrivains latins et grecs du IVᵉ à l'égard des deutérocanoniques."[152] This distinction extends also to Origen's voluminous œuvre, which contains no work devoted exclusively to the explanation of an ecclesiastical book. More to the point, no trace of any homily by Origen on an ecclesiastical book has been preserved, even for such a book as Wisdom which predicted the Passion of Christ so clearly to Origen.[153] This surely means that these books were not a part of the liturgy at Caesarea.[154]

Origen's ecclesiastical criterion was not based on a book's use in Christian worship, then, but on its broad use in the Church.[155] This principle is not as limitless as it may at first appear, for Origen did understand that some documents, though beneficial for certain purposes, were not to be used without extreme caution.[156] These would certainly not be included among those that could be described as "used by the Church," and this provides another justification for understanding Origen's statement at *Ep. Afr.* 19 as assuming the canonicity of Tobit. Origen's ecclesiastical criterion is very close to the one described by Augustine just before his list of canonical books: acceptance in the catholic churches.[157]

We have seen that Augustine has two different ways of formulating the ecclesiastical criterion: its public reading in the churches, and its acceptance by catholic churches. This is not all that Augustine says about the

---

[151] See Hengel, *Septuagint,* 68 and n. 33.

[152] Junod, "Formation," 118–119 n. 31.

[153] See our earlier discussion of Origen's treatment of Wisdom (p. 41, above), and cf. especially *Hom. Exod.* 6.1; *Hom. Jer.* 2.1.

[154] See Nautin's discussion of Origen's homilies on OT books (*Origène,* 401–405); also see Junod, "Formation," 119.

[155] On the private use which Origen expected Christians to make of the Bible, see A. Harnack, *Bible Reading in the Early Church,* trans. J.R. Wilkinson (New York, 1912), 68–75.

[156] Cf. Origen's *Comm. ser. Matt.* 28. On this passage, see the discussion of Hanson, *Doctrine,* 142–143. For Origen's use of Jewish pseudepigrapha, see Hanson, *Doctrine,* 134–136; Ruwet, "Les apocryphes"; Adler, "Pseudepigrapha," 215–224.

[157] See the discussion in Braverman, *Jerome's Commentary,* 35–43, especially p. 39: "Origen accepted as inspired a group of books not included in the Jewish canon. [...] His chief criterion for this recognition was use in the Church." Also Sundberg on Origen's canonical views (*Old Testament,* 137): "It would appear, therefore, that the use of the churches was the determining factor for him."

determination of the canon, and Wermelinger points to three criteria emphasized by the bishop of Hippo: apostolicity, reliable transmission, and the present consensus of churches.[158] Polman shows how each of these are inter-related in Augustine's thought,[159] and, for our purposes, they may each be considered aspects of the ecclesiastical criterion, together amounting to the document's widespread acceptance in the Church for a long time. Augustine's confidence in the Church's ability to determine its own canon should come as no surprise as it is completely in keeping with other statements on ecclesiastical authority as articulated by Augustine. Most famous is his statement: *Ego vero Euangelio non crederem, nisi me catholicae Ecclesiae commoueret auctoritas* ("But I would not believe the Gospel, unless the authority of the catholic Church moved me"; *Fund.* 5.6).[160] Thus, his criterion for canonicity could hardly be other than the ecclesiastical criterion. The apostles bore witness to authoritative writings and the Church has preserved their testimony.

## Conclusion

This chapter has outlined the major principles used by ancient Jews and Christians as they determined the precise extent and contents of the OT. A test fairly widespread among Jews involved the date of a work's composition: if it was written after a certain chronological limit, variously defined as the time of Artaxerxes or Ezra or Malachi, the work could not be considered canonical. This is probably related to the view that it was at this time that the inspiration or prophecy granted by the Holy Spirit ceased in Israel. This standard of canonicity was not influential in Christianity, though the Jewish biblical canon itself became determinative for many Christians. In fact, the Fathers generally debated whether the synagogue or the Church

---

[158] Wermelinger, "Le canon des Latins," 175–176; see also K.-H. Ohlig, "Canon scripturarum," in C. Mayer (ed.), *Augustinus-Lexikon*, vol. 1 (Basel, 1986–1994), 713–724 (721–722); La Bonnardière, *Livre de la Sagesse*, 56–57.

[159] Polman, *Word of God*, 190–198. This discussion is in the context of the NT canon, but would apply equally to the OT canon.

[160] For discussion of this statement, see K.-H. Lütcke, "Auctoritas," in Mayer, *Augustinus-Lexikon*, 498–510 (507–508); R.B. Eno, "Authority," in A.D. Fitzgerald (ed.), *Augustine through the Ages* (Grand Rapids, 1999), 80–82. Moreover, according to Augustine, one of the proofs for the doctrine of original sin is the very fact that the Church practices infant baptism; see E.R. Fairweather, "St. Augustine's Interpretation of Infant Baptism," in *Augustinus Magister. Congrès International Augustinien, Paris, 21–24 September 1954*, 3 vols. (Paris, 1954), 2.897–903.

had the right to specify the books in the OT. However, along with the synagogal criterion and the ecclesiastical criterion, patristic writers give testimony to a third major principle of OT canonicity. To this principle we now turn.

CHAPTER THREE

# HEBREW SCRIPTURE AND
# THE CANON OF THE OLD TESTAMENT

Having explored the two major principles which guided patristic thought concerning the OT canon, we are now in a position to appreciate another criterion that some Fathers employed. While the synagogal criterion and the ecclesiastical criterion shaped the debate about the canon throughout the patristic era, as the previous chapter established, many Christians nuanced these positions further. As Hanson says of Origen's adherence to the ecclesiastical criterion, "the tradition current in the Church concerning a book was something which, in Origen's view, should be given its true weight, but was not by any means decisive."[1] In this chapter we will see that, though they perhaps disagreed on how influential the Jewish reception or rejection of a work should be for the Church, both Origen and Africanus were united in affirming the important role that Hebrew scripture played in the way that Christians conceived of their OT. The statements in their correspondence, which we will investigate at the beginning of this chapter, demonstrate that they accepted as a necessary criterion for OT canonicity that the document in question must have originally been written in the Hebrew language. The explicit statements endorsing this criterion in these letters suggest that a wider exploration in patristic literature might reveal other Fathers sharing this notion. Such an exploration occupies the last half of this chapter.

## JULIUS AFRICANUS

There is very little extant information for Africanus' views on the OT canon, but he does make two important statements on the topic in his letter to Origen. The second of these we have already examined, finding that § 7 of his letter does not necessarily contain a general endorsement of the synagogal criterion, though Origen so understands it. The first statement comes at

---

[1] R.P.C. Hanson, *Origen's Doctrine of Tradition* (London, 1954), 142. Hanson says this with regard to Origen's attitude toward the Epistle to the Hebrews.

§ 5, which, in the edition of Walther Reichardt,[2] closes with these words: ἐξ Ἑβραίων δὲ τοῖς Ἕλλησι μετεβλήθη πάνθ' ὅσα τῆς παλαιᾶς διαθήκης φέρεται ("everything that circulates as part of the OT was translated from Hebrew to Greek").

This statement forms the conclusion to a discussion of the puns contained in the Greek text of Susanna 54–55 and 58–59. Daniel interrogates separately the two villainous elders, cleverly inducing them to implicate themselves. Theodotion's version of Daniel contains the following account of these interviews, with the crucial puns italicized.[3]

First Interview (Sus. 54–55)

> νῦν οὖν ταύτην εἴπερ εἶδες, εἶπον Ὑπὸ τί δένδρον εἶδες αὐτοὺς ὁμιλοῦντας ἀλλήλοις; ὁ δὲ εἶπεν Ὑπὸ *σχῖνον*. εἶπε δὲ Δανιηλ Ὀρθῶς ἔψευσαι εἰς τὴν σεαυτοῦ κεφαλήν· ἤδη γὰρ ἄγγελος τοῦ θεοῦ λαβὼν φάσιν παρὰ τοῦ θεοῦ *σχίσει* σε μέσον.

> "Now therefore, if you really saw this woman, tell: Under what tree did you see them having intercourse together?" Then he said, "Under *a mastich*." Then Daniel said, "Truly you have lied to the detriment of your own head, for already as the angel of God receives the sentence from God he *will split* you in two."

Second Interview (Sus. 58–59)

> νῦν οὖν λέγε μοι Ὑπὸ τί δένδρον κατέλαβες αὐτοὺς ὁμιλοῦντας ἀλλήλοις; ὁ δὲ εἶπεν Ὑπὸ *πρῖνον*. εἶπε δὲ αὐτῷ Δανιηλ Ὀρθῶς ἔψευσαι καὶ σὺ εἰς τὴν σεαυτοῦ κεφαλήν· μένει γὰρ ὁ ἄγγελος τοῦ θεοῦ τὴν ῥομφαίαν ἔχων *πρῖσαι* σε μέσον, ὅπως ἐξολεθρεύσῃ ὑμᾶς.

> "Now, therefore, tell me: Under what tree did you catch them having intercourse together?" Then, he said, "Under *an evergreen oak*." Then Daniel said to him, "Truly you also have lied to the detriment of your own head, for the angel of God is waiting with the sword *to saw* you in two so as to destroy you."

Africanus points out to Origen that the play on words indicates that the story of Susanna was written in Greek. Ἐν μὲν οὖν ἑλληνικαῖς φωναῖς τὰ τοιαῦτα ὁμοφωνεῖν συμβαίνει, παρὰ τὴν πρῖνον τὸ πρῖσαι καὶ σχίσαι παρὰ τὴν σχῖνον, ἐν δὲ τῇ ἑβραΐδι τῷ παντὶ διέστηκεν ("Now, using Greek words, such things happen to sound alike, *prisai* alongside *prinos* and *schisai* alongside *schinos*, but in Hebrew they are completely different"; § 5). He is not alone in his

---

[2] W. Reichardt, *Die Briefe des Sextus Julius Africanus an Aristides und Origenes*, TU 34.3 (Leipzig, 1909), 79.

[3] J. Ziegler, O. Munnich, D. Fraenkel (eds.), *Susanna, Daniel, Bel et Draco*[2], Septuaginta 16.2 (Göttingen, 1999), 231–233. The English translation is by R.T. McLay in NETS.

recognition of this point; in fact, Origen responds by saying that he has already perceived the problem (*Ep. Afr.* 10; cf. Origen, *apud* Jerome, *Comm. Dan.* 13:54–55). Jerome reports that a certain Jewish teacher mocked the story due to the presence of the Greek puns (*Praef. Dan.* 23–27), and he says that the puns led Porphyry to conclude that the entire book of Daniel was a Greek document (*Comm. Dan.*, prol.).[4]

Our interest in the way Africanus formulates this objection concerns the general principle that he articulates at the close of this point. Before we can draw out its implications, however, we must deal with a text-critical problem. The text Reichardt prints, which we saw earlier, differs slightly from de Lange's edition owing to the fact that, according to de Lange, "[l]e texte est manifestement corrompu."[5] The preserved text lacks a proper marker of disjunction between the discussion of the puns and the following point about the implausibility of there being a Jew as rich as Joachim (husband of Susanna) in the Babylonian exile (§ 6). Presented below is the transition between these two thoughts as found in the three best manuscripts and the two critical editions.[6] The section continues from Africanus' statement: ἐξ Ἑβραίων δὲ τοῖς Ἕλλησι μετεβλήθη πάνθ' ὅσα τῆς παλαιᾶς διαθήκης φέρεται.

| | |
|---|---|
| C* O | φέρεται παρὰ τὲ Ἰουδαίοις αἰχμάλωτοι ὄντες ἐν τῇ Βαβυλωνίᾳ |
| C^corr. | φέρεται παρὰ δὲ Ἰουδαίοις αἰχμάλωτοι ὄντες ἐν τῇ Βαβυλωνίᾳ |
| V | φέρεται παρὰ δὲ χαλδαίοις αἰχμάλωτοι ὄντες ἐν τῇ Βαβυλωνίᾳ |
| Reichardt^txt | φέρεται. Παρὰ δὲ Ἰουδαίοις αἰχμάλωτοι ὄντες ἐν τῇ Βαβυλωνίᾳ |
| Reichardt^app | φέρεται. Πρὸς δὲ Ἰουδαῖοι αἰχμάλωτοι ὄντες ἐν τῇ Βαβυλωνίᾳ |
| de Lange | φέρεται παρὰ Ἰουδαίοις. <***> αἰχμάλωτοι ὄντες ἐν τῇ Βαβυλωνίᾳ |

---

[4] P.M. Casey warns against deciphering Porphyry's exact opinion from Jerome's information ("Porphyry and the Origin of the Book of Daniel," *JTS* 27 (1976): 15–33 (19)). N. de Lange (ed.), *Origène, La Lettre à Africanus sur l'histoire de Suzanne*, in *Origène, Philocalie, 1–20: Sur les Écritures*, SC 302 (ed. M. Harl; Paris, 1983), 490, thinks that Porphyry was dependent on Africanus for his opinion, but it is more likely that he was relying on his own analysis of the text, as believed by R.M. Grant, "Historical Criticism in the Ancient Church," *JR* 25 (1945): 183–196 (194); and W. Adler, "'What the Hebrews Say': Translation, Authority, and the Story of Susanna and the Elders," in F.W. Knobloch (ed.), *Biblical Translation in Context* (Bethesda, Md., 2002), 19–39 (27). As Grant argues, Africanus knew that Daniel and Susanna were independent documents, and so would Porphyry had he known of Africanus' work. But Porphyry was misled by the Theodotion version of Daniel, in which Susanna comes first, and he concluded thereby that the entire book must have been written in the same language as its first part. For a survey of other recent interpretations of Porphyry's point about Susanna's puns, see J.G. Cook, *The Interpretation of the Old Testament in Greco-Roman Paganism* (Tübingen, 2004), 200–203.

[5] De Lange, *Lettre*, 518 n. 1.

[6] The manuscript evidence presented here is based on the collations of Reichardt and de Lange. For information about the state of the text, and the manuscripts C, O, and V, see Reichardt, *Briefe*, 66–69, and de Lange, *Lettre*, 502–508.

The text of V is certainly secondary, and de Lange provides a probable account for its origins: C was corrected from παρὰ τὲ Ἰουδαίοις to παρὰ δὲ Ἰουδαίοις, which produces "un non-sens" if taken with αἰχμάλωτοι ὄντες, and so the copyist of V replaced Ἰουδαίοις with χαλδαίοις.[7] This leaves the evidence of C and its correction to be explained. De Lange correctly avers that the most natural reading would take the παρὰ Ἰουδαίοις with φέρεται, but this requires omitting the conjunction and leaving a lacuna at the beginning of § 6. Thus, the result does not entirely please even de Lange.[8] Reichardt's text follows the correction found in C, which makes good sense of the end of § 5 but produces a difficult reading for the beginning of § 6. In his apparatus, Reichardt suggested that § 6 originally began with πρὸς δὲ Ἰουδαῖοι, which makes excellent sense and could plausibly produce the alternative readings extant in the manuscripts: πρὸς δὲ Ἰουδαῖοι → παρὰ δὲ Ἰουδαῖοι → παρὰ δὲ Ἰουδαίοις (→ παρὰ τὲ Ἰουδαίοις). However, de Lange points to the quotation of this passage in Origen's reply as evidence that would influence the textual decision here. Origen says, Πρὸς τούτοις ἐπαπορεῖς αὐταῖς λέξεσι· Πῶς αἰχμάλωτοι ὄντες ἐν τῇ Βαβυλωνίᾳ ("In addition to these things, you object with these words: 'How could those being captives in Babylon ...'"; § 19). De Lange remarks that if Reichardt's conjectural reading were correct, one should probably also include Origen's πῶς.[9] We cannot assume that Origen has quoted the beginning of Africanus' statement because Origen does not include a conjunction, but it does seem likely that the πῶς formed part of the text which Origen quotes. How it may have fallen out of the text of Africanus' letter is another problem that leads us to agree with de Lange that "aucune solution satisfaisante ne se présente."

Despite this difficulty, there are some indications that the text of Reichardt is preferable to that of de Lange. First, de Lange stresses the need for a conjunction at the beginning of § 6, but he eliminates the conjunction present in the best manuscripts so that παρὰ Ἰουδαίοις can go with φέρεται from § 5. As we will see in just a moment, the sense thus achieved does not warrant the adoption of a reading present in only a few late witnesses.[10] Moreover, Reichardt's conjecture Ἰουδαῖοι seems necessary at the beginning

---

[7] De Lange, *Lettre*, 518 n. 1.

[8] De Lange, *Lettre*, 518 n. 1: "aucune solution satisfaisante ne se présente."

[9] De Lange, *Lettre*, 518 n. 1.

[10] For the witnesses that read φέρεται παρὰ Ἰουδαίοις (without any conjunction), see Reichardt, *Briefe*, 69–70, who cites *Vat. gr.* 702 from the 15th century, and *Vat. gr.* 2261 from the 16th–17th century. De Lange merely cites "*recentiores*" for the reading he adopts (*Lettre*, 516, *app. crit.* to § 5, line 25).

of § 6 so that ὄντες can modify a noun in the text. De Lange also recognizes this problem, suggesting that the corruption of the text resulted from the similarity of the end of § 5 with the beginning of § 6, but this supposition only doubles the problems.[11]

A final indication that one should prefer Reichardt's text over that of de Lange derives from the resultant force of Africanus' argument in each case. De Lange's text would carry the meaning at the conclusion of § 5 that the Jewish Bible was written in Hebrew, and that this was translated into Greek.[12] Aside from the fact that these points are so obvious as to hardly need mentioning, one should also note that such a statement by Africanus would not form a very clear conclusion to the discussion of the puns, since it does not make explicit the connection between the Jewish Bible in Hebrew and the Greek puns. It would require the reader to infer several steps essential to the argument: (1) the Church's OT should be restricted to what is accepted by the Jews; (2) since the Jewish Bible originated in Hebrew and the puns cannot exist in Hebrew, the story of Susanna is not accepted into the Jewish Bible; (3) thus, it is disqualified from being in the Christian OT. Not only would it be strange for Africanus to leave the conclusion unexpressed in such an otherwise closely argued letter, but also the position maintained here would be redundant with that of § 7, which also assumes a direct connection between the Book of Daniel as accepted by the Jews and by the Christians. Would Africanus, who is far from verbose in this letter, have repeated himself in this way without indicating as much in the second occurrence?

On the other hand, if we follow Reichardt's text, all of these problems disappear: there would be no assertion that the Jewish Bible was composed in Hebrew and translated into Greek, no redundancy with § 7, and the text would offer a perfectly suitable conclusion to the discussion of the play on words. For Africanus would be saying, "everything that circulates as part of the OT was translated from Hebrew to Greek."[13] Therefore, Susanna cannot

---

[11]  De Lange, *Lettre*, 518 n. 1.

[12]  De Lange, "The Revival of the Hebrew Language in the Third Century CE," *JSQ* 3 (1996), 342–358, interprets the phrase thus: "In other words, the Hebrew Bible is the touchstone of what Jews consider authentic in the Greek Bible" (351). Such a statement only awkwardly suits the context of Africanus' letter.

[13]  Or, "transmitted from the Hebrews to the Greeks," as D. Barthélemy takes it; see "Origène et le texte de l'Ancien Testament," in J. Fontains and C. Kannengiesser (eds.), *Epektasis* (Paris, 1972), 247–261; repr. in *Études d'histoire du texte de l'Ancien Testament* (Göttingen, 1978), 203–217 (204). In any case, the statement would still have linguistic implications,

find a place in the Church's Bible because the puns prove its Greek origin, while the Church only admits OT literature originally written in Hebrew. Therefore, based on the overall argument presented by Africanus, it seems unlikely that he would have concluded § 5 with παρὰ Ἰουδαίοις, no matter how the beginning of § 6 is reconstructed.

Thus, Africanus makes a significant statement about the relationship between the Christian OT and the Hebrew language. In truth, even the text of de Lange would require the interpreter to assume this relationship, though we have seen that the logic would work more by implication, while the text as printed by Reichardt more clearly expresses its meaning. We should note that unlike § 7, the statement Africanus makes in § 5 cannot be restricted to this discussion of Daniel but must be interpreted as a general principle of biblical criticism, for it has in view "whatever circulates as part of the OT." Here, Africanus asserts without argument that the Christian OT comprises only documents composed in Hebrew—he presents no evidence in support of his assertion. He simply assumes that informed Christians generally acknowledge the Hebrew criterion for the OT canon.

Before leaving Africanus, we should take another look at what he says at § 7 of his letter to Origen. The text reads as follows: πρὸ δὲ τούτων ἁπάντων ἥδε ἡ περικοπὴ σὺν ἄλλαις δύο ταῖς ἐπὶ τῷ τέλει τῷ παρὰ τῶν Ἰουδαίων εἰλημμένῳ Δανιὴλ οὐκ ἐμφέρεται ("Before all these things, this pericope along with two others at the end [= Bel and the Dragon] does not circulate in the [version of] Daniel received from the Jews"). We saw in Chapter Two above that this statement could be interpreted specifically in reference to the text of Daniel rather than generally as a principle for the OT canon. However, within the present discussion the prepositional phrase παρὰ τῶν Ἰουδαίων takes on added significance. Translators usually render the phrase "among the Jews," which makes sense in the context.[14] But, such a translation would require a dative complement for the preposition (παρὰ τοῖς Ἰουδαίοις). On the contrary, the actual text with its genitive complement means "from the Jews," with a phrase such as ὑπὸ τῶν ἐκκλησίων understood.[15] Though the statement

---

and N. de Lange, *Origen and the Jews* (Cambridge, 1976), 29–30, has shown that 'Hebrew' as a description of a person in Greco-Latin sources usually (not always) implies facility in the Hebrew language.

[14] See the translations by F. Crombie in ANF 4.386; H. Engel, *Das Susanna-Erzählung*, OBO 61 (Göttingen, 1985), 18: "von den Juden akzeptierten"; Adler, "Hebrews," 25 (his translation differs only slightly from that of Crombie); de Lange, *Lettre*, 519: "reçu chez les Juifs"; J.W. Trigg, *Biblical Interpretation* (Wilmington, Del., 1988), 119: "that the Jews accept."

[15] Cf. the statement examined earlier (pp. 38, 46) in Origen's prologue to his *Comm. Cant.*: [...] *apud hebraeos, a quibus eloquia Dei ad nos videntur esse translata.*

may relate merely to the Book of Daniel, nevertheless, it does acknowledge the Church's debt to Judaism for its OT literature, a sentiment that ultimately derives from the NT (cf. Rom. 3:2). If we were to ask how Africanus knows that the version of Daniel received from the Jews does not contain Susanna when the LXX and Theodotion versions do, the answer would be that he has investigated the matter either directly from Jewish informants or indirectly through the version of Aquila. In either case, Africanus' presumed investigation would aim at ascertaining the contents of the Hebrew (and Aramaic) edition of Daniel. This, again, leads to the conclusion that for Africanus, the Christian OT must be restricted to translations from Hebrew. He assumes that Origen will hold the same view.

## ORIGEN

### *The* Stromata

In fact, Origen does agree with Africanus that OT literature must derive from an original Hebrew document. He first gives indications of this view in his *Stromata*, one of his earliest writings, a section of which he dedicated to providing exegetical notes to the Theodotion version of Daniel.[16] This work has been lost, but Jerome concluded his *Comm. Dan.* by excerpting Origen's exegesis of Susanna and Bel and the Dragon. Jerome states after the conclusion of his commentary on Daniel 12:

> *Expositis, ut potui, quae in Danielis libro iuxta hebraicum continentur, ponam*
> *breuiter quid Origenes, in decimo Stromatum suorum libro, de Susannae et Belis*
> *fabulis dixerit.*[17]

---

[16] Eusebius, *Hist. Eccl.* 6.24, reports that Origen composed ten books of the *Stromata* while still living in Alexandria. Hanson, *Doctrine*, 26, gives the *Stromata* the date of 222. In his commentary on Dan. 4:5 (Vul; Eng.: 4:8), Jerome preserves Origen's statement that he would begin using Theodotion's version (rather than the LXX) as his base text from this verse because of its closer proximity to the Hebrew text (cf. *Comm. Dan.* 13:8). Jerome says that these comments by Origen were in the ninth book of his *Stromata*, while the comments on Susanna and Bel and the Dragon were in the tenth book. For surveys of all that is known of Origen's *Stromata*, see P. Nautin, *Origène* (Paris, 1977), 293–302; and R.M. Grant, "The *Stromateis* of Origen," in J. Fontaine and C. Kannengiesser (eds.), *Epektasis* (Paris, 1972), 285–292.

[17] On Jerome's use of the term *fabula* in this context, see J. Ruwet "Les 'Antilegomena' dans les œuvres d'Origène: les antilegomena de l'Ancien Testament," *Bib* 24 (1943): 18–58 (31 n. 1), who claims that Jerome sometimes uses *fabula* not pejoratively but as an equivalent to *historia*, citing as evidence *Epist.* 68.2 and *Comm. Philm.* vs. 4. Jerome calls Susanna *historia* in his *Praef. Dan.* 21 (also line 24), and in the same line he describes as *fabulae* the Hymn

> Since what is contained in the Book of Daniel according to the Hebrew has
> been expounded as I have been able, I will briefly set out what Origen, in the
> tenth book of his *Stromata*, said concerning the stories of Susanna and Bel.

Certainly, Jerome did not provide a literal translation of Origen's words,
and some scholars have been doubtful of our deciphering Origen's true sentiments from Jerome's rendering.[18] Other scholars do not doubt Jerome's
fidelity; on the contrary, they believe we here get Origen's true view which
he later masked in his *Ep. Afr.*[19] As will be apparent in the course of the
discussion, both of these positions err in assuming that Origen expresses
diametrically opposing views in his *Ep. Afr.* and in the *Stromata* as transmitted by Jerome. As for Jerome's fidelity to his source, scholars generally
consider him a faithful translator, especially as compared to Rufinus, and
careful study of the contents of these particular thoughts from the *Stromata*
confirm their origination with Origen rather than Jerome.[20]

In these excerpts from Origen's *Stromata* we see that he had struggled
with the problem of the puns in Susanna fully two decades before Africanus
wrote to him. Jerome records one comment for the two different puns in
Susanna 54–55 and 58–59.

> *Quia Hebraei reprobant historiam Susannae, dicentes eam in Danielis uolumine*
> *non haberi, debemus diligenter inquirere: nomina 'schini' et 'prini'—quae Latini*
> *'ilicem' et 'lentiscum' interpretantur—si sint apud Hebraeos, et quam habeant*

---

of the Three Young Men and Bel and the Dragon. However, P.W. Skehan, "St. Jerome and the
Canon of the Holy Scriptures," in F.X. Murphy (ed.), *A Monument to St. Jerome* (New York,
1952), 257–287 (282–283), shows that *fabula* can have "pejorative implications," as seen in
the *Comm. Jer.* 5.67.

[18] E.g. C. Julius, *Die griechischen Danielzusätze und ihre kanonische Geltung*, Biblische
Studien 6.3–4 (Freiburg, 1901), 54; Engel, *Susanna-Erzählung*, 25. Ruwet, "Les Antilegomena
de l'Ancien Testament," 31, cautions against trusting Jerome completely, though he later (34)
points out that had Jerome doctored Origen's words to any great extent, it is inexplicable that
he would leave so many positive comments about Susanna in the text. J. Braverman, *Jerome's
Commentary on Daniel* (Washington, D.C., 1978), 126, shows that Jerome "did not translate
Origen's words verbatim," but he still considers these to be Origen's thoughts.

[19] N.R.M. de Lange, "The *Letter to Africanus*: Origen's Recantation?" *StPatr* 16.2 = TU 129
(1985): 242–247; Adler, "Hebrews," 32.

[20] Hanson, who generally distrusts the Latin translations of Origen (*Doctrine*, 40–47),
cites this passage as from Origen without batting an eye (134). Ruwet, "Les Antilegomena de
l'Ancien Testament," 34, thinks it unlikely that Jerome altered Origen's meaning very much.
De Lange (*Lettre*, 492; "Origen's Recantation?" 247) twice raises the question of Jerome's
fidelity to his source, but does not seriously explore the possibility of manipulation on
Jerome's part. On Jerome as a translator of texts outside the Bible, see F. Cavallera, *Saint
Jérôme* (Leuven, 1922), 2.78–80; J.N.D. Kelly, *Jerome* (New York, 1975), 77; Hanson, *Doctrine*,
43: "Where we are on sure ground with Jerome, for instance in his translation of the *Homilies
on Luke*, we cannot help noticing that he is a much more accurate translator than Rufinus."

ἐτυμολογίαν: *ut ab 'schino' 'scissio', et a 'prino' 'sectio' siue 'serratio' dicatur lingua eorum. Quod si non fuerit inuentum, necessitate cogemur et nos eorum acquiescere sententiae, qui graeci tantum sermonis hanc uolunt esse* περικοπὴν *quae graecam tantum habeat* ἐτυμολογίαν *et hebraicam non habeat; quod si quis ostenderit duarum istarum arborum scissionis et sectionis et in hebraeo stare* ἐτυμολογίαν, *tunc poterimus etiam hanc scripturam recipere.*

Because the Hebrews reject the Story of Susanna, saying that it is not contained in the Book of Daniel, we ought to investigate diligently if the nouns *schinos* and *prinos*—which Latins translate as 'oak' and 'mastic' trees—exist among the Hebrews and what etymology they have, so that in their language 'dividing' is derived from *schinos* and 'cutting' or 'sawing' is derived from *prinos*. But if it should not be found, we will necessarily be forced to acquiesce to the opinion of those who claim that this pericope is of the Greek language only, because it contains Greek etymologies and not Hebrew ones. But if anyone should show that the etymology of these two trees, *schinos* and *prinos*, exists in Hebrew, then we would be able to accept also this as scripture.

Aside from the obvious insertion by Jerome of the relevant Latin terms, these statements have many parallels with Origen's letter to Africanus, as we shall see in a moment. Here, Origen reports that the Hebrews lack the story of Susanna in their edition of Daniel, a fact that gives Origen pause due to the presence of the Greek puns in the Church's version of Daniel. Apparently, the absence of Susanna from the Jewish Bible is a problem only because it prevents Origen from checking the Greek puns in the original and allows for the possibility that there was no Hebrew original at all. Origen acknowledges that some people have already contested the authenticity of the story, declaring it to be an originally Greek document. Thus, it could be that Origen himself did not perceive the potential problem created by the puns until challenged on this point by certain others. It is impossible to know whether these others were Christians or Jews, but the linguistic awareness required to recognize the difficulty of the puns makes it altogether likely that they were Jews, of the sort whom Jerome reports to have ridiculed the story of Susanna as a Greek forgery (*Praef. Dan.* 20–27). For Origen, whether the Greek puns could reflect Hebrew puns, as a question bearing on the original language of composition, should be investigated with all care (*debemus diligenter inquirere*). This is because the canonicity of an OT document relates directly to its language of composition. The point comes across clearly in the final sentence of the paragraph, in which Origen says the document may be accepted (as canonical) only if it was composed in Hebrew.[21]

---

[21]  Cf. Ruwet, "Les Antilegomena de l'Ancien Testament," 32.

One further point from this passage: Origen again makes clear that he is not following the synagogal criterion for canonicity. If he were, then the Jewish rejection of Susanna would settle the matter. Instead, he evinces a desire to retain the story, and we can see elsewhere that Origen is not shy about citing Susanna.[22] His view is no doubt linked to Susanna's popularity within the Church, as shown both by the frequent citations of the story and the iconographic use of elements from it.[23] However, in his *Stromata*, Origen acknowledges the validity of the Hebrew criterion to determine whether the Church should accept Susanna. He does not here speculate on how an original part of Daniel might have dropped out of the Jewish edition of the book, but his *Stromata* is an early work in which his ideas have not fully ripened. There is the implication, which will later become an assertion, that the Church should not always trust the Jews when it comes to the Christian Bible.

The final passage excerpted by Jerome from Origen's *Stromata* should be mentioned here. Commenting on verse 17 of Bel and the Dragon, Origen returns to a theme he had highlighted earlier in his treatment of Susanna— that Scripture speaks of a person's 'voice' as 'great' only if that person is pious.

> *Hoc quod scriptura nunc dicit: 'Clamauit uoce magna,' quia de idolatra et igno-rante Deum dicitur, uidetur obseruationem nostram subuertere, qua dudum asseruimus uocem magnam in sanctis tantum reperiri. Quod soluet facile qui hanc historiam in libro Danielis apud Hebraeos dixerit non haberi; si quis autem eam potuerit approbare esse de canone, tunc quaerendum est quid ei respon-dere debeamus.*

> That which Scripture now says, 'He called out with a great voice,' because it is said with reference to an idolater ignorant of God, it seems to overturn our observation that we just made that a 'great voice' is found only with reference to saints. This problem is easily solved by the one who says that this story is

---

[22] Cf. *Comm. Jo.* 20.33; 28.34; and especially *Comm. ser. Matt.* 61, where he cites Susanna with the defense that he is not unaware of its rejection by the Jews, but cites it because it is accepted by the Church; cf. in the same vein *Hom. Lev.* 1.1.3. For other citations of the additions to Daniel in Origen, see E. Schürer, *The History of the Jewish People in the Age of Jesus Christ*, rev. G. Vermes et al., 3 vols. (Edinburgh, 1973–1985), 3.2.727. Ruwet, "Les Antilegomena de l'Ancien Testament," 32, 33–34, shows that Origen usually considers Susanna to be holy scripture, even in the *Stromata*.

[23] For the popularity of the Susanna story in patristic literature, see the new Schürer, *History*, rev., 3.2.726–727; for its use in Christian iconography, see P. Boitani, "Susanna in Excelsis," in E. Spolsky (ed.), *The Judgment of Susanna* (Atlanta, 1996), 7–19.

not contained in the Book of Daniel among the Hebrews. But if anyone can confirm that it is in the canon, then it would be necessary to seek out how we should respond to him.

Origen is strangely apathetic here.[24] He neither agrees with those who reject the passage, nor does he want to bother finding an alternative solution in order to preserve the validity of his exegetical theory regarding *magna vox*. It almost seems that he would prefer to keep his interpretation of *magna vox* at the expense of Bel and the Dragon. Obviously, he is not sure how best to approach the passage and simply notes the problems involved so that he can give more thought to the issues and furnish definitive answers later. This exactly corresponds to his approach regarding Susanna's puns. This passage does not provide evidence for Origen's canonical theory, except in showing that in his earlier years he was not so sure as he later became.

## Letter to Africanus

Origen did give all these matters much thought over the next two decades, so that when Africanus dispatched his letter, "il était en état de fournir une réponse immédiate et détaillée."[25] We have already seen that the first part of Origen's reply concerns Africanus' §7 where Africanus seemed to affirm the synagogal criterion. Origen strongly rejects this principle, based on the textual work that produced the *Hexapla*. His earlier uncertainty as to whether the Jewish dismissal of Bel and the Dragon would provide a satisfying answer to the appearance of a *magna vox* coming from King Darius has solidified into the firm resolve that it would not (cf. *Ep. Afr.* 3; 8). He does not here mention whether this has led him to abandon or modify his understanding of *magna vox*.

At §10, Origen turns to consider the puns. In 222, he articulated what he regarded as the proper course of action in response to this problem: "we ought to investigate diligently if the nouns *schinos* and *prinos* [...] exist among the Hebrews and what etymology they have." He has done this by now as well as he could.

---

[24] Ruwet, "Les Antilegomena de l'Ancien Testament," 33, describes Origen's attitude here as "la forme indécise, disons mieux, affectant l'indifférence." This greater apathy regarding Bel and the Dragon can be compared with Hippolytus' *Comm. Dan.*, wherein he dealt with Susanna and the Song of the Three Young men, but apparently not with Bel and the Dragon, though, according to Schürer, it "was certainly known to Hippolytus and regarded by him as an integral part of the book of Daniel" (*History*, rev., 3.2.726); cf. his *Comm. Dan.* 2.26.

[25] De Lange, *Lettre*, 493.

ἐπείπερ φροντίσας τῶν κατὰ τὸν τόπον, τῷ καὶ αὐτὸς ἠπορηκέναι αὐτοῖς, οὐκ ὀλίγοις Ἑβραίοις ἀνεθέμην πυνθανόμενος πῶς παρ' αὐτοῖς ὀνομάζεται πρῖνος καὶ πῶς λέγουσι τὸ πρίζειν, ἔτι δὲ εἰς τί μεταλαμβάνουσι τὴν σχῖνον τὸ φυτὸν καὶ πῶς τὸ σχίζειν ὀνομάζουσιν.

When I was considering this passage, for I myself was confused about it, I consulted not a few Hebrews, asking how the words *prinos* and *prizein* were said among them, and how they would translate *schinos* the tree, and how they say *schizein*.

For various reasons, Origen's investigation yielded no results—no one could tell him the Hebrew words corresponding to the Greek puns. One Jew told him that Jewish knowledge of Hebrew had declined generally so much that even the 'wise men' (σοφοί) could not always remember the correct words. In fact, the only way to be certain about a Hebrew word is to find that word in the Hebrew scriptures. Thus, Origen mocks Africanus' certainty on this point as naïve.

Τούτων οὖν ὅσον ἐπὶ ἐμῇ ἱστορίᾳ ὑπὸ Ἑβραίων οἷς συνέμιξα, εἰρημένων, ἐγὼ μὲν εὐλαβῶς ἔχω ἀποφήνασθαι πότερον καὶ παρ' Ἑβραίοις ἡ ἰσοδυναμία τῶν κατὰ ταῦτα παρωνυμιῶν σῴζεται ἢ οὔ· σὺ δὲ ὅπως διεβεβαιώσω, αὐτὸς ἴσως οἶδας.

These things are all that were said about the story by the Hebrews I encountered; therefore, I am cautious of affirming whether or not the significance of the play on words is preserved among the Hebrews. How you can be so confident you yourself probably know.

Later, in § 18, Origen returns to the puns to indicate one other possible solution that he had previously failed to mention. He notes that the scriptures contain many puns that make sense in Hebrew but not in Greek. However, he can cite Gen. 2:23 as an example of a Hebrew play on words that can successfully be brought over in translation, with two separate attempts given by Theodotion and Symmachus.[26] He draws this inference:

Οὐδὲν οὖν θαυμαστὸν ἑρμηνεύσαντάς τινας τὸ περὶ Σουσάννας ἑβραϊκόν [...] ἤτοι κυρίως ἐκδεδωκέναι τὰ τῆς λέξεως, ἢ εὑρηκέναι τὸ ἀνάλογον τοῖς κατὰ τὸ ἑβραϊκὸν παρωνύμοις, ἵνα δυνηθῶμεν οἱ Ἕλληνες αὐτοῖς παρακολουθῆσαι.

It should cause no surprise, then, if certain translators of the Hebrew text of Susanna [...] have given a literal translation or if they found an analogy to the play on words in Hebrew, so that we Greeks could understand it.

---

[26] De Lange, *Lettre*, 575–576, sorts out Origen's rather confused argument.

Even if the Greek puns are not a literal representation of the Hebrew text, it is certainly possible that they were contrived by the translators to reflect an analogous feature of the Hebrew text.[27]

In this way, Origen completely gets around the problem of the puns and no longer needs an answer to his question of their Hebrew equivalents. Though he cannot prove it, his inconclusive investigation allows him to assume a Hebrew original for Susanna, confident that no one else can disprove it. He can also assert that he stands firmly within ecclesiastical tradition, unlike Africanus, who wants to overturn this tradition based on dubious philology.[28]

However, when Origen supposes that Susanna was an original part of the Hebrew Daniel, he must offer an explanation as to why the edition of Daniel current among the Jews lacks the story. As suggested earlier, the germ for his answer was probably present already when working on his *Stromata*. He argues at length in his *Ep. Afr.* 13–15 that the Jewish leaders have removed passages from the Bible which paint them in a bad light. Susanna is one example, and Origen finds a parallel case in the poverty of references in the OT to the murder of Israelite prophets, despite the prevalence of this theme in the NT. This answer for Susanna's absence among the Jews has been echoed in modern times: a century ago D.M. Kay said, "The story would not be popular with elders, and it was the elders who fixed the Canon."[29] In fact, the charge cannot stand up to close scrutiny,[30] but for Origen it serves its purpose.

---

[27] This explanation has been accepted by, e.g., the new Schürer (*History*, rev., 3.2.724–725), though it was denied in the original Schürer (E. Schürer, *A History of the Jewish People in the Time of Jesus Christ* (ET: New York, 1885–1891), 2.3.184). The basic premise of the solution, that puns can be translated, is proven in the translations of Jerome into Latin (*Praef. Dan.* 27–30), Luther into German (see Reichardt, *Briefe*, 66), and, C.J. Ball into English ("The History of Susanna," in H. Wace (ed.), *The Holy Bible* [...]: *Apocrypha*, 2 vols. (London, 1888), 2.323–343 (341)). This last author provides several possible Hebrew equivalents for the puns (324).

[28] Cf. Adler, "Hebrews," 29, who argues that Origen opposes philology to the authority of the Church. On the contrary, Origen reveals Africanus' philological naïveté but does not disparage the philological approach. He shows that it comes to a dead-end in this case.

[29] D.M. Kay, "Susanna," in R.H. Charles (ed.), *Apocrypha and Pseudepigrapha of the Old Testament in English* (Oxford, 1913), 1.638–651 (642). C.A. Moore considers this statement "plausible" (*Daniel, Esther and Jeremiah: The Additions*, AB 44 (New York, 1977), 80–81).

[30] Solomon Zeitlin ("Jewish Apocryphal Literature," *JQR* 40 (1950): 223–250 (236–237)) has shown that Jews were not averse to transmitting "scandals connected with their leaders." See also H. Fisch, "Susanna as Parable: A Response to Piero Boitani," in Spolsky, *Judgment*, 35–41 (35–36).

Origen makes this accusation of Jewish suppression of Scripture also elsewhere, especially his roughly contemporaneous *Comm. ser. Matt.* 28,[31] and he had probably come across it in Hippolytus' *Comm. Dan.* Hippolytus explains the Jewish rejection of Susanna in this way:

Ταῦτα μὲν οὖν οἱ τῶν Ἰουδαίων ἄρχοντες βούλονται νῦν περικόπτειν τῆς βίβλου, φάσκοντες μὴ γεγενῆσθαι ταῦτα ἐν Βαβυλῶνι, αἰσχυνόμενοι τὸ ὑπὸ τῶν πρεσβυτέρων κατ᾽ ἐκεῖνον τὸν καιρὸν γεγενημένον, ἀγνοοῦντες τὴν τοῦ πνεύματος οἰκονομίαν.[32]                                (*Comm. Dan.* 1.15.2 on Sus. 8)

Therefore these things the leaders of the Jews wish now to cut out of the book, saying that these things did not happen in Babylon, being ashamed of the thing done by the elders at that time, being ignorant of the economy of the Spirit.

In addition to the charge of intentional suppression of Susanna by Jewish authorities, there is also the significant parallel between this passage and Origen's thought regarding the divine economy.[33] Gustave Bardy dates Hippolytus' commentary to 202–204,[34] so there was plenty of time for it to come into the hands of Origen. Perhaps this would have happened during Origen's visit to Rome about 215. Origen seems to have stayed there for a good while, perhaps even a year, so it is not unlikely that he would have met Hippolytus, as Jerome affirms (*Vir. ill.* 56).[35] Of course, this would be several years before writing his *Stromata*, in which his views were still not fully formed, so we may guess that Hippolytus' charge of rabbinic suppression of Susanna (mentioned only briefly by Hippolytus in his commentary) had provoked Origen's thoughts but had done little more than this by 222. Only later would he discover that the significant NT theme of the murder of the prophets was missing from the OT, and this provided the corroborating evidence to substantiate Hippolytus' accusation.

Why does Origen invest so much energy on the Greek puns? He says in his *Stromata* that it has bearing on the document's canonicity. As mentioned

---

[31] For more references, see de Lange, *Lettre*, 497.

[32] For the text, see M. Richard (ed.), *Hippolytus Werke I. Commentarius in Danielem*, GCS NF 7 (Berlin, 2000).

[33] Equivalent to Hippolytus' τοῦ πνεύματος οἰκονομία is Origen's mention of ἡ Πρόνοια in *Ep. Afr.* 8. For Origen, the 'divine economy' or 'Providence' ensured that the Church's Bible was accurate. See the discussion in A. Kamesar, *Jerome, Greek Scholarship, and the Hebrew Bible* (Oxford, 1993), 13–17. It is not clear from Hippolytus' passing reference whether he had the identical view, but it would seem to be similar.

[34] G. Bardy and M. Lefèvre, *Hippolyte. Commentaire sur Daniel*, SC 14 (Paris, 1947), 10.

[35] On the date of Origen's journey to Rome, see Nautin, *Origène*, 418; on the length of his stay, see p. 365.

earlier, some scholars suggest that the comments in the *Stromata* preserved by Jerome have been manipulated to suit the translator's views, while others affirm that the *Stromata* articulate Origen's true feelings absent from the *Ep. Afr.*, in which Origen attempts to ingratiate himself to the Church distrustful of his scholarly propinquity to the Jewish Bible. Both of these positions assume a wide gap between what we read in the *Ep. Afr.* and what we read in the *Stromata*. De Lange provides a good example. After reviewing the position taken in the *Stromata* and contrasting that with the *Ep. Afr.*, he says of Origen's stance in the latter work:

> il est loin d'admettre l'argument que l'œuvre ne peut être acceptée que si elle avait un original hébreu; au contraire, il soutient fortement que le critère qu'il faut adopter pour accepter une œuvre dans le canon biblique n'est pas la *langue* mais l'*usage*, celui de l'Église.[36]

However, as we have seen, in both works Origen affords great weight to the problem of the puns and the Jewish rejection of Susanna. Moreover, the 'dichotomy view' does not take into account Origen's statement in *Ep. Afr.* 10 as he turns to the problem of the puns: καὶ πρῶτόν γε ἀρξώμεθα ἀπὸ τοῦ δυνηθέντος ἄν δυσωπῆσαι πρὸς τὸ μὴ παραδέξασθαι τὴν ἱστορίαν ("And let us begin first from the point that would be able to shame us into not accepting the story"). This comment clearly grants immense power to the problem of the puns, and sounds very much like what we earlier read in the *Stromata*: "but if anyone should show that the etymology of these two trees, *schinos* and *prinos*, exists in Hebrew, then we would be able to accept also this as scripture." Origen is here turning his attention from Africanus' §7, regarding the absence of Susanna from the Jewish Bible, to Africanus' §5, where Africanus had exploited the puns to show that Susanna was composed in Greek. As we have seen, Africanus' conclusion to this point was an unambiguous articulation of the Hebrew criterion: "whatever circulates as part of the OT was translated from Hebrew to Greek." Origen's response to this statement is complete agreement—if the Greek puns can prove a Greek original for Susanna, then we cannot accept the story (πρὸς τὸ μὴ παραδέξασθαι τὴν ἱστορίαν).[37] Origen does not agree that the Greek puns can

---

[36] De Lange, *Lettre*, 492; see also de Lange, "Origen's Recantation?" 247; Adler, "Hebrews," 32.

[37] Engel, *Susanna-Erzählung*, 20: "Während Origenes die Voraussetzung des Africanus "echt"/kirchlich kanonisch = 'von den rabbinischen Juden anerkannt' zurückweist, scheint er mit ihm die Annahme zu teilen, die Ursprache solcher Schriften müsse habräisch (allenfalls syrisch = aramäisch) sein und ihr Stoff jüdischer Tradition entstammen." Though his book

prove a Greek original for Susanna, and he should know, for he has spent considerable time and energy in an attempt to determine this point. He conducted this fruitless investigation entirely because the issue was of the greatest importance: composition in Hebrew is a criterion of canonicity.

So, while it is true that Origen in his *Ep. Afr.* emphasizes the Church's right to determine its own Bible without being tied to what the Jews accept, the ecclesiastical criterion is not the only one he affirms. There is no great distinction between what he says here and what is found in his *Stromata*, with the necessary allowance made for riper and firmer views after two decades of thought and research. In neither case does he oppose the language of original composition to usage in the Church, but asserts that both principles must be taken into account to determine a document's canonicity.

### Suppression of Scripture

The above arguments from Origen's *Ep. Afr.* have sought to establish that the great Caesarean scholar regarded the Hebrew language as a necessary criterion for establishing the authenticity of OT material. However, some scholars have stressed that Origen's defense of Susanna should be interpreted as an issue of the text-form of Daniel rather than a matter of canonical books.[38] Four points tell against this idea. First, we will see later in Chapter Five (pp. 183–185) that Origen does occasionally explain textual divergences between the Hebrew text and the LXX as due to the Seventy translators, and he views these changes positively. In the case of Susanna, on the other hand, the divergence between Greek and Hebrew could lead to the rejection of the story, something that obviously troubles Origen a great deal. In other words, he views Susanna as something different from a textual concern. Second, while the first part of Origen's letter does focus on textual issues, the transition at §10 signals a change of subject, so that Origen now responds to Africanus' assertion that "whatever circulates as part of the OT was translated from Hebrew to Greek," a statement itself bearing wider implications than merely textual, thus demanding a commensurate response. Third, later

---

was published two years later, Engel (17 n. 23) is unaware of the edition by de Lange. On Origen's acceptance of the Hebrew criterion, see also F. Stuhlhofer, *Der Gebrauch der Bibel von Jesus bis Euseb* (Wuppertal, 1988), 129; A.E. Steinmann, *The Oracles of God* (St. Louis, 1999), 155.

[38] See, e.g., E.E. Ellis, *The Old Testament in Early Christianity* (Tübingen, 1991), 16–17; R. Beckwith, *The Old Testament Canon of the New Testament Church* (Grand Rapids, 1985), 393–394; cf. also the translation by Crombie, ANF 4.388–389.

in the discussion Origen compares the situation of Susanna with that of Tobit and Judith (§ 19). Fourth, the charge of Jewish suppression as articulated by Origen concerns documents rather than textual readings. This last point requires further discussion.

One must first distinguish between the common Christian accusation of Jewish falsification of scripture and the less frequent accusation that Jews suppressed certain documents.[39] The former charge deals specifically with textual issues in books accepted as canonical by Jews and Christians, as we see in Justin (*Dial.* 70–73), Irenaeus (*Haer.* 3.21.3), and others.[40] Origen himself generally rejected this notion, as Jerome reports in his *Comm. Isa.* 6:9–10.[41]

> *quod si aliquis dixerit, Hebraeos libros postea a Iudaeis esse falsatos, audiat Origenem quid in octauo uolumine Explanationum Esaiae huic respondeat quaestiunculae, quod numquam Dominus et apostoli, qui cetera crimina arguunt in scribis et pharisaeis, de hoc crimine, quod erat maximum, reticuissent.*

> But if anyone says that the Hebrew books were later falsified by the Jews, he should listen to how Origen responds to this query in the eighteenth volume of his *Explanations of Isaiah*, that the Lord and the apostles, who charged the scribes and Pharisees with other crimes, would never have kept silent concerning this crime, which was the greatest.

On the other hand, the accusation that the Jews suppressed entire documents finds expression only in Tertullian with regard to Enoch (*Cult. fem.* 1.3), Hippolytus with regard to Susanna (*Comm. Dan.* 1.15.2), and Origen with regard to Susanna and several documents narrating the murder of the ancient prophets (*Ep. Afr.* 13–15; *Comm. ser. Matt.* 28). Tertullian and Hippolytus hardly develop the argument at all, so it easily reaches its most sophisticated form in Origen. The extent to which Origen presents his case in his *Ep. Afr.*, and the fact that the same argument appears in his *Comm.*

---

[39] Note that both Ellis, *Old Testament*, 16, and Beckwith, *Old Testament*, 394, fail to distinguish between textual falsification and suppression of documents, so that they equate Origen's position with that of Justin.

[40] See W. Adler, "The Jews as Falsifiers: Charges of Tendentious Emendation in Anti-Jewish Christian Polemic," in *Translation of Scripture*, JQR Supplement (Philadelphia, 1990), 1–27. This accusation continued to be trumpeted against the Jews throughout the Middle Ages, on which see I.M. Resnick, "The Falsification of Scripture and Medieval Christian and Jewish Polemics," *Medieval Encounters* 2 (1996): 344–380.

[41] Adler ("Falsifiers," 9–10) cites also Jerome's translation of Origen's *Hom. Jer.* 16.10 (on Jer. 17:1), but the example loses some power because the Greek preserves no comment regarding Jewish falsification.

*ser. Matt.*, indicates that he had not hastily constructed it.[42] Adler's suggestion that "Origen may have said this only in the heat of argument" cannot be accepted, and seems to be based in part on his failure to distinguish between the accusations of falsification and suppression.[43]

It is true that Origen envisions the Jews as falsifying the suppressed documents in order to discredit them. He says regarding a certain Isaiah apocryphon, ὅπερ τάχα ἐπίτηδες ὑπὸ Ἰουδαίων ῥεραδιούργηται, λέξεις τινὰς τὰς μὴ πρεπούσας παρεμβεβληκότων τῇ γραφῇ ἵν' ἡ ὅλη ἀπιστηθῇ ("which perhaps has been intentionally corrupted by Jews, having interpolated into the writing certain improper expressions so that the entirety might be doubted"; *Ep. Afr.* 13). It does not seem to occur to Origen that this line of reasoning could lead to Christian acceptance of various apocrypha as scripture.[44] Elsewhere, he counsels against this very practice, due to the presence of many false teachings in these writings (*Comm. ser. Matt.* 28; *Comm. Cant.*, prol. *ad fin.*). Origen, of course, is quite familiar with text-critical research, and he is usually confident in his ability to determine whether the Greek text differs from the Hebrew due to textual error or Providence.[45] But, this concerns biblical texts, and he evinces no such confidence regarding apocryphal documents. Perhaps there were too few manuscript copies to inform his decisions; perhaps he perceived that the apocrypha were not preserved by Providence, and so the same rules would not apply. In any case, Origen's employment of these documents in no way implied their scriptural standing.

Probably the absence of available versions for apocryphal documents did factor into Origen's refusal to sort out systematically the alleged Jewish interpolations, for it is probable that he encountered these texts only in their Christian form. De Lange has presented a convincing case that the Jews with whom Origen conversed about Susanna actually did not know the story, and Origen's belief to the contrary resulted from a misunderstanding.[46] The same may have happened with regard to the Isaiah apocryphon

---

[42] De Lange (*Lettre*, 497) attempts to trace somewhat the process by which the idea of Jewish suppression developed in Origen's mind.

[43] Adler, "Falsifiers," 16; for his confounding falsification with suppression, see p. 9.

[44] Adler, "Falsifiers," 16, says that Origen here creates "the conditions for selective legitimization of Apocrypha."

[45] Cf. Kamesar, *Jerome*, 17–18; and see our discussion below in ch. 5, pp. 178–189.

[46] De Lange, *Lettre*, 485–488. He similarly explains Jerome's comments made at *Comm. Jer.* 5.67.3–7. De Lange's explanation for Origen's statements is accepted by G. Dorival, "Origène, témoin des textes de l'Ancien Testament," in J.-M. Auwers and A. Wénin (eds.), *Lectures et relectures de la Bible* (Leuven, 1999), 351–366 (355 n. 12).

which Origen mentions. Scholars commenting on Origen usually identify this document with the *Ascension of Isaiah*, a work completely extant only in an Ethiopic translation of its Greek Christian form.[47] Origen mentions this document several times, and it is clear that he thinks of it as Jewish, at least originally.[48] Scholars of the *Ascension* have long accepted that within the extant work there exists a Jewish substratum, typically called the *Martyrdom of Isaiah*, which was later expanded by Christian editors.[49] Apparently it is this *Martyrdom* which scholars have had in mind as the text to which Origen refers when speaking of a Jewish Isaiah apocryphon.

However, recent work on the *Ascension* would disallow this interpretation. While composite theories involving Jewish sources and Christian interpolations have dominated the history of scholarship on the *Ascension*, there has of late been a trend in the direction of seeing the entire document as essentially Christian, whether from a single author or not.[50] In fact, this trend has been so strong that Richard Bauckham has classified it as "complete unanimity" since 1980.[51] Thus, there seems to have been no written Isaiah apocryphon current among Jews, despite the fact that rabbinic tradition agrees with the *Ascension* in describing Isaiah's end as death-by-sawing

---

[47]  De Lange, *Lettre*, 543 n. 3; Adler, "Falsifiers," 16; Schürer, *History*, rev., 3.1.335.

[48]  See the quotations collected in Schürer, *History*, rev., 3.1.339.

[49]  Especially influential was the analysis of R.H. Charles, *The Ascension of Isaiah* (London, 1900), xxxvi–xliii; see also Schürer, *History*, rev., 3.1.337.

[50]  See esp. P. Bettiolo, et al. (eds.), *Ascensio Isaiae: Textus*, CCSA 7 (Turnhout, 1995); E. Norelli, *Ascensio Isaiae: Commentarius*, CCSA 8 (Turnhout, 1995); and the many important studies of the *Ascension* by Norelli which he lists in his "The Political Issue of the *Ascension of Isaiah*: Some Remarks on Jonathan Knight's Thesis, and Some Methodological Problems," in D.H. Warren, et al. (eds.), *Early Christian Voices* (Leiden, 2003), 267–279 (268 n. 7). Norelli considers the document a composite of two Christian writings, with the first five chapters (the account of the martyrdom) being the later of the two. For the view that the document is a unified Christian work, see R. Bauckham, *The Fate of the Dead* (Leiden, 1998), 363–390.

[51]  Bauckham, *Fate*, 365. Bauckham perhaps exaggerates; at any rate, J. Blenkinsopp, *Opening the Sealed Book* (Grand Rapids, 2006), 49–50 still maintains the Jewish origin of the *Martyrdom*, though he seems unaware of recent work in this area. M.A. Knibb considered part of the document Jewish in his "Martyrdom and Ascension of Isaiah," in J.H. Charlesworth (ed.), *Old Testament Pseudepigrapha*, 2 vols. (New York, 1983–1985), 2.143–176, but he later recanted this view; see his "Isaianic Traditions in the Apocrypha and Pseudepigrapha," in C.C. Broyles and C.A. Evans (eds.), *Writing and Reading the Scroll of Isaiah*, 2 vols. (Leiden, 1997), 2.633–650 (637). On the religious origins of the pseudepigrapha in general, see R.A. Kraft, *Exploring the Scripturesque* (Leiden, 2009), esp. chs. 1–2; J.R. Davila, *The Provenance of the Pseudepigrapha* (Leiden, 2005). Davila mentions the recent general agreement on the Christian origin of the *Ascension of Isaiah* (p. 78), but he does not otherwise discuss it.

at the command of Manasseh (*b. San.* 103b).[52] It may be that the traditions known to the Jews about Isaiah's death led Origen to believe that the *Ascension* had a Jewish core, just as Origen's interaction with Jews in reference to Susanna made him think that the story circulated among them. Origen asserted that the Jews had added certain heretical passages to the Isaiah apocryphon, but these apparently were actually Christian in origin.[53]

It seems probable, then, that contemporary Jews did not possess any of the documents which Origen accuses them of having suppressed. On the contrary, he likely developed this theory by piecing together various bits of information obtained through encounters with Jewish and Christian sources. It may be that the tradition of Ezra's reserving seventy books for the erudite as found in 4 Ezra 14 influenced Origen, as de Lange suggests, or that he knew the rabbinic practice of 'hiding' (גנז) books away for various reasons, as others think.[54] It is most likely that both of these traditions were known to him and provoked his thinking. It was suggested earlier that Origen had probably read the specific charge of Jewish suppression of Susanna in the *Comm. Dan.* by Hippolytus. These three sources contributed the idea that Jewish leaders hid certain documents. By the time he wrote his *Stromata* he already associated the Ahab and Zedekiah mentioned in Jer. 29:22–23 with the wicked elders of Susanna, and he claimed to have received this tradition from a Jew (*apud* Jerome, *Comm. Dan.* 13:6, 13:60). In the fragments of this work preserved by Jerome there is no indication that Origen deduced at this time that the traditions about Ahab and Zedekiah implied the continued existence of Susanna among certain Jews of his day, as he asserts to Africanus (*Ep. Afr.* 11–12). This idea came subsequent to his recognition that the 'killing the prophets' theme so prominent in the NT found little support in the OT,[55] and especially his familiarity with the *Ascension of Isaiah*, which

---

[52] For further references and analysis of the rabbinic traditions themselves, as well as their relationship to the *Ascension*, see G.G. Porton, "Isaiah and the Kings: The Rabbis on the Prophet Isaiah," in Broyles and Evans, *Writing*, 2.693–716 (701–715). Porton shows that the *Ascension* has almost nothing in common with the rabbinic legends outside of the 'wood saw' used to kill Isaiah.

[53] E. Norelli, "Ascension d'Isaïe," in F. Bovon and P. Geoltrain (eds.), *Écrits apocryphes chrétiens I* (Paris, 1997), 499–545, says that the *Ascension* was associated with heretics (501).

[54] On the rabbinic practice, see S.Z. Leiman, *The Canonization of Hebrew Scripture* (Hamden, Conn., 1976), 72–86. Those who associate it with Origen's views in the *Ep. Afr.* include Beckwith, *Old Testament*, 392; M. Hengel, *The Septuagint as Christian Scripture* (Grand Rapids, 2002), 71 n. 40, 91 n. 46. For de Lange's views, see *Origen*, 52, 175 n. 19.

[55] For a survey of the development of this theme in post-exilic Judaism, see D. Satran, *Biblical Prophets in Byzantine Palestine* (Leiden, 1995), 25–28.

he misconstrued as an ancient Israelite document, at least in part. Evidently, this broad theme, and the concrete evidence of the *Ascension* specifically, prompted Origen to develop his theory, a theory that essentially has nothing to do with Susanna.[56]

Although Origen formulates his theory of suppression only generally in terms of ὅσα περιεῖχεν αὐτῶν κατηγορίαν παρὰ τῷ λαῷ ("whatever entails an accusation against them among the people"; *Ep. Afr.* 14; cf. also §13), the manner in which he developed it suggests that he thought in terms of suppressed documents rather than falsified passages. Each of the influences outlined in the previous paragraph points in this direction, especially his main analogy with the *Ascension of Isaiah*. That Susanna itself could be conceived as an independent document is confirmed by some ancient witnesses and was probably suggested to Origen by its varying position in the LXX and Theodotion versions of Daniel.[57] Jerome reports that Origen began in the ninth book of his *Stromata* commenting on the LXX version of Daniel, but switched to Theodotion's text at Dan. 4:8 (*Comm. Dan.* 4:5). This explains why his comments on the Theodotion version of Susanna, which forms the first chapter in that edition, come only after his comments on the rest of the book.[58] Origen thus knew quite well that the Susanna story shared no intimate connection contextually with the rest of Daniel. His comparing its suppression to that of the *Ascension of Isaiah*, which was obviously independent from the Book of Isaiah, indicates that he likewise understood Susanna to be essentially an independent document attached to the rest of Daniel because of their shared characters and historical situation.

The context of Origen's discussion indicates that he was thinking of these suppressed documents as Hebrew compositions. We saw above in Chapter Two that Origen signals at the beginning of §10 that he is beginning a new topic, turning from the absence of Susanna among the Jews to the problem of the Hebrew original. The next time Origen signals a change of topic is at §16, where he begins to take Africanus' seven arguments in

---

[56] As de Lange, *Lettre*, 497, points out: "Cet argument n'a aucun rapport intrinsèque avec l'histoire de Suzanne."

[57] For canonical lists that include Susanna as a separate book, see the evidence for Ps.-Nicephorus and Ps.-Athanasius cited in G. Dorival, "L'apport des Pères de l'Église à la question de la clôture du canon de l'Ancien Testament," in J.M. Auwers and H.J. de Jonge (eds.), *The Biblical Canons* (Leuven, 2003), 81–110 (106).

[58] Jerome, *Comm. Dan.* 13:1, reports that Origen's commentary on Susanna formed part of the tenth book of his *Stromata*, whereas the other part of Daniel received comment in the ninth book.

order, one at a time. Not only does this exhibit the care with which Origen organized his response to Africanus, but it also indicates that §10–15 form a single unit in Origen's mind.[59] He announces at the beginning of the unit that he will now treat the matter of the puns and the original language of composition. Therefore, he intends the theory of Jewish suppression to support his belief in a Hebrew original of Susanna. Specifically, this theory answers the question as to why the Jewish Bible omits the story, given the existence of a Hebrew original and the continuing awareness of Susanna among certain Jews.[60] Origen says that other documents sharing these characteristics were also omitted, thus making his case for Susanna more plausible. The theory would not serve its main point if we were not to assume that Susanna, the *Ascension of Isaiah*, etc., were written in Hebrew.

## Conclusion

Our discussion up to this point in the chapter has attempted to establish that both Africanus and Origen agreed that the canonicity of an OT document required its original language of composition to be Hebrew. If this thesis proves persuasive, then de Lange's case for a disingenuous letter will be rendered invalid.[61] His argument is based on Origen's affirming the synagogal criterion everywhere but in his *Ep. Afr.*, where he denies it along with the Hebrew criterion.[62] Origen has supposedly designed this denial in the *Ep. Afr.* to garner favor with the churches at large, who remain uncertain about Origen's critical positions. However, not only does Origen everywhere reject the synagogal criterion, but he also quite openly affirms the Hebrew criterion in the *Ep. Afr.* If he were trying to disguise his requirement for a Hebrew original, he does a very poor job of it.

The exchange of letters between Africanus and Origen indicates that the Hebrew criterion was generally accepted in the Church of their day. Neither scholar argues for the principle; rather, both presuppose it and use it as the basis for further arguments. That this view was shared by two men otherwise so strongly at odds in matters of biblical criticism suggests that

---

[59] See similarly de Lange, *Lettre*, 480.

[60] At §13, Origen introduces his theory of suppression by placing this question in Africanus' mouth: Τί δήποτε οὐ φέρεται παρ' αὐτοῖς ἐν τῷ Δανιὴλ ἡ ἱστορία, εἰ, ὡς φῇς, τοιαῦτα περὶ αὐτῆς οἱ σοφοὶ αὐτῶν παραδιδόασι ("Why then does the story not circulate among them in Daniel, if, as you say, their wise men transmit such traditions about it").

[61] De Lange, "Origen's Recantation?"; Adler, "Hebrews," 32, seems to follow de Lange without citing him. See also [George] Salmon, "The Apocrypha: General Introduction," in Wace, *The Holy Bible* [...]: *Apocrypha*, 1.ix–xlvi (xxiv).

[62] De Lange does not actually distinguish between these two criteria.

they were both drawing on a belief more widely-held. The next section of this chapter explores evidence for the Hebrew criterion in patristic literature more generally.

OTHER EVIDENCE FOR THE
HEBREW CRITERION IN PATRISTIC LITERATURE

### The Hebrew Alphabet and the Canonical Books

Origen's charge of Jewish suppression of scripture apparently had very little effect on his followers, as there does not seem to be a later echo of it even among his ardent supporters. On the other hand, the comments with which Origen introduces the Jewish canon in his commentary on the first Psalm (*apud* Eusebius, *Hist. eccl.* 6.25, quoted above, p. 37) had a profound effect on later writers; the vast majority of early Christian canonical lists were influenced by this passage. For in it, Origen first spelled out for Christian readers the connection between the number of letters in the Hebrew alphabet and the number of books accepted as canonical by the Hebrews. It became commonplace in the Church to restrict the OT canon to 22 books in order to maintain a symbolic connection with the 22 letters of the Hebrew alphabet. This emphasis on the connection between the OT books and the Hebrew language provides evidence for the acceptance of the Hebrew criterion among those transmitting this tradition.

As mentioned earlier (p. 24), the number 22 is first encountered in Josephus (*C. Ap.* 1.37–43), though he refrains from naming the books of the Bible and does not mention the Hebrew alphabet. Scholars disagree over whether Josephus' canon is equivalent to the later rabbinic canon, or smaller in some way, and if smaller, which books are omitted by Josephus.[63] Nearly simultaneously with Josephus, the number 24 is attested in 4 Ezra 14:45 and *Gospel*

---

[63] S. Zeitlin, "An Historical Study of the Canonization of the Hebrew Scriptures," *PAAJR* 3 (1931–1932): 121–158; repr. in S.Z. Leiman (ed.), *The Canon and Masorah of the Hebrew Bible* (New York, 1974), 164–201, argued that the canon of Josephus omitted Ecclesiastes and Esther (172–178). Hengel, *Septuagint*, 101, thought Josephus may have omitted Song of Songs and Ecclesiastes. Beckwith, *Old Testament*, 80, thinks one or the other of these books may have been omitted. Many scholars do equate Josephus' canon with that of the later Rabbis; see S.Z. Leiman, "Josephus and the Canon of the Bible," in L.H. Feldman and G. Hata (eds.), *Josephus, the Bible, and History* (Detroit, 1989), 50–58 (53–54); Ellis, *Old Testament*, 7 n. 25; R. Hennings, *Der Briefwechsel zwischen Augustinus und Hieronymus* (Leiden, 1994), 139, and the literature cited by Hennings at 139 n. 35. S. Mason, "Josephus and His Twenty-Two Book Canon," in L.M. McDonald and J.A. Sanders (eds.), *The Canon Debate* (Peabody, Mass., 2002),

*of Thomas* 52. Rabbinic literature transmits this latter number exclusively, beginning with *b. B. Bathra* 14b, where it is assumed rather than articulated.[64] Dorival believes 22 to be the older number, and he dates the number 24 to the fourth century (based on Jerome's evidence), but this fails to explain the evidence of 4 Ezra, contemporary with Josephus.[65] Beckwith argues that 24 is the older number, but his evidence is also selective.[66] It is impossible to determine conclusively which reckoning is earlier or how it came about that they were simultaneously employed by Jews. Both Josephus and the account in 4 Ezra assume that the numbers they report have been well-known among Jews for a long time. The number 24 is unattested among the Fathers before the fourth century, though Christian writers probably would have been aware of this alternative from 4 Ezra, the Gospel of Thomas, or direct encounters with Jews.[67]

The more pressing issue here concerns the symbolic value of the numbers, especially the number 22. Origen links it to the Hebrew alphabet, and several Fathers follow suit.[68] Josephus does not mention the alphabet, nor

---

110–127, counters all of this, asserting that "[w]e presently have no way of recovering the internal shape of his [sc. Josephus'] Bible from *C. Ap.* 1 or from his actual use of scripture in *A.J.* 1–11" (127).

[64] This passage as reported in the Talmud is a baraita, which may suggest a date ca. 200 or earlier; so Beckwith, *Old Testament*, 122; emphasizing the lateness of the list is G. Veltri, *Libraries, Translations, and 'Canonic' Texts* (Leiden, 2006), 13–14; J.N. Lightstone, "The Rabbis' Bible: The Canon of the Hebrew Bible and the Early Rabbinic Guild," in McDonald and Sanders, *Canon Debate*, 163–184 (178 and n. 16), who "generally would not date *beraitot* any earlier than the second half of the third century, and many are probably later." H.-P. Rüger, "Le Siracide: un livre à la frontière du canon," in J.-D. Kaestli and O. Wermelinger (eds.), *Le Canon de l'Ancien Testament* (Geneva, 1984), 47–69 (55–56), cites for the number 24 also *Eccl. Rab.* 12.11; *Song Rab.* 4.22; *Pesiq. Rab.* 3; and *Num. Rab.* 14.29. See also Str-B 4.419–420; Schürer, *History*, rev., 2.314–321. Hennings, *Briefwechsel*, 138, inexplicably cites the Targum to Song of Songs (5.10) as the first rabbinic testimony to 24 books and dates this targum to 200. On the contrary, the targum was actually composed in the seventh or eighth century; see P.S. Alexander, *The Targum of Canticles*, Aramaic Bible 17A (Collegeville, Minn., 2003), 55–58.

[65] Dorival, "Pères," 97–98. He does acknowledge 4 Ezra (p. 97), but does not explain its number, given nearly three centuries before Jerome. For an influential study dating 22 before 24, see P. Katz, "The Old Testament Canon in Palestine and Alexandria," *ZNW* 47 (1956): 191–217; repr. in Leiman, *Canon and Masorah*, 72–98.

[66] Beckwith, *Old Testament*, 121–122, 235–273. See the criticisms of Beckwith in Hennings, *Briefwechsel*, 137 n. 25.

[67] The number 24 is first encountered among patristic writers in Victorinus of Pettau, *Comm. Rev.* 4:8. See above, pp. 52–53 and nn. 136–137; cf. Hengel, *Septuagint*, 62 n. 13.

[68] Origen apud Eusebius, *Hist. Eccl.* 6.25; Athanasius, *Ep. fest. 39*; Epiphanius *Pan.* 8.6.1–4; *Mens.* 4; 22–23; Gregory of Nazianzus, *Carm.* 1.12; Hilary, *Instr. Ps.* 15; Jerome, *Prol. gal.*

does Melito, whose canon list some have enumerated as 22.[69] In fact, no Jewish source transmits the connection between the number of biblical books and the alphabet, and even Origen himself, in the extract preserved by Eusebius (*Hist. eccl.* 6.25), does not say that the connection with the Hebrew alphabet formed part of the tradition that he received from the Jews.[70] Nevertheless, Origen does make this claim elsewhere: Διὰ τοῦτό φασιν Ἑβραῖοι τῆς παλαιᾶς γραφῆς ἰσαρίθμους τοῖς στοιχείοις εἶναι τὰς βίβλους ("Therefore, the Hebrews say that the books of the Old Testament are equivalent in number to the letters"; *Hom. Lam.* frg. 3).[71] Several scholars likewise have been willing to attribute a Jewish origin to the alphabet connection.[72]

However, scholars of the development of the canon often ignore the connection or deny its reality. For example, Peter Katz asserted that the number 22 in relation to the biblical books has no intrinsic significance.

> The number twenty-two is the sum total of the earliest arrangement of scrolls we are able to trace. It was not chosen to serve as an indication of anything else; it is not a symbol. As a matter of course, the identical number of letters of the Hebrew alphabet was snatched at in search for a deeper meaning. Who is likely to suppose that Homer aimed at writing as many books as represent the Greek alphabet?[73]

This final statement by Katz is odd, as it serves actually to support an intrinsic relationship between the enumeration and the alphabet. For, of course, the question is not what was in Homer's mind, but what was in the mind of those who edited his work. According to Michael Haslam, the scholars who divided Homer's two epics into 24 books each did so despite interrupting traditional episodic divisions and limiting the size of a book to much less than a scroll could actually contain. This they did specifically because they were concerned with the alphabet. "It is not a numerical system but an alphabetical one, and the α–ω partitioning must have been devised for its symbolism, advertising Homer's all-comprehensiveness."[74]

---

[69] E.g. Katz, "Old Testament," 77–78; see also Hengel, *Septuagint*, 61.

[70] As noted by Hengel, *Septuagint*, 62 n. 12.

[71] See the edition by E. Klostermann (ed.), *Origenes Werke III*, GCS 6 (Leipzig, 1901), 236.

[72] Cf. Nautin, *Origène*, 268; de Lange, *Origen*, 175 n. 24, who traces the alphabet connection to a rabbinic midrash on אשרי in the Psalms; Hennings, *Briefwechsel* 159–160 n. 123, who rejects de Lange's arguments and (precariously) supposes that Origen encountered the connection in Jubilees. See above, pp. 24–25 n. 41.

[73] Katz, "Old Testament," 82.

[74] M. Haslam, "Homeric Papyri and Transmission of the Text," in I. Morris and B. Powell (eds.), *A New Companion to Homer* (Leiden, 1997), 55–100 (58). The division of the Homeric poems into 24 books is impossible to date precisely, and there is no agreement even to

Comparing Homer's 24 books to the 22 canonical books of the OT would indicate an essential connection to the alphabet in both cases.[75]

In addition to the parallel case with Homeric literature, there is also the fact that the number 22 is an artificial reckoning of the canonical books. The rabbinic canon of 24 books does not contain any obviously unnatural combinations of books. The only combinations that could possibly qualify are Ezra-Nehemiah and the Twelve Prophets, but both of these combinations seem to be attested well before an enumeration of the canon is encountered.[76] However, the 22-book canon required the artificial joining of Ruth with Judges and Lamentations with Jeremiah. As for the Jewish evidence for such combinations, even if Josephus' canon is deemed smaller than the rabbinic canon and thus lacks these artificial bonds,[77] Origen's list provides evidence for these combinations among the Jews of his day. For Sundberg has shown that Origen derived his list of Hebrew titles from a Jewish source, while Origen himself attempted to harmonize it with the Greek tradition.[78] Since the list of Hebrew titles does not allow a separate space for Ruth or Lamentations, one must think that Origen's informant either combined these books with others or omitted them, and few scholars would be willing to accept the latter alternative. The Christian form of the 22-book canon included even more material; Origen's list shows how much must be squeezed into the one title, 'Jeremiah.' Therefore, the artificiality of the number is apparent in Judaism and Christianity.

From the time of Origen, the number 22 was frequently cited as encompassing the whole OT, and this number had to be preserved regardless of

---

attribute it to the Alexandrian scholars. Haslam considers the division "prealexandrian" and cites the relevant literature (58 n. 6). For a survey of evidence, see R. Pfeiffer, *History of Classical Scholarship* (Oxford, 1968), 115–116.

[75] Note also the possible parallel in some Hellenistic-era catalogues of indigenous Egyptian literature numbering 42 items. While this is not the number of any sort of Egyptian alphabet, the number 42 is significant for Egyptians, and serves as evidence that organizers of such catalogues may have aimed for a specific, important number of items. See D.M. Carr, *Writing on the Tablet of the Heart* (Oxford, 2005), 196–197; and for Carr's linking the 22 biblical books to an alphabetic principle in Jewish education, see pp. 249–251, 270–271.

[76] See H.G.M. Williamson, *Ezra, Nehemiah*, WBC (Waco, Tex., 1982), xxi–xxiii, xxxv–xxxvi; J. Nogalski, *Literary Precursors to the Book of the Twelve*, BZAW 217 (Berlin, 1993), 2–3.

[77] Hengel, *Septuagint*, 101 and n. 66, argues that Josephus did omit two books from the rabbinic canon in order to arrive at the number 22, and this was done because of the alphabet.

[78] A.C. Sundberg, *The Old Testament of the Early Church* (Cambridge, Mass., 1964), 134–135. But see Ellis, *Old Testament*, 13–19, who shows that Origen may well have obtained the entire list from a Jewish source, if the addition of 'the epistle' to Jeremiah be regarded as an interpolation, for which there is some evidence.

the actual contents of the canon. In order to include Baruch and the Letter of Jeremiah, Epiphanius followed others in counting these documents as part of the Book of Jeremiah, even though he knew that they were rejected by the Jews (*Mens.* 5). Athanasius and Gregory of Nazianzus preserved the number, despite the omission of Esther, by counting Ruth separately. In the fifth century, the *Dialogue of Timothy and Aquila* included Judith among the 22, compensating for it by combining Song of Songs with Ecclesiastes.[79] As Mogens Müller has said, the Hebrew Bible influenced Christians in "trivial matters"; the Fathers generally did not concern themselves with the Hebrew text, but with "its number of books."[80] This they did in spite of their probable familiarity with the alternative reckoning of 24, which would allow for a more natural enumeration and a parallel to their own alphabet (cf. Hilary, *Instr. Ps.* 15). For patristic authors even more than for Jewish authors, the number 22 possessed a symbolic value not to be relinquished.

Even Origen, who himself did not accept the limits of the Jewish canon, stressed the importance of the number 22. Part of the context for his canon list from the commentary on the first psalm is preserved as the third section of the Philocalia.[81]

Ἐπεὶ δὲ ἐν τῷ περὶ ἀριθμῶν τόπῳ, ἑκάστου ἀριθμοῦ δύναμίν τινα ἔχοντος ἐν τοῖς οὖσιν, ᾗ κατεχρήσατο ὁ τῶν ὅλων δημιουργὸς εἰς τὴν σύστασιν ὁτὲ μὲν τοῦ παντὸς ὁτὲ δὲ εἴδους τινὸς τῶν ἐν μέρει, προσέχειν δεῖ καὶ ἐξιχνεύειν ἀπὸ τῶν γραφῶν τὰ περὶ αὐτῶν καὶ ἑνὸς ἑκάστου αὐτῶν, οὐκ ἀγνοητέον ὅτι καὶ τὸ εἶναι τὰς ἐνδιαθήκους βίβλους, ὡς Ἑβραῖοι παραδιδόασι, δύο καὶ εἴκοσι, οἷς ὁ ἴσος ἀριθμὸς τῶν παρ' αὐτοῖς στοιχείων ἐστίν, οὐκ ἄλογον τυγχάνει. Ὡς γὰρ τὰ κβ στοιχεῖα εἰσαγωγὴ δοκεῖ εἶναι εἰς τὴν σοφίαν καὶ τὰ θεῖα παιδεύματα τοῖς χαρακτῆρσι τούτοις ἐντυπούμενα τοῖς ἀνθρώποις, οὕτω στοιχείωσίς ἐστιν εἰς τὴν σοφίαν τοῦ θεοῦ, καὶ εἰσαγωγὴ εἰς τὴν γνῶσιν τῶν ὄντων, τὰ κβ θεόπνευστα βιβλία.

---

[79] For the text, see F.C. Conybeare (ed.), *The Dialogues of Athanasius and Zacchaeus and of Timothy and Aquila* (Oxford, 1898), 66. On this passage, see L. Lahey, "Hebrew and Aramaic in the *Dialogue of Timothy and Aquila*," in W. Horbury (ed.), *Hebrew Study from Ezra to Ben-Yehuda* (Edinburgh, 1999), 106–121 (109–111). On the date of the *Dialogue*, see J.Z. Pastis, "Dating the *Dialogue of Timothy and Aquila*: Revisiting the Earlier *Vorlage* Hypothesis," *HTR* 95 (2002): 169–195, who argues for the existence of a substantial substratum dating to the third century, of which substratum our passage forms a part. See also the forthcoming monograph by L. Lahey, *The Dialogue of Timothy and Aquila: Critical Greek Text and English Translation of the Short Recension with an Introduction including a Source-critical Study* (Tübingen: Mohr [Siebeck]).

[80] M. Müller, *The First Bible of the Church* (Sheffield, 1996), 80.

[81] Text in Harl, *Philocalie*, 260. See also the analysis of Nautin, *Origène*, 267–268.

> Since in the passage concerning numbers (each number having a certain significance among the things that exist, which the Creator of all things used for the composition both of the universe and of the individual parts) it is necessary to pay attention and to investigate from the scriptures the matters concerning them and each one of them, we should not be ignorant that it is not without reason that even the covenantal books, as the Hebrews transmit them, happen to be twenty-two, which is the same as the number of letters among them. For as the twenty-two letters seem to be an introduction to wisdom and divine education fashioned with these characters for men, so the twenty-two inspired books constitute an alphabet for the wisdom of God and an introduction to the knowledge of the things that exist.

Origen declares it reasonable (οὐκ ἄλογος) for the Hebrews to possess 22 books, since they have 22 letters in their alphabet, and the books and letters function in similar ways as introductions to divine wisdom. Elsewhere, Origen acknowledges that Hebrew was the original language of mankind, and that the 22 letters were written into creation by God.[82] Though Origen accepts more than 22 books, he recognizes the importance of the 22 letters, and he acknowledges the reasonableness displayed by the Hebrews in limiting their canon to this number. This connection of the books with the letters shows Origen's concern to define the OT by the Hebrew language.[83]

Later authors who used Origen's work, whether directly or as extracted by Eusebius or the Philocalists, would certainly perceive a close relationship between the OT books and the Hebrew language. Basil and Gregory entitle Origen's comments on the number 22 preserved in Philocalia 3, Διὰ τί κβ τὰ θεόπνευστα βιβλία ("Why there are twenty-two inspired books"). This title, as a heading for Origen's comments on the Hebrew alphabet, implies that the canon numbers 22 books specifically because of the alphabet. Others who report the connection between the OT books and the Hebrew alphabet include Athanasius, Epiphanius, Hilary, and Jerome. Without mentioning the alphabet explicitly, the number 22 is also stressed by Cyril of Jerusalem and the Council of Laodicea. It has been argued that Melito and the Bryennios List of OT books also transmit the tradition of 22 books.[84] The importance of the Hebrew alphabet in Christian conception of the OT canon

---

[82] For Hebrew as the original language, cf. Origen, *Cels.* 5.30–31; and see M. Rubin, "The Language of Creation or the Primordial Language: A Case of Cultural Polemics in Antiquity," *JJS* 49 (1998): 306–333 (317–318); for the number 22 in creation, cf. *Hom. Num.* 4.1, and see Harl, *Philocalie*, 264–265.

[83] See Hennings, *Briefwechsel*, 161.

[84] See Katz, "Old Testament."

extended to the time of Augustine, who himself makes no mention of it, and passes on a number for the OT books, 44, that seems to have no symbolic value (*Doctr. chr.* 2.13). His abandonment of the "holy number," as Hengel has termed it,[85] arose from his inclusion of the deuterocanonicals within the canon itself; it was impossible for Augustine to count the canonical books as 22. Prior to Augustine, the number 22 and its connection to the alphabet dominated discussions of the OT canon. This importance of the Hebrew alphabet makes sense only if the 22 canonical books were seen to be Hebrew compositions. The alphabet connection with the canon implies that no document written in a language other than Hebrew can be canonical.

One of Origen's admirers who does not mention the number 22 is Rufinus. Meinrad Stenzel concluded that Rufinus rejected that number and any connection to the alphabet. "Rufin hatte sich offenbar längst von der Ansicht freigemacht, dass ein innerer Zusammenhang zwischen den Büchern des Alten Testamentes und der Anzahl der hebräischen Buchstaben bestehen müsse."[86] Stenzel finds support for this assertion in Rufinus' translation of Origen's *Hom. Num.* 4.1.2 at Num. 3:39, where the number of the Levites is given as 22,000. Here, Rufinus' translation contains references to the 22 Hebrew letters, 22 generations from Adam to Jacob, and 22 species of animals, but there is no mention of the 22 books. Stenzel thinks it unbelievable that Origen would omit reference to the books, especially in light of his comments on the first psalm, which we have already examined. Rufinus must have left out this statement because he disagreed with the sentiment.

However, this argument fails at a number of points. It is not certain, as Stenzel claims ("über allen Zweifel gewiss"), that Origen would have included a reference to the OT canon in his *Hom. Num.* 4.1.2. In this passage, Origen is apparently drawing on Jubilees 2:23, which also speaks of the generations from Adam to Jacob and the works of creation, but not the alphabet or the canon, at least, according to the form of Jubilees preserved in our manuscripts.[87] Moreover, Origen's comments on the first psalm provide dubious evidence for Stenzel's assertions, for Rufinus himself also translated those comments within his translation of Eusebius' *Historia Ecclesiastica* (6.25), and there the Latin version does mention the 22 letters and 22 books.

---

[85] Hengel, *Septuagint*, 61.

[86] M. Stenzel, "Der Bibelkanon des Rufin von Aquileja," *Bib* 23 (1942): 43–61 (45). Kelly, *Commentary*, 22, follows Stenzel.

[87] See Hennings, *Briefwechsel*, 160–161. For the tradition of the 22 works of creation, see C. Bandt, *Der Traktat "Vom Mysterium der Buchstaben"*, TU 162 (Berlin, 2007), 74–76.

If Rufinus does not omit the reference in his translation of Eusebius' *Historia Ecclesiastica*, it is precarious to argue that he omitted the reference in another passage when it cannot be proven that there was such a reference originally.

As for Rufinus' own canon list in *Symb.* 34–36, it is in fact quite clear that he does count the OT books as 22. There is no other reason that he should clarify that Judges and Ruth count as one (*Iudicum simul cum Ruth*), or that the Hebrews count the four books of Reigns as two, the two books of Ezra as one, and the Twelve Prophets as one. The result is a 22-book canon, and we have seen that Rufinus knows the significance of this number to lie in its connection to the alphabet. Apparently, the number and the alphabet connection had both become so standard that Rufinus could assume his readers' knowledge of them.

The delimitation of the OT by the 22 books "according to the Hebrews" extends through (nearly) all of the Greek canon lists of the first four centuries, whether the number was mentioned or not. Fewer Latin authors acknowledge the number 22, but Hilary, Jerome, and Rufinus may all be cited. The continuing influence of this number can be seen, e.g., in the *Dialogue of Timothy and Aquila* and certain Armenian canon lists discussed by Michael Stone.[88] The reason the number 22 was so important can only be that patristic authors desired to maintain the connection with the Hebrew alphabet, even when they do not make this connection explicit.

This prevalent theme makes it probable that the canonical views evident in the correspondence between Africanus and Origen could claim wider support. We have seen that both Africanus and Origen presupposed the Hebrew criterion of canonicity. The analogy between the alphabet and the canon indicates that others did as well. Christian authors emphasized the number 22 because the Hebrew alphabet had 22 letters; the mystical significance of this connection necessarily implies that only books originally written in the Hebrew language were canonical for the OT.

## The Extent of the Septuagint Translation

The earliest account of the translation of the LXX is the second-century BCE *Letter of Aristeas*, which tells of the translation of the Pentateuch by the 72 Jewish scholars. On the extent of the translation the Jewish sources uniformly agree, though this can be said for almost no other aspect of

---

[88]  M.E. Stone, "Armenian Canon Lists V—Anonymous Texts," *HTR* 83 (1990): 141–161 (146).

their accounts. Aristobulus (frg. 3), Philo (*Mos.* 2.25–44), Josephus (*A.J.* 12.11–118), and the Rabbis (e.g. *b. Meg.* 9a–b) all limit the activity of the original translators to the Books of Moses.[89] On the other hand, Christian sources almost uniformly agree, even while citing Aristeas in support, that the original translators produced the entire Greek OT.[90] It seems likely that this expansion of the translation activity resulted from an honest reading of the *Letter of Aristeas* (or the epitome by Josephus), with its references to the 'sacred law' or 'Jewish books' as the object of translation.[91] Christians naturally read the term 'law' from their own perspective as a reference to the entire Old Covenant.[92]

The importance for our purposes of ancient views on the extent of the LXX translation lies in its being a translation, with the implication that each document ascribed to the LXX was thought to have originally existed in Hebrew. Indeed, John Chrysostom introduces a brief account of the translation legend by saying, πᾶσαι αἱ θεῖαι βίβλοι τῆς Παλαιᾶς Διαθήκης τῇ Ἑβραίων γλώττῃ ἐξ ἀρχῆς ἦσαν συντεθειμέναι, καὶ τοῦτο πάντες ἂν ἡμῖν συνομολογήσαιεν ("all the divine books of the OT were originally composed in the language of the Hebrews, and everyone would agree with us about

---

[89] For the fragment of Aristobulus, see the collection by C.R. Holladay, *Fragments from Hellenistic Jewish Authors*, vol. 3, *Aristobulus* (Atlanta, 1995), 156. This fragment is preserved by Eusebius (*Praep. ev.* 13.12.2) and Clement of Alexandria (*Strom.* 1.148.1), the latter version containing a reference to a translation of the law and the prophets. As a general statement on the transmission of Aristobulus' fragments, Holladay says, "While Eusebius' quotations adhere more closely to Aristobulus' original text, Clement's are more paraphrastic and reflect stylistic improvements" (45). On Aristobulus in general, the standard work is still N. Walter, *Der Thoraausleger Aristobulos* (Berlin, 1964), who affirms that Aristobulus had only the Pentateuch in view (pp. 31–33), though Walter does not address Clement's addition of the prophets to the translation in frg. 3. The most thorough treatment of the legend of the LXX as it developed in antiquity is A. Wasserstein and D. Wasserstein, *The Legend of the Septuagint* (Cambridge, 2006). Chapters 1–4 concern the legend within the Jewish sources. Wasserstein and Wasserstein consider Aristobulus to be a Christian "invention" (32).

[90] Cf. Justin, *Apol.* 1.31.2–5; *Dial.* 68.7; Irenaeus, *Haer.* 3.21.2; Clement of Alexandria, *Strom.*, 1.148–149; Tertullian, *Apologet.* 18.5–9. Tertullian is the first Christian author to mention the *Letter of Aristeas*. Others who cite the *Letter* while speaking of the translation of the entire OT include Eusebius, *Praep. ev.* 8; Epiphanius, *Mens.* 9.

[91] Cf. *Ep. Arist.* 3, 5, 28, 30, etc. The *Letter* does not name Moses, nor does it use the word 'Pentateuch,' a term first found in Ptolemy's *Letter to Flora* from the second century CE.

[92] For 'law' as encompassing the whole OT in Jewish and Christian thought, see Str-B 2.542–543; 3.159, 462–463; Hengel, *Septuagint*, 27 with n. 5. Alternatively, Christians could use 'law' as a reference to the time period when the Old Covenant was in effect: Hilary describes the LXX translation as having been produced *mediis* [...] *legis temporibus* (*Tract. Ps.* 2.2). This use of the word 'law' would also support the present argument that Christian readers naturally understood the *Letter of Aristeas* to concern the whole OT.

this"; *Hom. Gen.* 4.4; PG 53.42). Given the widespread acknowledgement that the LXX translation constituted the Bible of the Church, documents known to have been written in Greek would carry less authority than original Hebrew compositions because the former could not belong to the LXX translation. Those authors who do not limit the OT to 22 books sometimes relied on the expansion of the LXX translation to include within the canon deuterocanonicals, even some that are now known to have been composed in Greek. In doing so, these authors apparently continued to assume the validity of the Hebrew criterion.

It was Philo who first attested the inspiration of the Seventy translators (*Mos.* 2.37–40), and this view became almost axiomatic in Christian circles. The Fathers added various embellishments to the translation story to enhance the glory of the LXX. Borrowing a theme found also in rabbinic literature and hinted at in Philo, the Fathers often insisted that King Ptolemy separated the translators to prevent collusion, yet each of the seventy-two scholars produced an identical translation, the obvious result of divine favor.[93] Moreover, the idea that the apostles sanctioned this particular translation by citing it exclusively in their writings joined with other arguments in establishing the LXX as the official version of the Christian OT.[94] The result was that any writing not attributed to the LXX became suspect because it did not benefit from their inspiration.[95]

The first Christian author on record who mentions the LXX translation speaks of it as a translation of the OT as a whole, not just the Pentateuch (Justin, *Apol.* 1.31.2–5). The Fathers after Justin commonly describe the work of the Seventy in rather general terms as a translation of the Jewish scriptures or prophecies.[96] Jerome routinely, especially in his commentaries, refers to the Greek text of books outside the Pentateuch as the LXX. Some writers are more explicit, attributing specific books to the LXX translation. Cyril of Jerusalem (*Catech.* 4.33) and Epiphanius (*Mens.* 4–5) both say that

---

[93] Philo does not say that the translators were separated, but his emphasis on their all using the same words to translate the Pentateuch (*Mos.* 2.37) implies that he did not regard the translators as collaborating, *contra Ep. Arist.* 300–311 and Josephus, *A.J.* 12.103. The rabbinic version of this story is found in, e.g., *b. Meg.* 9a–b. For Christian writers who transmit the story, see ch. 5 below. For analysis of this story among the Rabbis, see Wasserstein and Wasserstein, *Legend*, 84–94, and for the Christian tradition, pp. 95–131.

[94] For apostolic sanction of the LXX, cf. especially Rufinus, *Apol. Hier.* 2.37–38, and see Kamesar, *Jerome*, 28–33, for the various arguments used in behalf of the LXX.

[95] Cf. Hengel, *Septuagint*, 74.

[96] Cf. Irenaeus, *Haer.* 3.21.2; Clement of Alexandria, *Strom.* 1.148–149. Tertullian, *Apologet.* 18.5–9; Eusebius, *Praep. ev.* 8.

all 22 books were translated by the Seventy.[97] Hilary attributes the translation of the Psalter to the original translation under King Ptolemy (*Tract. Ps.* 2.3).[98] Theodoret asserts that the Seventy translated the superscriptions in the Psalter, as they did the rest of the scriptures (*Comm. Ps.* prol. 7). The *Dialogue of Timothy and Aquila* follows its listing of the 22 canonical books with the assertion that the Seventy translators delivered to the apocrypha for Christians (εἰς τὰ ἀπόκρυφα παρέδωκαν ἡμῖν) the books of Tobit, Wisdom of Solomon, and Sirach, apparently meaning that the Seventy translated these books and then separated them from the 22 canonical books. Expanding the scope of the Seventy's activities to include these books obviously implies that each of these writings, even Wisdom of Solomon, was written in Hebrew and later translated into Greek along with the rest of the Hebrew scriptures. Müller rightly perceives the implications of this widening of the LXX translation when he writes of Tertullian's defense of 1 Enoch, "Apparently he reckons this book among the writings translated."[99]

The idea that every OT document was a translation from Hebrew poses no difficulty for most of the OT, since it was, in fact, written originally in Hebrew. However, Wisdom of Solomon and 2 Maccabees were received into the canon of some of the Fathers, though they were composed originally in Greek. The reason for this may be that some early Christians assumed that even these documents had their origins in Hebrew and were translated by the inspired Seventy translators. Since there is not much patristic discussion in this regard revolving around 2 Maccabees,[100] our comments will focus on the Wisdom of Solomon.

---

[97] According to the critical Greek text of Elia D. Moutsoula, "Τὸ 'Περὶ μέτρων καὶ σταθμῶν' ἔργον 'Επιφανίου τοῦ Σαλαμῖνος," *Theologia* 44 (1973): 157–200, Epiphanius also attributes to the Seventy the translation of 72 apocryphal books (*Mens.* 5.147–148). This statement may rely upon the tradition found in 4 Ezra 14:44–47 in which God inspired Ezra to reconstruct 94 books, though there the division is between 24 books for the public (i.e., canonical books) and 70 for an inner circle of wise men. See M.E. Stone, *Fourth Ezra*, Hermeneia (Minneapolis, 1990), 441 and n. 20.

[98] For a discussion of this passage, see A. Kamesar, "Hilary of Poitiers, Judeo-Christianity, and the Origins of the LXX: A Translation of *Tractatus super Psalmos* 2.2–3 with Introduction and Commentary," *VC* 59 (2005): 264–285 (281–283).

[99] Müller, *First Bible*, 76. Tertullian defends the authenticity and canonicity of 1 Enoch in *Cult. fem.* 1.3; he asserts the exclusive authority of the LXX at *Apologet.* 18.5–9.

[100] For a recent survey, see D.R. Schwartz, *2 Maccabees* (Berlin, 2008), 57–59, 88–89. On the other hand, the stories of the Maccabean martyrs enjoyed a significant place in Christian literature and liturgy; see L.F. Pizzolato and Chiara Somenzi, *I sette fratelli Maccabei nella chiesa antica d'Occidente* (Milan, 2005); R. Ziadé, *Les martyrs Maccabées: de l'histoire juive au culte chrétien* (Leiden, 2007).

As we have seen (p. 43), Jerome knew that Wisdom was not written in Hebrew, and he substantiates this by saying that *ipse stilus graecam eloquentiam redolet* ("the style itself is redolent of Greek eloquence"; *Praef. lib. Sal.* 17–18). Nevertheless, it is impossible to tell who else may have recognized this fact. Jerome's evaluation of the style of Wisdom arises from his deep learning in both Greek and Hebrew, and he stood virtually alone among the Fathers in his mastery of this combination of languages.[101] Even Origen, whose Hebrew skills were meager,[102] may not have recognized that Wisdom "smelled Greek"—after all, it takes the Greek puns for him and others to say that Susanna may have been written in Greek. There was not a similar hint for Wisdom. At least some early Christians apparently thought that it was indeed written by Solomon, and, consequently, an original Hebrew document.[103] The book was written by a Jew for Jews, and if it did continue in some use among certain Jews into the third century, for which there is, admittedly, little evidence,[104] this may have misled Origen into thinking that there was a Hebrew original.

On the other hand, Martin Hengel has asserted, "Educated users observed already long before Jerome, that Wisdom—in itself quite significant for Christology—was originally written in Greek and could not have originated with Solomon."[105] It seems that Hengel has confused here two distinct issues—language and authorship. In Chapter Two above (pp. 42–45), we saw that several early Christians were aware that Solomon did not write the

---

[101] For the debate on Jerome's competence in Hebrew, see J.S. Cameron, "The *Vir Tricultus*: An Investigation of the Classical, Jewish and Christian Influences on Jerome's Translation of the Psalter *Iuxta Hebraeos*" (diss.; University of Oxford, 2006), 28–68; M. Graves, *Jerome's Hebrew Philology* (Leiden, 2007), 1–7. Graves estimates that Jerome attained a very good "passive" ability in the language (84–95); see also D.L. Everson, "An Examination of Synoptic Portions within the Vulgate," *VT* 58 (2008): 178–190. On "Hebrew Learning among the Fathers" generally, see the article under that title by C.J. Elliott in W. Smith and H. Wace (eds.), *Dictionary of Christian Biography*, 4 vols. (London, 1877–1887), 2.851–872.

[102] See the evaluation in de Lange, *Origen*, 21–23.

[103] See above, p. 44 with n. 108, as well as G.M. Hahneman, *The Muratorian Fragment and the Development of the Canon* (Oxford, 1992), 201. R.H. Pfeiffer, *History of New Testament Times with an Introduction to the Apocrypha* (New York, 1949), 319, notes that the attribution of the book to Solomon "naturally implied that it was originally written in Hebrew."

[104] But cf. W. Horbury, "The Christian Use and the Jewish Origins of the Wisdom of Solomon," in J. Day, R.P. Gordon, and H.G.M. Williamson (eds.), *Wisdom in Ancient Israel* (Cambridge, 1995), 182–196 (185–186). On the continuation of other Greek 'biblical' literature among Jews, cf. R.A. Kraft, "Philo's Bible Revisited: the 'Aberrant Texts' and Their Quotations of Moses," in F. García Martínez and M. Vervenne (eds.), *Interpreting Translation* (Leuven, 2005), 237–253, who suggests that Philo's works may have circulated in Jewish circles as late as the third century.

[105] Hengel, *Septuagint*, 69.

Book of Wisdom; Augustine states this explicitly more than once. However, this is no indication that these authors considered the work to be Greek. As evidence for his claim, Hengel cites only Jerome's comment that *nonnulli scriptorum veterum hunc* [sc. *librum Sapientiae*] *Iudaei Filonis adfirmant* ("several of the earlier writers affirm that it [i.e., the Book of Wisdom] was by Philo the Jew"; *Praef. lib. Sal.* 18–19). But Jerome's statement is the only certain testimony we have associating Philo with Wisdom of Solomon, and it seems that he is dependent for this report on the Muratorian Fragment.[106] But it is not at all certain that even the Mur. Frag. supports this tradition,[107] so Jerome may have been the first to articulate the idea that Philo authored Wisdom. One might also point to Wisdom's apparent position within the NT according to some ancient authorities (cf. Mur. Frag. 69–71; Epiphanius, *Pan.* 76) as indicating an early recognition of its Greek character.[108] This also is dubious, for Horbury has convincingly argued that the position of Wisdom in these works does not indicate an association with the NT but is a reflection of a wider practice of locating the *antilegomena* of both OT and NT after the lists of both Testaments.[109] The "educated users" mentioned by Hengel did know that Solomon did not write Wisdom, but they probably still assumed its Hebrew origin. It is likely that part of the reason for this was its standing within the LXX translation.

The role played by the Greek translation of the OT in early Christianity was significant, to say the least. That nearly every patristic author believed the entire OT had been translated by the original inspired Jewish scholars

---

[106] See S.P. Tregelles, *Canon Muratorianus* (Oxford, 1867), 53; Hahneman, *Fragment*, 201. After Jerome, we also find Julian of Eclanum reporting that some attribute Wisdom to Philo, a view Julian classifies as an *incerta opinio* (preserved by Augustine, *C. Jul. op. imp.* 4.123; PL 45.1420). On the continuance of this association, see D.T. Runia, *Philo in Early Christian Literature*, CRINT 3.3 (Assen, 1993), 235–236. Note, however, that the testimony of Isidore of Seville is contradictory, as he once attributes Wisdom to Philo (according to a Jewish tradition, he says; *Etymologiae* 6.2.30), and once to Solomon (*Eccl. off.* 1.12.9).

[107] The extant Latin says that Wisdom was written "by the friends of Solomon," and this reading has been defended as original by W. Horbury, "The Wisdom of Solomon in the Muratorian Fragment," *JTS* 45 (1994): 149–159 (149–152); cf. Davila, *Provenance*, 221. Even if the Mur. Frag. ascribes Wisdom of Solomon to Philo it is not clear in what language the author of the Frag. supposed Philo to have written it. Philo was thought to have authored an etymological list of Hebrew words (cf. Jerome's preface to his *Nom. Hebr.*; see Kamesar, *Jerome*, 104), for which presumably he would have required some knowledge of Hebrew. So, it seems possible that the author of the Frag. would have envisioned Philo writing Wisdom in Hebrew. Note, however, that Jerome's statements in his *Praef. lib. Sal.* assume that Philo writes only in Greek.

[108] See, e.g., Hengel, *Septuagint*, 69–70.

[109] Horbury, "Wisdom of Solomon," 152–156.

means that Christians commonly acknowledged every document of the OT to have a Hebrew original. As we have seen, some Christian authors include within the translation even documents known today to have been composed originally in Greek.[110] Therefore, even as Greek documents made their way into the OT canon of some of the Fathers, the authority of the LXX translation embraced them.

### Jerome, Augustine, and the Hebrew Criterion

Nevertheless, it cannot be said that the ascription of all canonical writings to the work of the Seventy was universal in the early Church. Though Jerome does not always maintain the distinction between the Greek Pentateuch and the Greek translation of other books, he does understand that all the early Jewish testimonies speak of the translation of the Pentateuch alone: *et Aristaeus et Iosephus et omnis schola Iudaeorum quinque tantum libros Moysi Septuaginta translatos asserant* ("Aristeas and Josephus and every school of the Jews assert that only the five Books of Moses were translated by the Seventy").[111] Of course, this in no way entails his rejection of the Hebrew criterion, but is rather a part of his argument in behalf of the *Hebraica veritas*.

Jerome's views of the canon were examined above in Chapter Two, where we saw that he typically restricts his OT to the Jewish Bible. However, at least one passage indicates that he is willing, at least in a polemical context, to transgress this principle if he may still maintain the Hebrew criterion. Of course, Jerome is well-known as an advocate for a return to the Hebrew text, and he rejected certain books from the canon, based both on their absence from the Jewish Bible and on their original language of composition (i.e. the Greek documents Wisdom of Solomon and 2 Maccabees; cf. *Praef. lib. Sal.* 19–21; *Prol. gal.* 52–57). His position in favor of the Hebrew text leads him to exclude the Greek additions to books such as Esther, Daniel, and Jeremiah, since these additions were not available in Hebrew in Jerome's day. Although he does translate the additions to Esther and Daniel, he advises his readers that they are not to be found in Hebrew and clearly marks them with their "death-warrant," the obelus; he justifies his translation by saying that had he omitted these familiar parts of the books, ignorant

---

[110] E.g., the *Dialogue of Timothy and Aquila* seems to make this claim for Wisdom of Solomon.

[111] *Comm. Ezech.* 5:12; cf. *Comm. Mich.* 2:9; *Qu. hebr. Gen.*, prol.

readers would raise a fuss.[112] In his commentary on Daniel, Jerome treats the Hymn of the Three Young Men very dismissively and refuses to comment on the other additions at all, instead providing the student with some excerpts from Origen's *Stromata*.[113] Baruch and the Epistle of Jeremiah are completely passed over in his translation of Jeremiah and his commentary (*Praef. Jer.* 12–14; *Comm. Jer.*, prol.).

Thus, it is surprising to encounter Jerome's ambiguous statements regarding the additions to Daniel in his *Apologia adversus Rufinum*.

> *Quod autem refero quid aduersum Susannae historiam et hymnum trium puerorum et Belis draconisque fabulas, quae in uolumine hebraico non habentur, Hebraei soleant dicere, qui id in me criminatur stultum se sycophantam probat. Non enim quid ipse sentirem, sed quid illi contra nos dicere soleant explicaui. Quorum opinioni si non respondi in prologo, breuitati studens, ne non praefationem, sed librum uiderer scribere, puto quod statim subiecerim. Dixi enim: "... de quo non est huius temporis disserere."*        (*Ruf.* 2.33)

> But what I report [in the *Praef. Dan.*]—what the Hebrews are accustomed to say against the History of Susanna and the Hymn of the Three Young Men and the stories of Bel and the Dragon, which are not contained in the Hebrew volume—the one accusing me of this crime proves himself to be a dolt and a sycophant. For I explained not what I myself think, but what they are accustomed to say against us. If I did not respond to their opinion in the prologue, striving for brevity, lest I should seem to be writing not a preface but a book, I think that I immediately added [such a comment], for I said, "concerning which it is not the time to discuss."

As Skehan points out, Jerome guards against saying anything definite.[114] Though his statements here imply that he would accept the additions to Daniel as authentic, Jerome probably was intentionally ambiguous as to his own position. He never did provide a response to the Jewish opinion of the additions, and when he wrote his commentary on Daniel a few years later, he definitely rejected them. By that time he had even devised an additional argument against their canonicity: the LXX version of Bel and the Dragon

---

[112] See Jerome's *Praef. Dan.*, where he describes the function of the obelus as "slaying" (*iugulans*) the passages to which it is attached (line 22; the term "death-warrant" comes from Skehan, "Jerome and the Canon," 281), and justifies his translation as for the *inperiti* (line 23). Jerome only alludes to the additions to Esther in his *Praef. Esth.*, but following his translation of the book as he found it in Hebrew, he includes the additions with a prefixed note and the obelus.

[113] Cf. his *Comm. Dan.* 3:23 and 3:91 for his statements about the Hymn, and 13:1 for Origen's *Stromata*.

[114] Skehan, "Jerome and the Canon," 281–282; see also Braverman, *Jerome's Commentary*, 50–51.

identifies Daniel as a priest (v. 2), while *sancta scriptura*, i.e. the Hebrew Bible (Dan. 1:6), reports that he was from the tribe of Judah.[115] So, perhaps in his *Ruf.* 2.33, Jerome's noncommittal language was merely an attempt to score polemical points.

Yet, if we continue reading in the *Adversus Rufinum*, we will see that even here Jerome affirms the authority of the Hebrew text. For in the same paragraph, Jerome goes on to say, *Qui istiusmodi nenias consectatur et Scripturae hebraicae ueritatem non uult recipere, audiat libere proclamantem: Nemo eum cogit legere quod non uult* ("The one who pursues nonsense of this sort and does not care to accept the truth of Hebrew scripture, should hear freely as I proclaim: no one forces him to read what he does not want").[116] And at the end of the next chapter (*Ruf.* 2.34):

> *Nec hoc dicimus quod Septuaginta interpretes suggillemus, sed quo apostolorum et Christi sit maior auctoritas, et ubicumque Septuaginta ab hebraico non discordant, ibi apostolos de interpretatione eorum exempla sumpsisse; ubi uero discrepant, id posuisse in graeco quod apud Hebraeos didicerant.*[117]

> Nor do we say this because we would deride the Seventy translators, but because the authority of the apostles and Christ is greater, and everywhere the LXX is not discordant with the Hebrew, there the apostles took examples from their translation; but where [the Hebrew and LXX] disagree, there they have put in Greek what they learned among the Hebrews.

It is impossible to believe, therefore, that Jerome's ambiguous response to Rufinus concerning the additions to Daniel intends to cast doubt upon the appropriateness of following the Hebrew text. On the contrary, he

---

[115] Cf. the preface to his *Comm. Dan.*, lines 55–58 in the edition of Glorie (CCSL 75A, 773–774), and see Braverman, *Jerome's Commentary*, 52, 69–70. A little further in the preface (lines 65–66), Jerome says that the additions to Daniel have *nulla scripturae sanctae auctoritas*.

[116] It is not clear to me why Fremantle's translation in NPNF² 3.517 omits the clause regarding Hebrew scripture, instead rendering the sentence: "If there is any one who pays attention to silly things like this, I must tell him loudly and freely, that no one is compelled to read what he does not want." The line in question appears both in the Migne edition (PL 23.455b) and in the edition of P. Lardet, *Saint Jérôme, Apologie contre Rufin*, SC 303 (Paris, 1983), 194.28–29, who translates it as "et ne veut pas admettre la vérité de l'Écriture hébraïque."

[117] For other references to Jerome's insistence that the apostles relied on the LXX only when it agreed with the Hebrew, see P. Lardet, *L'Apologie de Jérôme contre Rufin: un commentaire* (Leiden, 1993), 237, who cites *Praef. Jos.* 26–28 and *Comm. Isa. lib.* 15, prol. This is in direct response to the view of many early Christians, especially Rufinus (*Apol. Hier.* 2.37–38), that the apostles sanctioned the LXX for the Church by virtue of their quoting it rather than providing their own translation. See Kamesar, *Jerome*, 29–30. For the validity of Jerome's claim, see Cameron, "Vir Tricultus," 203–242.

apparently means that one may accept the authenticity of the additions if they could claim a share of the *Hebraica veritas*. A possible way of harmonizing Jerome's non-committal language in *Ruf.* 2.33 with his statements elsewhere more clearly in support of Hebrew text is to understand that even in *Ruf.* 2.33 he continues to endorse the Hebrew criterion (as evidenced by *Ruf.* 2.34), though he now assumes for argument's sake that Origen had been right rather than Africanus concerning the original language of the additions to Daniel. Indeed, we might understand his statements to Rufinus as repeating the position of Origen that Jerome recorded at the end of his *Comm. Dan* (13:54–59), namely, that Susanna could be received as scripture if a Hebrew etymology could be established for the puns.[118] That Jerome could see these additions as Hebrew compositions is also suggested by his Latin version of Susanna's puns (*Praef. Dan.* 27–30), which concedes one of Origen's major points in the *Ep. Afr.* (§18): puns can be translated. In any case, Jerome continues to advocate the authority of Hebrew scripture as determinative for the Christian OT.

At the other end of the spectrum, Augustine fully endorses the view that the Seventy translated all of the Jewish scriptures by the inspiration of God (*Civ.* 18.42–43). Unfortunately, determining how this impacts Augustine's views concerning the Hebrew criterion of canonicity proves very difficult. First of all, he does not make clear whether he imagined that the Greek text of every canonical book derived from the LXX translation. For, not only does he advocate the LXX as the Bible of the Church, but he allows into the canon certain books which a moment's thought would have shown could not have been translated by the Seventy. Sirach is an obvious example, if Augustine was familiar with its translator's preface. Moreover, Augustine affirms the canonicity of 1 and 2 Maccabees, which he knows to have post-dated the LXX translation and even the cessation of prophecy among the Jews.[119]

> *Ab hoc tempore apud Iudaeos restituto templo, non reges, sed principes fuerunt usque ad Aristobulum; quorum supputatio temporum non in Scripturis sanctis, quae appellantur canonicae, sed in aliis inuenitur, in quibus sunt et Machabaeorum libri, quos non Iudaei, sed Ecclesia pro canonicis habet, propter quorundam Martyrum passiones uehementes atque mirabiles, qui antequam Christus uenisset in carne, usque ad mortem pro Dei lege certarunt, et mala grauissima atque horribilia pertulerunt.* (*Civ.* 18.36)

---

[118] See Cook, *Interpretation*, 202 and n. 296, who attributes this position to Jerome based on his *Comm. Dan.* 13:54–59.

[119] Cf. Augustine, *Civ.* 18.45, in which chapter Augustine situates the cessation of prophecy after the construction of the Second Temple, mentions the LXX translation during the reign of Ptolemy Philadelphus, and then indicates that the wars of the Maccabees followed this.

From this time, when the Temple had been restored among the Jews, there were not kings but princes up until Aristobulus, whose dates are found not in the holy scriptures, which are called canonical, but in others, among which are the books of Maccabees, which not the Jews, but the Church holds as canonical on account of the severe and marvelous sufferings of certain martyrs, who, before Christ had come in the flesh, contended unto death for the law of God, and endured most serious and horrible calamities.

Augustine emphasized the authority of the LXX perhaps more than any other Father. He was aware that the translation did not replicate the Hebrew Bible, and he was willing to concede the authority of the original-language text, but he never wavered in asserting that the LXX is the Christian OT: *hanc tamen* [sc. *editionem*] *quae Septuaginta est, tanquam sola esset, sic recepit Ecclesia* ("but the Church has received this [edition] which is the LXX as if it were the only one"; *Civ.* 18.43). His correspondence with Jerome seems only to have solidified this idea in his mind.[120] Thus, it is surprising that he would accept into the canon documents which he knew to be later than the inspired translation, and it is difficult to settle on an explanation for this circumstance. Perhaps he did not perceive the implication of the relative dates of the translation of the LXX and the composition of the Books of Maccabees; he does not highlight the post-LXX origin of Maccabees. Or, it may be that Augustine thought that the Seventy translators produced a Greek version of the Jewish canon alone, and that Greek versions of the deuterocanonicals came only later. We have seen that the ecclesiastical tradition of reading these books liturgically controlled Augustine's view of them,[121] so maybe he did not feel it necessary to tie every canonical book to the LXX translation.

In the second place, if Augustine did not include the Greek text of every canonical book within the LXX, it is still uncertain which of these books he would have considered original Hebrew compositions and which ones original Greek compositions. Surely he did not believe that canonical documents not translated by the Seventy were, therefore, not translations at all. He himself would have no way of checking, but he would have the authority of Jerome for the belief that Sirach and 1 Maccabees were in Hebrew.[122] He

---

[120] Compare Augustine, *Doctr. chr.* 2.22 (ca. 397), with *Civ.* 18.43, written decades later.

[121] Both Jerome (*Praef. lib. Sal.* 19) and Rufinus (*Symb.* 36) testify that the Books of Maccabees were read publicly in churches. This seems to be a western phenomenon, since neither Athanasius (*Ep. fest.* 39) nor Cyril of Jerusalem (*Catach.* 4.33–37) are aware of the practice. See above, p. 54.

[122] On 1 Maccabees, cf. Jerome, *Prol. gal.* 55–57; on Sirach, cf. Jerome, *Praef. lib. Sal.* 14.

would have to reject Jerome's assurances if he were to believe that Wisdom of Solomon and 2 Maccabees were Hebrew, but this would not be the only instance in which Augustine's theology trumped Jerome's philology. While there is no evidence for his opinion on the original language of 2 Maccabees, it seems likely that Augustine's statement that Jesus Sirach authored both Wisdom [of Solomon] and Ecclesiasticus implies that he grouped them together as translations from the Hebrew.[123]

That said, it is possible that Augustine represents the rejection of the Hebrew criterion; after all, he has developed a sophisticated theory to account for the differences between the Hebrew and Greek texts (cf. *Civ.* 18.43; *Doctr. chr.* 2.22). We will show later, in Chapter Five, that in textual matters Augustine maintained the importance and originality of the Hebrew but rejected the idea that the Church's Bible should match textually the Hebrew Bible. Possibly he took a similar position for canonical matters, so that he was not concerned to accept books exclusively that had been written in Hebrew. Despite his frequent references to the OT as originally Hebrew (cf., e.g., *Doctr. chr.* 2.16; *Tract. Ev. Jo.* 117.4), we have seen that Augustine does not limit the OT to 22 books (pp. 90–91), nor does he unequivocally embrace all of the canonical books within the framework of the LXX. These two indicators for the acceptance of the Hebrew criterion, which we found in many other Christian writers, do not apply to Augustine. His firm stance that only the Church has the power to govern the scope of its Bible apparently stood alone as his criterion for canonicity.

## Conclusion

In the previous chapter, we examined the criteria which served the canonical theories of patristic authors. We saw that Christians generally debated whether the Christian OT should reproduce the Jewish Bible or whether the Christian Bible should comprise those documents that were useful to the Church. While the Fathers took sides on these issues, and accused those on the other side of perverting the Bible, most of them agreed on a third criterion: each OT document must have been composed in Hebrew.

Both Julius Africanus and Origen explicitly endorse the Hebrew criterion, though they differ as to its applicability in the case of Susanna. Furthermore, neither Africanus nor Origen argue in behalf of the Hebrew criterion, but

---

[123] Cf. Augustine, *Doctr. chr.* 2.13; he later corrected this attribution (*Retract.* 2.30.2), but the point made here still stands.

rather assume that it is generally accepted. Evidence for this general acceptance has been found in the extension of the LXX translation to the entire
OT and in the widespread analogy between the OT canon and the Hebrew
alphabet. One might also say that the Hebrew criterion is implied by the
common tradition associating Ezra with the rewriting of all OT scripture,
discussed above in the context of the Date criterion (pp. 18–19). At the end of
the period under examination, Jerome and Augustine take opposing views
on the proper Christian OT canon, and they probably also diverge on the
applicability of the Hebrew criterion for such questions. For his part, Jerome
usually follows the synagogal criterion, which necessarily allows for literature only in Hebrew, but he is able to be pushed in debate to the point
of permitting documents outside the Jewish canon if they are written in
Hebrew. The details of Augustine's position are ambiguous, but he seems to
reject the Hebrew criterion for canonicity, instead relying solely on Christian tradition to establish the content of the Bible. In fact, in his possible
rejection of the Hebrew criterion, Augustine's view challenges Christian tradition, which had generally upheld this standard.

# CHAPTER FOUR

## THE LANGUAGE OF HEBREW
## SCRIPTURE AND PATRISTIC BIBLICAL THEORY

The previous chapter argued that Hebrew scripture featured in important ways in Christian ideas about OT canonicity, to the point that early Christian writers accepted into their OT canon only documents which they believed to have been composed in the Hebrew language. This idea would seem to elevate Hebrew to an exalted status among the world's languages and might bring to mind the rabbinic designation of Hebrew as לשון הקודש (*leshon haqodesh*; 'the holy language').[1] This chapter explores what ideas Jews and Christians may have shared about the special status of Hebrew, and it suggests some ways in which the language of Hebrew scripture influenced patristic biblical theory.

Jewish ideologies of Hebrew have garnered quite a bit of scholarly attention over the past few decades. Some scholars date quite early the emergence of Jewish reverence for the language of the Bible, into the Hellenistic or even Persian period, while also showing that different individuals or groups within ancient Judaism approached this matter in different ways. Some Jewish groups before the turn of the era clearly deemed Hebrew unique and 'special' in its role as the first language, sometimes describing it as 'sacred.' The ideology of Hebrew reflected in rabbinic literature expanded on this reverence for לשון הקודש in several different directions.

Christian ideas about Hebrew have generated less interest among scholars, so it will be worth while to study these views here. Following an overview of Jewish ideologies of the Hebrew language, this chapter will investigate this theme in Christian sources. We will first have to examine whether the Fathers could differentiate between Hebrew and Aramaic, a quite difficult prospect for Christian readers who most often knew neither language. Then we will explore the ideas reflected in patristic literature in respect to both of these languages. Finally, we will make some proposals concerning how the Christian ideas about the status of Hebrew among the world's languages factored into their biblical theory.

---

[1] For other ways of construing this phrase, see below, pp. 116–117. 'Holy language' is the traditional interpretation.

## Hebrew: The Holy Language of Judaism

This section surveys some of the evidence highlighted in recent scholarship on Jewish ideologies of Hebrew in the Second Temple and rabbinic periods. Of course, scholars who work in this area have not achieved consensus in the interpretation of every detail or even in some of the major issues. Nevertheless, we will here attempt an overview, focusing on those data that seem to indicate that some ancient Jewish groups or individuals thought that the Hebrew language deserved a certain admiration in comparison with the world's other languages. We will first summarize some of the results of the well-trodden subject of language use among ancient Jews, and then we will chart a roughly chronological course through ancient Jewish evidence for reverence of the Hebrew language.

### The Languages of Early Judaism

It is clear that Palestine was a multi-lingual environment in the centuries surrounding the turn of the era, with Hebrew, Aramaic, and Greek each being spoken by a significant number of people, and other languages (e.g. Latin) represented as well.[2] Recent work has clarified two important aspects of this linguistic situation. On the one hand, scholars have shown, without much disagreement, that the Greek language played a rather significant role in ancient Palestine, even within the Jewish population. Several decades ago, Saul Lieberman showed that the Rabbis used Greek much more than previously realized, and Lieberman's insights have been echoed and expanded by subsequent scholarship.[3] While the evidence cited in these works illuminates the linguistic situation of Late Antique Palestine,

---

[2] See the surveys by J.A. Fitzmyer, "The Languages of Palestine in the First Century A.D.," *CBQ* 32 (1970): 501–531; J. Barr, "Hebrew, Aramaic and Greek in the Hellenistic Age," in W. Davies and L. Finkelstein (eds.), *The Cambridge History of Judaism*, vol. 2: *The Hellenistic Age* (Cambridge, 1989), 79–114; J.C. Poirier, "The Linguistic Situation in Jewish Palestine in Late Antiquity," *Journal of Greco-Roman Christianity and Judaism* 4 (2007): 55–134, available online at http://www.jgrchj.net/volume4/JGRChJ4-3_Poirer.pdf.; W. Smelik, "The Languages of Roman Palestine," in C. Hezser (ed.), *The Oxford Handbook of Jewish Daily Life in Roman Palestine* (Oxford, 2010), 122–141.

[3] S. Lieberman, *Greek in Jewish Palestine* (New York, 1942); see also idem, *Hellenism in Jewish Palestine*[2] (New York, 1962); and more recently D. Sperber, "Rabbinic Knowledge of Greek," in Sh. Safrai, et al. (eds.), *The Literature of the Sages: Second Part*, CRINT 2.3b (Minneapolis, 2006), 627–640. A brief survey of evidence is found in A. Paul, "La Bible grecque d'Aquila et l'idéologie du judaïsme ancien," in *ANRW* II.20.1 (New York, 1987), 221–245 (222–224). Another recent overview of the Greek language within Jewish society in Jerusalem, with a focus on Josephus, may be found in T. Rajak, *Josephus*[2] (London, 2002), 46–64.

Martin Hengel and others have argued that the same penetration of Greek into Jewish society can be demonstrated for the earlier period, also. Hengel cites inscriptions, epistles, the Greco-Jewish literature of Palestine, and the Greek fragments discovered at Qumran.[4] Some ability in Greek became essential for many Palestinian Jews in the centuries following Alexander's conquests.

In the second place, the old debate about whether Hebrew or Aramaic was the primary Semitic language of this period has resolved itself in favor of Aramaic, with Hebrew being a significant secondary language. Scholarship had once relied on the notion that Aramaic dominated Palestine to the complete exclusion of Hebrew as a vernacular, the latter being instead an 'artificial' academic language employed by the Rabbis. The twentieth century saw a drastic revision of that thesis, based first on the language of the Mishnah itself, and then on manuscript discoveries, both of which indicate that Hebrew survived as a spoken language until after the Second Revolt.[5] Nevertheless, it is becoming increasingly clear that the use of

---

[4] M. Hengel, *Judaism and Hellenism*, 2 vols. (trans. J. Bowden; Philadelphia, 1974), 1.58–61; see also Fitzmyer, "Languages," 512–515; J.N. Sevenster, *Do You Know Greek?* (Leiden, 1968); and the essays in J.J. Collins and G.E. Sterling (eds.), *Hellenism in the Land of Israel* (Notre Dame, 2001). For the epigraphic evidence, see now the edition by H.M. Cotton et al. (eds.), *Corpus inscriptionum Iudaeae/Palestinae. Vol. 1: Jerusalem, part 1: 1–704* (Berlin, 2010); this edition, and the second volume covering the rest of Palestine, will replace vol. 2 of *CIJ*. For a recent survey of Greek inscriptions in Palestine, see P.W. van der Horst, "Greek in Jewish Palestine in Light of Jewish Epigraphy," in Collins and Sterling, *Hellenism*, 154–174. For an analysis of the Greek manuscripts at Qumran, see E. Tov, "The Greek Biblical Texts from the Judean Desert," in S. McKendrick and O.A. O'Sullivan (eds.), *The Bible as Book: The Transmission of the Greek Text* (New Castle, Del., 2003), 97–122. Some scholars have gone so far as to anoint Greek the normal language of most Palestinian Jews, e.g., J.A. Overman, "The Diaspora in the Modern Study of Ancient Judaism," in Overman and R.S. MacLennan (eds.), *Diaspora Jews and Judaism* (Atlanta, 1992), 63–78 (65–68); H.B. Rosén, *Hebrew at the Crossroads of Cultures* (Leuven, 1995), 11–13.

[5] This second view is associated mostly with M.H. Segal, *A Grammar of Mishnaic Hebrew* (Oxford, 1927), 1–20; see more recently P.S. Alexander, "How Did the Rabbis Learn Hebrew?" in W. Horbury (ed.), *Hebrew Study from Ezra to Ben-Yehuda* (Edinburgh, 1999), 71–89 (74–75). For the impact of the discovery of the Dead Sea Scrolls on this question, see J.T. Milik, *Ten Years of Discovery in the Wilderness of Judaea* (trans. J. Strugnell; Naperville, Ill., 1959), 130–133, who considers these scrolls to have proven "beyond reasonable doubt that Mishnaic was the normal language of the Judaean population in the Roman period" (130). The popularization of the previous view—that Aramaic completely replaced Hebrew in the Greco-Roman period—is usually attributed to Abraham Geiger, *Lehr- und Lesebuch zur Sprache der Mischnah* (Breslau, 1845), as by, e.g., Barr, "Hebrew," 82; M. Graves, *Jerome's Hebrew Philology* (Leiden, 2007), 76 n. 2. Both of these latter works have brief overviews of the history of research, but see especially A. Sáenz-Badillos, *A History of the Hebrew Language* (Cambridge, 1993), 161–173, who also notes that Geiger had taken up "a widely held view" (162). For the

Hebrew in certain contexts, such as by the Qumran group or by the Rabbis, was motivated by a particular linguistic ideology, and so the Hebrew literary texts at hand may not provide the best indication of common language use in ancient Palestine. Other pieces of evidence, such as inscriptions and documentary texts, exhibit Aramaic much more often than Hebrew.[6] Thus, the late-twentieth-century revisers of Emil Schürer's late-nineteenth-century work judiciously updated his original opinion—Aramaic was "the sole popular language of Palestine"—to a more nuanced statement in keeping with current evidence: "The final conclusion must be that the principal language, spoken and written, used by Palestinian Jews during the inter-Testamental age was Aramaic. But mishnaic Hebrew served as an additional medium of oral communication."[7] It is generally believed that the fortunes of Hebrew declined further a few generations after the Second Revolt (132–135 CE), and its revival took place only after the close of the ancient period.[8]

Of course, the comments above describe circumstances in Palestine. The linguistic situation elsewhere was different, inasmuch as Hebrew "played an even smaller role in the Diaspora than in Roman Palestine."[9] Following Alexander's campaigns, Egyptian Jews became almost completely Greek-speaking, as even the few smatterings of Hebrew words (e.g. שלום) on

---

forerunners of Segal's and Geiger's views, see the notice by J. Fellman, "The Linguistic Status of Mishnaic Hebrew," *JNSL* 5 (1977): 21–22.

[6] On the epigraphic evidence for Aramaic as opposed to Hebrew, see the summary by D. Goodblatt, *Elements of Ancient Jewish Nationalism* (Cambridge, 2006), 52–55. As mentioned above, n. 4, a new edition of the inscriptions from ancient Palestine has begun to appear under the title *Corpus inscriptionum Iudaeae/Palestinae*, ed. H. Cotton et al.

[7] Compare the statements as found in the original edition, E. Schürer, *A History of the Jewish People in the Time of Jesus Christ* (ET: New York, 1885–1891), 2.1.9, with those of the revised edition, E. Schürer, *The History of the Jewish People in the Age of Jesus Christ*, rev. G. Vermes et al., 3 vols. (Edinburgh, 1973–1985), 2.28. For recent analyses of the early period in which Aramaic began to supersede Hebrew, see F.H. Polak, "Sociolinguistics and the Judean Speech Community in the Achaemenid Empire," in O. Lipschits and M. Oeming (eds.), *Judah and the Judeans in the Persian Period* (Winona Lake, Ind., 2006), 589–628; I. Kottsieper, "'And They Did Not Care to Speak Yehudit': On Linguistic Change in Judah during the Late Persian Era," in O. Lipschits, G.N. Knoppers, and R. Albertz (eds.), *Judah and the Judeans in the Fourth Century B.C.E.* (Winona Lake, Ind., 2007), 95–124. Both of these studies highlight the dominance of Aramaic as the vernacular and the retention of Hebrew in religious contexts.

[8] See Segal, *Grammar*, 15; Alexander, "Rabbis," 75 and n. 6; Poirier, "Linguistic Situation," 102; Sáenz-Badillos, *History*, 202–209; S. Schwartz, "Language, Power and Identity in Ancient Palestine," *Past & Present* 148 (1995): 3–47 (35); D. Noy, "'Peace upon Israel': Hebrew Formulae and Names in Jewish Inscriptions from the Western Roman Empire," in Horbury, *Hebrew Study*, 135–146 (145).

[9] Schwartz, "Language," 38.

tombstones attest.[10] This was apparently in keeping with the practice of pre-Hellenistic Egyptian Jews, whose use of Aramaic, the language of the Persian Empire, is attested by the Elephantine Papyri.[11] To be sure, some Hebrew documents have been discovered in Egypt, such as the Nash Papyrus, dated by W.F. Albright to the Maccabean Age, and the prayer edited by F. Klein-Franke and dating to the early second century CE.[12] However, the paucity of the evidence only highlights the dominance of the Greek language among these Egyptian Jews. This, in part, led to the need for the Hebrew Torah to be translated into the current vernacular of the Jews, and our earliest account of this translation, the *Letter of Aristeas*, takes it for granted that Jews competent in Hebrew would have to come from Judaea (§ 28–51). Indeed, Philo, the greatest representative of Alexandrian Judaism, probably did not know Hebrew at all, and, in any case, he cannot have made much use of it.[13]

Other Diaspora communities, for which our evidence is scantier, do not seem to have differed from their Egyptian counterparts in respect of Hebrew language usage.[14] Jerome (*Epist.* 36.1) testifies to the presence in a Roman

---

[10] The epigraphic evidence is presented in *JIGRE*; see p. 258 for an index of the inscriptions based on language. See also Barr, "Hebrew," 101–102; Schwartz, "Language," 42, who notes the sloppiness of the Hebrew lettering. The Jewish papyri from Egypt are published in *CPJ*.

[11] For a recent study of the Jewish Elephantine Papyri, with reference to their various editions, see A. Joisten-Pruschke, *Das religiöse Leben der Juden von Elephantine in der Achämenidenzeit* (Wiesbaden, 2008).

[12] For the Nash Papyrus, see W.F. Albright, "A Biblical Fragment from the Maccabaean Age: The Nash Papyrus," *JBL* 56 (1937): 145–176. For the Hebrew prayer from the second century CE, see F. Klein-Franke, "A Hebrew Lamentation from Roman Egypt," *ZPE* 51 (1983): 80–84. See the differing interpretations of such evidence in Schwartz, "Language," 38 and n. 82; and M.O. Wise, "Accidents and Accidence: A Scribal View of Linguistic Dating of the Aramaic Scrolls from Qumran," in T. Muraoka (ed.), *Studies in Qumran Aramaic*, AbrNSup 3 (Leuven, 1992), 123–166; repr. in *Thunder in Gemini* (Sheffield, 1994), 103–151 (143 n. 134). See also the cautious statements of C. Haas, *Alexandria in Late Antiquity* (Baltimore, 1997), 120–121 and the corresponding notes on pp. 419–420.

[13] See now A. Kamesar, "Biblical Interpretation in Philo," in Kamesar (ed.), *The Cambridge Companion to Philo* (Cambridge, 2009), 65–91 (65–72). For a strained attempt to allow Philo some knowledge of Hebrew, see T. Rajak, *Translation and Survival* (Oxford, 2009), 149–150.

[14] See the language indices in the new collections of inscriptions that replace *CIJ* vol. 1: *IJudO* 1.377–378; 2.630; 3.268–269; *JIWE* 1.310–311; 2.513–514. See also the recent two-part article by A. Edrei and D. Mendels, "A Split Jewish Diaspora: Its Dramatic Consequences," *JSP* 16 (2007): 91–137; 17 (2008): 163–187; and now Edrei and Mendels, *Zweierlei Diaspora* (Göttingen, 2010). Edrei and Mendels contend that European Jews were substantially alienated from the rabbinic Eastern Jews after 70 CE, due in large measure to the use of different languages (not Hebrew or Aramaic) among the Western communities. For their discussion of the European epigraphic evidence, see "Diaspora II," 175–177. But for cautions regarding the thesis of Edrei and Mendels, see F. Millar, "A Rural Jewish Community in Late Roman Mesopotamia, and the Question of a 'Split' Jewish Diaspora," *JSJ* 42 (2011): 351–374.

synagogue of some Hebrew manuscripts and at least one 'Hebrew' who could read them.[15] However, the epigraphic evidence in the city points to Greek and, to a lesser extent, Latin, as virtually the only languages in use among the Jews. According to Leonard Rutgers, of the "595 Jewish mostly funerary inscriptions" discovered in Rome by 1995, 467 (79%) were written in Greek, 127 (21%) in Latin, only one in Aramaic, and one bilingual inscription has Aramaic and Greek. Hebrew appears only as a concluding formula to six Greek inscriptions.[16] The same supremacy of Greek is also evident in the great synagogue at Sardis, where the 79 Greek inscriptions far outnumber the five written in Hebrew.[17]

---

[15] On the date of Jerome's *Epist.* 36, and the veracity of the book-borrowing incident related by Jerome, see A. Cain, "In Ambrosiaster's Shadow: A Critical Re-Evaluation of the Last Surviving Letter Exchange between Pope Damasus and Jerome," *REAug* 51 (2005): 257–277 (263–266).

[16] L.V. Rutgers, *The Jews in Late Ancient Rome* (Leiden, 1995), 176; see also Noy, "Peace upon Israel"; idem, "Writing in Tongues: The Use of Greek, Latin and Hebrew in Jewish Inscriptions from Roman Italy," *JJS* 48 (1997): 300–311; S. Cappelletti, *The Jewish Community of Rome* (Leiden, 2006), 177–191. Rutgers (p. 202) goes on to caution against concluding that the Roman Jews knew little Hebrew, as there may be other explanations for why Hebrew was not considered an appropriate inscriptional language, but the evidence certainly does not indicate that Hebrew was commonly used by the Roman Jews. Indeed, Noy ("Writing," 302) suggests that "Hebrew or Aramaic may in fact be overestimated" by these figures, because the very fact that these Semitic languages are one diagnostic feature indicating Jewishness means that genuinely Jewish inscriptions lacking any Hebrew or Aramaic are more likely to be overlooked by scholars. Rutgers is in constant interaction with the earlier study by H.J. Leon, *The Jews of Ancient Rome* (Philadelphia, 1960), who presents slightly different figures for the languages of the Roman Jewish inscriptions (75–92; see Rutgers, op. cit., 176 n. 1). For Jerome as a witness to Hebrew scholarship in Rome, see A. Kamesar, *Jerome, Greek Scholarship and the Hebrew Bible* (Oxford, 1993), 41–42, who shows that Jerome "consolidated his knowledge of Hebrew" during his second stay at Rome (ca. 382–385). For the existence of a rabbinic academy in Rome in the second century, cf. *b. San.* 32b, and see Rutgers, op. cit., 203–204.

[17] The inscriptions from Sardis have been published by J.H. Kroll, "The Greek Inscriptions of the Sardis Synagogue," *HTR* 94 (2001): 5–55; F.M. Cross, "The Hebrew Inscriptions from Sardis," *HTR* 95 (2002): 3–19; now also in *IJudO* 2, pp. 209–297. Cross publishes also a sixth Hebrew inscription found not at the Synagogue but near it. This sixth inscription evidences somewhat more sophisticated Hebrew (i.e., it contains a conjugated verb), which leads Fergus Millar to assert, "Its possible implications are therefore quite considerable" ("Christian Emperors, Christian Church and the Jews of the Diaspora in the Greek East, CE 379–450," *JJS* 55 (2004): 1–25 (12)). On the Sardis synagogue generally, see the several articles by A.T. Kraabel reprinted in Overman and MacLennan, *Diaspora Jews*. Note that Jodi Magness has recently redated the synagogue to the sixth century, instead of the previous fourth century date; see "The Date of the Sardis Synagogue in Light of the Numismatic Evidence," *AJA* 109 (2005): 443–475.

### Reverence for the Hebrew Language in Early Judaism

Thus, while Hebrew seems to have been almost non-existent among Jews outside of Palestine during the period under review, even within Palestine, Greek and Aramaic are better attested. This leads to the question of why Hebrew was preserved at all among these communities. Earlier it was suggested that ideological reasons may contribute to an answer; after all, Hebrew "has a theological significance in Judaism not commonly associated with language in any other religion."[18] Rabbinic exaltation of Hebrew as לשון הקודש (leshon haqodesh)[19] naturally points in this direction, and several scholars have tried to demonstrate the existence of an ideology surrounding the Hebrew language that predates the rabbinic period.

The Hebrew Bible never uses the term 'Hebrew' in reference to a language and in general has very little to say about the language of ancient Israel. Only two biblical passages acknowledge that the Israelite language, called יהודית (Yehudit; 'Judaean'), differed from others, and only Neh. 13:24 hints that this language was in any way desirable, and it may not even do that.[20] In short, the Hebrew Bible provides hardly any evidence for an ideology of Hebrew, though it does acknowledge that the Jews have their own particular language.

Despite the growing dominance of Aramaic as the Jewish vernacular in Palestine during the Second Temple Period, most Jewish coins and some Jewish literature continued to feature Hebrew prominently. Though some Persian-era coins display Aramaic inscriptions, others bear Hebrew writing.[21] The Hasmoneans minted coins mostly in Hebrew, while some

---

[18] M. Gruber, "Language(s) in Judaism," in J. Neusner, et al. (eds.), *The Encyclopaedia of Judaism*, 3 vols. (Leiden, 2000), 2.783–797 (783).

[19] This phrase may be rendered, "the holy language," or, as we will see, "the language of the sanctuary [i.e., Temple]." See below, pp. 116–117.

[20] The biblical passages naming יהודית as a distinct language are 2 Kings 18:26–28 (= Isa. 36:11–13; cf. 2 Chr. 32:18) and Neh. 13:24. On this last passage, see Poirier, "Linguistic Situation," 56: "the concern in Nehemiah was not directly that of linguistic corruption per se but rather the interreligious marriages signified by that corruption." See also D.H. Aaron, "Judaism's Holy Language," in J. Neusner (ed.), *Approaches to Ancient Judaism, New Series*, vol. 16 (Atlanta, 1999), 49–107 (60), who comments on the difficulty of determining whether the contrast in Nehemiah concerns distinct languages or dialects of a single language, which suggests that "it may be a matter of a cultural clash rather than a linguistic one." See also K.E. Southwood, "'And They Could Not Understand Jewish Speech': Language, Ethnicity, and Nehemiah's Intermarriage Crisis," *JTS* 62 (2011): 1–19.

[21] See Y. Meshorer, *A Treasury of Jewish Coins* (Jerusalem, 2001), 6–21. For a survey of evidence for Hebrew in this period, and an analysis of its linguistic features, see Sáenz-Badillos, *History*, 112–160.

bilingual coins included Hebrew and Greek. Alexander Jannaeus was the only Hasmonean who minted some coins without Hebrew inscriptions (bilingual coins with Aramaic and Greek), though many of his coins did include Hebrew.[22] Furthermore, admirers of the Hasmoneans produced literature that exalted the Hebrew language in varying ways: the author of 1 Maccabees composed his work in Hebrew, and 2 Maccabees, though written in Greek, frequently praises the 'ancestral language' (ἡ πάτριος φωνή).[23] Seth Schwartz attributes this emphasis on Hebrew to that language's position in the Torah and the Temple, the two objects most evocative of Judaism, and which were both desecrated in the Seleucid persecutions enacted by Antiochus Epiphanes.[24] Yet, already before the persecutions, Ben Sira composed his volume of instructions in Hebrew, which may also be attributable to his emphasis on the Hebrew Torah.[25] And, recently, David Goodblatt has argued that the composition of Persian-era biblical literature in Hebrew, at a time when Aramaic was already the first language of many Jews, suggests a nascent linguistic ideology: "the emergence of Hebrew as one of the indicia of Jewish identity is not much later than the construction of the Second Temple and perhaps simultaneous with the emergence of the Pentateuch."[26]

The documents associated with the Qumran group provide the first clear attestation of the sanctity of Hebrew. A very fragmentary scroll dated paleographically to the Herodian era (4Q464) contains the earliest extant reference to the phrase לשון הקודש, previously known only through rabbinic texts.[27] Another writing of great importance to the Qumran community, the

---

[22] See Meshorer, *Treasury*, 23–59; for Jannaeus' bilingual coins, see 37–40, 47. For the Hasmonean attitude toward Hebrew, see Barr, "Hebrew," 112, who is doubtful of a significant Hasmonean emphasis on Hebrew. B.Z. Wacholder suggests based on 2 Mac. 2:14 that "Judah Maccabee seemingly encouraged the renaissance of a Hebrew literary tradition," but the evidence is rather slight; see "The Ancient Judaeo-Aramaic Literature (500–164 BCE): A Classification of Pre-Qumranic Texts," in L.H. Schiffman (ed.), *Archaeology and History in the Dead Sea Scrolls* (Sheffield, 1990), 257–281 (273).

[23] Cf. 2 Mac. 7:8, 21, 27; 12:37; 15:39; and see J.W. van Henten, "The Ancestral Language of the Jews in 2 Maccabees," in Horbury, *Hebrew Study*, 53–68. For the original language of 1 Maccabees, see J.A. Goldstein, *1 Maccabees*, AB 41 (New York, 1976), 14. On the ideology associated by these works with the Maccabean Revolt, see Schwartz, "Language," 26–27.

[24] See Schwartz, "Language," 23–26. For Schwartz' argument that Hebrew continued throughout the Second Temple Period as the language of the Temple, see pp. 33–34.

[25] So J.K. Aitken, "Hebrew Study in Ben Sira's *Beth Midrash*," in Horbury, *Hebrew Study*, 27–37 (27).

[26] Goodblatt, *Elements*, 66.

[27] Cf. frg. 3, col. 1. The text is edited by E. Eshel and M. Stone, "4QExposition on the Patriarchs," in M. Broshi, et al. (eds.), *Qumran Cave 4, XIV, Parabiblical Texts, Part 2*, DJD 19 (Oxford, 1995), 215–230. On this text, see also S. Weitzman, "Why Did the Qumran Commu-

Book of Jubilees, contains our earliest attestation for the view that Hebrew was the original language of mankind, and was preserved through the line of Abraham following the confusion of languages at Babel.[28] Moreover, eighty percent of the documents found in the caves were written in Hebrew. Not all of these documents can be thought to have been composed at the site, but Armin Lange is probably correct in considering Hebrew to be a prerequisite for determining sectarian authorship for any of the scrolls.[29] William Schniedewind has proposed that the Hebrew language reflected in the Dead Sea Scrolls resulted from an attempt to speak not just biblical Hebrew but the very language of God, basing his case on several linguistic features which he considers unexplained by historical grammarians.[30] Steve Weitzman similarly classifies Hebrew in the Qumran mindset as "a supernatural language unlike any other, a transcendent tongue revealed to a divinely designated community in order to free it from Babel's curse."[31] Finally, some

---

nity Write in Hebrew?" *JAOS* 119 (1999): 35–45; J.C. Poirier, "4Q464: Not Eschatological," *RevQ* 20 (2002): 583–587; and esp. W. Smelik, "Language Selection and the Holy Tongue in Early Rabbinic Literature," in L. Teugels and R. Ulmer (eds.), *Interpretation, Religion and Culture in Midrash and Beyond* (Piscataway, N.J., 2008), 91–151 (95–99).

[28] Jubilees 12:25–27. 4Q464 may also allude to the Babel story as its mention of לשן הקודש comes just after the verb נבלת; cf. Gen. 11:7, and see Weitzman, "Qumran Community," 38. Whether Jubilees was composed before or after the establishment of the Qumran community, it was clearly important to the covenanters, as 14 or 15 copies (depending on the very fragmentary 4Q217) were found in the Qumran caves; moreover, the group shared certain controversial beliefs with Jubilees, such as adherence to the solar calendar. See J.C. VanderKam, "Jubilees, Book of," in L.H. Schiffman and J.C. VanderKam (eds.), *Encyclopaedia of the Dead Sea Scrolls*, 2 vols. (Oxford, 2000), 1.434–438.

[29] A. Lange, "Kriterien essenischer Texte," in J. Frey and H. Stegemann (eds.), *Qumran Kontrovers* (Paderborn, 2003), 59–69 (64).

[30] W.M. Schniedewind, "Qumran Hebrew as an Antilanguage," *JBL* 118 (1999): 235–252; idem, "Linguistic Ideology in Qumran Hebrew," in T. Muraoka and J.F. Elwolde (eds.), *Diggers at the Well* (Leiden, 2000), 245–255; see also idem, "Prolegomena for the Sociolinguistics of Classical Hebrew," *Journal of Hebrew Scriptures* 5 (2004): article 6, available online at http://www.arts.ualberta.ca/JHS/Articles/article_36.pdf. Schniedewind's 'antilanguage' proposal has been accepted by, e.g., J.H. Charlesworth, *The Pesharim and Qumran History* (Grand Rapids, 2002), 20; C. Hezser, *Jewish Literacy in Roman Palestine*, TSAJ 81 (Tübingen, 2001), 228 n. 13; D.M. Carr, *Writing on the Tablet of the Heart* (Oxford, 2005), 259. Schniedewind himself thinks the type of Hebrew reflected in the scrolls was actually spoken by the community, as does E. Qimron, "The Nature of DSS Hebrew and Its Relation to BH and MH," in Muraoka and Elwolde, *Diggers*, 232–244 (Qimron advocates the view that Qumran Hebrew reflects the colloquial Hebrew of the time, a view rejected by Schniedewind). On the other hand, several other scholars consider the language to be merely literary, e.g. Hezser, loc. cit.; A. Hurvitz, "Was QH a 'Spoken' Language? On Some Recent Views and Positions: Comments," in Muraoka and Elwolde, *Diggers*, 110–114; Poirier, "Linguistic Situation," 73–75.

[31] Weitzman, "Qumran Community," 43.

scholars have emphasized that these writings showcase a 'pure' Hebrew, relatively free from Grecisms and Aramaisms.[32] All of this suggests that the Qumran community cultivated their form of Hebrew as a distinctive part of their self-identity.

Other Jewish groups also considered Hebrew to be tied to their identity. While excavating the caves around Naḥal Ḥever, Yigael Yadin uncovered a collection of fifteen letters, most of which were written in the name of Shimeon bar Kosiba (better known as Bar Kokhba), the leader of the Second Jewish Revolt against Rome (132–135). Of the fifteen letters, nine are in Aramaic, four in Hebrew, and two in Greek. While those statistics favor Aramaic as the language commonly used, which accords with the evidence for Palestinian Judaism generally for this period, Hannah Cotton argues that the presence of Hebrew documents, however few, is significant, because of the utter lack of any Hebrew documentary texts from the period prior to this revolt.[33] Moreover, one of the Greek letters, *P. Yadin* 52, is well-known both for the apology offered therein for not writing in Hebrew, and for the difficulty (due to a lacuna) of interpreting the writer's excuse for his choice of language. In the recent official publication of the letter, Cotton reconstructs the sentence thus: ἐγράφη δὲ Ἑλληνεστὶ διὰ τὸ ἡμᾶς μὴ εὑρηκέναι Ἑβραεστὶ ἐγγράψασθαι, which may be translated, "it [the letter] was written in Greek because we could not write in Hebrew."[34] This statement would seem to testify both to the penetration of the Greek language in the Roman Near East and to the desirability on the part of Bar Kokhba's followers of communicating in Hebrew. However, Cotton inter-

---

[32] On the absence of Greek loanwords, see Hengel, *Judaism*, 60; for the relative lack of Aramaic influence on Qumran Hebrew, see Schniedewind, "Antilanguage," 242; Poirier, "Linguistic Situation," 75. For a caution against claiming too much for the limited and fragmentary evidence supplied by the Qumran caves, see Aaron, "Holy Language," 75–77.

[33] H.M. Cotton, "The Languages of the Legal and Administrative Documents from the Judaean Desert," *ZPE* 125 (1999): 219–231 (225). The Aramaic letters are *P. Yadin* 50, 53, 54, 55, 56, 57, 58, 62, 63; Hebrew: *P. Yadin* 49, 51, 60, 61; Greek: *P. Yadin* 52, 59. Yadin first reported his discovery in "Expedition D," *IEJ* 11 (1961): 36–52; idem, "Expedition D—The Cave of Letters," *IEJ* 12 (1962): 227–257. The final publication is in Y. Yadin, et al., *The Documents from the Bar Kokhba Period in the Cave of Letters: Hebrew, Aramaic, and Nabatean-Aramaic Papyri*, 2 vols. (Jerusalem, 2002). See also N. Lewis, *The Documents from the Bar Kokhba Period in the Cave of Letters: Greek Papyri* (Jerusalem, 1989).

[34] See Cotton's edition of the letter in Yadin, et al., *Documents: Hebrew*, 1.351–362 (354.11–15). The translation offered here does not agree with Cotton's own translation, as explained just below in the text. See also H.M. Cotton, "The Bar Kokhba Revolt and the Documents from the Judaean Desert: Nabataean Participation in the Revolt (*P. Yadin* 52)," in P. Schäfer (ed.), *The Bar Kokhba War Reconsidered* (Tübingen, 2003), 133–152, in which Cotton cites the many previous editions of the letter (143 n. 45).

prets the adverbs Ἑληνεστί/Ἐβραεστί as referring to script rather than language. To her mind, since the author of the letter seems to be Nabataean, he would naturally have written in the Aramaic language. He wrote in Greek instead because Jews and Nabataeans used different scripts for Aramaic. Thus, he meant, "I have written in Greek because I do not know the Hebrew script [= Jewish square script] to use for Aramaic."[35] Cotton admits the difficulty of this uncommon understanding of such adverbs as Ἑληνεστί/Ἐβραεστί ("in Greek/in Hebrew"), causing her to present her view as tentative.[36] Nevertheless, even if this interpretation of P. Yadin 52 proves correct, there still remains other evidence that some of those participating with Bar Kokhba in the revolt against Rome cultivated a particular admiration for the Hebrew language. Other Hebrew documentary texts from this time period have been discovered at Wadi Murabbaʿat and Naḥal Ḥever, and the coins minted by the rebels exclusively bore Hebrew inscriptions in paleo-Hebrew script.[37]

It is possible that language ideology also played a role in the First Revolt (66–73 CE). While formerly all of the Hebrew documents from Wadi Murabbaʿat were dated to the period of the Bar Kokhba War, several scholars have redated a few of them (Mur. 22, 29, 30) to the First Revolt. Cotton spells out the significance of redating these few Hebrew documents:

---

[35] This is my paraphrase of Cotton's interpretation. Cotton discusses this interpretation of P. Yadin 52 in both works mentioned in the previous note, but see esp. her article "The Bar Kokhba Revolt," 146–148; cf. J.J. Price and Sh. Naeh, "On the Margins of Culture: The Practice of Transcription in the Ancient World," in H.M. Cotton, et al. (eds.), From Hellenism to Islam (Cambridge, 2009), 257–288 (259–260). The Nabataean origin of the author of P. Yadin 52 was already suggested by D. Obbink, "Bilingual Literacy and Syrian Greek," BASP 28 (1991): 51–57; and accepted by H. Lapin, "Palm Fronds and Citrons: Notes on Two Letters from Bar Kosiba's Administration," HUCA 64 (1993): 111–135.

[36] Cotton, "The Bar Kokhba Revolt," 147 n. 61. Cotton also mentions the ambiguity in the word 'Hebrew' itself for this time period (does it mean what we think of as Hebrew or Aramaic?). This issue receives treatment below.

[37] For the coins, see L. Mildenberg, The Coinage of the Bar Kokhba War (Aarau, 1984); Meshorer, Treasury, 135–165. For the Hebrew documentary texts from Wadi Murabbaʿat, see P. Benoit, J.T. Milik, and R. de Vaux, Les grottes de Murabbaʿat, DJD 2 (Oxford, 1961). To isolate the Hebrew documents in this edition, use the index in E. Tov, et al., The Texts from the Judaean Desert: Indices and an Introduction to the DJD Series, DJD 39 (Oxford, 2002), 97–100, keeping in mind that all documents are in Hebrew unless otherwise noted. For the Hebrew documentary texts from Naḥal Ḥever, see H.M. Cotton and A. Yardeni, Aramaic, Hebrew and Greek Texts from Naḥal Ḥever and Other Sites with an Appendix Containing Alleged Qumran Texts (The Seiyâl Collection 2), DJD 27 (Oxford, 1997), in which only nos. 30 and 49, along with the lower half of no. 8, are in Hebrew, the rest being Aramaic and Greek. One other "apparently Hebrew" document was formerly attributed to 4Q but is now thought to come from Naḥal Ḥever, and so it is also published in DJD 27, 300–303 (quotation from p. 300).

It may not be a coincidence therefore that there are no documents in Hebrew which date to the years before the first revolt, or to the period between the two revolts. During the revolts Hebrew became, alongside Aramaic, the language of legal documents. The same ideology which inspired the decision to use Hebrew in legal documents of the second revolt may well have motivated also the freedom fighters of the first one.[38]

Of course, other languages were also used, as Greek and Aramaic are attested at Masada, the last stronghold maintained by the Jewish rebels.[39] Nevertheless, the few documents in Hebrew indicate an effort to write in this language, and, again, all the coins minted by the Jews at this time feature Hebrew in paleo-Hebrew script exclusively. The significance of this becomes clear in light of the absence of similar Hebrew inscriptions in the Herodian coins and those of the Roman Procurators of Judaea, all of which bear inscriptions only in Greek and, occasionally, Latin.[40] Since the paleo-Hebrew script had long been replaced for most functions by the 'Jewish' script, an adaptation of Aramaic script, Seth Schwartz describes the probable role of paleo-Hebrew writing on the coins of the two revolts as akin to a 'talisman,' a symbol of Jewish identity.[41]

We have mentioned the common view that the use of Hebrew declined following Bar Kokhba's war. However, at this time we also get the most explicit statements in favor of the Hebrew language. In rabbinic literature, Hebrew emerges fully as לשון הקודש. Whether this designation originally meant 'the language of the Sanctuary,' 'the language of the Holy One,' or simply 'the holy language,' is a contested issue; in any case, the phrase לשון הקודש clearly sets Hebrew apart from other languages.[42] This is especially

---

[38] Cotton, "Languages," 225; for her arguments favoring the earlier date, see pp. 221–223, where she discusses only Mur. 29 and 30. For the redating of Mur. 22 along with Mur. 25 (in Aramaic), see H. Eshel, "Documents of the First Jewish Revolt from the Judean Desert," in A.M. Berlin and J.A. Overman (eds.), *The First Jewish Revolt* (New York, 2002), 157–163.

[39] See the official publications of Yigael Yadin's excavations from the 1960s, especially Yadin and J. Naveh, *Masada I: The Aramaic and Hebrew Ostraca and Jar Inscriptions* (Jerusalem, 1989); H.M. Cotton and J. Geiger, *Masada II: The Latin and Greek Documents* (Jerusalem, 1989). The Latin documents were left by the Roman troops, not the Jewish rebels.

[40] For the coins of the revolt, see L. Kadman, *The Coins of the Jewish War of 66–73 C.E.* (Tel Aviv, 1960); Meshorer, *Treasury*, 115–134. For the Herodian coins, see Meshorer, *Treasury*, 61–114; the Herodian bilingual coins in Greek and Latin are described on pp. 111–112. For the coins of the Procurators of Judaea, see pp. 167–176.

[41] Schwartz, "Language," 27. On the ideology reflected in the coins of the two revolts, see also Meshorer, *Treasury*, 115–117, 163. On some of the problems related to the expression 'Jewish identity,' see, e.g., S.J.D. Cohen, *The Beginnings of Jewishness* (Berkeley, 1999).

[42] For the different interpretations of the phrase, see P. Schäfer, *Die Vorstellung vom heiligen Geist in der rabbinischen Literatur* (Munich, 1972), 127–129; see also Alexander, "Rabbis,"

clear in a Mishnaic ordinance concerning the appropriate language to use for different religious recitations: the *Shema*, blessings over food, etc., may be said in any language (כל לשון), while other (especially priestly) benedictions must be recited in לשון הקודש (*m. Sotah* 7.1–2). Therefore, translations are permitted early in rabbinic literature for certain functions, and this attitude finds an echo in other passages, as well.[43] However, David H. Aaron has argued that "rabbinic Judaism functioned with two sets of values simultaneously: an official sanctioning of vernaculars and an overt, unofficial preference for Hebrew ritual."[44] It was this latter 'preference' which eventually came to take preeminence, as reflected in the Talmudic debates concerning whether translated scriptures are really scriptures at all, or whether Hebrew itself confers sanctity on the volumes (cf. *b. Shab*. 115a–b); the Mishnaic ordinance (*Shab*. 16.1) had earlier considered translations to be sacred. Rabbi Yohanan's preference for Hebrew led him to declare Aramaic to be unsuitable for prayer because it is unintelligible to ministering angels (*b. Sotah* 33a; *b. Shab*. 12b). While Aramaic thrived for certain forms of religious compositions, Hebrew solidified its position as the liturgical language.[45]

---

75 n. 7. For discussions of rabbinic ideology of Hebrew, see the following works: H. Eilberg-Schwartz, "Who's Kidding Whom? A Serious Reading of Rabbinic Word Plays," *JAAR* 55 (1987): 765–788; S.D. Fraade, "Rabbinic Views on the Practice of Targum, and Multilingualism in the Jewish Galilee of the Third-Sixth Centuries," in L.I. Levine (ed.), *The Galilee in Latin Antiquity* (New York, 1992), 253–286; B. Spolsky, "Jewish Multilingualism in the First Century: An Essay in Historical Sociolinguistics," in J. Fishman (ed.), *Readings in the Sociology of Jewish Languages* (Leiden, 1985), 35–50; Paul, "La Bible grecque," 230–245; N. de Lange, "The Revival of the Hebrew Language in the Third Century CE," *JSQ* 3 (1996): 242–358; Schwartz, "Language," 31–35; Aaron, "Holy Language," 78–107; Smelik, "Language Selection," 99–151.

[43] See R. Langer, *To Worship God Properly* (Cincinnati, 1998), 22–23; W.F. Smelik, "Language, Locus, and Translation between the Talmudim," *JAB* 3 (2001): 199–224 (209–210); Aaron, "Holy Language," 83–87. Aaron points out (p. 85) that some synagogues, not only in the Diaspora, followed this allowance, if one can trust the report in the Jerusalem Talmud in which R. Levi bar Haitah was angered to hear the *Shema* recited in Greek in a Caesarean synagogue (*y. Sotah* 7.1, 21b). On this latter passage, see also L.I. Levine, "The Sages and the Synagogue in Late Antiquity," in Levine, *Galilee*, 201–222 (217–218). Cf. also *m. Meg*. 2.1 for the rules regarding the required language for reading Esther during Purim, and on this passage see J.E. Burns, "The Special Purim and the Reception of the Book of Esther in the Hellenistic and Early Roman Eras," *JSJ* 37 (2006): 1–35 (24–32); W. Smelik, "Code-switching: The Public Reading of the Bible in Hebrew, Aramaic and Greek," in L. Morenz and S. Schorch (eds.), *Was ist ein Text?* (Berlin, 2007), 123–151 (141–147).

[44] Aaron, "Holy Language," 88.

[45] On Hebrew as the language of the synagogue, see Aaron, "Holy Language," 81–87. Recent literature on the development of the synagogue liturgy is briefly surveyed by Richard S. Sarason in his introduction to the reissue of J. Heinemann and J. Petuchowski, *Literature of the Synagogue* (1975; repr. Piscataway, N.J., 2006), v*–viii*; see also R. Langer, "Revisiting Early Rabbinic Liturgy: The Recent Contributions of Ezra Fleischer," *Proof* 19 (1999):

The reason for emphasizing Hebrew is its relationship to Torah and especially to the Divine Author of the Torah. Genesis Rabbah makes this apparent, as other scholars have noted.[46] There, God is represented as speaking Hebrew to angels and others before the creation of humans (*Gen. Rab.* 8.4–5; 11.8). Furthermore, God used the Hebrew alphabet as an instrument in creation (12.10; 18.4; 31.8).[47] Since Hebrew is the original divine speech, it was constructed with more care than other languages, which allows it to convey meaning in seemingly insignificant details, including incidental resemblances between words (4.7) and even the shapes of the letters (12.10). At least for this particular rabbinic document, these details seem to flesh out what it means for Hebrew to be לשון הקודש.

It seems fairly clear that the dominant use of Hebrew in early rabbinic literature is in some way tied to the rabbinic linguistic ideology. Nicholas de Lange has constructed a case for the 'revival' of Hebrew as an academic and religious language based on several lines of evidence, most especially on the Mishnah as a Hebrew document emanating from a largely Aramaic-speaking rabbinate. We may accept his point that the early Rabbis composed their works in Hebrew intentionally without thinking that this entailed a 'revival,' for this survey of Jewish views has shown that a

---

179–204. On the ancient social location of the Aramaic targumim, see W.F. Smelik, *The Targum of Judges* (Leiden, 1995), 24–41. On Aramaic religious poetry, see J. Yahalom, "Angels Do Not Understand Aramaic: On the Literary Use of Jewish Palestinian Aramaic in Late Antiquity," *JJS* 47 (1996): 33–44. The debate at *b. Shab.* 115a–b concerns whether translations were holy enough to be saved from a fire on the Sabbath, or whether this applied only to Hebrew documents, concerning which see Paul, "Bible grecque," 230–235. Smelik, "Language," seeks to show that "rabbinic views on translation were not monolithic" (p. 207), to which end he details the variety of opinion to be found in the literature.

[46] See Eilberg-Schwartz, "Who's Kidding," 769–788; Aaron, "Holy Language," 96–100.

[47] For this idea, cf. also Jubilees 12:26; and the rendering of Gen. 11:1 in Targum Ps-Jonathan and Targum Neofiti. Jubilees has the loss of Hebrew occurring as a result of the Fall of man (Gen. 3), while rabbinic sources envision Hebrew continuing as the language of mankind until the Tower of Babel (Gen. 11:1–9). On the alphabet as an instrument of creation, see C. Bandt, *Der Traktat "Vom Mysterium der Buchstaben"*, TU 162 (Berlin, 2007), 72–73. For the creation of the Torah and, therefore, Hebrew, before the creation of the universe, cf. *Gen. Rab.* 1.1; *Abot R. Nat.* A 31; and see Paul, "Bible grecque," 237. According to some sources, animals could speak, presumably in Hebrew, before the Fall (Jub. 3:28; Philo, *QG* 1.32; Josephus, *A.J.* 1.41). On Hebrew as the original language of mankind, restricted to the ancestors of Abraham following the incident at Babel, see the sources cited by L. Ginzberg, *The Legends of the Jews*, 7 vols. (Philadelphia, 1909–1938; repr. Philadelphia, 1998), 5.205–206 n. 91. Contrast this view, however, with that of Rav (*b. San.* 38b), who says that Adam spoke Aramaic. The whole tradition receives detailed treatment in M. Rubin, "The Language of Creation or the Primordial Language: A Case of Cultural Polemics in Antiquity," *JJS* 49 (1998): 306–333. See also Paul, "Bible grecque," 240–243; U. Eco, *The Search for the Perfect Language* (Oxford, 1995).

developing ideology of Hebrew is traceable to Maccabean times, if not earlier.[48] Seth Schwartz concludes similarly that the composition of the Mishnah in Hebrew "constituted an act of appropriation, an assertion of rabbinic control over what was symbolically central in Judaism."[49] A comparison between *m. Kil.* 1.1 and *y. Kil.* 1.1, 27a suggests that some of the statements preserved in Hebrew in the Mishnah may have originally been spoken in Aramaic and maybe Greek.[50]

It was, in fact, Aramaic and Greek, but especially Aramaic, that were pushed to the side as the prestige of Hebrew grew. Though the initial stages of the developing Hebrew ideology may have been in reaction against Hellenistic culture and language, it is difficult to find specific Jewish groups who took this stand. The Hasmoneans did not stress Hebrew to any great extent, and, in any case, they did not abandon Greek in favor of the ancestral language. The Qumran documents contain disparaging references to the language of their opponents, but this apparently indicates Aramaic rather than Greek.[51] The Rabbis themselves have a rather lenient attitude toward Greek, reserving their harsher statements for the Aramaic language. Rabbi Judah's comment is the clearest evidence of this view (*b. B. Qam.* 83a): בארץ ישראל לשון סורסי למה או לשון הקודש או לשון יונית ("In the Land of Israel—why [use] the Syrian language [= Aramaic]? [Use] either the holy language or the Greek language").[52]

---

[48] See de Lange, "Revival"; for another recent criticism of de Lange, see Graves, *Jerome's Hebrew Philology*, 77 n. 5.

[49] Schwartz, "Language," 34.

[50] See Hezser, *Literacy*, 242 n. 127; idem, "The Mishnah and Ancient Book Production," in A.J. Avery-Peck and J. Neusner (eds.), *The Mishnah in Contemporary Perspective* (Leiden, 2002), 167–192 (179); De Lange, "Revival," 345. For further on this topic, see Aaron, "Holy Language," 95–96.

[51] The Qumran references to their opponents' language are found in CD 5.11–12; 1QH 10.18; 12.16. This is probably Aramaic, as believed by E. Qimron, "Observations on the History of Early Hebrew (1000 BCE–200 CE) in the Light of the Dead Sea Documents," in D. Dimant and U. Rappaport (eds.), *The Dead Sea Scrolls: Forty Years of Research* (Leiden, 1992), 349–361; Wacholder, "Judaeo-Aramaic," 274; Poirier, "Linguistic Situation," 76 n. 64. Others think the Qumranites stressed biblical Hebrew as opposed to Mishnaic Hebrew; see Ch. Rabin, "The Historical Background of Qumran Hebrew," in Rabin and Y. Yadin (eds.), *Aspects of the Dead Sea Scrolls*, ScrHier 4 (Jerusalem, 1958), 144–161; Schniedewind, "Antilanguage." G. Vermes, *Discovery in the Judean Desert* (New York, 1956), 70, thinks the linguistic enemy was Greek.

[52] See also *b. San.* 21b for the statement that Hebrew is for Israel while Aramaic is reserved for the הדיוטות ('commoners'; from Gr. ἰδιώτης). Another well-known passage favorable to Greek is *b. Sotah* 49b, which says that half of Rabban Gamaliel's 1000 students studied Torah, while the other half studied Greek. On rabbinic statements concerning Greek, see Spolsky, "Jewish Multilingualism," 38–39; Aaron, "Holy Language," 79; G. Veltri, *Libraries, Translations, and 'Canonic' Texts* (Leiden, 2006), 100–106. For a more positive evaluation of

Thus, beginning no later than the mid-Hellenistic Period, when Hebrew had ceased to be the language commonly spoken by most Jews, it became the language most evocative of Judaism. This means, in the words of David Goodblatt, that "the language had some connection to Jewish identity," though it was not a criterion of Jewishness, as most Jews did not speak Hebrew. This latter point allows for the elevation of Hebrew even in the Diaspora. As Goodblatt goes on to note, even those without the ability to speak or read the language could still recognize written or spoken Hebrew and associate it with their Jewish identity.[53] There is some evidence that this association did indeed take place for at least some Diaspora Jews. Although Hebrew is very poorly attested in the Diaspora, the few Hebrew inscriptions demonstrate perhaps recognition of the primacy of the Hebrew language.[54] Philo's exegetical works rely completely on the Greek text, which he believes to be the inspired equivalent of the Hebrew (cf. *Mos.* 2.38–40), but he does recognize the originality of the Hebrew text and imparts not a few (sometimes fanciful) Hebrew etymologies.[55] Moreover, Origen reports on a practice current in his day among the 'most accurate' manuscripts of the Greek Bible: καὶ ἐν τοῖς ἀκριβεστέροις δὲ τῶν ἀντιγράφων Ἑβραίοις χαρακτῆρσι κεῖται τὸ ὄνομα, Ἑβραϊκοῖς δὲ οὐ τοῖς νῦν, ἀλλὰ τοῖς ἀρχαιοτάτοις ("and in the most accurate of the copies, the Name [of God] is put in Hebrew characters, not the current Hebrew characters [= the Jewish script], but the most ancient [= paleo-Hebrew]").[56] Extant Greek manuscripts bear out Origen's assertion that some copies did follow the practice of including the Tetragrammaton in

---

Aramaic as reflected in rabbinic literature, see J.F.A. Sawyer, *Sacred Languages and Sacred Texts* (London, 1999), 35–37; but see also Smelik, "Language," 218–222.

[53] Goodblatt, *Elements*, 69. Here, Goodblatt is explicitly drawing on Seth Schwartz' concept of Hebrew as talisman, mentioned earlier in the present chapter.

[54] Later inscriptions incorporating Hebrew result from the resurgence of this language in the Late Antique Diaspora. See especially Sh. Simonsohn, "The Hebrew Revival among Early Medieval European Jews," in *Salo Wittmayer Baron Jubilee Volume*, 3 vols. (Jerusalem, 1974), 2.831–858. Also see Tcherikover, *CPJ*, 2.101–102; Noy, "Peace Upon Israel," 145, with reference to Southern Italy; N.R.M. de Lange, "A Thousand Years of Hebrew in Byzantium," in Horbury, *Hebrew Study*, 147–161; F. Millar, "The Many Worlds of the Late Antique Diaspora: Supplements to the 'Cambridge History of Judaism' vol. IV," *JJS* 59 (2008): 120–138 (125; see also 126); Edrei and Mendels, "Diaspora, II," 176.

[55] See L.L. Grabbe, *Etymology in Early Jewish Interpretation* (Atlanta, 1988); and on Philo's view of language, see D. Winston, "Aspects of Philo's Linguistic Theory," *SPhA* 3 (1991): 109–125; Weitzman, "Qumran Community," 39. On Hebrew in the Jewish Diaspora generally, see Schwartz, "Language," 40–43.

[56] Origen, *Sel. Ps.* 2 (PG 12.1104b). See B.M. Metzger, *Manuscripts of the Greek Bible* (Oxford, 1981), 33–35.

Hebrew script. Scholars disagree on the significance of such manuscripts for determining the practice of the original translators, but it is clear that those who copied and used these texts considered Hebrew a more appropriate medium to record God's name, probably because Hebrew was considered holier than Greek.[57]

For the Rabbis, of course, Hebrew was something more than just the Jewish language; it was, indeed, the divine language, with special properties distinct from any other speech. Some pre-rabbinic documents contain hints at this view (e.g. Jubilees, 4Q464), but the implications are fully elaborated only by the Rabbis. Many Jews from the Hellenistic period onward seem to have recognized that the Hebrew language was tied to their identity as Jews. Some rabbinic statements imply that the Hebrew language ties the speaker to God.

Before concluding our discussion of Judaism, we should briefly note some notions about the script in which Hebrew was written. Joseph Naveh has documented the transition from the paleo-Hebrew script to the Aramaic script for the copying of documents in the Hebrew language, locating the change in the third century BCE.[58] At least by this time, scribes began copying biblical texts in the Jewish square script. However, as we have seen, the paleo-Hebrew script appears on most of the Jewish coins of the Hellenistic and Roman periods. Ya'akov Meshorer has said that the ancient script on the coins was a matter of "political significance."

> The rulers who minted the coins sought to make them especially prestigious by means of symbols of Jewish significance and inscriptions written in letters from the glorious days of the kingdom of Judah in the First Temple period.[59]

---

[57] For discussion of this phenomenon, see G. Howard, "The Tetragram and the New Testament," *JBL* 96 (1977): 63–83; P.W. Skehan, "The Divine Name at Qumran, in the Masada Scroll, and in the Septuagint," *BIOSCS* 13 (1980): 14–44; A. Pietersma, "Kyrios or Tetragram: A Renewed Quest for the Original LXX," in Pietersma and C. Cox (eds.), *De Septuaginta* (Mississauga, Ont., 1984), 85–101; M. Rösel, "The Reading and Translation of the Divine Name in the Masoretic Tradition and the Greek Pentateuch," *JSOT* 31 (2007): 411–428.

[58] J. Naveh, *Early History of the Alphabet*[2] (Jerusalem, 1987), 112–124. In the brief discussion in the present chapter, the terms 'Jewish script' and 'Aramaic script' will be used interchangeably, while the Hebrew script will be referred to as such or with the modifier 'paleo,' with no distinction in meaning. Professional paleographers use more precise terminology not called for here; see F.M. Cross "The Development of the Jewish Scripts," in G.E. Wright (ed.), *The Bible and the Ancient Near East* (1961; repr. Winona Lake, Ind., 1979), 133–202 (189–190 n. 5).

[59] Meshorer, *Treasury*, 48; see also 39–41. In saying that most Jewish coins of the Hellenistic and Roman periods included paleo-Hebrew script, we are not including the Herodian coins, which do not have Hebrew inscriptions, nor the coins of Alexander Jannaeus in Aramaic and Greek, mentioned above.

Paleo-Hebrew script apparently conveyed to some scribes greater dignity or sanctity, as we not infrequently find it used for the Tetragrammaton in documents otherwise written completely in the Aramaic script, or even in Greek biblical manuscripts.[60] The Hebrew script on the coins minted by the Jewish rebels of the two revolts against Rome almost certainly played a symbolic role. However, even among those groups that promoted the Hebrew language and used the Hebrew script for certain purposes, Hebrew was typically written in the Aramaic script. The Qumran Scrolls and the Hebrew documents emanating from the First and Second Jewish Revolts have provided many examples of this, with the exception of only twenty paleo-Hebrew manuscripts from Qumran, all of the Torah and Job.[61] For these groups, though the ancient Hebrew script continued to resonate in important ways, it featured less prominently in their practice than the Hebrew language itself.

This distinction between script and language becomes heightened among the Rabbis. They do not call the ancient script 'holy' as they do the language, but rather call it simply כתב עברי ("Hebrew writing"; *m. Yad.* 4.5) or even, disparagingly, רועץ ("broken, rugged"; *b. San.* 22a); moreover, the Rabbis associate this 'broken' script alternately with Israelite sinfulness or with the heretical Samaritans, the preservers of the ancient writing. Texts written in the ancient script do not defile the hands (*m. Yad.* 4.5). Ezra is said to have effected the change in script, but the Rabbis disagree on the original script in which the Torah appeared. Some say it was given in Hebrew writing, now reserved for the הדיוטות ('commoners'), while Rabbi Judah declared that the 'Assyrian' writing (i.e., the Jewish square script) was original, and only became 'broken' when Israel sinned.[62] Though the reasons for the original

---

[60] See the discussion just above, and also see Metzger, *Manuscripts*, 33–35; Skehan, "Divine Name"; E. Tov, *Scribal Practices and Approaches Reflected in the Texts Found in the Judean Desert* (Leiden, 2004), 238–246. The DSS sometimes employ still other techniques to differentiate the Divine Name from the writing surrounding it; see Tov, op. cit., 218–221.

[61] A list of twenty Qumran manuscripts written wholly in paleo-Hebrew is given in Tov, *Texts* (הנה 39), 214. See also the entire discussion in Tov, *Scribal Practices*, ch. 6, "Scripts," but esp. pp. 246–248, "Texts written completely in paleo-Hebrew characters." Cross, "Development," 189 n. 4, thinks that these paleo-Hebrew manuscripts reflect a re-awakening of the use of this ancient script "in the era of nationalistic revival of the second century B.C." On the use of paleo-Hebrew at Qumran, see E. Ulrich, "The Palaeo-Hebrew Biblical Manuscripts from Qumran Cave 4," in D. Dimant and L. Schiffman (eds.), *Time to Prepare the Way in the Wilderness* (Leiden, 1995); repr. in *The Dead Sea Scrolls and the Origins of the Bible* (Grand Rapids, 1999), 121–147.

[62] Cf. *t. San.* 4.7–8; *b. San.* 21b–22a; and see E. Tov, *Textual Criticism of the Hebrew Bible*[3] (Minneapolis, 2012), 207. Rabbi Judah's opinion is echoed by other Rabbis; cf. *y. Meg.* 1.11 71b–71c; *Esth. Rab.* 4.12. Some of the Church Fathers cite the tradition that Ezra changed the

change are unknown, the transition was complete. Eventually, a branch of mystical theology developed around the square script as if it were ordained by God.[63]

### The Relationship between Hebrew
### and Aramaic According to the Fathers

When we begin to pursue a possible ideology of Hebrew in Greco-Latin sources, we immediately encounter a problem of terminology. To give a famous example, the Fourth Gospel occasionally cites Aramaic words with the term Ἑβραϊστί ("in Hebrew"), e.g., Βηθζαθα in 5:2, Γαββαθα in 19:13, Γολγοθα in 19:17, and ραββουνι in 20:16. The evangelist is not unique in his terminology: Philo says that the Ἑβραῖοι use the Aramaic word πάσχα according to their πάτριος γλώττη ("ancestral language"; *Decal.* 159; cf. *Spec.* 2.145), and Josephus designates the Aramaic form σάββατα as κατὰ τὴν Ἑβραίων διάλεκτον ("according to the dialect of the Hebrews"; *A.J.* 1.33; cf. 3.252 on ἀσαρθά). To add to the confusion, Philo regularly uses the term 'Chaldean' to designate the original language of scripture (cf., e.g., *Mos.* 2.38), a practice for which Jerome criticizes him (*Comm. Dan.* 1:6).[64] Due to this puzzling

---

script, e.g. Jerome, *Prol. gal.* 5–8. For references to other rabbinic and patristic testimonia, see S.A. Birnbaum, *The Hebrew Scripts* (Leiden, 1971), 71–75; Ginzberg, *Legends*, 6.443–444 n. 44.

[63] See Aaron, "Holy Language," 50 n. 5, 100–105. For more on the change of script, including some guesses at the cause of the change, see Birnbaum, *Scripts*, 74; A. Yardeni, *The Book of Hebrew Script* (London, 2002), 44; F.M. Cross, "The History of the Biblical Text in the Light of Discoveries in the Judaean Desert," *HTR* 57 (1964): 281–299 (289, 297–298); repr. in Cross and S. Talmon (eds.), *Qumran and the History of the Biblical Text* (Cambridge, Mass, 1975), 177–195 (185, 193–194); idem, *From Epic to Canon* (Baltimore, 1998), 223; Naveh, *Alphabet*, 122; idem, "Scripts and Inscriptions in Ancient Samaria," *IEJ* 48 (1998): 91–100; idem, "Hebrew Texts in Aramaic Script in the Persian Period?" *BASOR* 203 (1971): 27–32; D. Diringer, "Early Hebrew Script versus Square Script," in D.W. Thomas (ed.), *Essays and Studies Presented to Stanley Arthur Cook* (London, 1950), 35–49; R.S. Hanson, "Paleo-Hebrew Scripts in the Hasmonean Age," *BASOR* 175 (1964): 26–42; K.A. Matthews, "The Background of the Paleo-Hebrew Texts at Qumran," in C.L. Meyers and M. O'Connor (eds.), *The Word of the Lord Shall Go Forth* (Winona Lake, Ind., 1983), 549–568.

[64] For further references in Philo to 'Chaldean' as a designation for Hebrew, see the indices to Philo's works in LCL 10.298–299; Supplement 2.280. For further data and analysis of Philo's terminology, see C.-K. Wong, "Philo's Use of Chaldaioi," *SPhA* 4 (1992): 1–14. As for Philo's reasons for calling the biblical language 'Chaldean,' inadequate explanations are suggested by Schürer, *History*, rev., 2.28 n. 118; Weitzman, "Qumran Community," 39. Rather, see A.D. Roitman, "'This People Are Descendants of Chaldeans' (Judith 5:6): Its Literary Form and Historical Setting," *JBL* 113 (1994): 245–263 (254–262, esp. 262 n. 67), who argues that

terminology, together with the antiquated view that Hebrew was not spoken at the turn of the era, scholars have long concluded that Greek and Latin
sources regularly mean Aramaic when they use the designation 'Hebrew.'
This has led some English translators of the NT to render the phrase τῇ
Ἑβραῖδι διαλέκτῳ as "in Aramaic."[65] Philo's peculiar use of 'Chaldean' for
Hebrew may then be explained as necessitated by the fact that 'Hebrew' is
used for Aramaic.[66]

However, we have seen that the demise of Hebrew as a spoken language,
at least for the period of the NT, no longer commands a scholarly consensus. Furthermore, two recent studies, an article by John C. Poirier and an
unpublished paper by Ken Penner, have argued that 'Hebrew' does in fact
mean Hebrew in the first century. Examining the usage of τῇ Ἑβραῖδι διαλέκτῳ in Acts, Poirier shows that the phrase probably means 'in the Hebrew
language' in Acts 21:40; 22:2; and 26:14.[67] Penner has tried to demonstrate
that many of the examples used to establish the equation Hebrew = Aramaic are precarious at best. The three place names from the Fourth Gospel
may accurately reflect the correct form used even by Hebrew speakers, just
as the Latin form 'Nova Scotia' is the correct name in English. The Kaufmann

---

some Jews identified their origins with the prestigious Chaldeans in order to counteract anti-
Jewish polemic that propagated a lower pedigree for Jews. As Roitman notes (and see already
Jerome, *Comm. Dan.* 1.6), Philo has biblical precedent for tracing the origins of the Hebrew
people to the Chaldeans. Philo probably thought that Abraham spoke Hebrew (Winston,
"Aspects," 119), which must have been the native language of his Chaldean homeland (cf. Gen.
15:7); thus Chaldean = Hebrew. See below for Jerome's alternative use of the term 'Chaldean'
for Aramaic.

[65] See the NIV and NLT at Acts 21:40; 22:2; 26:14. The NRSV, NASB, and ESV give 'Hebrew'
in the text, but include notes indicating that the reader should understand by this 'Aramaic.'

[66] This is the explanation given in the new Schürer, *History*, rev., 2.28 n. 118. For other
discussions of this problem which conclude that 'Hebrew' can mean 'Aramaic,' see A. Meyer,
*Jesu Muttersprache* (Leipzig, 1896), 39–42; G. Dalman, *Grammatik des jüdisch-palästinischen
Aramäisch*[2] (Leipzig, 1905), 1; P. Ellingworth, "Hebrew or Aramaic?" *BT* 37 (1986): 338–341;
F.J. Thomson, "SS. Cyril and Methodius and a Mythical Western Heresy: Trilinguism. A
Contribution to the Study of Patristic and Mediaeval Theories of Sacred Languages," *AnBoll*
110 (1992): 67–122 (75–77); Veltri, *Libraries*, 198. D.R.G. Beattie and P.R. Davies, "What Does
Hebrew Mean?" *JSS* 56 (2011): 71–83, argue that the term 'Hebrew' in the ancient period
actually does mean 'Aramaic' (not just sometimes), and it only later came to be associated
with the biblical language, apparently during the rabbinic period (p. 82). They base this
opinion mostly on the NT evidence, but also on some rabbinic passages, one of which (*m. Yad.*
4.5) they recognize as counter-evidence (p. 75). They do not mention Philo, whose use of both
'Chaldean' and 'Hebrew' for the language of the Bible would seem to tell against their theory;
see Wong, "Philo's Use of Chaldaioi." Nor have they considered that in Josephus' retelling of
the story found in 2 Kings 18 (cf. *A.J.* 10.8), he has changed the Ἰουδαϊστί of the biblical text
(v. 26, reflecting יהודית) to Ἑβραϊστί, which in this context is contrasted with Συριστί (ארמית).

[67] See Poirier, "Linguistic Situation," 79–82.

manuscript of the Mishnah attests the form רבונו at Taanit 3.8 (rather than the רבונו of the printed versions), indicating that ραββουνι (John 20:16) may be considered Hebrew. Finally, though Philo and Josephus do call Aramaic forms 'Hebrew,' they merely adopt their terminology from the LXX, which regularly uses σάββατα (e.g. Exod. 16:29) and πάσχα (e.g. Exod. 12:11).[68] Thus, Penner and Poirier have struck a significant blow against the view that 'Hebrew' means 'Aramaic'; in the first century, it seems that Hebrew meant Hebrew.

Nevertheless, later writers did sometimes use 'Hebrew' in reference to a language they knew to be Aramaic.[69] The Greeks designated ארם by the term Συρία, and so the normal designation for Aramaic in Greek and Latin sources was 'Syriac' (e.g. Συριστί/Syriace), which is the translation for ארמית in its five biblical occurrences: 2 Kings 18:26 // Isa. 36:11 (contrasted in both passages with יהודית/'Ιουδαϊστί, or Ἑβραϊστί in Jos. A.J. 10.8); Ezra 4:7, twice; Dan. 2:4.[70] The same terminology is reflected in Classical Greek and most patristic authors, and even occasionally in rabbinic literature.[71] The lone

---

[68] K. Penner, "What Language Did Paul Speak in Acts 21–22? Ancient Names for Hebrew and Aramaic" (paper presented at the annual meeting of the Canadian Society of Biblical Studies, Halifax, 2003; available at http://stfx.academia.edu/KenPenner/Teaching). The passage from the Kaufmann Codex of the Mishnah may be checked in G. Beer, *Faksimile-Ausgabe des Mischnacodex Kaufmann A. 50* (Haag: M. Nijhoff, 1929), 157 line 2. For a discussion of the terms 'Hebrew' and 'native language' in the writings of Josephus, see Rajak, *Josephus*, 230–232.

[69] Penner ("Language," 7) allows for a "blurring of the distinction" beginning in the fourth century, and cites Eusebius (*Theoph.* 4.12), Epiphanius (*Pan.* 26.1.5; 69.68.3), and Joannes Moschus (*Prat. spir.* 136) to this effect. (The precise references are not found in Penner's paper but were supplied, along with other helpful information, through personal communication. I thank Dr. Penner for this help.) The *Theophania* of Eusebius, which has been preserved complete only in Syriac (edition by S. Lee (London, 1842); ET idem, *Eusebius, Bishop of Caesarea, on the Theophania* (Cambridge, 1843), 234 and n. 1), cites a passage from the 'Hebrew' Gospel, though Eusebius elsewhere affirms that this Gospel at least contains 'Syriac' (e.g. *Hist. eccl.* 4.22.8). For discussion of this latter passage, and the citations of Epiphanius and Joannes Moschus, see below.

[70] Two other 'biblical' references in Greek: 2 Mac. 15:36 explains that Adar is the name of a month in ἡ Συριακὴ φωνή, and the LXX Job has an epilogue taken from ἡ Συριακὴ βίβλος, which F.M. Cross thinks may have come from 11QtgJob (*The Ancient Library of Qumran*³ (Sheffield, 1995), 38 n. 1), but see also A.Y. Reed, "Job as Jobab: The Interpretation of Job in LXX Job 42:17b–e," *JBL* 120 (2001): 31–55, esp. 35–37. Neh. 13:24 may refer to an Aramaic dialect in its contrasting אשדודית with יהודית, but the identification of the former language is by no means certain; see J.M. Myers, *Ezra, Nehemiah*, AB 14 (Garden City, N.Y., 1965), 216–217; Southwood, "And They Could Not Understand Jewish Speech," 14–15. In any case, אשדודית had no influence on later terminology for Aramaic.

[71] For classical authors, see LSJ, 1732 s.v. Συριστί. For rabbinic usage, see M. Jastrow, *Dictionary of the Targumim, the Talmud Babli and Yerushalmi, and the Midrashic Literature* (1903; repr. Peabody, Mass.: Hendrickson, 2005), 970 s.v. סורסי; Dalman, *Grammatik*, 2–3.

exception is Jerome, who refers to biblical Aramaic as 'Chaldean.'[72] Jerome and Epiphanius, both of whom are reputed to have at least studied both Hebrew and Aramaic,[73] attest some level of understanding that Jews in the first century communicated in Aramaic rather than Hebrew.[74] Moreover, Nonnus of Panopolis realized that the two words labeled 'Hebrew' in John 19:13, 17 were Aramaic in form and the sign over the cross (John 19:20) may also have been Aramaic rather than Hebrew.[75] Thus, early Christians understood that there was a 'Syriac' language distinct from Hebrew, and

---

[72] Cf. *Praef. Dan.* 8–9; *Comm. Dan.* 2:4; *Praef. Tob.* 3; *Praef. Jud.* 2–3. Jerome does use the term 'Syriac' for other Aramaic (e.g. *Comm. Isa.* 36:11; *Comm. Matt.* 6:24). Jerome's practice reflects the two different appellations for the language of the Chaldeans in the LXX of Daniel 2:4 and 2:26. The Greek of Dan. 2:4 (LXX and Theodotion) indicates that the language spoken by the Χαλδαῖοι was termed Syriac (Συριστί), but Dan. 2:26 in the LXX explains Daniel's alternative name Belteshazzar as Χαλδαϊστί, apparently in reference to its Akkadian origin (so Schürer, *History*, rev., 2.28 n. 118). The term Χαλδαϊστί in the LXX of Dan. 2:26 has no equivalent in the Hebrew of that verse or in Theodotion's version. Cf. also Dan. 1:4 in Greek (LXX and Theodotion), where the Jewish youths are required to learn διάλεκτος Χαλδαϊκή.

[73] Jerome calls Epiphanius *quinque linguis* and says that he knew Greek, Syriac, Hebrew, Egyptian, and some Latin (*Ruf.* 2.22; 3.6). Jerome calls himself only *trilinguis*, which does not include Aramaic (*Ruf.* 3.6), but he does report that he struggled to learn Aramaic (*Praef. Dan.* 11–19) and even (sarcastically? See A. Fürst, *Hieronymus* (Freiburg, 2003), 76) calls himself *eloquentissimus homo in syro sermone vel graeco* (*Epist.* 17.2). Of course, he translated the Aramaic of Daniel (on which he also wrote a commentary) and Ezra into Latin, though he did not take the trouble to do this for Tobit (*Praef. Tob.* 9–11). On Jerome's knowledge of Aramaic, see D. Brown, *Vir Trilinguis* (Kampen, 1992), 82– 85; D. King, "*Vir Quadrilinguis?* Syriac in Jerome and Jerome in Syriac," in A. Cain and J. Lössl (eds.), *Jerome of Stridon* (Surrey, 2009), 209–224. On Jerome's competence in Hebrew, see the recent studies by Graves, *Jerome's Hebrew Philology*; J.S. Cameron, "The *Vir Tricultus*: An Investigation of the Classical, Jewish and Christian Influences on Jerome's Translation of the Psalter *Iuxta Hebraeos*" (diss.; University of Oxford, 2006), 28–68; H.I. Newman, "How Should We Measure Jerome's Hebrew Competence?" in Cain and Lössl, *Jerome of Stridon*, 131–140; for Epiphanius' knowledge of languages, see J. Dummer, "Die Sprachkenntnisse des Epiphanius," in F. Altheim and R. Stiehl (eds.), *Die Araber in der alten Welt*, 5.1 (Berlin, 1968), 392–435; repr. in *Philologia Sacra et Profana* (Stuttgart, 2006), 29–72, especially 35–47.

[74] In the *Nom. Hebr.*, Jerome explains many of the Semitic terms appearing in the Gospels as *Syrum est, non hebraeum* (cf. also *Comm. Matt.* 6:24). Note especially the passages in which Jerome classifies the words of Jesus as *syrum* (*Nom. Hebr.* 63.20; cf. Mark 14:36; *Nom. Hebr.* 63.29–30; cf. Mark 5:41) and people's names as *syrum* ('Bartholomaeus' at *Nom. Hebr.* 60.20–21; 'bar' at 60.23; 'Barrabban' at 60.28–29; 'Maria' at 62.19–20; 'Zachaeus' at 63.16–18; 'Martha' at 65.11–13). [The references to Jerome's *Nom. Hebr.* are according to the page and line numbers of the first edition of P. de Lagarde, *Onomastica Sacra* (Göttingen, 1870).] Epiphanius recognized that Jesus, while on the cross, quoted Ps. 22:1 mostly in Aramaic (*Pan.* 69.68.3).

[75] Cf. Nonnus of Panopolis, *Paraphrasis S. evangelii secundum Ioannem*, canto 19.65, 91, 109, in the edition of A. Scheindler, *Nonni Panopolitani S. Evangelii Ioannei* (Leipzig, 1881), 201–203.

some even attest that 'Syriac' had been a common language of the Jews from the time of Jesus.

And yet, both Epiphanius and Jerome classify as Hebrew certain texts or words which are in fact Aramaic. For Jerome's part, this may be due only to a slip of the memory, as he sometimes labels as Hebrew even the Aramaic on which he is commenting in the book of Daniel, though he does also call it Chaldean on occasion.[76] However, it also may be that Jerome regarded the relationship between Hebrew and Aramaic to be so close as to allow for a common designation ('Hebrew'). After all, in the *Praef. Tob.* (8–9) he writes, *vicina est Chaldeorum lingua sermoni hebraico* ("the language of the Chaldeans is close to Hebrew speech"; cf. *Prol. gal.* 1–2).[77] This may explain his several references to the original Hebrew form of the First Gospel in use among the Nazarenes and Ebionites, which he professes even to have translated *de Hebraeo sermone* (*Comm. Matt.* 12:13). However, elsewhere he says that the language of the Gospel is actually Aramaic, but is written in Hebrew characters: [sc. *Evangelium iuxta Hebraeos*] *Chaldaico quidem Syroque sermone, sed Hebraicis litteris scriptum est* ("The Gospel according to the Hebrews was written in the Chaldean and Syrian language, but in Hebrew letters"; *Pelag.* 3.2).[78] It appears that the close

---

[76] Jerome calls the language Hebrew at *Comm. Dan.* 2:16, 27; 3:23; he calls it Chaldean at *Comm. Dan.* 4:5; 4:10; 5:11; 6:4. In each of these four latter passages Jerome cites a specific Aramaic word, except in 5:11, where he writes: *Praeter Symmachum, qui chaldaicam veritatem secutus est, ceteri 'spiritum Dei' interpretati sunt.* But in this instance Jerome's distinction between 'spirit of gods' versus 'spirit of God' follows from his prior discussion in 4:5, where he does cite the Aramaic words and uses the term *lingua chaldaea*.

[77] Cf. Eusebius, *Praep. ev.* 10.5.2, where he equates the Syrians who are reputed to have invented the alphabet with the Hebrews: Σύροι δ' ἂν εἶεν καὶ Ἑβραῖοι [...].

[78] For other patristic references to the original Hebrew form of the First Gospel, or some other Semitic-language Gospel, see W.C. Allen, *A Critical and Exegetical Commentary on the Gospel According to S. Matthew*, ICC (Edinburgh, 1907), lxxix–lxxxiii. For a recent analysis of "The Jewish Christian Gospel Tradition," see the article under that name by C.A. Evans in O. Skarsaune and R. Hvalvik (eds.), *Jewish Believers in Jesus* (Peabody, Mass., 2007), 241–277; and for Jerome's evidence particularly, see O. Skarsaune, "Evidence for Jewish Believers in Greek and Latin Patristic Literature," in Skarsaune and Hvalvik, *Jewish Believers*, 505–567 (541–549); also Fürst, *Hieronymus*, 67–69. There seems to be evidence for multiple Semitic Gospels under various titles, sometimes associated with Matthew, but Jerome apparently knows of only one such Gospel, though he attests several names for it (*Comm. Matt.* 12:13; *Pelag.* 3.2; and see Skarsaune, "Evidence," 543–544). Jerome mentions this 'Hebrew' Gospel several times (*Epist.* 20.5; 120.8; *Vir. ill.* 3; *Comm. Isa.* 11.2), and says that he translated it into Greek and Latin (*Vir. ill.* 2; cf. *Comm. Matt.* 12:13; *Comm. Mich.* 7.7). His calling the Aramaic of this Gospel 'Hebrew' may find a parallel in Eusebius, who says of the second-century Christian Hegessipus, ἔκ τε τοῦ καθ' Ἑβραίους εὐαγγελίου καὶ τοῦ Συριακοῦ καὶ ἰδίως ἐκ τῆς Ἑβραΐδος διαλέκτου τινὰ τίθησιν (*Hist. eccl.* 4.22.8). If this difficult clause concerns only one

connection between Hebrew and Aramaic, and especially the shared script, led to Jerome's encompassing both languages under one appellation.

In Epiphanius we have explicit confirmation of this latter idea. In *Pan.* 26.1.5, he explains the folly of relating Νωρία, the supposed wife of Noah, to Πύρρα of Greek mythology, based on the etymology of their names.

> ἐπειδὴ γὰρ νοῦρα ἐν τῇ Ἑβραΐδι πῦρ οὐ κατὰ τὴν βαθεῖαν γλῶσσαν ἑρμηνεύεται ἀλλὰ Συριακῇ διαλέκτῳ (ἠσάθ [= אש] γὰρ τὸ πῦρ παρὰ Ἑβραίοις καλεῖται κατὰ τὴν βαθεῖαν γλῶσσαν) [...].[79]

> For since *noura* in Hebrew means 'fire' not according to the deep language but in the Syriac dialect (for fire is called *asath* among Hebrews according to the deep language) [...].

In the view of Epiphanius, 'Hebrew' may be divided into 'the deep language' and 'the Syriac dialect.' He thus indicates that Syriac is a recent adaptation of the ancient, or 'deep,' Hebrew language.[80] It may be that Jerome's *Epist.* 18A.10 reflects a similar idea, since there he boasts of having studied under a Jew so expert at Hebrew as to be called a 'Chaldean.'

If Jerome and Epiphanius could classify Aramaic within the general category 'Hebrew,' then it is likely that others who claimed no knowledge of either language would have done the same. It is possible that the NT and contemporary Greek literature (e.g. Philo and Josephus) may have contributed to the terminological confusion, since, as we have seen, these

---

"Syriac Gospel according to the Hebrews" from which Hegessipus takes Hebrew extracts, then we have an instance in which 'Hebrew' includes Aramaic. This view is advocated by R. Handmann, *Das Hebräer-Evangelium* (Marburg, 1888), 31–34. His reasoning involves the elimination of the καί between εὐαγγελίου and τοῦ Συριακοῦ, though he admits that Rufinus' translation (*disseruit autem et de euangelio secundum Hebraeos et Syros et quaedam etiam de lingua Hebraica disputavit*) already attests the καί. An English translation following this line of reasoning is offered by A.C. McGiffert in NPNF² 1.200: "And from the Syriac Gospel according to the Hebrews he quotes some passages in the Hebrew tongue." The translation by K. Lake (LCL; Cambridge, Mass., 1926), on the other hand, renders the clause, "and he makes extracts from the Gospel according to the Hebrews, and from the Syriac and particularly from the Hebrew language" (1.377). On patristic references to and citations from the Hebrew Gospel, see now the first two chapters in J.R. Edwards, *The Hebrew Gospel and the Development of the Synoptic Tradition* (Grand Rapids, 2009), 1–96.

[79] Later in the same work, Epiphanius again seems to classify Συριακή as a subcategory of the Ἑβραϊκή διάλεκτος (69.68.3). For a further instance in which Epiphanius may speak of Aramaic as 'Hebrew,' see A. Hilhorst, "The Prestige of Hebrew in the Christian World of Late Antiquity and Middle Ages," in A. Hilhorst, et al. (eds.), *Flores Florentino* (Leiden, 2007), 777–802 (795–796).

[80] See G.W.H. Lampe (ed.), *A Patristic Greek Lexicon* (Oxford, 1961), 282 s.v. βαθύς, where "ancient, original" is listed as a possible definition, with a citation of our passage from Epiphanius. No other author is cited for this usage.

sources do label as Hebrew what are in fact morphologically Aramaic terms, as some later writers recognized.[81] This may explain why Joannes Moschus reported that the common language in Palestine of his day (ca. 600) was Hebrew (*Prat. spir.* 136), though it was generally known to have been Aramaic. There is even one passage in the Talmud (*b. Meg.* 18a) that seems to refer to Aramaic by the term עברית (*'Ivrit;* 'Hebrew').[82]

There are a few reasons why late antique Christians may have encompassed Aramaic under the designation 'Hebrew.' First, it may be that the most appropriate label for the 'language of the Hebrews' was deemed to be 'Hebrew,' whether they actually spoke Hebrew or Aramaic. This could only be the case if their language was Semitic, for there is no instance in which Latin- or Greek-speaking Jews are said to have spoken Hebrew. Furthermore, authors could, of course, be more specific if needed, such as when Origen wanted to explain why he had such a difficult time discovering the Hebrew term for the trees mentioned in the Story of Susanna (*Ep. Afr.* 10). There it was necessary to point out that Jews sometimes employ Aramaic terms in place of those proper to Hebrew. But when Christians thought about Palestinian Jews, they generally thought of them as speaking Hebrew. The similarity between Hebrew and Aramaic, especially from an outsider's perspective, and the prominence of (the idea of) Hebrew in Judaism and Christianity due to its status as the biblical language, probably contributed to this conception.

In the second place, a few Christians may have perceived an actual linguistic relationship between the two languages. For instance, when Epiphanius classifies 'Syriac' as a 'Hebrew' language and opposes it to 'the deep language,' he implies a historical connection between Hebrew and Aramaic. This historical connection may be related to the widespread notion of Hebrew as the primordial language. This view, which we have already seen in Judaism and will see again in Christian sources, granted Hebrew the status of the original language spoken by the first generations of humans.

---

[81] See again Nonnus of Panopolis (cited above, n. 75) and Jerome, *Nom. Hebr.* 61.22–23, where he classifies as *syrum* the word 'Golgotha' (within his listing of words in the Gospel of Matthew) though John 19:17 labels this word 'Hebrew.'

[82] The context concerns reading the Book of Esther in a language other than the original. A list of non-Hebrew languages is given, including Coptic, עברית, Elamean, Median, and Greek. Maurice Simon says of the mention of עברית: "Apparently the reference is to a kind of Aramaic spoken by the Bene Eber, or 'on the other side' (*be'eber*) of the Euphrates" (*The Babylonian Talmud*, ed. I. Epstein, pt. 2: *Seder Mo'ed*, vol. 8: *Megillah* (London, 1938), 18a, p. 110 n. 4). See also G. Schramm, "Languages (Hebrew): A. Hebrew as a Language Name," *ABD* 4.203–204; K.G. Kuhn, Ἑβραῖος, *TDNT* 3.366–367; Beattie and Davies, "What Does Hebrew Mean," 74.

Other languages originated only after the 'confusion of tongues' associated with the Tower of Babel (Gen. 11). Some forms of this tradition imply that the world's languages are lineally descended from Hebrew; indeed, Jerome draws such a connection between Latin and Hebrew in his *Comm. Soph.* 3:18, where he connects the Latin *nugae* to the Hebrew נוגים (*nugim*; √ יגה) and comments, *ut nosse possimus linguam Hebraicam omnium linguarum esse matricem* ("so that we should know that the Hebrew language is the mother of all languages"). Given this view, considering Aramaic to be derived from Hebrew would have been relatively obvious. Since Aramaic continued to share many characteristics with its 'parent tongue,' it could be classified as a type of Hebrew.

A third reason for designating Aramaic by the term 'Hebrew' may be related to the script in which it was written. Again, Jerome's comments provide a hint toward this possibility. He says of the change of language from Hebrew to Aramaic in the Book of Daniel, *hebraicis quidem litteris sed lingua scribuntur chaldaica, quam hic syriacam vocat* ("they are written in Hebrew letters but in the Chaldean language, which it here calls 'Syriac'"; *Comm. Dan.* 2:4; cf. *Praef. Dan.* 8–10; *Pelag.* 3.2). We have already observed that the Rabbis knew the square script they used was borrowed from Aramaic, and they attributed its introduction to Ezra (p. 122). Origen (*Sel. Ps.* 2) and Jerome (*Prol. gal.* 3–8) are also familiar with the tradition concerning Ezra, but they do not say that he introduced the 'Chaldean' or 'Syriac' alphabet to Hebrew; rather, they apparently think Ezra's script was completely new. According to Jerome, *certumque est Ezram scribam legisque doctorem post captam Hierosolymam et instaurationem templi sub Zorobabel alias litteras repperisse, quibus nunc utimur* ("and it is certain that Ezra the scribe and teacher of the law, after the captivity of Jerusalem and the restoration of the Temple under Zerubbabel, invented other letters, which we now use"; *Prol. gal.* 5–7). Though Jerome knew that the current Hebrew script was not the original script preserved now among the Samaritans (*Prol. gal.* 7–8),[83] he did not think that the script now in use had come from Aramaic. He rather thought the reverse was the case: Aramaic-speaking Jews borrowed the Hebrew script to write their native language. The association of a script with a particular language would be natural for Westerners for whom one of the first steps toward learning either Greek or Latin was familiarity with

---

[83] On the Samaritan script, see Dan Barag, "Samaritan Writing and Writings," in Cotton, et al., *From Hellenism to Islam*, 303–323.

the writing system.[84] The custom of using the same script for Hebrew and Aramaic probably explains why Jerome sometimes terms as 'Hebrew' both the Aramaic of Daniel and the Aramaic "Gospel according to the Hebrews." The shared script led to a shared designation—Hebrew.

Therefore, while recent research has weakened the idea that 'Hebrew' might have meant Aramaic at the turn of the era, such terminology is confirmed for the later period, at least by the fourth century. The earlier period affords no strong evidence for the mixing of terms which may indicate confusion of the two languages. However, some later Fathers do explicitly categorize Aramaic as a type of Hebrew. The close relationship between these two languages, as it was articulated by patristic authors, must factor into our examination of the idea of Hebrew in the ancient Church.

### The Idea of Hebrew in Patristic Literature

Patristic ideas concerning the Hebrew language share some important elements with the views we have observed in Jewish sources. The Fathers considered Hebrew to be distinctive among the world's languages because it was the original language of mankind and it was the language characteristic of Jews. This latter point becomes important due to the Jewish position within the divine economy; it was they, after all, to whom were entrusted 'the oracles of God' (Rom. 3:2). However, Christian authors apparently did not attribute to Hebrew the status of 'sacred language' in the rabbinic sense of לשון הקודש, just as Greek, the language of the NT, largely failed to achieve this status.

The non-sanctity of Hebrew within early Christianity is indicated by the position of translations of the Hebrew scriptures in the Church and by the advocacy of vernacular languages in Christian liturgy. As for the second point, if Christians ever used Hebrew as their primary liturgical language, the practice waned and ceased with the success of the Gentile mission.[85] After this time, the liturgical use of Hebrew was limited to only a few words such as 'amen' and 'hallelujah.'[86] Origen declares that the God of all nations accepts prayers in all languages (*Cels.* 8.37), and other Fathers express the

---

[84] On the relationship between script and language, see Price and Naeh, "On the Margins of Culture."

[85] The NT evidence indicates that the liturgical language of earliest Christianity was more likely Aramaic; see the first chapter of J.A. Fitzmyer, *A Wandering Aramean* (Missoula, Mont., 1979), 1–27.

[86] On the significance of these terms in Christian liturgy, see Hilhorst, "Prestige of Hebrew," 799–800.

same sentiment.[87] As for the position of biblical translations within the Church, the LXX is the obvious example of a translation that largely displaced the original Hebrew text. This was true even within certain streams of Judaism, as attested by Philo, according to whom the LXX Pentateuch constituted a perfect *ad litteram* and *ad sensum* translation (*Mos.* 2.38–40). Christians expanded this legend, not only by applying it to the entire OT but also, occasionally, by ascribing inspiration to the translation even in deviations from the current Hebrew text.[88] The favorable attitude toward scriptural translations agrees with the theory articulated in the Mishnah, though we saw earlier that rabbinic literature increasingly tended to emphasize the original language of scripture. Thus, it does not seem that early Christians considered Hebrew a 'holy language,' as some Jews did.

That is not to say that there may not be indications to the contrary. For example, Jerome constantly speaks admiringly of the *Hebraica veritas*; however, since he can also speak of the *Graeca veritas* (*Praef. Evang.* 4) in reference to the NT, and the *Chaldaica veritas* (*Comm. Dan.* 5:11) in reference to the Aramaic of Daniel, the phrase has less to do with any particular language than with the original language of scripture as the proper basis of study. The 'scriptural' status of Hebrew, Greek, and Latin also explains the designation of these three languages by Isidore of Seville as *linguae sacrae* (*Etymologiae* 9.1.3).[89]

More problematic is Origen's classifying Hebrew as the primordial θεῖα διάλεκτος ("divine language"; *Cels.* 5.30–31). Origen does not explain this term, and this is apparently the only time in his writings when he seems to ascribe a sacred status to Hebrew. Moreover, Origen nearly always contents himself to rely on the Greek LXX or a more literal Greek rendering of the current Hebrew text. This fact alone casts doubt on the claim of Matthew J. Martin that "translation of Hebrew Scripture for Origen presented something of a problem."[90] Martin bases this conclusion on the research into Origen's theory of names conducted by Naomi Janowitz, who showed that Origen attributed great power to the Hebrew pronunciation of certain biblical

---

[87] For references and discussion, see Thomson, "Cyril and Methodius," 79–80.

[88] See the survey of authors in A. Wasserstein and D.J. Wasserstein, *The Legend of the Septuagint* (Cambridge, 2006), 95–131; and see ch. 5 below.

[89] For discussion of this passage, see Thomson, "Cyril and Methodius," 84; Hilhorst, "Prestige of Hebrew," 782–784.

[90] M.J. Martin, "Origen's Theory of Language and the First Two Columns of the Hexapla," *HTR* 97 (2004): 99–106 (102); see also idem, "Writing Divine Speech: Greek Transliterations of Near Eastern Languages in the Hellenistic East," in C. Cooper (ed.), *Politics of Orality* (Leiden, 2007), 251–273 (esp. 263–267).

names, including the names of the patriarchs and the names for God.[91] However, Martin misunderstands the evidence as presented by Janowitz, both by failing to perceive that Greek names for God carry similar power according to Origen (*Cels.* 1.24–25; 5.45),[92] and by extending Origen's emphasis on Hebrew from personal names to the entire language. This will not work, for, as Marguerite Harl says, "La doctrine des 'noms', ici [i.e., *Philoc.* 17] et ailleurs dans l'œuvre d'Origène, concerne en fait, comme nous allons le voir, les noms propres: noms propres des dieux, noms propres bibliques."[93] It does not seem that the reason Origen thought Hebrew 'divine' was that it possessed any efficacy, religious or otherwise, more than other languages.

Origen designates Hebrew as the θεία διάλεκτος in *Cels.* 5.30–31 while explaining the beginnings of linguistic diversity among humans. Relying on the Babel story of Gen. 11, Origen says that mankind originally spoke a single 'divine language' until the sin of the Tower prompted God to assign each nation an angel who would impart to that people a new language (*Cels* 5.30; cf. *Hom. Num.* 11.4). The only people who preserved the original language (ἡ ἐξ ἀρχῆς διάλεκτος) was Israel (*Cels.* 5.31). In what sense is this language divine? Perhaps Origen simply means that God used Hebrew in his speaking the world into existence, and he subsequently taught this language to the first humans. Again, there is no indication that Hebrew's status as 'divine' gave it any special properties, of the sort, for instance, that we saw reflected in *Gen. Rab.* Even if Hebrew was the mother tongue of God, still one should remember that he is ὁ πάσης διαλέκτου κύριος ("the Lord of every language"; *Cels.* 8.37).

Nevertheless, the Fathers did not regard Hebrew as on par with the world's other languages. On the contrary, Hebrew was special and important for at least two reasons: first, it represented the first human speech, and, second, it was the language of the Jews, the people of the Old Covenant. As for the first point, Greek and Latin Fathers frequently echo the traditional Jewish understanding of Hebrew as the language of creation. Augustine (*Civ.* 16.11) is representative in saying that the primordial language was

---

[91] N. Janowitz, "Theories of Divine Names in Origen and Pseudo-Dionysius," *HR* 30 (1991): 359–372.

[92] Martin ("Origen's Theory," 101) is aware of Janowitz's discussion of these passages, for which see Janowitz, "Theories," 360–365; see also Harl's treatment of *Philocalia* 17 (= *Cels.* 1.24–25 and 5.45–46) in *Origène, Philocalie, 1–20: Sur les Écritures*, SC 302 (Paris, 1983), 447–457 (see also pp. 387–397 on *Philocalia* 12). On Celsus' opinion concerning the names of God, see J.G. Cook, *The Interpretation of the Old Testament in Greco-Roman Paganism* (Tübingen, 2004), 117–119.

[93] Harl, *Philocalie*, 448.

preserved only through the descendants of Heber (= Eber; Gen. 10:21) as those alone who did not participate in the sin of the Tower of Babel.[94] Related to this is the idea that the Hebrew letters represent the first alphabet, a view first affirmed by the Hellenistic Jewish author Eupolemus in a fragment (frg. 1) preserved by several later writers.[95] One of these, Eusebius, goes beyond Eupolemus by providing the evidence that the Greek letter names are meaningless in Greek but do make sense in Hebrew (*Praep. ev.* 10.5). However, Milka Rubin has shown that the reason for the ready acceptance of Hebrew as the first language on the part of Greek and Latin Christians was not the prominence of Hebrew in the Christian mindset, but rather the lack of a suitable alternative for the primordial language. The Bible itself advocates the view that all mankind spoke one language for a time (Gen. 11:1), and Hebrew would seem to be a reasonable candidate to identify with this language, judging from the biblical evidence. It should not be surprising that the Fathers typically draw this conclusion. Bede, for one, explicitly bases himself on the biblical evidence: *Primam autem linguam fuisse generi humano hebream uidetur, ex eo quod nomina cuncta quae usque ad diuisionem linguarum in Genesi legimus, illius constat esse loquelae* ("It seems that the first language for humankind was Hebrew, because it is agreed that all the words which we read in Genesis up to the division of languages are of that speech"; *Hexaemeron* 1.2).

On the other hand, Gregory of Nyssa accepts the opinion that Hebrew was invented following the exodus, and he attributes this view to τινες τῶν ἐπιμελέστερον ταῖς θείαις γραφαῖς ἐπηκολουθηκότων ("some of those who

---

[94] For additional patristic references and analysis, see Rubin, "Language," 317–322; and add to her references Origen, *Hom. Num.* 11.4; Jerome, *Epist.* 18A.6.7. In regard to the 'exceptions,' Eusebius (*Praep. ev.* 1.7) should be omitted. The passage does present the view that no one language can claim originality, but Rubin (p. 320) fails to realize that Eusebius is quoting from Diodorus Siculus, as Eusebius says at the end of *Praep. ev.* 1.6. Cf. Diod. Sic., *Bibliotheca historica* 1.6–8, and, for his views on the origins of language particularly, 1.8.3–4. Eusebius himself, after quoting Diodorus, expresses his general disagreement with the latter's position on the origin of mankind. While Eusebius does not mention specifically the origins of language, one may presume that he opposed Diodorus' views on this matter, as well.

[95] Cf. the edition by C.R. Holladay, *Fragments from Hellenistic Jewish Authors*, vol. 1: *Historians* (Chico, Calif., 1983), 112. The primary transmitters of the fragment are Clement of Alexandria (*Strom.* 1.23.153.4) and Eusebius (*Praep. ev.* 9.25.4–26.1); for later Greek authors who cite this fragment, see pp. 136–137 (n. 1) of Holladay's work. Holladay points out that classical authors typically (not unanimously) attributed the invention of the alphabet to the Phoenicians (138 n. 6, with references), while Eupolemus asserts that the Phoenician alphabet was derived from the Hebrew alphabet. In the seventh century, Isidore of Seville omits reference to the Phoenicians in his concern to show that the Latin and Greek alphabets are derived from the Hebrew one (*Etymologiae* 1.3.4–5).

have pursued very carefully the divine scriptures"). His discussion shows his disinterest in the question of the original language, for he is at pains to prove that human language is conventional rather than created by God.[96] It may be that the biblical scholars cited by Gregory also influenced Theodoret, who likewise assigns the origins of the Hebrew language to the Mosaic period. The etymologies of the names of the patriarchs (e.g. Adam, Cain, Abel, Noah) show that the original language of mankind was not Hebrew but Syriac, Theodoret's own native language. Yet, in the end he disallowed any theological value to attach to his conclusions (*Quaest. Gen.* 60–62). In this he agreed with most other patristic authors. Though the status of a particular language as 'original' might occasionally have exegetical importance (cf. e.g. Jerome, *Comm. Soph.* 3:18, quoted above, p. 130), it did not make that language 'holy.'

The second aspect that made Hebrew distinctive among the world's languages was its association with the ancient Jews. Naturally, the Fathers knew that not all Jews spoke Hebrew. Origen had difficulty tracking down a Jew who could inform him of the Hebrew name for two types of trees (*Ep. Afr.* 10). The NT apparently identifies as Ἑλληνισταί Jews who spoke Greek rather than Hebrew (Acts 6:1),[97] and the Fathers were thoroughly familiar with the Jewish Greek translations of scripture required for Greek-speaking Jews (cf. Origen, *Ep. Afr.* 4). Philo uses Ἑβραῖοι in reference to Jews who speak the language, as opposed to himself (*Conf. Ling.* 129), and Jerome at least knew that Philo characteristically wrote Greek (*Praef. lib. Sal.* 17–19).

However, all of this evidence for linguistic diversity among Jews concerns the 'modern' descendants of ancient Israel. Early Christians recognized that Hebrew was uniquely associated with the Israelites of the biblical period. Indeed, the ancient Jews were the only people who spoke Hebrew. It was, after all, their ancestor Heber who alone preserved this primordial language. In fact, Augustine affirms not only that Heber alone preserved the language, but also that he transmitted it only to that part of his progeny that led to Abraham, and Abraham taught the language only to his descendants that led to Jacob (= Israel; *Civ.* 16.11). This allows him to assert: *linguam* [sc.

---

[96] *Contra Eunomium*, book 2 (= 12b), § 252–261; pp. 299–302 in W. Jaeger (ed.), *Contra Eunomium Libri I et II*, GNO 1 (Leiden, 1960). Gregory's statement about Hebrew's post-exodus origins is at § 256. While Gregory attributes the view to certain biblical scholars, it also corresponds to the view of the anti-Christian writer Celsus, refuted by Origen at *Cels.* 3.6. On Gregory's theory of language, see M. La Matina, "Philosophy of Language," in L.F. Mateo-Seco and G. Maspero (eds.), *The Brill Dictionary of Gregory of Nyssa* (Leiden, 2009), 604–611.

[97] On the identity of these Ἑλληνισταί, see C.K. Barrett, *A Critical and Exegetical Commentary on the Acts of the Apostles*, 2 vols., ICC (Edinburgh, 1994–1998), 1.307–309.

*hebraicam*] *solus Israel populus potuit obtinere* ("only the people Israel were able to maintain the [Hebrew] language"; *Civ.* 16.3).

This view may reflect the Jewish position that associated Hebrew with Jews at least since biblical times (2 Kings 18:26; Neh. 13:24) and developed during the Second Temple Period into the language ideology that we examined before. Whether Christians interacted with Palestinian or Diaspora Jews, they would discover that the Jews themselves considered Hebrew to be characteristically their language. Furthermore, the NT identifies the language of Jesus and his contemporaries as Hebrew, and this probably had some influence on the Fathers. According to early Christians, as also according to ancient Jews, Hebrew was the typical Jewish language.

The import of this observation concerns the language in which the ancient Israelites composed their sacred literature. The greatest significance of the Hebrew language for the Fathers lay in its role within the divine economy as the language of the OT. Augustine expresses this point clearly: *Hebraea vocatur lingua, quam Patriarcharum et Prophetarum, non solum in sermonibus suis, verum etiam in Litteris sacris custodivit auctoritas* ("It is called the Hebrew language, which the authority of the Patriarchs and Prophets preserved, not only in their speech but also in their sacred writings"; *Civ.* 16.11). Therefore, knowledge of Hebrew is helpful for biblical interpretation, especially when the translations are obscure, as Augustine (*Doctr. chr.* 2.16) and Isidore (*Etymologiae* 9.1.3) counsel their readers. There is no need to document Jerome's ubiquitous citation of the *Hebraica veritas* as the original language of the OT. Furthermore, we saw in the previous chapter that every patristic passage that argues for the use of the LXX against the Hebrew concedes that the OT was written originally in Hebrew, as does the consistent limiting of the OT canon to 22 books, equivalent to the 22 letters of the Hebrew alphabet. In this connection, Origen's insistence on discovering the Hebrew terms for Susanna's trees becomes comprehensible (*Ep. Afr.* 10). The Jews whom he interrogated suggested that they might be able to supply the relevant words in Aramaic, but it seems not to have occurred to Origen that Aramaic may have been the original language of Susanna. The language of ancient Israel was Hebrew, and so this was the language of scripture.

One exception to the association of Hebrew with ancient Israel is found in Theodoret. The bishop of Cyrus seems to think that Hebrew was never the vernacular of the Jews, but only a 'religious' or 'hieratic' language for the scriptures. He thus compares Hebrew to the 'hieratic' writing of other cultures:

οἶμαι αὐτὴν [sc. τὴν Ἑβραῖαν γλῶσσαν] ἱερὰν εἶναι φωνήν· ὥσπερ γὰρ ἐν τοῖς ἑλλη-
νικοῖς ναοῖς ἴδιοί τινες ἦσαν χαρακτῆρες γραμμάτων, οὓς ἱερατικοὺς προσηγόρευον,
οὕτω διὰ τοῦ Μωϋσέως ὁ τῶν ὅλων Θεὸς ταύτην ἔδωκε τὴν γλῶτταν, διδακτὴν οὐ-
σαν, οὐ φυσικήν.                                                                    (*Quaest. Gen.* 61)

I think it [the Hebrew language] to be a hieratic speech. For just as in Greek
temples there are certain characters of the alphabet that are peculiar, which
they call 'hieratic', so through Moses the God of all things gave this language,
being a taught language, not a natural one.

As evidence, Theodoret notes that Jewish children in his day first learn
the language of the surrounding culture, and then study Hebrew when
they become teenagers (μειράκια).[98] He denies that Hebrew is named after
Heber as the lone preserver of the primordial language (*Quaest. Gen.* 62).
Theodoret connects Abraham's designation as a Hebrew (עברי; cf. Gen.
14:13) not to his language but to his crossing (עבר) the Euphrates. Implied in
Theodoret's reasoning is that Abraham and his descendents did not speak
Hebrew but Syriac, his candidate for the primordial language. Presumably,
Theodoret would say that the ancient Israelites also used Syriac as a vernac-
ular, since Hebrew was only their *hieratic* language. Yet, Theodoret certainly
does not intend by this to disassociate Hebrew from scripture; indeed, scripture is precisely the area to which he limits Hebrew.

The general patristic notion, then, is that the Hebrew language was the
original human language and the language exclusive to biblical Israel, and
thus the language of the Bible. The one exception to seeing Hebrew as the
vernacular of the ancient Israelites still affirms that it is the language of their
scripture. These elements clearly connect the patristic ideas to their Jewish
counterparts, though not to the extent of some rabbinic formulations of
לשון הקודש. Furthermore, we should note that few Christians of the patristic
period troubled themselves to learn Hebrew, so that the Hebrew text rarely
became the basis for Christian exegesis. The unique status of Hebrew as the
primordial and biblical language remained for the most part a matter of
theory that did not stimulate an active interest in the language for Christians
as it did for some Jews.

---

[98] On possible influences on Theodoret in this regard, see F. Millar, "Christian Emperors,"
18.

## *The Idea of Aramaic in Patristic Literature*

Earlier we saw that the fourth-century Fathers sometimes classified Aramaic as a type of Hebrew. This contrasts somewhat sharply with some rabbinic statements concerning Aramaic, examined above, that disparage Aramaic in behalf of Hebrew. If the Fathers could categorize Aramaic as a sub-branch of Hebrew, might they have considered Aramaic a possible biblical language, especially given the fact that the Hebrew Bible features substantial Aramaic sections? Early Christians do not discuss the Aramaic language very frequently, but the available evidence indicates that Aramaic was not considered a 'biblical' language in the same way that Hebrew was.

Indeed, it is difficult to determine which Christian authors other than Jerome perceived that parts of the Bible were written in Aramaic. None of the Fathers except Jerome seems to realize that Dan. 2:4 begins an extensive Aramaic section in that book. Though Theodoret's native language was Syriac, he interprets the reference to Aramaic (Συριστί in his Greek version) in Dan. 2:4 as conveying only that the astrologers spoke this language, not that the text was written in this language.[99] Augustine read some of Jerome's writings and so may have understood through these, if in no other way, that certain parts of the Bible were written in Aramaic, but he does not regard this as significant since he counsels Latin speakers to learn the biblical languages of Hebrew and Greek *ad Scripturarum divinarum cognitionem* ("for the knowledge of the divine Scriptures"), with no mention of Aramaic (*Doctr. chr.* 2.16). Later, Augustine acknowledges that Aramaic words do appear in the Bible (2.59), but he means only individual words scattered throughout scripture, and he mentions also Hebrew and Egyptian words that have been usefully interpreted in onomastic lists. Origen probably knew very little about the Hebrew language,[100] but at least he knew that Hebrew and Aramaic ('Syriac') were distinct languages and that 'modern' Jews, in some cases, spoke the latter more proficiently than the former (*Ep. Afr.* 10). But not only does he accept Africanus' principle that the OT was entirely written in Hebrew, but also his investigation into the Hebrew names for Susanna's trees exhibits the practical consequences of this principle, since the Aramaic terms will not suffice.

---

[99] See the text and translation given by R.C. Hill, *Theodoret of Cyrus: Commentary on Daniel* (Atlanta, 2006), pp. 34–37, and Hill's n. 45 on p. 37.

[100] See N.R.M. de Lange, *Origen and the Jews* (Cambridge, 1976), 21–23.

Of course, Jerome did know that Aramaic appeared in the Bible, and he typically designates this biblical Aramaic by the term 'Chaldean.' Since he translated the entire Hebrew Bible, he would naturally recognize each time the text changed from Hebrew to Chaldean, which language was much more challenging for him.[101] Where the original language of scripture is Chaldean, one may speak of the *Chaldaica veritas*, as Jerome does in his comment on Dan. 5:11.

However, the existence of Aramaic portions of scripture does not lead Jerome to regard Aramaic as a true biblical language. He implies that one reason Tobit and Judith are unworthy of inclusion within the canon is because they were composed in Chaldean.[102] The preface to his translation of Tobit begins: *Mirari non desino exactionis vestrae instantiam. Exigitis enim, ut librum chaldeo sermone conscriptum ad latinum stilum traham, librum utique Tobiae* ("I do not cease to be surprised at the earnestness of your command. For you order me to translate into Latin style a book written in the Chaldean language, the Book of Tobit"; 2–3). A little later he writes, *Arguunt enim nos Hebraeorum studia et inputant nobis, contra suum canonem latinis auribus ista transferre* ("Hebrew studies condemn us and accuse us of transferring those things for Latin ears against their own canon"; 6–7). Jerome's devotion to Hebrew presented an obstacle to his translating a book written in Chaldean, and he expresses surprise that anyone would demand such a translation. That Jerome lacks enthusiasm for the task is shown both by his own words (*Feci ... non tamen meo studio*, "But I did not do it by my own eagerness"; lines 5–6) and by his unwillingness to struggle with the Chaldean text itself, as he did with Daniel (*Praef. Dan.* 11–19). Instead, Jerome secured the services of a Jew who translated from Chaldean to Hebrew, which Jerome then rendered into Latin (*Praef. Tob.*

---

[101] The four passages in the Bible containing Aramaic are all noted by Jerome: cf. *Qu. hebr. Gen.* for Laban's language in Gen. 31:47 (which Jerome calls 'Syriac'); for the Aramaic portions of Ezra and Daniel, as well as the single Aramaic verse Jer. 10:11, cf. *Praef. Dan.* 8–10 (all are 'Chaldean'). For Jerome's difficulty with 'Chaldean,' cf. *Praef. Dan.* 11–19.

[102] Modern scholars would be very hesitant to endorse Jerome's opinion as to the original language of these books. Most consider Judith to have been Hebrew; see the evidence given by C.A. Moore, *Judith*, AB 40 (Garden City, N.Y., 1985), 66–67. About Tobit there is more debate. M. Hallermayer, *Text und Überlieferung des Buches Tobit* (Berlin, 2008), examines in detail all of the available texts, especially the four Aramaic fragments and one Hebrew fragment of the book found in Qumran Cave 4, but her summary of the evidence for the original language (on pp. 175–179) concludes that no sure result can be reached from the available texts. Hallermayer herself cautiously leans toward Aramaic (179), based on the testimony of Origen and Jerome, as well as Tobit's absence from the Jewish canon.

8–11). Any chance that the *veritas* may thus have been obscured by being "poured into the third jar" (cf. *Praef. lib. Sal.* 24) seems not to have been a concern.[103] As for Ezra and Daniel, the abundance of Hebrew text in both books, especially as a frame for the Aramaic, allowed them to be considered basically Hebrew books. That Jerome did so consider them is clear from his failure even to mention the Aramaic of Ezra in the preface to his translation of that book, and from his concluding note in his commentary on the proto-canonical part of Daniel, where he says that he has interpreted Daniel *iuxta hebraicum* (*Comm. Dan.* 13:2).

Nevertheless, though the Aramaic of Tobit and Judith became an argu-ment against them for Jerome, other early Christians, such as Origen (*Ep. Afr.* 19), did accept these books into the canon. Most of these Christians had no way of determining the original language of the books, and they no doubt assumed their Hebrew origin due to their Jewish composition. How-ever, Origen, for one, is aware that the Jews contemporary with him did not possess Tobit or Judith in Hebrew: Ἑβραῖοι τῷ Τωβίᾳ οὐ χρῶνταί, οὐδὲ τῇ Ἰου-δίθ· οὐδὲ γὰρ ἔχουσιν αὐτὰ κἄν ἐν ἀποκρύφοις ἑβραϊστί, ὡς ἀπ' αὐτῶν μαθόντες ἐγνώκαμεν ("The Hebrews do not use Tobit or Judith, for they do not have them even in the apocrypha in Hebrew, as we know having learned it from them"; *Ep. Afr.* 19). J. Ruwet thought there was a "sérieuse probabilité" that this sentence implies that Tobit and Judith did feature among the Jewish apocrypha not in Hebrew, but in Aramaic, as Jerome later testifies (*Praef. Tob.* 4–5; *Praef. Jud.* 1).[104] If this is true, then we may have a case in which Origen consciously accepted the canonicity of an Aramaic composition.

However, it is difficult to accept this conclusion. First, Origen previously affirmed the Hebrew criterion for canonicity in this same letter, so it would be strange now to openly reject it. His Hebrew criterion could be reconciled with Ruwet's interpretation of *Ep. Afr.* 19 by speculating that Origen deemed the extant Aramaic of Tobit and Judith to be translations from Hebrew. This would be little different from the situation he imagines regarding Susanna, which he knows only in its Greek form but considers this to be a translation from a lost (or suppressed) Hebrew original. Alternatively, Origen may have considered Aramaic to be a form of Hebrew, as Epiphanius did. Yet,

---

[103] For a brief commentary on Jerome's prefaces to Tobit and Judith, together with an evaluation of the quality of Jerome's translations of these books, see P.-M. Bogaert, *Judith*, Vetus Latina 7/2, fasc. 1 (Freiburg, 2001), 30–32. On Tobit, see also V.T.M. Skemp, *The Vulgate of Tobit Compared with Other Ancient Witnesses* (Atlanta, 2000); idem, "Jerome's Tobit: A Reluctant Contribution to the Genre Rewritten Bible," *RBén* 112 (2002): 5–35.

[104] J. Ruwet, "Les apocryphes dans les œuvres d'Origène," *Bib* 25 (1944): 143–166 (151).

it is not clear that Ruwet's interpretation of *Ep. Afr.* 19 should be followed, and, in truth, few scholars have followed it. For instance, de Lange translates the passage, "ils ne les ont pas en hébreu, même pas dans les apocryphes," which in no way implies an Aramaic form of Tobit and Judith.[105] It seems that Origen's statement here should be read in the light of his earlier argument that the Jewish authorities suppressed certain works, some of which (but certainly not all, e.g., Susanna) remain in the Jewish non-canonical literature (*Ep. Afr.* 13: ὧν τινὰ σώζεται ἐν ἀποκρύφοις). Given Origen's extended defense of Susanna's Hebrew composition despite the absence of that original Hebrew text, we should probably see in his comment about Tobit and Judith a reference to the earlier discussion, such that Tobit and Judith offer a further example of good canonical literature now completely non-extant in Hebrew. Aramaic does not enter the picture and has nothing to do with the argument.

## CONCLUSION

This chapter has attempted to outline some of the ideas about the Hebrew language commonly accepted in ancient Judaism and Christianity. We have seen that Hebrew commanded a special status among many Jews and Christians because of its role as the primordial language and the language of scripture. However, while this motivated some Jews to cultivate a use of the language at least for certain circumstances, a similar situation hardly ever obtained in Christianity. Moreover, even the elements of the tradition shared by Jews and Christians may not have resulted from direct influence. Patristic interpretation of the Bible was sufficient to generate both the idea of Hebrew as the first language and its association with ancient Israel, and thus with Israelite scripture. Naturally, the agreement between patristic ideas stemming from the Bible and Jewish teaching could only have reinforced these beliefs.

We have also noticed the significance of these results for the Hebrew criterion of canonicity examined in the previous chapter. If the language

---

[105] N. de Lange (ed.), *Origène, La Lettre à Africanus sur l'histoire de Suzanne*, in Harl, *Philocalie*, 469–578 (563). Other translations that do not imply the existence of Aramaic versions of Tobit and Judith include those by A.C. Sundberg, *The Old Testament of the Early Church* (Cambridge, Mass., 1964), 137; A. Salvesen, "A Convergence of the Ways? The Judaizing of Christian Scripture by Origen and Jerome," in A.H. Becker and A.Y. Reed (eds.), *The Ways that Never Parted* (Tübingen, 2003), 233–258 (235).

of ancient Israel was Hebrew, then the sacred literature produced by that nation must also be in Hebrew. The language of a document may then be used as a control for the reception of the authentic OT into the Church. In other words, even if Jews contemporary with the Fathers could not be fully trusted to transmit the word of God as they received it (because of their falsifying or suppressing documents, discussed in the previous chapter), one may still use their language as a criterion for eliminating spurious documents. While no Christian writer formulates the principle in these terms, our discussion from the previous chapter shows that at least Origen and Africanus conceived of the criterion in this way.

Of course, the criterion proves useful only if one knows which works were originally composed in Hebrew and which works were not. When originally Greek documents were added into the Christian OT canon, documents such as Wisdom of Solomon and 2 Maccabees, those responsible for their inclusion may have done so with the understanding that their presumed ancient Jewish composition entailed an original Hebrew text. Our previous chapter's argument about the general acceptance of the Hebrew criterion would indicate as much. That Jerome had to point out that Wisdom and 2 Maccabees were actually late Greek works (*Prol. gal.* 56; *Praef. lib. Sal.* 17–18) implies that other Christians did not understand this. Even when there seemed to be sufficient evidence to exclude a candidate from canonicity, as in the case of Susanna, Origen's *Ep. Afr.* shows that attachment to the text also played a major role in decisions. And yet, it still had to be shown that the document could have been written in Hebrew, the language of the ancient Jews.

# CHAPTER FIVE

# HEBREW SCRIPTURE AND THE TEXT OF THE OLD TESTAMENT

Concerns about the correct OT text demanded as much or more attention from the Fathers as did concerns about the canon. Indeed, our earliest witness to textual problems associated with the OT (Justin) precedes by some decades our earliest witness to similar problems with the canon (Melito). Scholars have often explored this area, some producing learned studies on patristic textual theory. However, our study advances the discussion by focusing on the role that Hebrew scripture played in patristic arguments about the OT text. While recent work tends to suggest that it played a minor role, or even a negative one (i.e., LXX against Hebrew text), we will find that the Fathers typically endeavored to equate their Greek text with the Hebrew.

Of course, concern for the relationship between the Greek LXX translation and the original Hebrew text preceded the Christian era. Some Jewish sources, such as Philo, Josephus, the *Letter of Aristeas*, and even the Rabbis evince an interest in highlighting or denying variation between the Greek and Hebrew Bibles. These Jewish ideas have also received their share of attention, but again our particular perspective—emphasizing Hebrew scripture in their theory—will allow us to suggest new ways of understanding their views. Following an examination of these Jewish sources, we will turn our attention to the Fathers. The nature of the evidence and its usual interpretation by modern readers demand a lengthy and detailed discussion. Once again, the results emphasize the positive role of Hebrew scripture in patristic biblical theory.

## THE TEXT OF THE SEPTUAGINT IN EARLY JUDAISM

### *The Text of the Bible in Early Judaism*

The discovery of the biblical scrolls from Qumran and elsewhere in the Judaean Desert has illuminated the plurality of Hebrew textual forms for many biblical books in antiquity. Before the mid-twentieth century, textual witnesses were restricted (more-or-less) to the Masoretic Text (MT), the Samaritan Pentateuch (SP), and the LXX with its presumed Hebrew *Vorlage*.

The Dead Sea Scrolls bear witness to forms, sometimes incipient, of each of these textual streams, at least. Various theories have sought to explain this situation, without any consensus.[1]

However, the proto-MT textual tradition of most biblical books held a prominent, if not dominant, position in Judaism and grew in prominence throughout the centuries surrounding the turn of the era. Taking the Hebrew Bible as a whole, Emanuel Tov provides the following statistics classifying the textual form of the Qumran scrolls:[2]

|  | Torah | Remaining Books |
|---|---|---|
| Proto-MT | 52% | 44% |
| pre-SP | 6.5% | |
| LXX *Vorlage* | 4.5% | 3% |
| non-aligned | 37% | 53% |

There are certainly a large number of non-aligned scrolls that conform to none of the previously known categories, and these scrolls cover most books of the Hebrew Bible. Yet, this category encompasses a wide range of divergences from the proto-MT, varying in degree, not all of the same signifi-

---

[1] For the history of research and a presentation of his own view, see E. Tov, *Textual Criticism of the Hebrew Bible*[3] (Minneapolis, 2012), 155–190. For a response to Tov, see F.M. Cross, *The Ancient Library of Qumran*[3] (Sheffield, 1995), 177–181. Tov responds to Cross in *The Text-Critical Use of the Septuagint in Biblical Research*[2] (Jerusalem, 1997), 183–187. E. Ulrich critiqued the views of Cross, Tov, and Sh. Talmon in "Horizons of Old Testament Textual Research at the Thirtieth Anniversary of Qumran Cave 4," *CBQ* 46 (1984): 613–636 (619–624), and then he developed his own ideas in a series of articles now collected in *The Dead Sea Scrolls and the Origins of the Bible* (Grand Rapids, 1999). See now, for the history of research, analysis of data, and a new theory of textual standardization, A. Lange, "'They Confirmed the Reading' (*y. Ta'an.* 4.68a): The Textual Standardization of Jewish Scriptures in the Second Temple Period," in Lange, M. Weigold, and J. Zsengellér (eds.), *From Qumran to Aleppo* (Göttingen, 2009), 29–80.

[2] E. Tov, "The Biblical Texts from the Judaean Desert—An Overview and Analysis of the Published Texts," in E.D. Herbert and E. Tov (eds.), *The Bible As Book: The Hebrew Bible and the Judaean Desert Discoveries* (New Castle, Del., 2002), 139–166 (152–156). J. VanderKam and P. Flint, *The Meaning of the Dead Sea Scrolls* (New York, 2002), 146, have criticized Tov's statistics as unduly favoring the proto-MT, since he includes in this category even texts that are equally close to the pre-SP or to the LXX *Vorlage*. However, this criticism is irrelevant because when either the LXX or SP agree with the MT and with a Qumran scroll, there is even greater evidence of a dominant textual tradition. Other, more useful criticisms of Tov's classification of the Qumran biblical scrolls are given by B. Chiesa, "Textual History and Textual Criticism of the Hebrew Old Testament," in J. Trebolle Barrera and L. Vegas Montaner (eds.), *The Madrid Qumran Congress*, 2 vols. (Leiden, 1992), 1.257–272; P.J. Gentry, "The Septuagint and the Text of the Old Testament," *BBR* 16 (2006): 193–218 (210–212). These scholars think that Tov focuses too much on the diversity of the texts and should rather highlight their similarities.

cance. Even though Qumran attests a great deal of textual diversity, still the high percentages of proto-MT scrolls show that it held a respected position among the textual options in antiquity. The prominence of the MT becomes apparent also in several other ways: the twenty-three biblical scrolls discovered in other areas of the Judean Desert all featured the proto-MT textual form; the Rabbis adopted the proto-MT as their single authoritative text; the various translators who produced the LXX by and large used proto-MT texts as their *Vorlagen*; and the so-called καίγε revision of some books of the LXX apparently intended to bring the LXX into conformity with the proto-MT.[3] Naturally, one should allow for the prominence of other text-types for some biblical books before the rabbinic period, as for instance the text of Samuel reflected in 4QSamᵃ. Nevertheless, the proto-MT text of Samuel gradually displaced other types.[4] By the second century CE, Hebrew texts for all biblical books survived almost exclusively in the textual traditions of the proto-MT and the SP.[5] Because by this time the Samaritans had long distinguished themselves from Judaism, one may limit the Jewish biblical texts in Hebrew to the proto-MT.[6] From the end of the of the first century CE, this latter was essentially the only Hebrew textual tradition extant.[7]

---

[3] See F.M. Cross, *From Epic to Canon* (Baltimore, 1998), 213–218 for his account of how the proto-MT became dominant. On the rabbinic adoption of the proto-MT, see P.S. Alexander, "Why no Textual Criticism in Rabbinic Midrash? Reflections on the textual culture of the Rabbis," in G.J. Brooke (ed.), *Jewish Ways of Reading the Bible* (Oxford, 2000), 175–190. For a recent argument that the LXX does not attest non-MT *Vorlagen* as much as is often thought, see Gentry, "Septuagint," 213–218.

[4] On Samuel, see E. Ulrich, "Josephus's Biblical Text for the Books of Samuel," in L.H. Feldman and G. Hata (eds.), *Josephus, the Bible, and History* (Detroit, 1989), 81–96; repr. in Ulrich, *Scrolls and Origins*, 184–201 (190); idem, *The Qumran Text of Samuel and Josephus* (Missoula, Mont., 1978); F.M. Cross, "The History of the Biblical Text in the Light of Discoveries in the Judaean Desert," *HTR* 57 (1964): 281–299; repr. in F.M. Cross and S. Talmon (eds.), *Qumran and the History of the Biblical Text* (Cambridge, Mass, 1975), 177–195 (191–192).

[5] For a recent book-by-book analysis of the textual evidence, see A. Lange, *Handbuch der Textfunde vom Toten Meer*, vol. 1 (Tübingen, 2009).

[6] For a recent treatment of the Samaritan Pentateuch, see R. Pummer, "The Samaritans and Their Pentateuch," in G.N. Knoppers and B.M. Levinson (eds.), *The Pentateuch as Torah* (Winona Lake, Ind., 2007), 237–269.

[7] See Tov, *Textual Criticism*, 27–36. For the view that Josephus' comments on textual uniformity (*C. Ap.* 1.42) accurately reflects the reality of his own time, see G.W. Anderson, "Canonical and Non-Canonical," in P.R. Ackroyd and C.F. Evans (eds.), *The Cambridge History of the Bible*, vol. 1 (Cambridge, 1970), 113–159 (116–117); Cross, *Epic to Canon*, 205; Lange, "They Confirmed," 29–31. However, Josephus' portrayal of Jewish unwillingness to alter the biblical text may, in context, be merely rhetorical. See the analysis of his similar statements on biblical translation in S. Inowlocki, "'Neither Adding nor Omitting Anything': Josephus' Promise not to Modify the Scriptures in Greek and Latin Context," *JJS* 56 (2005): 48–65.

The growing prominence of the proto-MT in the centuries surrounding the turn of the era had consequences for the Greek translations of the OT. The LXX often presents readings different from the proto-MT in either minor or major details. Following the "typologie des divergences" set out by Marguerite Harl, we can classify the divergences between the LXX and the proto-MT as arising for a variety of reasons. (1) The LXX *Vorlage* may have differed from the proto-MT. On the other hand, if the LXX *Vorlage* was identical to the proto-MT, differences between the LXX and MT may still arise because (2) the translators understood their *Vorlage* differently from modern Hebraists; (3) the Greek and Hebrew languages are so different; (4) the translators made "targumique" redactional moves; or (5) the translators rendered their passage according to their own theological interpretation.[8] In any case, the result was sometimes unacceptable for those Jews who considered the proto-MT the authoritative text form and desired a translation that reflected it as closely as possible. Origen incorporated within his *Hexapla* three recent translations (Aquila, Symmachus, and Theodotion) which he knew corresponded more closely to the current Hebrew text than did the LXX.[9] Besides these Greek minor versions, scholars have identified two substantial pre-Christian recensions of the LXX designed to bring the Greek of certain biblical books into better accord with a Hebrew text. The proto-Lucianic recension (the existence of which is disputed) and the καίγε revision had a significant impact on the subsequent reception of the Greek OT, as later writers often exhibit influence from these revisions when citing the LXX.[10]

---

[8] See M. Harl, "Les divergences entre la Septante et le Texte Massorétique," in G. Dorival, M. Harl, and O. Munnich, *La Bible grecque des Septante* (Paris, 1988), 201–222. Harl outlines this typology on p. 203, and then proceeds to discuss each point except for the third.

[9] For analysis of the ancient *testimonia* and modern debates about Aquila, Symmachus, and Theodotion, see Munnich in Dorival, Harl, and Munnich, *Bible grecque*, 143–157; N. Fernández Marcos, *The Septuagint in Context* (Leiden, 2000), 109–154.

[10] For an assessment of these revisions, see Fernández Marcos, *Septuagint*, 247–252. Fernández Marcos accepts Cross' theory of local texts, and accordingly classifies the proto-Lucianic recension as an attempt to align the Greek text with a Palestinian type of Hebrew text (though see his more hesitant statement on p. 235), while the later καίγε revisers sought to align the Greek text with a Babylonian type of Hebrew text (= proto-MT). For Cross' earlier presentation of these same ideas, see "The Evolution of a Theory of Local Texts," in Cross and Talmon, *Qumran*, 306–320; and, more recently, *Epic to Canon*, 216–217. For the debate on the existence of the proto-Lucianic recension, see Fernández Marcos, *Septuagint*, 234–235; Munnich in Dorival, Harl, and Munnich, *Bible grecque*, 169–170.

## Jewish Sources on Greek Scripture

With apparently so many textual choices for those Jews who required (or simply preferred) a Greek translation of scripture, how did they evaluate their options? By which criteria did they judge what should constitute the Bible in Greek? The Jewish reception of the Greek forms of scripture has commanded the attention of scholars for decades. Many studies have focused on the various Greek hebraizing revisions and what these might tell us about the status of the biblical texts in Alexandrian and Palestinian Judaism.[11] Others have examined the tradition of the LXX found in rabbinic literature.[12] Recently, the continued use of Greek scripture among Jews into Late Antiquity has stimulated research.[13] And, of course, the various ancient retellings of the translation story have always featured prominently in such discussions.[14] It is with these retellings that we begin our investigation.

The basic story is well-known and has already received some treatment in this monograph (Chapter Three). According to the *Letter of Aristeas*, written about a century after the events it portrays,[15] Demetrius of Phalerum advised

---

[11] A seminal study is D. Barthélmy, *Les Devanciers d'Aquila* (Leiden, 1963); see also, e.g., S.P. Brock, "To Revise or Not to Revise: Attitudes to Jewish Biblical Translation," in G.J. Brooke and B. Lindars (eds.), *Septuagint, Scrolls, and Cognate Writings* (Atlanta, 1992), 301–338; S. Kreuzer, "From 'Old Greek' to the Recensions: Who and What Caused the Change of the Hebrew Reference Text of the Septuagint," in W. Kraus and R.G. Wooden (eds.), *Septuagint Research* (Atlanta, 2006), 225–237.

[12] G. Veltri, *Eine Tora für den König Talmai* (Tübingen, 1994); idem, "The Septuagint in Disgrace: Some Notes on the Stories on Ptolemy in Rabbinic and Medieval Judaism," in N. de Lange, J.G. Krivoruchko, and C. Boyd-Taylor (eds.), *Jewish Reception of Greek Bible Versions* (Tübingen, 2009). 142–154; E. Tov, "The Rabbinic Tradition concerning the 'Alterations' Inserted into the Greek Translation of the Torah and Their Relation to the Original Text of the Septuagint," *JSJ* 15 (1984): 65–89; repr. in *The Greek and Hebrew Bible* (Leiden, 1999), 1–20; idem, "The Evaluation of the Greek Scripture Translations in Rabbinic Sources," in F. García Martínez and M. Vervenne (eds.), *Interpreting Translation* (Leuven, 2005), 385–399; repr. in *Hebrew Bible, Greek Bible, and Qumran* (Tübingen, 2008), 365–377; A.I. Baumgarten, "Bilingual Jews and the Greek Bible," in J.L. Kugel (ed.), *Shem in the Tents of Japhet* (Leiden, 2002), 13–30; M. Simon-Shoshan, "The Tasks of the Translators: The Rabbis, the Septuagint, and the Cultural Politics of Translation," *Proof* 27 (2007): 1–39.

[13] See esp. T. Rajak, *Translation and Survival* (Oxford, 2009); de Lange, Krivoruchko, and Boyd-Taylor, *Jewish Reception of Greek Bible Versions*.

[14] For the ancient sources of this legend, see P. Wendland, *Aristeae ad Philocratem Epistula* (Leipzig, 1900), which includes an appendix with various Jewish and Christian *testimonia*. The most complete analysis of the legend is A. Wasserstein and D.J. Wasserstein, *The Legend of the Septuagint* (Cambridge, 2006).

[15] Rajak, *Translation and Survival*, 50, represents the consensus when she says about the date of the composition of the *Letter of Aristeas*: "perfectly sustainable hypotheses fall anywhere between c.200 and c.100 BCE." For a justification for designating the author as 'Aristeas' rather than 'Ps-Aristeas,' see S. Honigman, *The Septuagint and Homeric Scholarship*

Ptolemy II Philadelphus, the Hellenistic king of Egypt in the early third century BCE, to acquire for his famous library the divine law of the Jews. The king's interest in this proposal was not dampened when Demetrius told him that these books required translation. He forthwith dispatched a letter to Eleazar, high priest in Jerusalem, requesting accurate scrolls of the Jewish law and sages who could translate them. The seventy-two Jewish scholars who came to Alexandria for the task completed their work in seventy-two days, "as if according to some design" (§ 307). Demetrius gathered the Alexandrian Jews and read out the translation to their hearty approval.

Almost as early as the *Letter of Aristeas*, the obscure figure Aristobulus, a Jewish Hellenistic author of the mid-second century BCE, confirms the basic outline of the *Aristeas* story—King Ptolemy II commissioned Demetrius of Phalerum to oversee the production of a translation of the Jewish law. Josephus also transmits the same basic narrative, which is to be expected since his account (*A.J.* 12.11–118) epitomizes the *Letter of Aristeas*.[16]

We do find important new elements to the developing legend in Philo. For instance, Philo is the first author explicitly to declare the translators inspired.

> καθάπερ ἐνθουσιῶντες προεφήτευον οὐκ ἄλλα ἄλλοι, τὰ δ' αὐτὰ πάντες ὀνόματα καὶ ῥήματα, ὥσπερ ὑποβολέως ἑκάστοις ἀοράτως ἐνηχοῦντος.    (*Mos.* 2.37)

> [The translators ...] as if possessed, prophesied, in the course of translating, not each one something different, but all of them the same nouns and verbs, as if a prompter were invisibly giving them instructions.[17]

What seems to be implied here, and what we encounter explicitly only through later sources, is the separation of the translators from one another, so that they each worked separately on the same portions of the Pentateuch, and each translated in exactly the same way.[18] This is miracle enough, and later Christian writers will employ this tradition as a sign of the authenticity of the LXX. Yet, Philo has another miracle to relate. In the next paragraph he speaks of the relationship between the translation and its *Vorlage*.

---

*in Alexandria* (New York, 2003), 1; Rajak, *Translation and Survival*, 31. For whether we should designate his composition as a 'book' or 'letter,' see the contrasting answers by the same two authors, *locc. citt.* Honigman prefers 'book,' while Rajak prefers the traditional 'letter.'

[16] For Aristobulus, cf. the edition by C.R. Holladay, *Fragments from Hellenistic Jewish Authors*, vol. 3, *Aristobulus* (Atlanta, 1995), frg. 3, p. 156.

[17] This translation is by A. Kamesar, "Biblical Interpretation in Philo," in Kamesar (ed.), *The Cambridge Companion to Philo* (Cambridge, 2009), 65–91 (66).

[18] See, e.g., Simon-Shoshan, "Tasks of the Translators," 15. This interpretation of Philo is rejected by Wasserstein and Wasserstein, *Legend*, 45, who say that the separation of the translators was invented by the Rabbis.

καίτοι τίς οὐκ οἶδεν, ὅτι πᾶσα μὲν διάλεκτος, ἡ δ' Ἑλληνικὴ διαφερόντως, ὀνομάτων πλουτεῖ, καὶ ταὐτὸν ἐνθύμημα οἷόν τε μεταφράζοντα καὶ παραφράζοντα σχηματίσαι πολλαχῶς, ἄλλοτε ἄλλας ἐφαρμόζοντα λέξεις; ὅπερ ἐπὶ ταύτης τῆς νομοθεσίας οὔ φασι συμβῆναι, συνενεχθῆναι δ' εἰς ταὐτὸν κύρια κυρίοις ὀνόμασι, τὰ Ἑλληνικὰ τοῖς Χαλδαϊκοῖς, ἐναρμοσθέντα εὖ μάλα τοῖς δηλουμένοις πράγμασιν.

(*Mos.* 2.38)

Yet who does not know that every language, and Greek in particular, is rich in vocabulary, and it is possible to adorn the same thought in many different ways by metaphrasing and paraphrasing, applying [to the thought] different words on different occasions? It is denied that this occurred in the case of the present translation, but words in their proper meanings corresponded to words in their proper meanings, the Greek to the Chaldean (i.e., Hebrew), with the same sense, perfectly suited to the external realities intended.[19]

A perfect word-for-word and sense-for-sense translation, Philo knows, is impossible; translation is an inexact science, always entailing loss of meaning or nuance because expressions do not transfer perfectly between languages.[20] And yet, says Philo, in the case of this translation by the Seventy sages, the Greek and the Hebrew do match word-for-word and sense-for-sense (ἔν τε τοῖς πράγμασι καὶ τοῖς ὀνόμασι). The translators found Greek words that not only corresponded etymologically to the Hebrew words,[21] but they also perfectly expressed the meaning of the original. The result, as Philo says a couple of paragraphs later, is that a comparison of the Hebrew text and its Greek translation reveals no difference whatsoever between the two. Rather, they are ἀδελφαὶ μᾶλλον δὲ [...] μία καὶ ἡ αὐτὴ ἔν τε τοῖς πράγμασι καὶ τοῖς ὀνόμασι ("sisters, or rather [...] one and the same both in sense and in words"), while the translators were οὐχ ἑρμηνῆς [...] ἀλλ' ἱεροφάνται καὶ προφῆται ("not translators [...] but hierophants and prophets"; *Mos.* 2.40). For Philo, the inspiration of the Seventy translators—their status as "hierophants and prophets"—manifests itself specifically in their ability to produce a Greek version that precisely reproduces its *Vorlage*. This view effectively eliminates the possibility of a hebraizing revision, for any change in the text would constitute a move away from the Hebrew. Certainly Philo has not arrived at this view as a result of his own research into the Greek and

---

[19] Again, the translation (complete with brackets) is by Kamesar, "Biblical Interpretation in Philo," 66–67. See also Kamesar's wider discussion of this passage, pp. 65–71. For Philo's use of the term 'Chaldean' for biblical Hebrew, see above, pp. 123–124, n. 64.

[20] On this aspect of Philo's translation theory as it applies to his views of the LXX, see Simon-Shoshan, "Tasks of the Translators," 8–9.

[21] On Philo's use of the term κύρια in *Mos.* 2.38, see Kamesar, "Biblical Interpretation in Philo," 69.

Hebrew texts; on the contrary, his ignorance of Hebrew no doubt strength-
ened his belief in the authenticity of the LXX. For Philo, the perfection of the
LXX is a matter of dogma likely based on the tradition of reading the Greek
text as the authoritative word of God.

Indeed, several scholars have proposed just this reasoning as an explanation for the *Letter of Aristeas*. This view of the *Letter* entails that its author
aimed in part to canonize the LXX in parallel fashion to the giving of the
Torah on Sinai, thus sanctioning the use of a translation (as opposed to
the original) as sacred literature. Honigman asserts that the growing sanctity of the LXX required justification, because "it is doubtful whether anyone in Ptolemaic Egypt, or indeed the Graeco-Roman world at large, would
have ever considered a freshly made translation of any sacred text as sacred
itself."[22] A survey of the *Letter* suggests that Aristeas intended to sanctify the
translation by equating it with the Hebrew text. A royal initiative secured
the best Hebrew *Vorlagen* from Jerusalem and seventy-two of the best translators (six from each of the by-now theoretical twelve tribes; §§ 28–40), who
demonstrate abundantly their wisdom and adequacy for the task (§§ 187–
294). The translators work together on a secluded island where they complete their work in seventy-two days (§§ 301–307). The king bows before the
translation (§ 317) just as he had earlier bowed before the Hebrew scrolls
(§§ 176–179). The Greek translation has obtained a standing equivalent to

---

[22] Honigman, *Septuagint*, 95. This interpretation of the *Letter* was first worked out in
detail by H.M. Orlinsky, "The Septuagint as Holy Writ and the Philosophy of the Translators," *HUCA* 46 (1975): 89–114. It has largely been accepted by Honigman, op. cit., 53–59; and
B.G. Wright III, "Translation as Scripture: The Septuagint in Aristeas and Philo," in Kraus
and Wooden, *Septuagint Research*, 47–61 (53–57); see also H. Karpp, "'Prophet' oder 'Dolmetscher'? Die Geltung der Septuaginta in der Alten Kirche," in W. Schneemelcher (ed.)
*Festschrift für Günther Dehn* (Neukirchen, 1957), 103–117; repr. in Karpp, *Vom Umgang der
Kirche mit der Heiligen Schrift* (Cologne, 1983), 128–150 (132). While Orlinsky (*art. cit.*, 95, etc.)
and Honigman (op. cit., 125) explicitly endorse the terminology of 'canonization' in this context, Wright does not use this word, but rather speaks of the *Letter* as justifying use of the
translation as "an independent, scriptural authority" (*art. cit.*, 54). Rajak (*Translation and
Survival*, 51) asserts that canonizing the LXX cannot be the "basic reason" for composing the
entire *Letter*, which, to be sure, spends little time addressing the translation itself. However,
Rajak proceeds to note the parallels between our *Letter* and the Sinai narrative in Exodus,
and admits: "The sensitive analysis by Orlinsky 1975 of the working out of the typology of
the Sinai revelation within *Aristeas* remains valuable independently of his conclusions on
canonization" (52 n. 81). But, apart from assigning the various possible purposes of the *Letter*
the status of 'primary' or 'secondary' (see Honigman, op. cit., 37–63, for her view on this), we
may say that if Aristeas depicted the translation in terms of the original giving of the Law, this
would seem necessarily to put the translation on par with the Hebrew text, thus canonizing
it (inasmuch as the Hebrew text itself was deemed 'canonized').

that of the Hebrew text. Indeed, it is this correspondence of the translation to the original that prompts the Alexandrian Jews to pronounce a curse on anyone who would dare modify the translation (§§ 310–311).

> ἐπεὶ καλῶς καὶ ὁσίως διηρμήνευται καὶ κατὰ πᾶν ἠκριβωμένως, καλῶς ἔχον ἐστίν,
> ἵνα διαμένῃ ταῦθ' οὕτως ἔχοντα καὶ μὴ γένηται μηδεμία διασκευή.          (§ 310)

> Since it has been translated well and in a sacred manner and accurately in every way, it is good that it remain just as it is and no alteration should happen.

Again, as for Philo, the exact equivalence between translation and *Vorlage* implies that any alteration in the translation would, in Aristeas' theory, constitute a move away from the Hebrew.[23]

Two significant results emerge from the preceding discussion. (1) The original Hebrew text retained a vital place in the theory of those Jews who relied on the Greek translation. It would seem that Philo and Aristeas, especially, could not bear any deviation whatsoever between the original text and the Bible they used. Aristobulus provides too little information to say what he thought about this issue. As for Josephus, his summary of *Aristeas* softens the rhetoric somewhat but maintains that the Jews decided at the promulgation of the LXX that any subsequent corruption in the Greek text should be corrected (*A.J.* 12.108–109). He does not address himself to the relationship between the LXX and Hebrew text specifically, but his positive portrayal of the translation and his own employment of the LXX allows one to guess that he would have said the two texts were very close.[24] This evaluation of the LXX did not command a consensus of Jewish opinion. We may preview our later discussion of the prologue to Sirach and the rabbinic statements (cf. esp. *b. Meg.* 9a–b) by saying that both represent the LXX as only an imperfect reflection of the original, with the Rabbis even enumerating certain changes made by the translators.

---

[23] On the curse formula, see Orlinsky, "Septuagint," 95–96; Honigman, *Septuagint*, 123–127. For a different view, see Brock, "To Revise," 307, discussed below. M.R. Niehoff, *Jewish Exegesis and Homeric Scholarship in Alexandria* (Cambridge, 2011), 30–37, also emphasizes that *Aristeas* raises the profile of the Hebrew text for his Greek Jewish readers.

[24] On Josephus' views of the LXX, see A. Pelletier, *Flavius Josèphe adaptateur de la Lettre d'Aristée* (Paris, 1962); Brock, "To Revise," 308–309. Ulrich has analyzed Josephus' biblical text for the Books of Samuel and found that he uses the Greek version to the extent that there is no evidence that he so much as refers to the Hebrew; see his *Qumran Text of Samuel*, 223–256; "Josephus's Biblical Text." On the other hand, M. Hengel, *The Septuagint as Christian Scripture* (Grand Rapids, 2002), 77, interprets Josephus as "aware that the Alexandrian translation of the Torah required improvement, and thus justifying the efforts at correction originating in Palestine [...]."

Nevertheless, the Jewish authors encountered in this section who relied on Greek scripture each considered their Bible a (miraculously) accurate translation. Still, they conceived of the Hebrew text as authoritative, and each argued that the translation achieved an authoritative status inasmuch as it corresponded to the Hebrew. We began this section asking how they evaluated the textual options confronting them. We might say that they judged the value of a biblical translation by a 'Hebrew criterion,' and it was the faithfulness, so they argued, of the translation to its Hebrew *Vorlage* that secured the sacred status of the LXX. Of course, we cannot imagine Aristeas and Philo busily comparing their copy of the LXX to the Hebrew text in order to confirm this theory. However, their theory that God was somehow involved in ensuring the accuracy of the LXX meant that they could only evaluate any Greek text deviating from the LXX as an inaccurate translation of the Hebrew.

(2) The second major result echoes a theme we noticed above in Chapter Three: the Jewish sources, including the Rabbis (*b. Meg.* 9a), all limit the translation of the Seventy sages to the Greek Torah. The implications of this fact have been under-appreciated in scholarship. For instance, H.B. Swete opened the second chapter of his *Introduction to the Old Testament in Greek*: "At Alexandria and in Egypt generally the Alexandrian version was regarded, as Philo plainly says, with a reverence scarcely less than that which belonged to the original."[25] Swete was talking about the entire Greek Old Testament; Philo was not. If Philo confined the translation of the Seventy to the Pentateuch, then his reverence for the LXX, his belief in its inspiration, his assertion that it precisely replicated the Hebrew original, also applies only to the Books of Moses. Likewise for Aristeas, Aristobulus, Josephus, and the Rabbis. Whereas the Greek Pentateuch enjoyed widespread esteem and, in the minds of some Jews, divine sanction, this lofty status applied to no other Greek translation. No ancient Jew says in any extant work that the Greek form of any non-Pentateuchal book is inspired, sacred, or even a very good translation.

### Septuagint versus Hebrew in Early Judaism

Scholars often depict ancient Jewish attitudes toward the Greek translations as one of opposition: some Jews favored the original Greek translation of their Bible—here we have especially Philo and the *Letter of Aristeas*—and

---

[25] H.B. Swete, *An Introduction to the Old Testament in Greek*[2], rev. R.R. Ottley (Cambridge, 1914), 29.

these fiercely opposed other Jews who wanted to revise the Greek translation to be more in line with a particular Hebrew text, a position represented especially by the revisers of the proto-Lucianic and καίγε texts, as well as Sirach's grandson. Sebastian Brock famously described this ancient debate with the words, "To Revise or Not To Revise."[26] The two representatives of the 'conservative' position (opposed to revision) both hail from Egypt, where familiarity with Hebrew was rare, while the hebraizing recensional activity took place in Palestine among those who could consult the Hebrew text, just as Ben Sira's grandson migrated to Egypt from Palestine.[27]

This analysis thus neatly divides the Jewish positions into two camps, one pro-LXX, the other pro-Hebrew. Some scholars have seen a similar division in Christian authors and have asserted that it is a reflection of or inheritance from Judaism.[28] However, the problems with such a stark opposition should be obvious by now. While we may concede the existence of a pro-Hebrew group and a pro-LXX group, these categories require further refinement. For one thing, it is not clear that these two groups would have seen themselves as opposed to each other. After all, Philo and Aristeas revered the Hebrew text and denied that the LXX diverged from the original in any way. This corresponds to the first major result in the previous section. But the more pressing issue arises from the second major result, the Jewish restriction of the LXX to the Torah. The proposed opposition between pro-LXX and pro-Hebrew groups obscures the fact that those who praised the LXX were speaking of the Pentateuch alone, while pre-Christian evidence for revisions of the Greek text comes almost entirely from outside the Pentateuch.[29] According to recent introductions to the Greek Bible, neither

---

[26] Brock, "To Revise." Brock's view is now widely accepted; see e.g., Hengel, *Septuagint*, 62; J.W. Wevers, "The Dead Sea Scrolls and the Septuagint," *BIOSCS* 38 (2005): 1–24 (21–22); N. Fernández Marcos, "*Non placet Septuaginta*: Revisions and New Greek Versions of the Bible in Byzantium," in de Lange, Krivoruchko, and Boyd-Taylor, *Jewish Reception of Greek Bible Versions*, 39–50 (39–40).

[27] Brock notices this distinction; "To Revise," 325, 326; and S.P. Brock, "The Phenomenon of Biblical Translation in Antiquity," *Alta* II 8 (1969): 96–102; repr. in S. Jellicoe (ed.), *Studies in the Septuagint* (New York, 1974), 541–571 (553); see also S.P. Brock, "Aspects of Translation Technique in Antiquity," *GRBS* 20 (1979): 69–87.

[28] M. Müller, *The First Bible of the Church* (Sheffield, 1996), 46–97; R.B. ter Haar Romeny, *A Syrian in Greek Dress* (Leuven, 1997), 106–107; R.T. McLay, *The Use of the Septuagint in New Testament Research* (Grand Rapids, 2003), 103; R.G. Wooden, "The Role of 'the Septuagint' in the Formation of the Biblical Canons," in C.A. Evans and E. Tov (eds.), *Exploring the Origins of the Bible* (Grand Rapids, 2008), 129–146 (138–143).

[29] Note how Brock, "To Revise," 303–304, blurs this distinction by speaking of Philo's defense of the Septuagint and the revision of the Septuagint observable in the Greek Minor Prophets Scroll. Similarly, Müller, *First Bible*, 43–44: "already in pre-Christian Judaism we find

the καίγε 'revision' nor the proto-Lucianic recension have left any trace in the Pentateuch, while they are attested for several prophetic, poetic, and historical books.[30] Would Aristeas or Philo have objected to a revision of the Minor Prophets or the historical books of the Bible? They say nothing to indicate that they would have. Presumably the original translators of the Minor Prophets into Greek would not have found a revision of their work necessary, but no evidence suggests that they or those who used their translation would have attributed inspiration or any sort of sanctity to the Old Greek Minor Prophets. The fact that some later καίγε revisers produced a hebraizing revision of the Minor Prophets shows that they had different ideas about what a good translation should look like, but it does not constitute evidence for different views on the sanctity of the Old Greek translations. The same is true for the Greek texts of all the books affected by the proto-Lucianic and καίγε revisions (i.e., books outside the Pentateuch)—apparently they were not considered inspired, whether in Egypt or Palestine. Thus, it is not clear that Aristeas and Philo were reacting against revisions on the order of the καίγε—they apparently did not care about such revisions.

Since the Pentateuch alone among the Greek translations attained a revered and sanctified standing in some ancient Jewish communities, an exploration of ancient Jewish attitudes toward revising the LXX should limit itself to this portion of scripture. Possibly, the translation experienced some revision very early, as some scholars think with regard to the Tabernacle Account at the end of Exodus.[31] But, in fact, the pre-Christian evidence to hand exhibits very little indication of a desire to revise the Greek Pentateuch so that it would match the Hebrew more closely.

---

evidence of a wish to revise the old Greek translation to make it conform to the Hebrew Bible text [...]." This statement is only true for non-Pentateuchal books. The same ideas form the background for the essay by Kreuzer, "From 'Old Greek' to the Recensions."

[30] See Munnich in Dorival, Harl, and Munnich, *Bible grecque*, 159–160; Fernández Marcos, *Septuagint*, 249–250; for the proto-Lucianic recension specifically, see N. Fernández Marcos, "Some Reflections on the Antiochian Text of the Septuagint," in D. Fraenkel, U. Quast, and J.W. Wevers (eds.), *Studien zur Septuaginta—Robert Hanhart zu Ehren* (Göttingen, 1990), 219–229 (220–222). For the possible appearance of the καίγε group in Exodus, see below. On the problem of terminology for what Barthélemy called 'le groupe καίγε,' see L.J. Greenspoon, "The *Kaige* Recension: The Life, Death, and Postmortem Existence of a Modern—and Ancient—Phenomenon," in M.K.H. Peters (ed.), *XII Congress of the IOSCS, Leiden, 2004* (Atlanta, 2006), 5–16.

[31] See S. Jellicoe, *The Septuagint and Modern Study* (Oxford, 1968), 272–276; Munnich in Dorival, Harl, and Munnich, *Bible grecque*, 173–174.

The extant pre-Christian manuscripts of the Greek Pentateuch total nine, five from Qumran and four from Egypt.

| Name | Rahlfs Number | *Verzeichnis* page numbers[32] | Date | Contents |
|---|---|---|---|---|
| P. Ryl. 458 | Ra. 957 | 241–242 | II BCE | Deut. 23–28 |
| P. Fouad 266a | Ra. 942 | 170–171 | I BCE | Gen. 3–38 |
| P. Fouad 266b | Ra. 848 | 171–177 | I BCE | Deut. 17–33 |
| P. Fouad 266c | Ra. 847 | 177–178 | I BCE | Deut. 10–33 |
| 7QLXXExod | Ra. 805 | 154 | 100 BCE | Exod. 28:4–7 |
| 4QLXXLev<sup>a</sup> | Ra. 801 | 150–151 | late II–I BCE | Lev. 26:2–16 |
| pap4QLXXLev<sup>b</sup> | Ra. 802 | 151–152 | I BCE | Lev. 1:11–6:5 |
| 4QLXXNum | Ra. 803 | 152–153 | turn of era | Num. 3:40–4:16 |
| 4QLXXDeut | Ra. 819 | 153–154 | II BCE | Deut. 11:4, etc.? |

Sometimes these witnesses do attest a textual form slightly different from the great Uncials of the fourth century, but there is no consensus on how to interpret this evidence. Some scholars think the early scrolls exhibit hebraizing revision, while other scholars think the scrolls transmit the authentic Old Greek and the later uncials exhibit revision. J.W. Wevers, the editor of the Greek Pentateuch in the Göttingen edition, argued in several publications that even when an early scroll exhibits a hebraized text in certain places, unless one can show a consistent pattern of revision, such instances should be considered unintentional, the product of a scribe saturated with the Hebrew text carelessly copying his Greek *Vorlage*.[33] Wevers' category of 'unconscious revision' easily explains many of the apparent pre-hexaplaric revisions we will notice, and it has thus been echoed by several scholars. For example, Charles Perrot attributes these unconscious revisions to Alexandrian scribes who "*instinctivement*" eliminated differences between Greek and Hebrew based on their theory (which found expression in Philo and Aristeas) that the Greek Pentateuch matched perfectly the Hebrew Torah.[34] In the following survey, we will be looking for evidence of intentional hebraizing revision of the Greek Pentateuch dating to before the turn of the era, or at least by the mid first century CE, so that such

---

[32] A. Rahlfs and D. Fraenkel, *Verzeichnis der griechischen Handschriften des Alten Testaments*, I.1 (Göttingen, 2004).

[33] J.W. Wevers, "Die Methode," in R. Hanhart and Wevers (eds.), *Das Göttinger Septuaginta-Unternehmen* (Göttingen, 1977), 12–19 (17); for other references, see below.

[34] C. Perrot, "L'inspiration des Septante et le pouvoir scripturaire," in G. Dorival and O. Munnich (eds.), Κατα τους ο'—*Selon les Septante* (Paris, 1995), 169–183 (177).

revision could provide background for the statements in the *Letter of Aris-teas* and Philo.

One seemingly clear example of early revision of the Greek Pentateuch is the very fragmentary Exodus scroll from Qumran Cave 7, which preserves 56 letters from Exodus 28:4–7 and is, in the words of its editors, "generally closer to the MT than to the LXX."[35] The fragment as reconstructed in DJD 3 is given below, along with the MT (BHS) and LXX (Wevers). The main differences between the scroll and the LXX have been italicized.[36]

| | MT | 7QLXXExod | Göttingen LXX |
|---|---|---|---|
| verse 4c | ועשו בגדי קדש<br>לאהרן אחיך ולבניו<br>לכהנו לי: | [καὶ ποιήσουσιν στολὰς<br>ἁγίας ᾿Ααρὼν τῷ<br>ἀ]δ[ελ]φ[ῷ σου καὶ τοῖς<br>υἱοῖς α]ὐτοῦ ἱερα[τεύειν<br>αὐτὸν ἐμ]οί. | καὶ ποιήσουσιν στολὰς<br>ἁγίας ᾿Ααρων καὶ τοῖς υἱοῖς<br>αὐτοῦ *εἰς τὸ* ἱερατεύειν μοι. |
| verse 5 | והם יקחו את הזהב<br>ואת התכלת ואת<br>הארגמן ואת תולעת<br>השני ואת השש: | Καὶ αὐ[τοὶ λήμψονται] τὸ<br>χρυσίον [καὶ τὸν ὑάκιν]θον<br>καὶ τὴ[ν πορφύραν καὶ] τὸ<br>κόκκι[νον καὶ τὴν βύσσο]ν. | καὶ αὐτοὶ λήμψονται τὸ<br>χρυσίον καὶ τὴν ὑάκινθον<br>καὶ τὴν πορφύραν καὶ τὸ<br>κόκκινον καὶ τὴν βύσσον. |
| verse 6 | ועשו את האפד זהב<br>תכלת וארגמן תולעת<br>שני ושש משזר מעשה<br>השב: | Κα[ὶ ποιήσουσιν τὴν<br>ἐ]πω[μίδα ἐκ χρυσίου<br>καὶ ὑα]κίν[θου καὶ<br>πορφύρας καὶ κοκκίνου<br>νενησμένου καὶ βύσσου<br>κεκλωσμένης, ἔργον<br>ὑφάντου[37] ποικιλτοῦ·] | Καὶ ποιήσουσιν τὴν<br>ἐπωμίδα *ἐκ βύσσου<br>κεκλωσμένης, ἔργον<br>ὑφαντὸν ποικιλοῦ·* |
| verse 7 | שתי כתפת חברת<br>יהיה לו אל שני<br>קצותיו וחבר | [δύο ἐπωμίδες<br>συνέχουσαι ἔ]σον[ται<br>αὐτῷ ἑτέρα τὴν ἑ]τέρα[ν,<br>ἐπὶ τοῖς δυσὶ μέρεσιν<br>ἐξηρτισμέναι·] | δύο ἐπωμίδες<br>*ἔσονται αὐτῷ* συνέχουσαι<br>ἑτέρα τὴν ἑτέραν, ἐπὶ τοῖς<br>δυσὶν μέρεσιν *ἐξηρτημέναι·* |

---

[35] M. Baillet, J.T. Milik, and R. de Vaux, *Les 'Petites Grottes' de Qumran*, DJD 3 (Oxford, 1962), 142–143.

[36] The transcription reproduced here omits the dots below letters that indicate uncertain readings. No effort has been made to reproduce the line spacing. See also the collation of this fragment and the other Greek biblical texts from Qumran, by Wevers, "Dead Sea Scrolls and the Septuagint," 1–10.

[37] J.W. Wevers, *Exodus*, Septuaginta 2.1 (Göttingen, 1991), gives evidence in his apparatus for both ὑφάντου and ὑφάντον. The DJD editors chose to reconstruct this section of the scroll with the genitive, while Wevers chose the accusative for his text.

The pluses in verses 4 and 6 in 7QLXXExod vis-à-vis the LXX reflect the MT more closely. Perhaps this points to a more extensive effort to revise the Greek Pentateuch in Palestine before the Common Era. Yet, the extreme limitations of the evidence counsels caution in postulating how extensive such a hebraizing effort was. Wevers has evaluated the evidence of pre-Origen recensional activity in Exodus with these words: "the type of possible recensional activity found was on the whole casual. No trace whatsoever was found of the kind of revision identified by Barthélemy as belonging to revisers of the καίγε group."[38] Other texts that might reflect revision of the Greek Pentateuch have also been evaluated in alternative ways. For example, Eugene Ulrich has argued that 4QLXXLev[a] and 4QLXXNum are not revisions but good witnesses to the Old Greek, while Wevers has classified them both as representatives of his 'unconscious revision' category.[39] None of the Qumran LXX fragments necessarily reflects revised texts.

As for the other scrolls, Wevers has discussed in detail the text of P. Fouad 266b (Ra. 848).[40] He does not characterize its text in general as hebraizing, but as a good early witness to the LXX text. Wevers cites only six verses that possibly display influence of the Hebrew text, but he does not conclude for any of these that the scribe intentionally revised the LXX toward the

---

[38] J.W. Wevers, *Text History of the Greek Exodus* (Göttingen, 1992), 40. Here, Wevers refers to his earlier study, "PreOrigen Recensional Activity in the Greek Exodus," in Fraenkel, Quast, and Wevers, *Studien zur Septuaginta*, 121–139. In this paper, Wevers says on the basis of the clear addition in 7QLXXExod (Ra. 805) which brings it into better accord with the MT: "The conclusion that this early Palestinian text was the result of revision based on the Hebrew is inescapable" (123). However, he makes clear at the end of the article that this revision should not be considered systematic (i.e., not like Barthélemy's καίγε group).

[39] Ulrich's evaluation and critical text are found in P.W. Skehan, et al., *Qumran Cave 4, IV*, DJD 9 (Oxford, 1992), 187–194; for analysis, see E. Ulrich, "The Septuagint Manuscripts from Qumran: A Reappraisal of Their Value," in Brooke and Lindars, *Septuagint, Scrolls and Cognate Writings*, 49–80; repr. in *Scrolls and Origins*, 165–183. Agreeing with Ulrich is E. Tov, "The Greek Biblical Texts from the Judean Desert," in S. McKendrick and O. O'Sullivan (eds.), *The Bible as Book: The Transmission of the Greek Text* (London, 2003), 97–122 (106–110 on 4QLXXLev[a], 114–116 on 4QLXXNum). Munnich in Dorival, Harl, and Munnich, *Bible grecque*, 157–158, considers them both literary (non-hebraizing) revisions of the OG, as does Fernández Marcos, *Septuagint*, 251–252. Recently, Nicholas Petersen has also argued that these two scrolls do represent (mostly stylistic) revisions of the Greek text; see "An Analysis of Two Early LXX Manuscripts from Qumran: 4QLXXNum and 4QLXXLev[a] in the Light of Previous Studies," *BBR* 19 (2009): 481–510. For Wevers' opinion, see immediately below.

[40] J.W. Wevers, *Text History of the Greek Deuteronomy* (Göttingen, 1978), 64–85. The three parts of P. Fouad 266 have been published in Z. Aly and L. Koenen (eds.), *Three Rolls of the Early Septuagint* (Bonn, 1980).

Hebrew.[41] Elsewhere, in his article on P. Ryl. 458, Wevers has written that it "illustrates the phenomenon of 'unconscious' revision on the part of a bilingual scribe, a phenomenon also present in 848, and in the Qumran Greek fragments of Exodus, Leviticus and Numbers."[42] In this one statement, Wevers attributes all manuscript evidence of early revision in the Greek Pentateuch to his category of unconscious revision, so that, even where Jewish Greek papyri reflect the Hebrew more closely than does the LXX, this should usually be attributed to unintentional alteration on the part of a scribe imbued with the Hebrew text. If Wevers is correct, there is no evidence in the pre-Christian manuscripts for systematic revision in the Pentateuch toward the Hebrew text before the second century CE.

Other scholars also have a difficult time pinpointing such evidence for revision. Olivier Munnich invokes, besides 7QLXXExod, only the category of unconscious revision formulated by Wevers.[43] Natalio Fernández Marcos cites D.W. Gooding's *Recensions of the Septuagint Pentateuch* in which Gooding sought, in part, to demonstrate the existence of a pre-hexaplaric hebraizing recension of Deuteronomy, based on 235 variants scattered among several Greek manuscripts. Wevers mentions no such recension in his *Text History of the Greek Deuteronomy*, nor does he ever cite Gooding's lecture. In any case, Gooding himself made no attempt to date his proposed recension before the Christian era, so it would not exactly provide the evidence we are seeking.[44]

Dominique Barthélemy cites P. Fouad 266, along with individual words in Aristobulus and Ezekiel the Tragedian.[45] We saw above that Wevers interprets P. Fouad 266b as a good witness to the OG with minor, unintentional revision toward the Hebrew. The examples from Aristobulus and Ezekiel should probably be explained similarly. Barthélemy cites Aristobulus' text of Exod. 3:20 as coming from a revised text. The various readings are as follows.

---

[41] The six verses are Deut. 19:10; 20:20; 22:9b; 31:16, 21, 27. These are discussed in Wevers, *Greek Deuteronomy*, 69–71. For a criticism of Wevers on this point, see the review by K.G. O'Connell in *JBL* 99 (1980): 597–599.

[42] J.W. Wevers, "The Earliest Witness to the LXX Deuteronomy," *CBQ* 39 (1977): 240–244 (quotation from p. 244).

[43] See Munnich in Dorival, Harl, and Munnich, *Bible grecque*, 157–158.

[44] D.W. Gooding, *Recensions of the Septuagint Pentateuch* (London, 1955), 8–14; see Fernández Marcos, *Septuagint*, 251–252; Wevers, *Greek Deuteronomy*.

[45] D. Barthélemy, "Pourqoui la Torah a-t-elle été traduite en grec?" in M. Black and W.A. Smalley (eds.), *On Language, Culture, and Religion* (Paris, 1974), 23–41; repr. in *Études d'histoire du texte de l'Ancien Testament* (Göttingen, 1978), 332–340 (332 n. 24, 333–334 n. 29).

| MT | ושלחתי את ידי והכיתי את מצרים | And I will send my hand and I will strike Egypt |
| LXX | ἐκτείνας τὴν χεῖρα πατάξω τοὺς Αἰγυπτίους | Having stretched out the hand I will strike the Egyptians |
| Aristobulus[46] | ἀποστελῶ τὴν χεῖρά μου καὶ πατάξω τοὺς Αἰγυπτίους | I will send my hand and I will strike the Egyptians |

Aristobulus' text more literally represents the Hebrew than does the LXX, but this meager evidence should be interpreted as reflecting a text 'unconsciously revised,' unless we are able to find more indications of a revised text of Exodus. Aristobulus directly quotes the text of Exodus only three times, all in the same few lines. The LXX of Exod. 13:9 corresponds closely to the MT, so there is no room for a hebraizing revision. For Exod. 9:3, the LXX again closely matches the MT, except that for 'heavy pestilence' (דֶּבֶר כָּבֵד) the LXX has 'great death' (θάνατος μέγας). Whereas Aquila and Symmachus will later produce a more literal rendering of the MT (λοιμὸς βαρύς), Aristobulus does not present a hebraized version, but retains the LXX reading. Thus, the singular reading for Exod. 3:20 offers no warrant for hypothesizing that Aristobulus read an Exodus text intentionally revised toward the Hebrew.

Similarly, Barthélemy claims that Ezekiel the Tragedian used a Greek text for Exodus revised toward the Hebrew,[47] but this evaluation has not been confirmed by later research. Howard Jacobson has shown that where the LXX and MT diverge, Ezekiel consistently follows the LXX.[48] The one passage mentioned by Barthélemy to substantiate a hebraizing recension used by Ezekiel is Exod. 1:5, where Ezekiel agrees with the MT concerning the 70 descendants of Jacob that entered Egypt, while the Septuagint gives the number 75 (though cf. LXX Deut. 10:22).[49] Jacobson questions whether this verse suggests that Ezekiel consulted the Hebrew text directly and concludes that while it is the "most impressive piece of evidence" in this regard, it still does not persuade.[50] We may conclude likewise with regard to the question of whether Ezekiel used a hebraized Greek text. For this

---

[46] For the text of Aristobulus, see fragment 2, line 46 in Holladay, *Fragments*, 3.138. This reading for Exod. 3:20 is found only in Aristobulus, according to the apparatus in Wevers, *Exodus*, 88.

[47] Barthélemy, "Pourquoi," 333–334 n. 29.

[48] H. Jacobson, *The Exagoge of Ezekiel* (Cambridge, 1983), 40–41.

[49] For Ezekiel's text, see Jacobson, *Exagoge*, 50 line 2; or C.R. Holladay, *Fragments from Hellenistic Jewish Authors*, vol. 2: *Poets* (Atlanta, 1989), 346 (frg. 1, line 10).

[50] Jacobson, *Exagoge*, 81.

single instance it would be easy to imagine again an 'unconscious revision,' though Jacobson discusses the matter at length and offers several other possibilities.[51]

As mentioned earlier, the καίγε revision has not been identified for the Pentateuch. However, since the time of Barthélemy the revision/translation under the name of Theodotion has been associated with the καίγε revision, and K.G. O'Connell has presented a detailed argument for locating Theodotion's revision of Exodus within the καίγε tradition and dating it prior to Aquila, i.e., in the first century CE.[52] There are problems with this conclusion. For example, recent work has made the identification of authentic Theodotion material more complicated, as it can no longer be taken for granted that marginalia designated 'θ' in manuscripts derives from this reviser.[53] Also, in his review of O'Connell's monograph, Tov notes that the nature of the evidence ("marginal readings isolated from their context") entails that the demonstration of Theodotion's priority vis-à-vis Aquila is not as convincing as it could be. Nor is it necessarily the case that the more literal version (Aquila) must be subsequent to the less literal version (Theodotion).[54] Finally, scholars no longer envision the καίγε group as a homogenous school, but as a long-standing tradition of literalizing translation that first appears in an incipient form already in the Greek Pentateuch and culminates in the work of Aquila.[55] In light of this last point, locating

---

[51] Jacobson, *Exagoge*, 81–84.

[52] K.G. O'Connell, *The Theodotionic Revision of the Book of Exodus* (Cambridge, Mass., 1972). For reviews of O'Connell's monograph, see those by D. Barthélemy in *Bib* 55 (1974): 91–93, repr. in *Études*, 304–306; and E. Tov in *JBL* 93 (1974): 114–115, both of whom generally endorse O'Connell's conclusions. Note also the recent assessment by Fernández Marcos, *Septuagint*, 147 n. 23: "O'Connell has shown that the θ'-material of Exodus belongs to the καίγε revision." It is unclear how Fernández Marcos reconciles this with his later statement: "It has not been possible to identify either of these two revisions [καίγε or proto-Lucian] in the Pentateuch" (248). J.W. Wevers has not been convinced by O'Connell's attempt to locate Theodotion's Exodus within the καίγε tradition; see "The Interpretive Character and Significance of the LXX," in M. Saebø (ed.), *Hebrew Bible/Old Testament: The History of Its Interpretation* I 1 (Göttingen, 1996), 84–107 (89–90).

[53] See the brief discussion in Fernández Marcos, *Septuagint*, 145–146; T.M. Law, "Origen's Parallel Bible: Textual Criticism, Apologetics, or Exegesis?" *JTS* 59 (2008): 1–21 (8). O'Connell describes his method for isolating readings from Theodotion at *Theodotionic Revision*, 7–8.

[54] For this point, see E. Schürer, *The History of the Jewish People in the Age of Jesus Christ*, rev. G. Vermes et al., 3 vols. (Edinburgh, 1973–1985), 3.1.503.

[55] See the assessment of P. Gentry, *The Asterisked Materials in the Greek Job* (Atlanta, 1995), 495–499; idem, "The Place of Theodotion-Job in the Textual History of the Septuagint," in A. Salvesen (ed.), *Origen's Hexapla and Fragments* (Tübingen, 1998), 199–229; [R.]T. McLay, *The OG and Th Versions of Daniel* (Atlanta, 1996), 219–222. See also O. Munnich, "Contribution à l'étude de la première révision de la Septante," *ANRW* II.20.1 (New York, 1987), 190–220.

the Theodotion version of Exodus within the καίγε tradition and prior to Aquila would not require a date earlier than the early second century CE; in fact, this dating roughly corresponds to O'Connell's suggestion that the final form of Theodotion's Exodus existed "at least by the late first century A.D."[56]

All the examples of systematic hebraizing revision of the Greek Pentateuch by Philo's time amount to very little. Revisers certainly were at work, as attested most dramatically by the Greek Minor Prophets Scrolls, but the Greek Pentateuch seems to have been largely immune to such activity. As Charles Perrot has written, "Le Pentateuque grec, au statut normatif solide, a mieux résisté que les autres livres à ce mouvement de <<retour à hébreu>> qui traversa apparemment la Diaspora dès le premier siècle avant notre ère."[57] The significance of this fact has largely gone unnoticed as scholars pit Philo and Aristeas against the revisers in a battle over the LXX. Even Wevers, whom we have cited frequently in these pages as denying systematic pre-hexaplaric revision of the Pentateuch, considered the revision evident in the Greek Minor Prophets Scrolls to represent an opposition to Philo's insistence on the inspiration of the LXX.[58] Our discussion has demonstrated the weakness in this analysis. Philo's views would not necessarily entail any opposition to revision outside the Pentateuch, and revision of the Pentateuch itself is only poorly attested by his time.

If there is yet evidence for an ancient Jewish debate concerning the best text of the Greek Bible, perhaps it appears in Sirach's prologue or the curse formula in Aristeas (§§ 310–311). As for the prologue to Sirach, the crucial sentence says, οὐ γὰρ ἰσοδυναμεῖ αὐτὰ ἐν ἑαυτοῖς Ἑβραϊστὶ λεγόμενα καὶ ὅταν μεταχθῇ εἰς ἑτέραν γλῶσσαν, translated in the NRSV as "For what was originally expressed in Hebrew does not have exactly the same sense when translated into another language."[59] This text and translation seems to indicate that the Greek and Hebrew texts diverge in meaning—they are not exact equivalents, *contra* Philo and Aristeas. However, Benjamin Wright interprets these words not as pointing to the inadequacy of the Greek translations vis-à-vis the Hebrew, but as pointing to their inadequacy vis-à-vis literary Greek. According to Wright, the statement from the Sirach prologue should be read in view of the audience for which it was written,

---

[56] O'Connell, *Theodotionic Version*, 292.
[57] Perrot, "L'inspiration des Septante," 177.
[58] Wevers, "Dead Sea Scrolls and the Septuagint," 21.
[59] This sentence forms lines 21–22 in the critical edition by J. Ziegler, *Sapientia Iesu Filii Sirach²*, Septuaginta 12.2 (Göttingen, 1980), 125.

i.e., a Jewish readership ignorant of Hebrew and unable to compare the two texts. This, along with the fact that the grandson's translation itself exhibits poor literary Greek, indicates that the clause οὐ ... ἰσοδυναμεῖ does not refer to a distinction in meaning between original and translation, but should be given a different interpretation. In Wright's view,

> the grandson is claiming that because his product is a *translation* it does not have the same *rhetorical power or force* in Greek as the original Hebrew, not necessarily that things in Hebrew do no have the same *meaning* when translated into another language. And, in fact, the lack of rhetorical power in the Greek of the translation is apparent throughout.[60]

If this interpretation is correct, Ben Sira's grandson will not have considered hebraizing recensions particularly useful or necessary. However, even if Wright's views are overturned and the traditional interpretation represented above by the NRSV is vindicated, still the prologue would not necessarily favor revisions of the Greek. For, the grandson seems to be resigned to the fact that the Hebrew and Greek will be different, without much possibility of closing the gap, whether semantic or literary. Thus, though this prologue does offer important evidence for the view that the LXX does not replicate the Hebrew Torah, contrary to Philo and Aristeas, it seems best to leave it out of the discussion of ancient attitudes toward revisions of the LXX.

The curse concluding the translation story in the *Letter of Aristeas* might reflect a negative attitude toward revisions that had already begun appearing.[61] However, we earlier noted the interpretation of the *Letter* that con-

---

[60] B.G. Wright, III, "Why a Prologue? Ben Sira's Grandson and His Greek Translation," in S. Paul, et al. (eds.), *Emanuel* (Leiden, 2003), 633–644 (quotation from p. 640, italics in original). For clues in the prologue to the translation's intended audience, see Wright's discussion on p. 636. See also idem, "Access to the source: Cicero, Ben Sira, the Septuagint and their Audience," *JSJ* 34 (2003): 1–27. Wright's reading of Sirach's prologue is accepted by Honigman, *Septuagint*, 125. For another view, see G. Veltri, *Libraries, Translations, and 'Canonic' Texts* (Leiden, 2006), 197–201. On the semantic range of the verb ἰσοδυναμέω, see D. De Crom, "Translation Equivalence in the Prologue to Greek Ben Sirach," in M.K.H. Peters (ed.), *XIII Congress of the IOSCS. Ljubljana, 2007* (Atlanta, 2008), 99–111. Wright responds to criticisms of his proposal in "Translation Greek in Sirach in Light of the Grandson's Prologue," in J.-S. Rey and J. Joosten (eds.), *The Texts and Versions of the Book of Ben Sira* (Leiden, 2011), 75–94. On the literary character of the translation, see, in the same volume, J.K. Aitken, "The Literary Attainment of the Translator of Greek Sirach," 95–126.

[61] So Brock, "To Revise," 334, who cites (n. 11) in favor of this view A.F.J. Klijn, "The Letter of Aristeas and the Greek Translation of the Pentateuch in Egypt," *NTS* 11 (1965): 154–158; Barthélemy, "Pourquoi," 331–333; and Orlinsky, "Septuagint." However, I have not discovered where Orlinsky advocates the view that the *Letter of Aristeas* sought to discourage revision of

siders it as promoting the Greek text as a reproduction of the Hebrew, thus sanctioning its use as holy scripture. On this view, the curse may be merely a formula involved in canonizing documents.[62] As for the 'anti-revision' interpretation, Rajak offers the perceptive criticism that such an understanding of the *Letter* "requires extensive reading between the lines, as well as a focus restricted to a very small part of the narrative."[63]

Thus, the case for an ancient dispute between those favoring and those opposing revision of the LXX requires some nuancing. There were some Jews in the Diaspora, especially as represented by the Alexandrians Aristeas and Philo, who revered the Greek Pentateuch as possessing a sanctity independent of the Hebrew. There were also some Jews, especially in Palestine, who produced hebraizing revisions of Greek biblical books outside the Pentateuch. Evidence for pre-hexaplaric revision of the Greek Pentateuch is meager and ambiguous. As Olivier Munnich has said in regard to the LXX Pentateuch:

> L'absence d'une recension lucianique—si exceptionnelle dans la Bible grecque—prouve indirectement que la traduction a été jugée satisfaisante et qu'elle n'a donné lieu ni à contestation ni à refection. En somme, le texte grec du Pentateuque apparaît exceptionnellement unifié et stable par rapport à celui de nombreux livres historiques et prophétiques.[64]

The Judaean Desert Discoveries have shown that multiple Hebrew textual forms of certain biblical books circulated in ancient Palestine, and the evidence for these Hebrew textual forms includes the Pentateuch. We also have evidence for multiple Greek textual forms for certain biblical books, but this evidence does not include the Pentateuch. Perhaps future discoveries will provide such evidence. The Greek revisional activity for which we do

---

the Greek Pentateuch. Rather, as we saw earlier, Orlinsky interprets the *Letter* as canonizing the Greek text, thereby justifying its use as opposed to the Hebrew text, rather than as opposed to Greek revisions.

[62] On the curse formula, compare Brock, "To Revise," 307; and Orlinsky, "Septuagint," 95–96. Honigman (*Septuagint*, 123–127) argues also that any dissatisfaction with the LXX evident in the curse may have arisen from the instability in the manuscript tradition (attested by the extant early papyri) rather than any misgivings about the quality of the original translation. Niehoff, *Jewish Exegesis*, 20–25, associates the curse formula with textual scholarship on the Homeric epics, so that *Aristeas* would be discouraging the application of Aristarchus' methods to the Greek biblical text.

[63] Rajak, *Translation and Survival*, 51.

[64] O. Munnich, "Le texte du Pentateuque grec et son histoire," in C. Dogniez and M. Harl (eds.), *Le Pentateuque d'Alexandrie* (Paris, 2001), 51–59 (55). Munnich's later statement on the same page that Jews began revising the LXX perhaps at the end of the first century BCE (though, to be sure, he suggests this date with a question mark) is not borne out by the evidence he cites.

have direct evidence at present, however, such as is provided by the Greek Minor Prophets Scroll, would not have caused a problem for Philo or Aristeas. These authors concerned themselves only with the Greek version of the Pentateuch.

If we ask why there might have been a reluctance to revise the LXX Pentateuch but no similar reluctance to revise other Greek biblical translations, the answer would surely point to the prestige achieved by this text among Jews in antiquity, a prestige arising from its time-hallowed use among Greek-speaking Jews (in the Diaspora and Palestine) and from the translation legend.[65] Even the Rabbis echo this legend, including the attribution of the translation to an act of God (*b. Meg.* 9a). In fact, a search for criticism directed toward the Greek Pentateuch in Early Judaism produces surprisingly few results. Only Sirach's prologue might imply a criticism, but it probably simply addresses a perennial problem of the nature of translation, an activity in which the author of the prologue himself participates. Only with Aquila's translation in the second century CE do we have evidence that someone thought to improve upon the LXX Pentateuch. Before that, it would seem, the unique status of the Greek Pentateuch may have played a role in averting revisional activity within this portion of the Greek Bible.

## The Continued Use of Greek Scripture in Judaism

We turn now to the later period, from the second century CE and on, a time when Greek-speaking Jews had some choices for their preferred Bible. Did the newer versions by Aquila, Symmachus, and Theodotion make any headway among Jewish communities, or did they instead use the OG translations? Unfortunately, for this period we run up against the problem of a severe lack of evidence. How do we know what Bible translation Greek-speaking Jews used in the second to fifth centuries, and later? What evidence could there be? For the earlier period, concluding with the first century CE, we have relied on the literature produced by the Greek-speaking Jews themselves, but we discover a remarkable dearth of literary production for the later period. There are, perhaps, some examples, but none that would provide ready information about the nature of the biblical text in use among these Jews.[66]

---

[65] On the status of the LXX Pentateuch in Egypt and Palestine, see Dorival in Dorival, Harl, and Munnich, *Bible grecque*, 119–125; for Alexandria, see Barthélemy, "Pourquoi," 336–337.

[66] For a recent argument that the Jews of the Western Diaspora produced much of the pseudepigrapha, see A. Edrei and D. Mendels, "A Split Jewish Diaspora: Its Dramatic Consequences," *JSP* 16 (2007): 91–137; 17 (2008): 163–187. However, see also on the pseudepigrapha

Fergus Millar notes this lack of literature and advises that any historical information about Diaspora Jews at this time must come from inscriptions, iconography, and Christian sources.[67] We could also add, for our purposes, biblical manuscripts. However, while there do seem to be preserved Common-Era Jewish papyri of Greek translations for some books, the evidence is fragmentary and highly ambiguous because it is often difficult to conclude whether a given biblical fragment is Jewish or Christian.[68] For example, even the palimpsest fragments of Aquila found in the Cairo Genizah could very well have been Christian copies that Jews later acquired as scrap for the purpose of re-using for other documents, though Septuagint scholars usually assume the Jewish origin of these fragments.[69] The present state of research does not permit firm conclusions based on the preserved papyri. So too with regard to iconography; it just does not offer much help in deciphering the textual choices of ancient Jews. And so, James Aitken remarks of inscriptions, "they are our only Jewish Greek sources from this period (third to seventh centuries)."[70] We should also add, as Millar advises us, Christian *testimonia* as a possible avenue of research, and we must take into account the complex attitudes evident in rabbinic literature. What do these say about the Jewish Greek biblical text in the second century and later?

---

J.R. Davila, *The Provenance of the Pseudepigrapha* (Leiden, 2005). For other literature possibly produced by Diaspora Jews, see L.V. Rutgers, *The Hidden Heritage of Diaspora Judaism* (Leuven, 1998), 235–284. But according to F. Millar, there is no Diaspora literature after Josephus; see "The Many Worlds of the Late Antique Diaspora: Supplements to the *Cambridge History of Judaism* vol. IV," *JJS* 59 (2008): 120–138 (122). For a response to the theory of Edrei and Mendels, see F. Millar, "A Rural Jewish Community in Late Roman Mesopotamia, and the Question of a 'Split' Jewish Diaspora," *JSJ* 42 (2011): 351–374.

[67] F. Millar, "Christian Emperors, Christian Church and the Jews of the Diaspora in the Greek East, CE 379–450," *JJS* 55 (2004): 1–25 (3).

[68] See R.A. Kraft, "The 'Textual Mechanics' of Early Jewish LXX/OG Papyri and Fragments," in McKendrick and O'Sullivan, *Bible as Book: Greek Text*, 51–72, updated online at http://www.sas.upenn.edu/religious_studies/rak/earlylxx/jewishpap.html.

[69] See E.L. Gallagher, "The Religious Provenance of the Aquila Fragments from the Cairo Genizah," *JJS* (forthcoming). The fragments were first published in F.C. Burkitt, *Fragments of the Books of Kings according to the Translation of Aquila* (Cambridge, 1897); C. Taylor, *Hebrew-Greek Cairo Genizah Palimpsests from the Taylor-Schechter Collection* (Cambridge, 1900). Paleographical analysis suggests a date in the sixth century; see N. Tchernetska, "Greek Oriental Palimpsests in Cambridge: Problems and Prospects," in C. Holmes and J. Waring (eds.), *Literacy, Education and Manuscript Transmission in Byzantium and Beyond* (Leiden, 2002), 243–256 (246–247). An argument in behalf of a Christian origin was presented in M. Sokoloff and J. Yahalom, "Christian Palimpsests from the Cairo Geniza," *Revue d'Histoire des Textes* 8 (1978): 109–132 (109–111).

[70] J.K. Aitken, "Jewish Use of Greek Proverbs," in de Lange, Krivoruchko, and Boyd-Taylor, *Jewish Reception of Greek Bible Versions*, 53–77 (61).

The number of Jewish inscriptions containing a quotation of the Bible in Greek is quite small, and therefore the evidence is not very impressive.[71] Most striking are the three quotations of Prov. 10:7, all in Roman catacombs, perhaps all from the third century, and each transmitting a different text. One of them transmits Aquila's reading (*JIWE* 2.112), one is closer to the OG (*JIWE* 2.307), and the third exhibits a mixture of these two (*JIWE* 2.276).[72] A couple of inscriptions in Acmonia, apparently from the Jewish community there, reflect the OG of Zech. 5:1 (*IJudO* 2.175, 176).[73] Another inscription in a synagogue in Nicaea contains a Psalms verse apparently according to Aquila's version (*IJudO* 2.153).[74]

Finally, an inscription from what may be a synagogue in Caesarea Maritima contains a quotation from Isaiah 40:31—εἰ ὑπομέ[ν]ονταις [τόν θ(εὸ)ν ἀ]λλάξο(υ)σιν [ἰσχύ]ν.[75] If this reconstruction by L. Michael White is correct, it matches precisely the OG reading. Since it is in a site that has been classified by some as a synagogue, this could be evidence for continued use of the OG in Judaism. However, it is not at all clear that the site actually is a

---

[71] On the current state of research into ancient Jewish inscriptions, see P.W. van der Horst, "*Inscriptiones Judaicae Orientis*: A Review Article," *JSJ* 36 (2005): 65–83. Epigraphic biblical quotations have recently received attention from S. Cappelletti, "Biblical Quotations in the Greek Jewish Inscriptions of the Diaspora," in de Lange, Krivoruchko, and Boyd-Taylor, *Jewish Reception of Greek Bible Versions*, 128–141; Aitken, "Jewish Use," 61–65; D. Lincicum, "The Epigraphic Habit and the Biblical Text: Inscriptions as a Source for the Study of the Greek Bible," *BIOSCS* 41 (2008): 84–92; P.W. van der Horst, *Ancient Jewish Epitaphs* (Kampen, 1991), 37–39. See also the indices of biblical passages in each of the recent collections of Jewish inscriptions (except for *IJudO* 2): *JIGRE* 282–286 (though Cappelletti, *art. cit.*, 138, says of Egypt: "no evidence of clear quotations has been found"); *JIWE* 1.332; 2.540; *IJudO* 1.387; 3.276.

[72] See van der Horst, *Epitaphs*, 37–38; M. Williams, *The Jews among the Greeks and Romans* (Baltimore, 1998), 121; Aitken, "Jewish Use," 61–65; Cappelletti, "Biblical Quotations," 131–132.

[73] On the Jewishness of these inscriptions, see the discussion by Ameling in *IJudO* 2, pp. 373–374, p. 375, who leaves open the possibility of a Christian origin for both inscriptions; see also P. Trebilco, *Jewish Communities in Asia Minor* (Cambridge, 1991), 74–76. Both inscriptions contain the phrase τὸ ἀρᾶς δρέπανον, a reflection of LXX Zech. 5:1, which speaks of a δρέπανον πετόμενον, whereas the MT reads מגלה עפה. For the reading of the Greek minor versions, which all reflect MT accurately, see Jerome's comment on Zech. 5:1.

[74] See A. Salvesen, "Psalm 135(136):25 in a Jewish Greek Inscription from Nicaea," in G. Khan (ed.), *Semitic Studies in Honour of Edward Ullendorff* (Leiden, 2005), 212–221. Salvesen concludes (p. 219) that even if the inscription does not represent Aquila's translation, it still represents a preference for his literal style of translation.

[75] See M. Govaars, M. Spiro, and L.M. White, *Field O: The "Synagogue" Site* (Boston, 2009), inscription 2 on pp. 159–161, where White discusses his reconstruction and the orthography. I thank Prof. Jodi Magness for referring me to this inscription and its publication, and for sharing with me her review, published in *AJA* 114 (2010), online at http://www.ajaonline.org/pdfs/book_reviews/114.1/23_Magness.pdf.

synagogue, as the quotation marks in the title of the volume indicate (*The "Synagogue" Site*) and as Govaars makes clear.[76] Indeed, it would be quite surprising to find a Jewish community still reading the OG of Isaiah at this time—White suggests that the orthography points to a date in the early seventh century[77]—especially since it was this very version and book that created so much controversy earlier with its translation παρθένος ('virgin') at Isa. 7:14.[78] Moreover, the preserved portion of the inscription does not necessarily point exclusively to the OG of Isa. 40:31. While Aquila is unattested for the first part of this verse, he did use the same translation equivalents as we see in the inscription: קוה = ὑπομένω; hiphil of חלף = ἀλλάσσω; כח = ἰσχύς.[79] If Aquila's rendering of this verse were similar to that of the OG, this could explain why we have no evidence for it. As Alison Salvesen says, "often only the more interesting changes from LXX have been recorded."[80]

This limited epigraphic evidence indicates that while some Jews used the OG of Proverbs and the Minor Prophets, and maybe other books, into Late Antiquity, other Greek-speaking Jews began adopting Aquila's version, at least for some books. We do not know, however, what these Jews thought about these two versions, or even if they made their textual choices based on anything other than the availability of a particular scroll.

The Christian evidence is somewhat more explicit, even if also limited and open to various interpretations. There are, apparently, only two Church Fathers during the classical Patristic period who plainly assert that contemporary Jews use the translation by Aquila.[81] Augustine's information (*Civ.* 15.23) could well derive from other Christians, and so one may question its value as an independent report. The testimony of Origen is all-together different. In his *Ep. Afr.* 4, he explains that Aquila is:

---

[76] See her "Final Analysis and Conclusions," in Govaars, Spiro, and White, *Field O*, 123–143, esp. on Strata IV and V, pp. 127–136.

[77] Govaars, Spiro, and White, *Field O*, 161.

[78] For this controversy, see below in our discussion of the pre-Origen Fathers.

[79] For Aquila's translation equivalents, see J. Reider and N. Turner, *An Index to Aquila* (Leiden, 1966); for the attestation of Aquila for Isa. 40:31, see the second apparatus in J. Ziegler, *Isaias*, Septuaginta 14 (Göttingen, 1983), 271. Aquila's translation would have diverged from the OG in its rendering of the Tetragrammaton in the MT of Isa. 40:31, which appears in the OG, and in White's reconstruction, as ὁ θεός.

[80] Salvesen, "Jewish Greek Inscription," 215. See Salvesen's entire study for a good example of how to compare the biblical text in inscriptions to the ancient Greek translations known to us.

[81] This is according to the article by J.R. Labendz, "Aquila's Bible Translation in Late Antiquity: Jewish and Christian Perspectives," *HTR* 102 (2009): 353–388.

φιλοτιμότερον πεπιστευμένος παρὰ Ἰουδαίοις ἡρμηνευκέναι τὴν γραφήν, ᾧ μάλιστα εἰώθασιν οἱ ἀγνοοῦντες τὴν Ἑβραίων διάλεκτον χρῆσθαι, ὡς πάντων μᾶλλον
ἐπιτετευγμένῳ.

believed among Jews to have translated Scripture more zealously, whose
translation those not knowing the language of the Hebrews have become
especially accustomed to use, considering it the most successful of all.

One should not lightly dismiss Origen's testimony, for he certainly interacted with Jews and took great care not only to debate them but also to
learn from them.[82]

Precisely such Christian testimony serves as part of the foundation for
the traditional view that Jews from the second century CE forward rejected
the LXX, either because of its appropriation by Christians or because of
its divergences from the newly canonical MT, or both.[83] Some passages in
rabbinic literature seem to bear this out. Whereas the LXX is never cited
in rabbinic literature, except in the context of certain changes made by
the translators (cf. *b. Meg.* 9a–b), the translation of Aquila seems to meet
rabbinic approval and is cited ten times in the literature.[84] At about the
same time as Aquila, Justin Martyr bemoans the dissatisfaction with the
LXX among the Jewish teachers and asserts that they have made their own
translation (*Dial.* 68.7). At *Sop.* 1.7, the Rabbis compare the production of

---

[82] The basic study in this regard is N.R.M. de Lange, *Origen and the Jews* (Cambridge, 1976).

[83] E.g. Jellicoe, *Septuagint and Modern Study*, 74–76; Tov, *Textual Criticism*, 141; Hengel, *Septuagint*, 43–47; Müller, *First Bible*, 40–41; Karpp, "'Prophet' oder 'Dolmetscher'," 133–134; Dorival in Dorival, Harl, and Munnich, *Bible grecque*, 120–124.

[84] On the reception of Aquila among the Rabbis, see G. Veltri, "Der griechische Tar-gum Aquilas: Ein Beitrag zum rabbinischen Übersetzungsverständnis," in M. Hengel and A.M. Schwemer (eds.), *Die Septuaginta* (Tübingen, 1994), 92–115; repr. in Veltri, *Gegenwart der Tradition* (Leiden, 2002), 75–103; idem, *Libraries*, 168–189; Tov, "Evaluation," 373; Labendz, "Aquila's Bible Translation." For lists of the quotations of Aquila in rabbinic literature, see J. Reider, *Prolegomena to a Greek-Hebrew and Hebrew-Greek Index to Aquila* (Philadelphia, 1916), 151–155 (who omits the quotation of Aquila's translation of Prov. 25:11 in *Gen. Rab.* 93 3); Veltri, "Griechische Targum," 83–90, but he incorrectly lists the citation in *Esth. Rab.* 2.7 as from Esth. 2:13, when it is actually from Esth. 1:6 (correctly cited in Veltri, *Libraries*, 183); Labendz, "Aquila's Bible Translation," 365, who includes in her list two citations (Lev. 19:20 in *y. Qidd.* 1:1, 59a; Dan. 8:13 in *Gen. Rab.* 21.1) that appear only in Hebrew (no Hebrew translit-eration of the Greek). She also excludes the citation in *Esth. Rab.* 2.7 because of the late date of this midrash (see her principles regarding this on p. 354). For the view that the Rabbis pro-moted some Greek translations, including Aquila, Symmachus, and some elements of the καίγε revision, see P.S. Alexander, "The Cultural History of the Ancient Bible Versions: The Case of Lamentations," in de Lange, Krivoruchko, and Boyd-Taylor, *Jewish Reception of Greek Bible Versions*, 78–102 (80–90); but this idea is directly challenged by Labendz, "Aquila's Bible Translation."

the LXX to that of the golden calf (*Sop.* 1.7), and elsewhere they lament that by its use the Gentiles could claim, "We are Israel."[85]

On the other hand, these last statements come in only very late documents,[86] and quite a bit of recent scholarship has attempted to demonstrate that the Jews did not abandon the LXX in the first few centuries CE. Wasserstein and Wasserstein cast doubt on the two alleged motives for the rabbinic rejection of the LXX—Christian appropriation and a desire for a Greek translation matching the MT. They assert that "[t]here is evidence of Jewish use of the LXX for many generations after Aquila," but to substantiate this statement they can cite only the limited and ambiguous epigraphic evidence along with Justinian's *Nov.* 146.[87] This decree allows for Jewish reading of scripture in the vernacular (as opposed to exclusive use of Hebrew) and names the LXX as the primary translation to be used in a Greek context. Perhaps this attests a continuing use of the LXX in Judaism, though recent studies have doubted its value as a historical witness to Judaism, and in any case, its grudging allowance for the use of Aquila might instead imply that the Jews receiving this decree would rather read the more literal translation.[88] Veltri points out that Tertullian (*Apologet.* 18.9) represents Jews as still reading the LXX during his time, a rare patristic acknowledgment of this.[89] Aitken looks for evidence of familiarity on the part of the Rabbis with the

---

[85] For this latter statement, cf. Tanhuma, *Ki Tissa* 34; and see Wasserstein and Wasserstein, *Legend*, 62.

[86] However, see Simon-Shoshan, "Tasks of the Translators," 24, for an argument that these sentiments, and even the documents transmitting them, may be rather early, Amoraic or even Tannaitic.

[87] Wasserstein and Wasserstein, *Legend*, 61–63. Rajak, *Translation and Survival*, 302–303, also makes the argument from Justinian's *Nov.* 146. On the theme of continuing Jewish use of the LXX, see also W. Adler, "'What the Hebrews Say': Translation, Authority, and the Story of Susanna and the Elders," in F.W. Knobloch (ed.), *Biblical Translation in Context* (Bethesda, Md., 2002), 19–39 (19–21).

[88] Cf. Swete, *Introduction*, 33; Jellicoe, *Septuagint and Modern Study*, 77; Munnich in Dorival, Harl, and Munnich, *Bible grecque*, 147. For the text of Justinian's decree, see A. Linder, *The Jews in Roman Imperial Legislation* (Detroit, 1987), 402–411. For recent studies doubting the usefulness of the decree for supplying information about Judaism, see G. Veltri, "Die Novelle 146 περὶ Ἑβραίων: Das Verbot des Targumvortrags in Justinians Politik," in Hengel and Schwemer, *Die Septuaginta*, 116–130; L.V. Rutgers, "Justinian's Novella 146 between Jews and Christians," in R. Kalmin and S. Schwartz (eds.), *Jewish Culture and Society under the Christian Roman Empire* (Leuven, 2003), 385–406; repr. in *Making Myths* (Leuven, 2009), 49–77. For a more positive evaluation of the historical usefulness of the decree, see W. Smelik, 'Justinian's Novella 146 and Contemporary Judaism,' in T.M. Law and A.G. Salvesen (eds.), *Greek Scriptures and the Rabbis* (Leuven, *forthcoming*). (I thank Prof. Smelik for sharing with me his essay prior to its publication.)

[89] Veltri, *Libraries*, 51.

OG Proverbs, but his three examples of shared exegetical features (*m. Yoma* 3.9–11; *Avot* 4.1; *Lev. Rab.* 21.5) do not demonstrate any direct influence.[90] Rajak deconstructs the 'abandonment theory' long held by scholars and suggests alternative interpretations to the Christian sources that are usually cited as evidence that Jews gave up on the LXX. But again, she can find very little positive evidence for continued Jewish use of the traditional translations.[91] These studies have successfully called into question the view that Jews stopped using the LXX early in the second century CE, but they have failed to produce much new evidence with which to construct an alternative view.

We have seen that the limited epigraphic evidence indicates that some Jews in Late Antiquity used the OG of some books, other Jews used the translation of Aquila for some books. Origen claims that Jews use Aquila, while Tertullian says they use the LXX. The sanctity of the LXX within Judaism, as attested explicitly by Philo and Aristeas, probably anchored the traditional translation within some streams of Judaism, so that they would resist exchanging their Bible for a new one.[92] However, we should remind ourselves once again that all of our Jewish sources speak only of the Pentateuch as the LXX, and it was this portion of scripture alone that was ever deemed an 'inspired' translation among Jews.[93] Therefore, while the LXX Pentateuch might have enjoyed an entrenched place in Jewish society, this was not necessarily true for any other Greek translation.

Furthermore, Philo and Aristeas locate the element of inspiration specifically in the miraculous (at least for Philo) correspondence between the Greek translation and the Hebrew *Vorlage*. These Hellenistic Jewish authors evince a concern for a translation agreeing completely with the Hebrew text. Of course, Philo did not understand the extent to which the Greek Pentateuch differed from the Hebrew Torah. When once these differences became common knowledge, surely a great many Jews, now forced to choose between the LXX and the Hebrew text, would follow their theoretical position that a good translation must match the Hebrew. How much more would this be the case with regard to the non-Pentateuchal books, whose OG translations did not command the same level of esteem. Earlier

---

[90]  Aitken, "Jewish Use," 65–76.

[91]  Rajak, *Translation and Survival*, 278–313.

[92]  See esp. Rajak, *Translation and Survival*, 303–313.

[93]  Rajak, *Translation and Survival*, 313, acknowledges this, but the general tenor of her final chapter seems insufficiently to take it into consideration.

we saw that Origen depicts precisely this scenario as an actual fact—Jews who could not read Hebrew adopted Aquila's version because it was the closest to the Hebrew (*Ep. Afr.* 4).

When did the divergences between the Hebrew Torah and LXX Pentateuch become more widely publicized? Our earlier discussion highlighted the stability of the text of the Greek Pentateuch through the first century CE, so apparently divergences between translation and original did not at this time cause concern. During the second century, we have two indications that, at least within the rabbinic movement, the differences between the texts were more clearly perceived. First, the very production of Aquila's translation, which had some association with the Rabbis, and perhaps Symmachus' version as a successor, suggests some dissatisfaction with the traditional translation.[94] The nature of Aquila's translation demonstrates that the dissatisfaction would have resulted from a perceived failure in the LXX to render precisely its source text.

Second, probably around the same time as Aquila's activity the Rabbis formulated the list of changes made by the Seventy-two sages in their translation.[95] The Rabbis say that the king separated the translators and commanded them to 'write' the Torah of Moses. With the help of the Holy One, they produced identical translations, which included a number of changes in the text (*b. Meg.* 9a–b). This complex story has elicited various contradictory interpretations; scholars do not even agree as to whether the Rabbis evaluate these 'inspired changes' positively or negatively.[96] We

---

[94]  For the reception of Aquila's translation among the Rabbis, see our discussion above, along with A. Paul, "La Bible grecque d'Aquila et l'idéologic du judaïsme ancien," in *ANRW* II.20.1 (New York, 1987), 221–245; but for a more skeptical assessment of Aquila's relationship to the Rabbis, see Labendz, "Aquila's Bible Translation." For Symmachus' association with the rabbinic movement, see A. Salvesen, *Symmachus in the Pentateuch* (Manchester, 1991), 283–297; Alexander, "Cultural History," 80–90.

[95]  Wasserstein and Wasserstein, *Legend*, 68, locate the origins of the 'alterations' tradition in the Yavnean Period (ca. 80–117 CE); Tov, "Evaluation," 375, dates it to the first century BCE, but this is probably too early, as it is based on Tov's assumption that this is the time when "the differences between the Palestinian Hebrew text and the LXX [= OG Pentateuch] were recognized." We have seen that this assumption appears to be invalid.

[96]  For the positive view, see esp. G. Veltri, *Eine Tora*; idem, *Libraries*, 100–146. For the negative view, see Simon-Shoshan, "Tasks of the Translators"; Tov, "Evaluation," 376–377, which in some ways supersedes his previous study "Rabbinic Tradition." See also Wasserstein and Wasserstein, *Legend*, 51–94; R. Kalmin, 'The Miracle of the Septuagint in Ancient Rabbinic and Christian Literature,' in Z. Weiss, et al. (eds.), *"Follow the Wise"* (Winona Lake, Ind., 2010), 241–253. Jerome takes up the rabbinic tradition of the alterations in the LXX and uses it to cast doubt on the fidelity of the LXX; see A. Kamesar, *Jerome, Greek Scholarship, and the Hebrew Bible* (Oxford, 1993), 66–67.

cannot explore these complicated issues here. But we should notice that whereas Philo and Aristeas established the LXX Pentateuch's sacred status by virtue of its exact conformity to the Hebrew, this rabbinic tradition affirms the exact opposite. God did not help the translators create a perfect translation in complete harmony with the original; rather, he helped them produce a translation distinct from the original in several important ways.[97] Whereas the miraculous translation obviated any need for the Hebrew text for Philo and thus replaced the Hebrew, the legend transmitted in *b. Meg.* 9a–b eliminated this option. Whether the rabbinic sources view the changes positively or negatively, the tradition of the changes rules out this 'inspired' translation from being an accurate representation of the Hebrew text, as Philo believed.

The evidence for the continuing use of the Septuagint in Late Antique Judaism is extremely limited and, partly for this reason, open to various interpretations. While scholarship continues to demonstrate the abiding importance of the Greek language in some Jewish communities,[98] we have few data on which to base a judgment as to which Greek Bible version these Jews used. Both the patristic and the inscriptional evidence caution us against assuming that either Aquila or the OG was dominant among all Greek-speaking Jews of our period. We should not expect a Christian writer to comment if he has encountered some Jews who do, in fact, use the OG translations, because such usage would be unremarkable from the Christian perspective. The evidence that we have does not allow for certainty in any direction.

Nevertheless, the limited evidence at hand does suggest that some Jewish communities who would have formerly used the OG translations came to use Aquila's translation, instead. As Late Antiquity transitioned into the Byzantine Era, it seems that Aquila's translation, or at least his principles of translation, continued to appeal to Greek-speaking Jews, as recent research indicates. According to de Lange, in Byzantine Judaism "[v]arious Greek translations were used, the most popular apparently being that attributed

---

[97] See Tov, "Evaluation," 366, who describes the changes as "misrepresenting the content of the Hebrew Torah"; see also pp. 371–372, 375: "In the present context, the only examples provided for the content of the miraculous translation are these 'distorted' renderings." Along the same lines, see Simon-Shoshan, "Tasks of the Translators," 15. Baumgarten, "Bilingual Jews and the Greek Bible," 26–28, argues that the Rabbis were actually attempting to guard the authentic LXX against hebraizing revision.

[98] See recently de Lange, Krivoruchko, and Boyd-Taylor, *Jewish Reception of Greek Bible Versions.*

to Aquila [...]."[99] When one recalls that the revered Septuagint for Greek-speaking Jews amounted only to the Pentateuch, and nothing else, and that even this portion of Greek scripture they defended as an exact match to the Hebrew, the later adoption, by at least some Jews, of different versions is not at all so hard to explain. The newer translations will have indicted the OG as a sometimes inaccurate representation of the Hebrew, and this will have motivated some Jews to adopt a more faithful Bible.

## The Biblical Text in Early Christianity

Our earliest accounts of Christian reflection on critical issues regarding the Bible reveal that the LXX had become the authoritative text. This view is reminiscent of the Jewish pro-LXX view, so we are not surprised to find that the Christian sources also echo the insistence of Philo and Aristeas on the conformity between Hebrew and LXX. The majority of the Fathers were ignorant of Hebrew and rejected later Greek translations which, unbeknownst to them, agreed more closely with the MT than did the LXX. However, their ignorance of Hebrew allowed the Fathers to champion the LXX as the most accurate representation of the Hebrew text in Greek. Like Philo, Christians attributed inspiration to the translation sanctified by tradition, and they formulated an array of arguments to substantiate this claim.[100] But this usually did not entail a theoretical rejection of the Hebrew text, even though patristic theory in this regard rarely led to the practical consequence of incorporating Hebrew study within an exegetical program. In fact, there was no need to do so as long as one could convincingly assert that the Greek text under examination reflected exactly the original Hebrew text.

Christians did realize early that newer Greek translations of the OT—especially 'The Three': Aquila, Symmachus, and Theodotion—often disagreed with the received text of the LXX. This circumstance caused no little anxiety for Christian apologists and exegetes, and it prompted them to devise various explanations for the differences between the texts. Very

---

[99] N. de Lange, "Jews in the Age of Justinian," in M. Maas (ed.), *The Cambridge Companion to the Age of Justinian* (Cambridge, 2005), 401–426 (417). De Lange also highlights the continuing importance of Aquila as one of the major conclusions arising from the papers presented in de Lange, Krivoruchko, and Boyd-Taylor, *Jewish Reception of Greek Bible Versions*. See the last page of the "Introduction," 1–6.

[100] On the LXX in the Church of the patristic age, see Harl in Dorival, Harl, and Munnich, *Bible grecque*, 289–320; Kamesar, *Jerome*, 1–40. For the arguments used in support of the LXX's inspiration, see P. Benoit, "L'inspiration des Septante d'après les Pères," in *L'homme devant Dieu* (Paris, 1963–1964), 1.169–187; Kamesar, op. cit., 28–34.

rarely, however, did the Fathers admit that these newer translations represented the Hebrew text more accurately than did the LXX. Whereas modern scholars understand these later translations to be stimulated largely
(though not exclusively) by a desire to conform the Greek Bible more closely
to the current Hebrew text, ancient Christians usually considered anti-
Christian bias a more likely impetus. The wording of the LXX was deemed
the criterion by which the accuracy of other translations should be judged,
which implies that the LXX is the most accurate translation of the Hebrew.
When Christians did admit that the newer translations reflected the Hebrew
faithfully, they still usually thought that the 'original' LXX translated accurately the 'original' Hebrew text, and that either the LXX or the Hebrew
had now become corrupt. We will see examples of each of these views in
our examination below. Only very infrequently before Jerome and Augustine would a Christian suggest that the Seventy translators had intentionally
changed the biblical text. The essential identity of the original LXX and the
original Hebrew was preserved, so that, in effect, the Fathers maintained the
Hebrew criterion for the biblical text just as much as for the biblical canon.

While recent scholarship has illuminated the practical consequences
that comprehension of the Bible's Hebrew origins had on a few great Fathers
such as Origen and Jerome,[101] the role of the Hebrew text in the general biblical theory of the Fathers has not received sufficient attention. Consequently,
this section aims to clarify Hebrew's place in the Church's textual theory
through an analysis of patristic comments on the relationship between the
LXX and its parent text. Although only a few of the Fathers will feature in this
study, we will attempt to highlight some of the most significant statements
on the topic and thereby demonstrate the value of re-examining patristic
theory from this angle.

### Patristic Textual Theory before Origen

The earliest Christian author to mention the LXX was Justin Martyr in the
middle of the second century.[102] He tells the story of the translation in his
first *Apologia* (§ 31), where we see for the first time that the LXX had become
in Christian minds the entire Greek OT. In Chapter Three above we saw

---

[101] See, e.g., A. Salvesen, "A Convergence of the Ways? The Judaizing of Christian Scripture
by Origen and Jerome," in A.H. Becker and A.Y. Reed (eds.), *The Ways That Never Parted*
(Tübingen, 2003), 233–258.

[102] For a recent survey of the story in patristic literature, see Wasserstein and Wasserstein,
*Legend*, 95–131. Many of the sources in their original languages were collected by Wendland,
*Aristeae ad Philocratem Epistula*, 121–166.

that this expansion of the LXX beyond just the Pentateuch had important implications for the way Christians understood the scope of their Bible. Since the Seventy were viewed as authoritative translators into Greek, any book not translated by them was held in suspicion. With regard to the biblical text, extending the LXX to the whole OT meant that the traditional Greek form of each book was now seen to be authoritative. The Jewish proponents of the LXX did not necessarily feel compelled to defend the Greek form of non-Pentateuchal books. For Christians, the ascription of the entire Greek OT to the authoritative Seventy translators was advantageous because it allowed them a convenient way to defend the wording of their entire OT.

This is precisely how Justin uses the expanded scope of the LXX in his *Dialogus cum Tryphone.* Certain passages in this work are concerned with establishing the accuracy of the LXX version of Isaiah 7:14, with its translation παρθένος ('virgin') instead of νεᾶνις ('young woman'), this latter reading being supported, Justin says, by contemporary Jewish teachers and their new translation/interpretation.[103] Justin can support the reading παρθένος only by appealing to the authority of the Seventy translators, and since the miracle story elsewhere associated with the translation does not feature in Justin's account,[104] he can establish the authority of the LXX only by emphasizing that it is a Jewish translation made for a famous king (*Dial.* 68.7). But how to explain the recent Jewish insistence that the translation is wrong? Justin responds that the Jews have falsified the text out of malice toward Christ.[105]

’Αλλ’ οὐχὶ τοῖς διδασκάλοις ὑμῶν πείθομαι, μὴ συντεθειμένοις καλῶς ἐξηγεῖσθαι τὰ ὑπὸ τῶν παρὰ Πτολεμαίῳ τῷ Αἰγυπτίων γενομένῳ βασιλεῖ ἑβδομήκοντα πρεσβυτέρων, ἀλλ’ αὐτοὶ ἐξηγεῖσθαι πειρῶνται. καὶ ὅτι πολλὰς γραφὰς τέλεον περιεῖλον ἀπὸ τῶν ἐξηγήσεων τῶν γεγενημένων ὑπὸ τῶν παρὰ Πτολεμαίῳ γεγενημένων

---

[103] On Justin's terminology for 'to translate' and 'to interpret' (ἐξηγεῖσθαι rather than ἑρμηνεύειν), see Müller, *First Bible*, 71 n. 6.

[104] Some scholars have failed to recognize this: e.g., M.W. Holmes, "The Biblical Canon," in S.A. Harvey and D.G. Hunter (eds.), *The Oxford Handbook of Early Christian Studies* (Oxford, 2008), 406–426, who says that Justin "argued for the divine inspiration of the entire LXX" (411). To be sure, Justin assumed the authority of the entire LXX, but he nowhere explicitly ascribed inspiration to the translation.

[105] On the accusation of Jewish falsification of the Bible, see W. Adler, "The Jews as Falsifiers: Charges of Tendentious Emendation in Anti-Jewish Christian Polemic," in *Translation of Scripture* (Philadelphia, 1990), 1–27, where Justin receives attention at pp. 3–7; see also in this connection O. Skarsaune, "The Question of Old Testament Canon and Text in the Early Greek Church," in Saebø, *Hebrew Bible/Old Testament*, 443–450.

πρεσβυτέρων, ἐξ ὧν διαρρήδην οὗτος αὐτὸς ὁ σταυρωθεὶς ὅτι θεὸς καὶ ἄνθρωπος καὶ σταυρούμενος καὶ ἀποθνήσκων κεκηρυγμένος ἀποδείκνυται, εἰδέναι ὑμᾶς βούλομαι. (*Dial.* 71.1–2)

But I do not trust your teachers, who do not agree that the things were translated well by the Seventy elders with Ptolemy who was king of the Egyptians, but they try themselves to translate. And I want you to know that they completely omitted many scriptures from the translation accomplished by the elders who were with Ptolemy, from which it is expressly shown that this crucified one himself is proclaimed as God and man and crucified and dying.

Justin seems to think that the Hebrew text itself is not corrupt but only the more recent translation made by the Jews, for earlier he had accused the Jewish leaders of saying that whatever contradicts their own opinions "was not written this way" (μὴ οὕτω γεγράφθαι) in the Hebrew text (*Dial.* 68.8). Since Justin is criticizing this attitude, it would appear that he thinks these things are written in the current Hebrew text. Later he will say that the recent translations cancel (παραγράφω) or misinterpret (παρεξηγέομαι) the prophecies (*Dial.* 84.4), a statement also implying that the corruption is to be found in the Greek rather than the Hebrew. Clearly, Justin thinks the LXX alone can be trusted to represent accurately the original wording of the Hebrew prophecies. In other words, the very charge of Jewish falsification of scripture resulting in a text that disagrees with the LXX implies that the LXX will have corresponded more precisely with the original Hebrew text than the more recent Jewish texts.

On a theoretical level, therefore, Justin does not reject the original Hebrew text. He argues that the wording of the LXX reflects the wording of the Hebrew original. Nor is this just an incidental point in Justin's argument, but the correspondence between Hebrew and LXX is essential. If he had been content to argue that the LXX did not need to correspond with the Hebrew, he would not have needed to say that the newer Jewish translation was corrupt. The basis of his argumentation is that the true text is the one that conforms to the ancient Hebrew prophecies.

Irenaeus of Lyons emphatically affirms the miraculous nature of the LXX translation. Taking up a Jewish elaboration of the legend in which the translators were separated from one another in order to prevent collusion,[106] Irenaeus declares that all the Gentiles present at Ptolemy's court perceived the inspiration of the translation because the individual translators each

---

[106] On this rabbinic account, see our earlier discussion of rabbinic views on the LXX.

produced identical versions (*Haer.* 3.21.2). Irenaeus knows about two more recent translations, those by Theodotion and Aquila, but he asserts that the wording of the LXX alone is to be trusted because (1) it was translated by the Jews themselves (*Haer.* 3.21.1), (2) there was no possibility of Christian influence since the translation preceded Christ (3.21.1, 3), (3) the miraculous agreement of the translators confirms the inspiration of this version (3.21.2), and (4) the apostles themselves agree with the wording of the LXX (3.21.3).

Does Irenaeus see an opposition between the wording of the LXX and the wording of the Hebrew text? Hengel thinks that this is a possible implication of Irenaeus' version of the translation legend:

> In a certain sense, it [the LXX] can thus even be regarded as superior to the Hebrew text since any variations or instances of greater precision in relation to the original that may appear in the Greek version can be regarded as divinely legitimized through the agreement of the Seventy.[107]

Müller also sees this as a possibility: "Though it is not said *expressis verbis*, Irenaeus' formulations do not eliminate the possibility that there might be some discrepancy between the Hebrew and the Greek texts."[108]

However, Irenaeus' description of the translation makes it highly improbable that he himself thought it possible that the Seventy translators changed the wording of the Hebrew text. In fact, he says that by changing the word παρθένος to νεᾶνις in Isa. 7:14 the newer translations are *frustrantes prophetarum testimonium, quod operatus est Deus* ("frustrating the testimony of the prophets, which God provided"; *Haer.* 3.21.1). He refers here to the ancient Hebrew prophets, for he goes on to say that these prophesied before the Babylonian captivity. If Aquila and Theodotion are rejecting the testimony of the Hebrew prophets, then their text does not agree with the Hebrew text. This latter is reflected more accurately by the LXX, according to Irenaeus. Of course, he cannot verify this idea, for he does not know Hebrew. Yet, the four arguments listed earlier confirming the authority of the LXX establish it as the true translation: *Cum tanta igitur veritate et gratia Dei interpretatae sint Scripturae* [...] ("Since therefore the Scriptures were translated with such great accuracy and grace from God ..."; *Haer.* 3.21.3). Therefore, it represents most accurately the original Hebrew prophecies: *in Senioribus autem interpretatus est bene quae bene prophetata fuerant* ("But in the Elders what had been prophesied well was translated well"; *Haer.* 3.21.4). In Irenaeus'

---

[107] Hengel, *Septuagint*, 39.
[108] Müller, *First Bible*, 74.

mind, just as in Justin's, there is no opposition between Hebrew and LXX; the opposition is between Hebrew/LXX and the newer Jewish translations that misrepresent the Hebrew text.[109]

The remaining pre-Origen witnesses to the LXX tradition offer less detail on the wording of the LXX vis-à-vis the Hebrew text, mostly because they do not argue against the newer translations, which go unmentioned in these sources. Clement of Alexandria (*Strom.* 1.22) and Ps.-Justin (*Cohort. Graec.* 13) emphasize the miraculous agreement of the separated translators. This may well imply that the translation accurately represents its source text, for we have seen that Irenaeus says the translators were separated to prevent them from conspiring to alter the message. Tertullian certainly thinks the LXX accurately represents the Hebrew. In his account, which contains no miraculous elements, he says that the original translation is on display at the Serapeum, along with the Hebrew originals (*Apologet.* 18.8).[110] The reason for including the Hebrew is probably to allow visitors to confirm the accuracy of the translation, which again indicates that the Seventy translators necessarily translated what was in the Hebrew.

### Origen's Textual Theory

The five pre-Origenian Fathers whose views we have surveyed either ignore differences between the LXX and newer Greek translations of the OT (Clement, Tertullian, Ps.-Justin) or they affirm that the LXX more accurately reflects the Hebrew text while the newer translations corrupt messianic prophecies, especially Isa. 7:14, out of anti-Christian zeal (Justin, Irenaeus). Origen's approach to the text incorporated a much more sophisticated analysis of the types of variation between the LXX and newer translations. His extensive text-critical research prevented him from either ignoring the differences among the texts or attributing all of these differences to Jewish malice; indeed, Origen understood that Aquila, Symmachus, and Theodotion sometimes produced translations more useful for Christian exegesis than the LXX itself.[111] However, Origen's theory proves difficult to ascertain because his extensive œuvre contains seemingly contradictory statements

---

[109] See Karpp, "'Prophet' oder 'Dolmetscher'," 135–136, for a similar evaluation of Irenaeus' views.

[110] For the historical value of this statement from Tertullian, see Rajak, *Translation and Survival*, 43–46.

[111] Salvesen, "Convergence," 240, notes Origen's awareness that textual variants were not all due to Jewish hostility toward Christians. For Origen's awareness that the *recentiores* were at times useful for Christian interpretation, see Kamesar, *Jerome*, 27–28 n. 78, 37 n. 107.

embedded in vastly different types of work, such as scholarly writings, homilies, and apologetic treatises.

One point that is clear, and which represents a departure from previous Christian thought, is that Origen's research demonstrated that the divergences between the LXX and the newer translations reflect divergences between the LXX and the current Hebrew text.[112] This could not fail to become obvious while he was compiling his six-columned OT, the *Hexapla*, which Eusebius (*Hist. eccl.* 6.16) and others (e.g. Epiphanius, *Mens.* 7; 18) report as including the Hebrew text in Hebrew script, as well as its transliteration into Greek.[113] The focus of our discussion concerns how Origen conceived of these divergences between Greek and Hebrew, specifically, whether he thought that the LXX should conform to the Hebrew. Unfortunately, the evidence from the *Hexapla* and Origen's exegetical method do not unambiguously point to an answer. However, a careful examination of these sources does permit some conclusions.

Scholars have devoted much work to Origen's textual theory, and the uncertainty of the evidence has allowed for contradictory conclusions on many issues.[114] There seems to be at least general agreement on the following five points, which provide a brief overview of Origen's position and of its inherent difficulties. First, Origen concentrates his work on the LXX; though he does not transmit the legend of the translation, his exegetical and text-critical work fully bears out his stated commitment to the Bible of the Church as guaranteed by Providence (cf. *Ep. Afr.* 8).[115] Second, his research

---

[112] See Karpp, "'Prophet' oder 'Dolmetscher'," 136–138, for the view that this recognition of differences between Hebrew and Greek texts led to the development of the idea that the LXX formed a vital point in salvation history (*Heilsgeschichte*), surpassing for the church the original text. Some elements of this view by Karpp will receive critique in the present analysis.

[113] Eusebius himself does not describe the transliterated column, but Epiphanius does, and both of our fragmentary manuscript copies of the *Hexapla* (Ra. 1098, Ra. 2005) have the transliterated column. P. Nautin, *Origène* (Paris, 1977), 303–333, has denied the existence of a column in Hebrew characters. For critique of Nautin's position, see R.G. Jenkins, "The First Column of the Hexapla: The Evidence of the Milan Codex (Rahlfs 1098) and the Cairo Genizah Fragment (Rahlfs 2005)," in Salvesen, *Origen's Hexapla*, 88–102; and, in the same volume, G.J. Norton, "Observations on the First Two Columns of the Hexapla," 103–124.

[114] For an overview, see Fernández Marcos, *Septuagint*, 204–222.

[115] See Kamesar, *Jerome*, 3–28; B. Neuschäfer, *Origenes als Philologe*, 2 vols. (Basel, 1987), 1.100–103; Benoit, "L'inspiration des Septante," 178–179; R. Clements, "Origen's *Hexapla* and Christian-Jewish Encounter in the Second and Third Centuries," in T.L. Donaldson (ed.), *Religious Rivalries and the Struggle for Success in Caesarea Maritima* (2000), 303–329 (321–328). This is against the view of Nautin, *Origène*, 351–353, that Origen aimed for the original Hebrew text. Origen regards the LXX as given to the Church by God, but he does not transmit the translation legend; see C.P. [Hammond] Bammel, "Die Hexapla des Origenes: Die *Hebraica Veritas* im Streit der Meinungen," *Aug* 28 (1988): 125–149 (129–130).

assured him that the current text of the LXX was in some places corrupt, as evidenced by divergent readings in the LXX manuscripts.[116] Third, the Hebrew text as witnessed by the *recentiores* served as an important criterion in correcting the LXX (cf. *Comm. Matt.* 15.14).[117] Fourth, Origen's different statements concerning his objectives in his text-critical work (*Comm. Matt.* 15.14; *Ep. Afr.* 9) correspond to the tension in Origen's own theory as to whether it is preferable to have a LXX corrected according to the Hebrew or a 'pure' LXX.[118] Fifth, determining that a given LXX variant is secondary from a text-critical perspective does not prevent Origen from incorporating it into his exegesis (cf. *Hom. Jer.* 14.3; 15.5).[119] Kamesar's discussion of these and other points reveals that Origen was primarily committed to the exegetically significant text ("exegetical maximalism"), sometimes regardless of the authenticity of a particular reading, and he does not always disclose his reasoning behind his textual preferences.[120]

Origen's text-critical work led him to make three types of changes in his text of the LXX, only one of which he marked with the famous critical signs derived from Alexandrian Homeric scholarship. The changes he did not mark include the correction of proper names to agree more closely

---

[116] Origen often notes variants among the LXX manuscripts in his exegetical writings; for references, see below. Cf. also *Comm. Matt.* 15.14.

[117] Clements, "Origen's *Hexapla*," 325, has suggested that the 'healing' of the LXX did not rely even theoretically on the Hebrew, but only on the Three, and that the text marked with critical signs showing disagreements with the Hebrew is not a product of this 'healing.' However, her article provides insufficient detail regarding the specifics of this interpretation.

[118] Contrast the views of S.P. Brock, "Origen's Aims as a Textual Critic of the Old Testament," *StPatr* = TU 107 (1970), 215–218; and N.R.M. de Lange, "The *Letter to Africanus*: Origen's Recantation?" *StPatr* 16.2 = TU 129 (1985), 242–247. See also Kamesar, *Jerome*, 17–21; J. Schaper, "The Origin and Purpose of the Fifth Column of the Hexapla," in Salvesen, *Origen's Hexapla*, 3–14 (5, 12–14); J.N.B. Carleton Paget, "The Christian Exegesis of the Old Testament in the Alexandrian Tradition," in Saebø, *Hebrew Bible/Old Testament*, 478–542 (503–508); A. Grafton and M. Williams, *Christianity and the Transformation of the Book* (Cambridge, Mass., 2006), 117–132; Law, "Origen's Parallel Bible"; P.B. Decock, "Jerome's Turn to the Hebraica Veritas and His Rejection of the Traditional View of the Septuagint," *Neot* 42 (2008): 205–??? (210–213)

[119] R.P.C. Hanson, *Allegory and Event* (Richmond, Va., 1959), 175; Carleton Paget, "Christian Exegesis," 506 n. 168. Benoit ("L'inspiration," 179 and n. 64) notes that Origen does not attribute 'errors' to the original LXX but to subsequent scribes. Nevertheless, he exegetes even these scribal errors. Note the somewhat similar method found in *Gen. Rab.* 20.12 on Gen. 3:21, on which see Alexander, "Why No Textual Criticism," 177 and n. 4.

[120] For the first point, see especially Kamesar, *Jerome*, 19, 25, 27–28; and for the second point, 17–18. On Origen's exegetical goals behind his textual criticism, see also J. Wright, "Origen in the Scholar's Den: A Rationale for the Hexapla," in C. Kannengiesser and W.L. Petersen (eds.), *Origen of Alexandria* (Notre Dame, Ind., 1988), 48–62; Carleton Paget, "Christian Exegesis," 506; Schaper, "Origen," 13–14; Law, "Origen's Parallel Bible."

with the Hebrew spelling and conforming the word order to that of the Hebrew text.[121] Given his view that the Church quite rightly uses the LXX, his willingness to thus modify the Greek text to accord with the Hebrew, without so much as indicating the change, implies that the former had become corrupt and would originally have matched the Hebrew in these characteristics. Origen did mark with asterisks and obeli the quantitative differences between the extant Hebrew and the extant LXX, whether or not these differences corresponded to variants in the manuscript tradition of the LXX itself (*Comm. Matt.* 15.14; *Ep. Afr.* 7).[122] This change may again imply the importance of the current Hebrew text as a witness to the original form of the LXX. In fact, Kamesar says of Origen's phrase τὰ ἀκριβέστατα [sc. ἀντίγραφα] καὶ συμφωνοῦντα τοῖς Ἑβραϊκοῖς ("the most accurate [copies] and those harmonious with the Hebrew"; *Hom. Jer.* 14.3), "he seems almost to define more accurate codices as those which agree with the Hebrew."[123]

This side of Origen's textual position has a certain affinity with the earlier Christian views we have examined. Like his predecessors, Origen assumes that the LXX was a faithful translation of the Hebrew. However, whereas others had said that the newer translations are corrupt because they disagree with the faithful LXX, Origen recognizes that the newer translations are often very faithful, so he naturally infers that the LXX has become corrupt in the manuscript tradition. Therefore, he corrects the LXX to agree with the Hebrew; that is, he removes the corruption and restores the LXX to its pristine state of fidelity to the Hebrew text.[124]

Nevertheless, Origen's position cannot be reduced to the advocacy of a hebraized LXX. For one thing, the interpretation of his critical signs has caused some disagreement. Origen says that he used the obelus to mark pluses in the LXX vis-à-vis the Hebrew because he did not dare to eliminate these passages completely (οὐ τολμήσαντες αὐτὰ πάντη περιελεῖν; *Comm.*

---

[121] See Kamesar, *Jerome*, 10–12.

[122] Note that Origen's *Comm. Matt.* 15.14 does not at all imply that one may use the method indicated therein "as a means of determining where the LXX had omitted or added something to its translation," as asserted by Carleton Paget, "Christian Exegesis," 505. Under discussion in that passage is only textual corruption in the Greek manuscript tradition. Origen did not assume that the LXX text of his day replicated the original LXX. The 'additions' and 'omissions' that Origen identifies and 'corrects' serve the purpose of 'healing' the Greek text, i.e., removing the corruption it had suffered through transmission. The 'additions' and 'omissions' are not the products of the original translators but of subsequent scribes.

[123] Kamesar, *Jerome*, 10.

[124] For references to other scholars who emphasize this aspect of Origen's theory, see Law, "Origen's Parallel Bible," 9–11.

*Matt.* 15.14). Why did he not dare to eliminate the pluses? Was this decision made reluctantly because he was afraid of the public outcry that would
result, or did he not dare to omit this material because he genuinely believed
that one should not thus alter the ecclesiastical text ordained by Providence?[125] At issue is whether Origen intended the obelus to mark passages
which should be athetized, or whether he used the sign simply to signal a
variant without implying that the traditional LXX should be altered. Perhaps
most likely is a third possibility: Origen did not wish to imitate the reckless
scribes he castigates earlier in the same passage for wantonly altering a text
that may not be corrupt.[126] If this is the true interpretation of Origen's comment, it would reveal that he was not so bold as to presume that he could
make an adequate judgment on every variation. Origen's hesitancy in this
regard would probably be due to his recognition that the very Hebrew text
he was using for comparison may itself have become corrupt.[127]

Another reason that we cannot think that Origen always favored a LXX
text corrected against the Hebrew is that he argues extensively against
this view in the first section of his *Ep. Afr.* There, he enumerates some of
the "myriad" (§3) passages that diverge between the Greek and Hebrew
texts, sometimes in very major ways. Origen mocks the notion that Jewish
manuscripts are better than those possessed by Christians, and he offers the
theological argument that God would not allow that to happen (§8).

The two previous paragraphs establish that Origen did not always think
that the Church's Bible should be corrected according to the current Hebrew

---

[125] For the first interpretation, see Neuschäfer, *Origenes*, 1.102; de Lange, "Origen's Recantation?" 245–246. For the second interpretation, see Wevers, "PreOrigen Recensional Activity,"
125; C. Larcher, *Études sur la livre de la Sagesse* (Paris, 1969), 46 n. 2. De Lange (*art. cit.*, 247)
does admit that Origen was "restrained" in his wholesale adoption of the Hebrew "partly perhaps by a sincere regard for the Septuagint and the place it had won for itself in the church
by long usage."

[126] For this view, see N. Fernández Marcos, *Scribes and Translators* (Leiden, 1994), 4. For
a similar idea, see the statement by Kamesar, *Jerome*, 19: "In the textual sphere, Origen's
practice of using the longer text is probably better explained as a conservative desire to
'play it safe', i.e. to avoid excluding even a possibly authentic passage from his Bible." Origen
did not have available to him a plethora of established critical signs (see Fernández Marcos,
*Septuagint*, 210), which situation may have led him to re-interpret the signs that were in use.

[127] Cf. *Sel. Ps.* 3:8 (PG 12.1129b–c); *Sel. Ezech.* 7:27 (PG 13.796a). For this aspect of Origen's
thought, see Law, "Origen's Parallel Bible," 12, who criticizes those who have asserted that
Origen assumed the Hebrew text remained in its pristine state (for which, see, e.g., Salvesen,
"Convergence," 241). Origen typically envisions this textual corruption to be due to accidents
of transmission; he does not think the same applies to the Greek minor versions because
they are more recent; cf. *Comm. Jo.* 6.212, where he speaks of αἱ μηδέπω διαστραφεῖσαι ἐκδόσεις
Ἀκύλου καὶ Θεοδοτίωνος καὶ Συμμάχου.

text. However, most of Origen's statements are most easily understood if he generally presupposes that the original LXX did correspond to the original Hebrew, and that one of the two texts has become corrupt. We have already seen that Origen acknowledges the possibility that the Hebrew text has changed over time, and he certainly argues at length that the Jewish leadership might have suppressed documents from the Bible (*Ep. Afr.* 13–15). His insistence earlier in his *Ep. Afr.* that Christian Bibles are just as valid as, or more valid than, Jewish Bibles probably reflects this same viewpoint. Origen satirically imagines Christians pleading with Jews for copies of the Bible that are καθαροὶ καὶ μηδὲν πλάσμα ἔχοντες ("pure and having no forgery"; §8). His sardonic tone implies that he is not at all convinced that Jewish Bibles may be characterized in these terms. If they are in fact ἀκάθαρτοι καὶ πλάσμα ἔχοντες ("impure and having forgery"), then it would be foolish indeed for Christians to adopt Jewish manuscripts. Therefore, in these cases in which Origen hesitates to revise the LXX toward the Hebrew, the probable reason is that he does not consider the current Hebrew text always the correct text; it cannot be "the final court of appeal," as Hanson would have it.[128] However, he maintains even in these instances that the original LXX faithfully represented the original Hebrew. Thus, just as Origen advocated the Hebrew criterion for the OT canon, so also he generally endorses a Hebrew criterion for the OT text.

This view of Origen's thought can explain nearly all of his statements. However, some of Origen's comments indicate that he did consider it possible that the Seventy translators intentionally and providentially altered the biblical text. We will discuss several of the passages in which such a view is discernable.

Origen thinks that the Seventy have changed (ἐναλλάσσω; *Sel. Ps.* 42:3; PG 12.1420d) the grammatical tense from future to past in several messianic prophecies in the Psalms. He observes that the LXX and Theodotion put everything in the past, whereas Aquila makes some things past and some future, and Symmachus makes everything future. Ἔθος γὰρ τοῖς Ἑβδομή-κοντα πολλάκις τὰς περὶ Χριστοῦ προφητείας ὡς ἤδη γενομένας ἀπαγγέλλειν ("For it is the custom of the Seventy often to announce the prophecies concerning Christ as if they had already happened"). Origen goes on to ascribe this custom to the Seventy's desire to depict God as omniscient (*Sel. Ps.* 2:1; PG 12.1104c). The other translators speak σαφέστερον ("more clearly") because they render these verbs with future tenses (*Sel. Ps.* 42:3;

---

[128] Hanson, *Allegory*, 165.

PG 12.1420d). The change Origen envisions is rather small and, by his own admission, not universal, for he notes that the Seventy translate some messianic prophecies with the future tense (e.g. Isa. 52:13; cf. *Sel. Ps.* 2:1; PG 12.1104d). Yet, if readers of the LXX interpret the tenses as Origen does (i.e., as displaying God's omniscience), it is a change that would edify their faith.

The MT of Ps. 3:8 (Eng.: 3:7) contains the phrase כי הכית את כל איבי לחי ("for you have struck all my enemies on the cheek"), for which the LXX has ὅτι σὺ ἐπάταξας πάντας τοὺς ἐχθραίνοντάς μοι ματαίως ("for you struck all those hostile to me without cause"). Origen wonders about the difference between "cheek" (לחי) in the Hebrew text, as reflected in the newer Greek translations, and "without cause" (ματαίως) in the LXX (*Sel. Ps.* 3:8; PG 12.1129b–c). Some Ἑβραῖοι have suggested to him that the Hebrew text itself may have changed, but he also considers the possibility that the Seventy intentionally altered the text: ἢ [sc. εἰκός ἐστι] τὸ εὐτελὲς περιϊστάμενους τοὺς Ἑβδομήκοντα τῆς λέξεως, τετολμηκέναι ἀντὶ τοῦ 'σιαγόνα' ποιῆσαι 'ματαίως' ("or [it is possible] that the Seventy, avoiding the poverty of the letter, have dared to put 'without cause' instead of 'cheek'"). In any case, he accepts the LXX reading and proceeds to interpret it. His suggestion that the Seventy 'dared' to replace 'cheek' with 'without cause' attributes to the translators the motive of 'avoiding the poverty of the letter' (τὸ εὐτελὲς περιϊστάμενοι [...] τῆς λέξεως). Here, λέξις does not refer only to the words 'cheek' and 'without cause' but to literalism as opposed to the more spiritual ways of reading texts.[129] The Seventy have produced a good interpretation of the OT not because they found fault with the Hebrew text but because they eschewed rendering it literalistically (at least, in this case). For this reason, their translation is rich (not εὐτελής) in meaning.

In a manner similar to his handling of Ps. 3:8, Origen suggests in *Sel. Ezech.* 7:27 (PG 13.796a) that the Seventy did not translate the phrase ὁ βασιλεὺς πενθήσει ("the king will mourn") either because it was not in their Hebrew *Vorlage* or as a result of their consciously omitting it. In this case, Origen thinks their motivation for omitting the phrase would have been that they considered it inappropriate to depict the Savior as mourning. Origen points out, though, that even if one retains the reading, it may be harmonized with the life of Jesus, who does, in fact, mourn over Jerusalem (cf. Matt. 23:37–39). This is a case in which Origen seems convinced that the original LXX

---

[129] For this meaning, see G.W.H. Lampe (ed.), *A Patristic Greek Lexicon* (Oxford, 1961), 797 s.v. λέξις, definition 9; also see p. 577 s.v. εὐτέλεια, definition 1b: "of the inferiority of the 'letter' opp. spiritual exegesis."

did not contain a phrase, but then he proceeds to interpret that phrase, a phenomenon comparable to his willingness to incorporate scribal errors into his exegesis. Origen does not discuss how the Seventy translators would have been justified to omit material out of the false assumption that it does not apply to Jesus.

The changes that Origen attributes to the Seventy translators constitute providentially guided alterations that point toward a sense beyond the literal. At the same time, they are very limited in scale, consisting of the substitution of a single word, or merely a tense, or at the most omitting a few words. Nevertheless, the only change that Origen confidently attributes to the Seventy is that of the tense of some prophecies, whereas the other proposed changes are only possibilities that could have other explanations. Origen allows that the Seventy translators did not always adhere strictly to the text before them, but he actually invokes this option rather infrequently.

Some other comments by Origen may imply that the Seventy intentionally diverged from the Hebrew, but in light of Origen's general textual theory, these passages probably have alternative explanations. For example, in his *Hom. Lev.* 12.5.5, Origen considers why the LXX's phrase ἐκ τοῦ γένους αὐτοῦ ("from his relatives"; Lev. 21:13; cf. 21:14) has no counterpart in the Hebrew text available to him, where it says only that the Israelite high priest should take a virgin as a wife. He does not offer an explanation as to how the two texts came to differ, but he does think it appropriate that the Hebrews lack the phrase in question.

> *Illud tamen nolo vos lateat, quod Hebraei negant se scriptum habere, quod nos apud septuaginta interpretes invenimus, "de genere suo." Et recte illi non habent scriptum. Ablata est enim ab illis propinquitas Dei, ablata est adoptio filiorum, et translata est ad Ecclesiam Christi. Illi ergo non habent scriptum quia de genere Christi sint, sicut nec esse meruerunt.*

> But I do not wish it to escape your notice that the Hebrews deny that they have the thing written which we find in the LXX, "from his relatives." And rightly do they not have it written. For intimacy with God has been taken from them, the adoption of sons was taken away, and it was transferred to the Church of Christ. Therefore, they do not have it written because they are not from the relatives of Christ, just as they have not merited to be so.

We have seen that in *Sel. Ps.* 3:8 and *Sel. Ezech.* 7:27 Origen considers two possibilities for explaining a divergence between the Greek and Hebrew text: either the Hebrew text has changed during its transmission history since the time of the translation or the Seventy translators purposefully made the change. Origen does not discuss these possibilities here, but his comments tend to support the first explanation. After all, the *propinquitas Dei* that has been taken from the Jews did formerly belong to them. Presumably, at that time it would have been appropriate for their texts to reflect that fact with the reading ἐκ τοῦ γένους αὐτοῦ. This understanding of Origen's thought by an appeal to textual corruption in the Hebrew receives additional support later in the discussion where Origen admonishes his audience to beware lest they should prove unworthy of being Christians, "although we are the relatives of Christ" (*cum genus simus Christi*). The implication is that if Christians were to abandon their faith, it would be appropriate for their texts to reflect this through the omission of ἐκ τοῦ γένους αὐτοῦ. Therefore, this is probably not a case in which Origen would explain the LXX text by appealing to intentional alteration on the part of the translators. Rather, he probably thinks that the Hebrew text has become corrupt (whether intentionally or accidentally), and that this has ironically (providentially?) resulted in a reading appropriate to the current situation of the Jews.

Another example comes from Origen's comments on Ps. 4:8 (Eng.: 4:7), which, in the LXX edition of Rahlfs, contains the phrase ἀπὸ καιροῦ ("from the time"), a reading that agrees with the Hebrew.[130] Origen informs us the that the LXX manuscripts of his day have instead ἀπὸ καρποῦ ("from the fruit"), but he is aware of the wording in Hebrew. Origen's exegesis of the LXX reading (ἀπὸ καρποῦ) emphasizes that it has reference to the "time" (καιρός) when the fruit (καρπός) is harvested and abundant (*Sel. Ps.* 4:8; PG 12.1168a). He thus implies that the Hebrew and Greek give the same sense and are not really divergent. One may compare Origen's observation about the difference between the LXX of Isa. 6:10 and the quotation of this verse in John 12:40.

Περὶ δὲ τοῦ μὴ αὐταῖς λέξεσιν εἰρῆσθαι παρὰ τῷ προφήτῃ τὸ κείμενον ἐν τῷ εὐαγγελίῳ οὐ θαυμαστόν, πολλαχοῦ τοῦτο ποιησάντων τῶν διακονησαμένων τὰ τῆς καινῆς διαθήκης λόγια, ὡς καὶ ἐν ἄλλοις τετηρήκαμεν. πλὴν ἰσοδυναμεῖ τὰ τοῦ Ἡσαΐου ῥητὰ τοῖς ἐγκειμένοις ἐν τῷ εὐαγγελίῳ.[131]

But there is no surprise concerning the fact that what lies in the Gospel is not said with the same words in the prophet, since those who furnished

---

[130] A. Rahlfs, *Psalmi cum Odis*, Septuaginta 10 (Göttingen, 1931), 84. Rahlfs here relies on the *Vetus Latina*, since all Greek manuscripts apparently have καρποῦ for καιροῦ, the former being reflected also in Jerome's 'Gallican Psalter.' For Rahlfs' defense of such a method for establishing the OG, see pp. 45–46 of his edition.

[131] *Comm. Jo.* frg. 92; cf. E. Preuschen, *Origenes Werke IV: Der Johanneskommentar*, GCS 10 (Leipzig, 1903), 555.26–556.5.

the oracles of the new covenant have done this frequently, as also we have observed in other passages. But the words of Isaiah have the same meaning as what lies in the Gospel.

The principle Origen identifies here, along with the related example from Ps. 4:8, confirms that one cannot always label textual variants as true differences because they may produce the same meaning.

In another passage, Origen wonders about the absence of the word δικαί-ας ("righteous") in the Hebrew text and newer Greek versions of Ps. 2:12 where the LXX reads δράξασθε παιδείας μήποτε ὀργισθῇ κύριος καὶ ἀπολεῖσθε ἐξ ὁδοῦ δικαίας ("seize instruction lest the Lord become angry and you perish from the righteous way"). He suggests that the difference may stem either from the Seventy translators' adding the word providentially (or "economically"; κατ' οἰκονομίαν)[132] or from corruption within the Greek manuscripts attesting this word. Origen explains the verse twice, each time according to one of his two proposed explanations. First, he interprets the verse as if the Seventy had 'economically' added the word:

Κατ' οἰκονομίαν μὲν, ἵν' οὕτως νοήσωμεν· Ἐὰν μὴ δράξασθε παιδείας, ἀπολεῖσθε ἐξ ὁδοῦ δικαίας, καὶ ἐκπεσεῖσθε αὐτῆς, ὀργισθέντος ὑμῖν τοῦ Κυρίου.    (PG 12.1116d)

According to [the divine] economy, so that we should understand it thus: If you do not seize instruction, you will perish from the righteous way, and you will fall from it, the Lord having become angry with you.

After some further explanation, he offers a second interpretation, this time in accordance with the possibility that the Greek manuscripts err.

Ἐὰν μὴ ᾖ κείμενον τὸ, 'δικαίας,' ἐπεὶ οἱ μὴ δραξάμενοι παιδείας πάντως εἰσὶν ἐν ὁδῷ οὐκ ἀγαθῇ, δύναται λεληθότως λέγεσθαι, ὅτι μὴ δρασσομένων ὑμῶν παιδείας ὀργισθήσεται Κύριος, ἐκ τοῦ ἀπολέσθαι ὑμᾶς ἐκ τῆς ὁδοῦ ἐν ᾗ διατρίβετε, ἵνα μηκέτι ὑπάρχητε ἐν αὐτῇ.    (PG 12.1116d–1117a)

But if the word 'righteous' should not be here, since those who have not seized instruction are in a way that is not good, it is possible that it [the word 'righteous'] is said implicitly, because if you do not seize instruction the Lord will become angry, because of your perishing from the way in which you walk, so that you are no longer in it.

It is clear from this dual exegesis that the Seventy were guided by God to make their translation and that where they depart from the Hebrew text, the Church should follow the LXX. It is not clear what exegetical difference Origen sees between the two texts. It seems that with or without δικαίας,

---

[132] For this concept, see Kamesar, *Jerome*, 13–17.

Origen thinks the meaning of the passage is the same: one who does not pursue discipline will perish from the good or righteous path, and God will become angry. The difference is that with δικαίας the 'path' is explicitly qualified as 'righteous,' whereas without δικαίας, this qualification is subtle (δύναται λεληθότως λέγεσθαι) and must be inferred. Therefore, in this case, if the Seventy did 'economically' add the word δικαίας, this constituted an 'economic' clarification of the actual meaning of the Hebrew text; it was not a deviation.

In *Hom. Jer.* 16.5, Origen observes that his Greek text of Jer. 16:18 says that God will doubly recompense the Israelites for their sin, but it does not say that he will do this 'first,' which qualification is present in Hebrew. Once more, Origen proposes two explanations for this difference: either ignorant scribes removed 'first' from the Greek text in the course of its transmission, or the Seventy translators themselves 'economically' removed it. At first he seems quite unsure about the correct view, for he says about choosing between these two options, θεὸς ἂν εἰδείη ("God knows"). His subsequent discussion takes up only the first possibility (accidental omission of 'first') because it agrees with the other versions. Nor does Origen propose any theological reason why the Seventy translators would have left this word out, and indeed the passage has much the same sense with or without it. Therefore, this does not seem to be a case in which Origen seriously considers economic deviation on the part of the translators.

Thus, there are few passages in which Origen sees a genuine difference between the original LXX and the original Hebrew text. This conclusion differs from some previous scholarship which has sought to show either that Origen promoted the Hebrew text at the expense of the LXX, or that he advocated the LXX as a text differing from and surpassing the Hebrew.[133] On the contrary, building on Kamesar's demonstration that Origen was essentially "LXX-centered," we have shown that this emphasis on the LXX did not usually entail changes from the Hebrew text. In fact, one of the LXX's most admirable features, according to Origen, is the accuracy with which it renders the Hebrew text.[134] As Mogens Müller puts it: "as dedicated as he

---

[133] For the first view, see Nautin, *Origène,* 351–353; de Lange, "Origen's Recantation?" For the second view, see especially D. Barthélemy, "Origène et le texte de l'Ancien Testament," in J. Fontaine and C. Kannengiesser (eds.), *Epektasis* (Paris, 1972), 247–261; repr. in Barthélemy, *Études d'histoire du texte de l'Ancien Testament* (Göttingen, 1978), 203–217 (214–217); and idem, "La place de la Septante dans l'église," in *Aux grands carrefours de la révélation et de l'exégèse de l'Ancien Testament* (Paris, 1967), 13–28; repr. in the author's *Études,* 111–126 (112–114).

[134] For references and discussion, see Kamesar, *Jerome,* 15–16.

was to the Septuagint, he was convinced that this translation reflected the original Hebrew text."[135]

Origen was the first Christian to take seriously the differences between the LXX and the Hebrew text, and he dealt with these differences in various ways. He did allow some slight qualitative changes on the part of the LXX that were designed to point toward a sense deeper than the letter and highlight certain aspects of Christian theology. However, he did not develop these ideas into any sustained theory, as this type of explanation for textual variants features rarely in Origen's comments. We will see that his followers did not echo his concepts in this regard. Origen generally considered the LXX translation to be a faithful rendering of the Hebrew, and divergences between the two arise mostly from corruption in one of the two texts. Though the Hebrew is always "subordinate to the LXX" in Origen's thought,[136] nevertheless, the LXX imparts to the Church essentially the contents of the original Hebrew text.

### The Textual Theory of the Greek Fathers after Origen

Origen's textual work established that the extant LXX diverged often from the extant Hebrew text and not just from the newer Greek translations. This presented a challenge to his successors, for they could only with difficulty claim, with Justin and Irenaeus before Origen, that the LXX corresponds to the Hebrew text and any divergence derives from distorted translations by the Three. We will see that these Fathers responded to the challenge presented by Origen in various ways. On the whole, however, they followed through with few of the implications of Origen's textual research. They did not accord any practical importance to the Hebrew text, they rarely used the newer Greek translations to understand better the biblical text, and they hardly gave any thought at all to the text from which the LXX was translated.[137] So little did the Hebrew text bear upon the imagination of the Church that the contentious debate concerning the proper understanding of the prophecy in Isa. 7:14 provoked hardly any Christian to look behind the LXX at the original wording; they based their arguments solely on translations.[138]

---

[135]  Müller, *First Bible*, 81.

[136]  Kamesar, *Jerome*, 20.

[137]  See Kamesar, *Jerome*, 34–40.

[138]  See A. Kamesar, "The Virgin of Isaiah 7:14: The Philological Argument from the Second to the Fifth Century," *JTS* 41 (1990): 51–75 (57–58).

It seems that part of the reason for their ignoring Hebrew was that many Christians after Origen continued to assume that the best way to access the original Hebrew writings was through the LXX. The Fathers of this period took up previous arguments for establishing the authority of the LXX: (1) the translation that preceded Christ would not exhibit bias for or against the Christian message, and (2) the agreement of seventy(-two) translators trumps that of three (i.e., Aquila, Symmachus, and Theodotion), especially when the latter sometimes present divergent renderings.[139] These two arguments, the early date of the translation and the agreement among the translators, demonstrate that the Seventy deserve more respect and trust as faithful and accurate translators than do the Three; that is, the LXX translation matches the Hebrew text more closely. Moreover, the Fathers not infrequently charged the Three with distorting the OT, which again implies that the Hebrew text will not correspond to the newer translations.[140] Christians between Origen and Jerome did not take up Origen's suggestion that the Seventy translators occasionally altered the text to suit the Christian message. Indeed, this idea would have directly contradicted the two usual arguments for the authority of the LXX.[141] Whereas some scholars, such as Müller, have argued that the Fathers subsequent to Origen viewed the LXX as an advancement upon the Hebrew such that the translators were free to make inspired changes in the text,[142] our analysis will show that they typically sought to maintain the link between their Greek text and the original Hebrew Bible.

Eusebius of Caesarea and Gregory of Nyssa explain the variation between their LXX and the Hebrew as resulting from intentional corruption of the Hebrew text by the Jews. This judgment by Eusebius appears in the context of a discussion of the numbers in the biblical genealogies, which Eusebius wishes to exploit for chronological calculations in his *Chronicon*.[143] He trusts

---

[139] Both arguments appear in Chrysostom, *Hom. Matt.* 5.2; Theodoret, *Comm. Is.* 7:14. For the first argument, cf. also Hilary, *Tract. Ps.* 2.3; for the second, Epiphanius, *Mens.* 17; Augustine, *Epist.* 28.2.

[140] Cf. Chrysostom, *Hom. Matt.* 5.2; Theodoret, *Comm. Is.* 7:14; for references in Epiphanius, see the discussion below.

[141] Origen himself did not rely on these usual proofs for the LXX's authority. He establishes the authority of the Church's Bible by appealing to tradition as guided by Providence (*Ep. Afr.* 8–9).

[142] See, e.g., Müller, *First Bible*, 78. For further analysis of this position and the patristic sources relevant to it, see E.L. Gallagher, "The Septuagint's Fidelity to Its *Vorlage* in Greek Patristic Thought," in M.K.H. Peters (ed.), *XIV Congress of the International Organization for Septuagint and Cognate Studies: Helsinki, 2010* (Atlanta: SBL, *forthcoming*, 2012).

[143] See the edition by J. Karst, *Eusebius Werke V: Die Chronik, aus dem Armenischen über-*

the figures in his LXX more than the Hebrew text, partly because the Greek occasionally received confirmation from the Samaritan Pentateuch.[144] Nevertheless, Eusebius is confident that the LXX corresponds to the original Hebrew text because the Greek translation was made "from ancient and uncorrupted copies of the Hebrew."[145] Gregory offers a similar assessment of the relationship between the LXX and the current Hebrew text in his treatise *In inscriptiones psalmorum*. One section of this work (2.8–9) treats psalm superscriptions present in Gregory's copy of the LXX but absent from the Hebrew text. Because Gregory considers these superscriptions to bear messianic significance—they are ἐκκλησιαστικαί τε καὶ μυστικαὶ καὶ τῆς κατὰ τὸ μυστήριον ἡμῶν εὐσεβείας σημαντικαί ("ecclesiastical and mystical and indicative of the piety related to our mystery"; 91.27–92.4)—he accuses the Jews of 'silencing' (σιγάω; 95.23; 103.6) them through their 'unbelief' (ἀπιστία; 93.14) and 'wilful misunderstanding' (ἀγνωμοσύνη; 94.2).[146]

Two important and related differences from the pre-Origen Fathers emerge from these passages in Eusebius and Gregory. First, these two fourth-century writers trust the Greek Minor Versions, at least in the instances under discussion, to reflect accurately the contents of the Hebrew text extant among Jews. We have seen that especially Justin and Irenaeus deny this precise point. The second-century Fathers accuse the more recent Jewish translators of malicious intent in desiring to disprove Christianity, thus condemning themselves as unfaithful to their source text. The LXX, therefore, must correspond to the Hebrew. On the contrary, Eusebius and Gregory, both disciples of Origen, have apparently accepted their master's confidence in the authenticity of the Three, so that the LXX text stands opposed to the Hebrew itself, and not just to Aquila, Symmachus, and Theodotion. Thus forced to choose between LXX and Hebrew—something

---

*setzt*, GCS 20 (Leipzig, 1911), 40.13–20, who presents a German translation of the extant Armenian text. On the state of the text of the *Chron.*, see A. Drost-Abgarjan, "Ein neuer Fund zur armenischen Version der Eusebios-Chronik," in M. Wallraff (ed.), *Julius Africanus und die christliche Weltchronistik* (Berlin, 2006), 255–262.

[144] Cf. *Chron.*, ed. Karst, 44.20–23. Presumably Eusebius accessed the Samaritan Pentateuch through the Samareitikon, on which see R. Pummer, "The Samareitikon Revisited," in A.D. Crown and L. Davey (eds.), *Essays in Honour of G.D. Sixdenier: New Samaritan Studies* (Sydney, 1995), 381–455.

[145] Or, in Karst's German: "aus alten und fehlerlosen Vorlagen der Hebräer übersetzt worden ist"; *Chron.*, ed. Karst, 45.13–15. See [Hammond] Bammel, "Hexapla," 134.

[146] Page and line numbers refer to the edition of J. McDonough in GNO 5 (Leiden, 1962). On Gregory's discussion of these psalm superscriptions, see R.E. Heine, *Gregory of Nyssa's Treatise on the Inscriptions of the Psalms* (Oxford, 1995), 145 n. 85; Gallagher, "Septuagint's Fidelity."

the second-century Fathers did not have to do—Eusebius and Gregory both side with the LXX and accuse the Jews of tampering with the text of the Hebrew Bible. This represents the second difference from the pre-Origen writers. Whereas Justin and Irenaeus attributed corruption to the Jewish Minor Versions under the assumption that the LXX matched the Hebrew, Eusebius and Gregory assert that the Hebrew text itself has suffered (intentional) corruption. Origen had been unwilling to deem the existing Hebrew text always pristine; Eusebius and Gregory develop this idea further. Their discussions suggest that the original LXX replicated the original Hebrew and the latter has undergone alteration since the days of Ptolemy. Once again, this view might result from Origen's work. After all, Eusebius is credited in antiquity with promoting Origen's hexaplaric text of the LXX.[147] Presumably, then, he (and perhaps Gregory, also) felt confident that Origen had successfully 'healed' the Greek text (cf. Origen, *Comm. Matt.* 15.14), so that any variation between the hexaplaric LXX and the Hebrew must be the fault of corruption in the Hebrew text.

One might assume that Epiphanius of Salamis would present a more nuanced picture of the relationship between the LXX and Hebrew text, for he received the admiration of even Jerome (*Ruf.* 2.22; 3.6) for his broad linguistic competence, which included a knowledge of Hebrew.[148] Indeed, Epiphanius' views are somewhat complex, and his lengthy discussion in *De mensuris et ponderibus* introduces certain new elements.[149] The complexity of his position has engendered some misunderstanding by modern scholars, who interpret his statements as denying the essential identity of the LXX with the Hebrew. For example, Müller has asserted that Epiphanius "admitted to some discrepancies between the Greek translation and Hebrew text which were not owing to later correction."[150] However, Epiphanius shares

---

[147] Cf. Jerome, *Praef. Paralip. IH*, lines 10–12; and see Gentry, *Asterisked Materials*, 8–9 n. 19; Nautin, *Origène*, 354–358.

[148] See J. Dummer, "Die Sprachkenntnisse des Epiphanius," in F. Altheim and R. Stiehl (eds.), *Die Araber in der alten Welt*, 5 1 (Berlin, 1968), 392–435; repr. in Dummer, *Philologia Sacra et Profana* (Stuttgart, 2006), 29–72, who is skeptical of Epiphanius' knowledge of Hebrew and Aramaic (35–47).

[149] I have used the edition by Elia D. Moutsoula, "Τὸ Περὶ μέτρων καὶ σταθμῶν ἔργον Ἐπιφανίου τοῦ Σαλαμῖνος," *Theologia* 44 (1973): 157–200; indications of lines numbers in the present context refer to this edition. I have also consulted the English translation of the Syriac text found in James E. Dean, *Epiphanius' Treatise on Weights and Measures: The Syriac Version* (Chicago: University of Chicago Press, 1935). For references to other editions of Epiphanius' work, see Veltri, *Libraries*, 59–60 n. 116.

[150] Müller, *First Bible*, 78; see also Karpp, "'Prophet' oder 'Dolmetscher'," 138; Kamesar, *Jerome*, 34; Veltri, "Septuagint in Disgrace," 143.

with his predecessors and contemporaries a belief in the fidelity of the Seventy translators to their *Vorlage*, so that any differences between the Greek and Hebrew text should be interpreted as either irrelevant or a product of Jewish falsification.[151]

Epiphanius first explains that the asterisk (*Mens.* 2) and obelus (*Mens.* 3; 6) appearing in hexaplaric manuscripts signal quantitative differences between the Greek and Hebrew, this latter being reflected in Aquila and Symmachus, and "occasionally" (σπανίως; *Mens.* 2.17) Theodotion, at least with regard to passages under asterisk. Epiphanius characterizes most of these differences between the LXX and the Hebrew as the natural result of translation. The Seventy omitted certain 'superfluous' expressions in order to conform the Bible to Greek style; that is, these expressions are appropriate to Hebrew style but would sound strange in Greek, as Aquila's translation demonstrates (*Mens.* 2). Likewise, the translators added some words σαφηνείας ἕνεκα τοῦ λόγου ("for clarity of expression"; *Mens.* 17.465–466), or εἰς φράσιν καὶ ὠφέλειαν ("for literary style and for assistance"; *Mens.* 6.171). The examples Epiphanius chooses to illustrate the point further accentuate the insignificance of such changes for the meaning of the text. As for the type of material omitted by the Seventy, Epiphanius points to Gen. 5:5, which gives Adam's age as τριάκοντα ἔτος καὶ ἐννακόσια ἔτος according to the Hebrew text and Aquila (*Mens.* 2.23–24). The LXX appropriately smoothes out the text for Greek readers by omitting one ἔτος, thus: τριάκοντα καὶ ἐννακόσια ἔτη (*Mens.* 2.31). Turning to the additions made by the Seventy, Epiphanius quotes Ps. 140:1 (LXX) according to the Hebrew as πρόσχες τῇ φωνῇ (*Mens.* 6.164), to which the Seventy have added the clarifying expression τῆς δεήσεώς μου. In Epiphanius' view, the vast majority of differences between the Greek and Hebrew represent immaterial changes wrought by the Seventy simply to make a foreign text clear to Greek speakers. They are, in fact, no real changes at all.

With this context in view, one may properly understand Epiphanius' report about the translation in *Mens.* 6.

> Καὶ ὅπου μὲν προσέθεντο λόγον πάντες ὁμοῦ προσέθεντο, ὅπου δὲ ἀφείλοντο πάντες ἐπ' ἴσης ἀφείλοντο. Καὶ ὧν μὲν ἀφείλοντο οὐκ ἔστι χρεία, ὧν δὲ προσέθεντο ἔστι χρεία.    (*Mens.* 6.155–157)

> And wherever they added a word, they all added it together, and wherever they omitted something, they all equally omitted it. And the things they omitted were unnecessary, but the things they added were necessary.

---

[151] For a more extensive and detailed treatment of Epiphanius' views on the relationship between the LXX and the Hebrew text, see Gallagher, "Septuagint's Fidelity."

It is this passage that has caused some scholars to attribute to Epiphanius the view that the Seventy translators altered the biblical text. But in light of his earlier discussion of the words added and omitted by the translators, it is clear that Epiphanius denied that these changes bore such an implication. Rather, the additions and omissions constituted insignificant details designed to allow the biblical text to speak clearly to a Greek audience. In fact, in the same context, Epiphanius says that the translations were compared with the Hebrew text, with no contradiction discovered (*Mens.* 6.149–152). Throughout this discussion of passages added and subtracted, Epiphanius endeavors to acquit the translators of the charge of altering the biblical text.

Epiphanius also believes that certain apparent contradictions between the LXX and Hebrew are actually cases in which the Three have offered perverse translations. In this, he revives the views of Justin and Irenaeus. According to Epiphanius, Aquila distorted messianic prophecies (*Mens.* 15.414–418), Symmachus obscured passages relevant to the Samaritans (*Mens.* 16.445–447), and, while Theodotion usually agreed with the LXX, he did work 'alone' (ἰδίως; *Mens.* 17.454)[152] and stands together with Aquila and Symmachus against the 'truth' of the LXX (*Mens.* 17.458).

In comparison to Eusebius and Gregory of Nyssa, Epiphanius has several different opinions. He does not, as a rule, trust the Three to reflect accurately the current Hebrew text. Rather, the Three have often distorted the text to serve their own agendas. Neither does Epiphanius give serious consideration to textual corruption in the Hebrew as an explanation for divergences from the LXX. On the whole, he seems to assume, with Justin and Irenaeus, that the extant LXX corresponds to the extant Hebrew text, with due allowance being made for the nature of a translation, which cannot achieve one-to-one correspondence, not even an inspired translation.[153] This evaluation perhaps results from a more comprehensive examination of textual variation between Greek and Hebrew than that conducted by Eusebius or Gregory. Epiphanius saw that the majority of differences were inconsequential, and this realization shaped the way he discussed the matter.

---

[152] For the possibility that this is a criticism of Theodotion, see Salvesen, "Convergence," 247.

[153] Epiphanius' position thus matches more closely that of Sirach's grandson rather than that of Philo (*Mos.* 2.40). Note also that Epiphanius is willing to allow some variation in wording even among the original translators (*Mens.* 8.204–225; *Mens.* 17.477–482).

Theodoret of Cyrus, like Eusebius and Gregory, does trust the Three to represent the Hebrew text, but, unlike them, when confronted with a divergence between his LXX and the Hebrew, he tends to attribute corruption to the LXX manuscript tradition. This view becomes apparent in his *Comm. Psal.*, when he encounters superscriptions that diverge between his copy of the LXX and the Hebrew text. He concludes that an interpolator has added these superscriptions in the LXX after the time of the Seventy. He continues to assume, like the Fathers before him, that the original LXX matched precisely the original Hebrew. So, he says of the superscription appearing before Ps. 93 (LXX), which finds no correspondence in the Hebrew: Δῆλον, ὡς τὴν ἐπιγραφὴν ἄλλοι τινὲς τεθείκασι, καὶ οὔτε ὁ προφήτης, οὔτε οἱ τοῦτον ἐξ ἀρχῆς ἑρμηνεύσαντες ("It is clear that some others have inserted the superscription, not the prophet or the original translators").[154] Since Theodoret believes that the Seventy translators closely adhered to the Hebrew text (τῇ Ἑβραίων γλώττῃ δουλεύσαντες),[155] he must assume that the Hebrew prophet (i.e., David) and the original translators would have agreed in omitting the spurious superscription.[156]

Theodoret was one of the later members of the Antiochene School of biblical interpretation. While Theodoret maintained a very traditional approach to the LXX, some of his predecessors actually doubted its flawless reliability as a translation and attributed ultimate authority to the Hebrew text. Eusebius of Emesa based his exegesis on the text of the LXX, but he did not accord inspiration to this translation and he often sought to improve it with reference to what he termed ὁ Ἑβραῖος ('the Hebrew') and ὁ Σύρος ('the Syrian'). It seems that, as a native speaker of Syriac and author of Greek exegetical works, Eusebius understood the perils of translating and refused to ascribe authority to any text but the original. When he believed he encountered errors in the LXX, he attempted to determine the reading in Hebrew (which language he did not know) by exploiting a Syriac translation.[157] Eusebius' work formed the basis of that of his student, Diodore of

---

[154] PG 80.1629b–c; cf. Ps. 95 (LXX), PG 80.1644c–d; Ps. 96 (LXX), PG 80.1652b. Theodoret mentions that he has checked the reading in the *Hexapla*; on his access to the *Hexapla*, see J.-N. Guinot, "La fortune des *Hexaples* d'Origène aux IVe et Ve siècles en milieu antiochien," in G. Dorival and A. Le Boulluec (eds.), *Origeniana Sexta* (Leuven, 1995), 215–225 (esp. 219 n. 22).

[155] *Comm. Cant.* 3:6 (PG 81.120a); see J.-N. Guinot, "Théodoret de Cyr: une lecture critique de la Septante," in G. Dorival and O. Munnich (eds.), *Κατα τους ο'—Selon les Septante* (Paris, 1995), 393–407 (esp. p. 396).

[156] For further discussion of Theodoret's position, see Gallagher, "Septuagint's Fidelity."

[157] See Haar Romeny, *Syrian*, esp. 106–112.

Tarsus, who also did not scruple to criticize the LXX.[158] Theodore of Mopsuestia, like his predecessors, recognized the priority and authority of the
Hebrew text (*Comm. Ps.* 35:2a) and considered the LXX an imperfect translation (*Comm. Ps.* 55:7).[159] However, he rejected the methods of his teachers;
instead of using the Syriac translation to arrive at a better understanding of
the Hebrew, Theodore lambasted use of the Syriac as a departure from the
Hebrew (*Comm. Hab.* 2:11). He advocated access to the Hebrew only through
the LXX. Flawed as it might be, it still presented the Hebrew more accurately
than any other translation because those who produced it were experts both
in their own language and in the divine scriptures (*Comm. Soph.* 1:4–6).[160]

This brief survey has shown some of the ways the Fathers subsequent to
Origen attempted to deal with the textual evidence compiled by the great
scholar of Caesarea. Most of them continued to attribute inspiration to the
original Seventy translators, but they devised different means by which to
explain the deviations between the extant LXX and the extant Hebrew.
Eusebius of Caesarea and Gregory of Nyssa trusted the accuracy of the Three
as translators of the current Hebrew text, but they cast a suspicious eye at
that Hebrew text as it then existed among the Jews. Epiphanius considered
his copy of the LXX to be equivalent to the contemporary Hebrew text (thus,
like Justin and Irenaeus), and he emphasized that most perceived variations
were simply the necessary consequence of competent translation. However,
he also thought that the Three sometimes distorted the text. The Antiochenes generally trusted the current Hebrew text but had conflicting views
on the LXX. Theodoret of Cyrus believed that the original translation perfectly matched the Hebrew but that it had suffered through transmission,
while Eusebius of Emesa, Diodore of Tarsus, and Theodore of Mopsuestia
each deemed the LXX a flawed translation. Thus, these fourth- and fifth-
century Greek Fathers responded to the challenge presented by Origen's
text-critical work in various ways, but each either explicitly or implicitly
affirmed the authority and originality of the Hebrew text, though they sometimes thought it had not been preserved in its pristine state. For those

---

[158] See Haar Romeny, *Syrian*, 131–135; C. Schäublin, *Untersuchungen zu Methode und Herkunft der antiochenischen Exegese* (Cologne, 1974), 125.

[159] For further references, see Schäublin, *Untersuchungen*, 126 n. 165.

[160] See Haar Romeny, *Syrian*, 135–138; Kamesar, *Jerome*, 39–40. For the textual position of
Theodore's brother Polychronius of Apamea, see P. Bruns, "Polychronius von Apamea—Der
Exeget und Theologe," *StPatr* 37 (2001), 404–412, who writes, "Maßgebend ist für den Bischof
von Apamea bei der Interpretation des Daniel-Textes allein der aramäisch-hebräische Ur-
text" (407).

Fathers who continued to trumpet the LXX as an inspired translation, this Greek text constituted the authoritative form of the OT because it reflected the original Hebrew so accurately.

### The Textual Theory of Jerome and His Opponents

Jerome would not allow discussion concerning the biblical text to continue along the path just outlined. His motivations for beginning a study of the Hebrew language and the chronology of his developing views on the biblical text are issues that have been studied often and will not receive treatment here.[161] Instead, we will explore the way Jerome's textual theory differed from that of his predecessors. Rather than attempting a comprehensive treatment, we will continue our narrow focus, here exploring how Jerome conceived of the faithfulness of the LXX translators to their Hebrew *Vorlage*.

More than any previous Christian, Jerome invested substantial time in serious textual research, which allowed him to perceive the vast differences between the LXX and Hebrew. This in itself would not inevitably result in an innovative textual theory; Origen had also done extensive textual research, but he was generally content to explain textual variation in terms of corruption in the LXX or Hebrew, a view accepted by many other Christians. Jerome refused to follow this reasoning, believing instead that both texts remained essentially in their original form. We turn now to a demonstration of this point.

It may be thought that Jerome's promotion of the hexaplaric LXX as the authentic LXX suggests that Jerome regarded the Greek text as having suffered significant corruption through the course of its transmission, and that Origen's text-critical work had restored the LXX to its pristine state. After all, Jerome describes the hexaplaric LXX as *incorrupta et inmaculata septuaginta interpretum translatio* ("the incorrupt and undefiled translation of the Seventy interpreters"; *Epist.* 106.2), *emendata et vera exemplaria Septuaginta* ("the corrected and true copies of the LXX"; *Comm. Isa.* 58:11), and as *ipsi*

---

[161] For the older view of Jerome's 'conversion' to the *Hebraica veritas* following his move to Bethlehem see W. Schwarz, *Principles and Problems of Biblical Translation* (Cambridge, 1955), 26–34; M.E. Schild, *Abendländische Bibelvorreden bis zur Lutherbibel* (Heidelberg, 1970), 21–31. Kamesar's revised chronology (*Jerome*, 41–72), which locates Jerome's acceptance of the *Hebraica veritas* about a decade earlier, is reflected in, e.g., C.T.R. Hayward, *Saint Jerome's Hebrew Questions on Genesis* (Oxford, 1995), 10; A. Fürst, *Hieronymus* (Freiburg, 2003), 102–106; Salvesen, "Convergence," 248–250; S. Rebenich, *Jerome* (London, 2002), 29; M.H. Williams, *The Monk and the Book* (Chicago, 2006), 81–95 (see also pp. 60, 65 n. 6).

*Septuaginta* ("the LXX itself"; *Comm. Ezech.* 4:4–6).[162] However, Jerome can also present a completely opposite viewpoint, as when he criticizes Augustine for using the hexaplaric LXX instead of the genuine translation:

> *et miror, quomodo septuaginta interpretum libros legas non puros, ut ab eis editi sunt, sed ab Origene emendatos sive corruptos per obelos et asteriscos.*
>
> (*Epist.* 112.19)

> and I am amazed that you read the books of the Seventy interpreters not in their pure form, as they were edited by them, but corrected or rather corrupted by Origen with obeli and asterisks.

Though Jerome is being sarcastic here, this statement does show that he can represent Origen's textual achievement as either a return to the authentic LXX or a departure from the original translation, whichever his rhetorical point demands. Scholars have recognized the need for caution in interpreting Jerome's statements on the LXX, since he changes his evaluation of it depending on the audience and occasion of his writing.[163] We should probably use the same caution when interpreting Jerome's appraisal of the hexaplaric form of the LXX.

Some of Jerome's later commentaries provide evidence that he generally considered the traditional LXX, and not the hexaplaric edition, to best represent the original translation. For instance, at *Comm. Isa.* 2:20, Jerome says that the Seventy translators omitted a particular phrase, and that Origen added it into his edition under asterisk. At Isa. 40:7, the hexaplaric LXX includes a phrase under asterisk, which prompts Jerome's comment: *ex quo manifestum est, vel a LXX praetermissum, vel paulatim scriptorum vitio abolitum* ("from which it is manifest that either it was omitted by the Seventy or it was gradually abolished by the fault of the scribes").[164] It is important to note that in these passages, Jerome does not take it for granted that the hexaplaric LXX should be identified with original LXX; on the contrary, he suggests that the Seventy translators were responsible for errors in the Greek text and that Origen's work corrected these errors. Jerome's *Comm. Jer.* offers explanations on several occasions as to why the Seventy

---

[162] These citations are collected by Kamesar, *Jerome*, 56. See also the statement in *Praef. Paralip.* (*IH*) as cited by Kamesar on p. 61.

[163] See, e.g., [Hammond] Bammel, "Hexapla," 142.

[164] P. Jay, *L'exégèse de saint Jérôme d'après son 'Commentaire sur Isaïe'* (Paris, 1985), 114–119, shows that Jerome generally presents the Origenian recension as the LXX in his *Comm. Isa.*, but the comments we have noticed suggest that he did so not because this recension was an accurate representation of the original translation, but because it was an improvement on the original translation. For Jerome's view that passages under obelus in Isa. were added by the Seventy, see his comments on Isa. 40:1; 51:9; 60:1.

excluded material from their translation, material that is known to have been included by Origen under asterisk in his hexaplaric edition.[165] Far from deeming the hexaplaric LXX to be *ipsi Septuaginta* (cf. *Comm. Ezech.* 4:4–6), Jerome indicates in these passages that Origen's work changed the traditional and authentic LXX so that it would be more in line with the Hebrew. Certainly, this change met Jerome's approval, and it is likely that his promotion of the hexaplaric LXX was based solely on its proximity to the Hebrew rather than on any claim it might have to represent the original translation. Indeed, when Jerome describes the hexaplaric LXX as 'correct,' he probably means this in so far as it approximates the Hebrew, without any real regard for how closely it approximates the OG.[166] On the whole, it is doubtful whether Jerome judged the original Greek translation to have suffered more than minor textual corruption during the course of its transmission.

Jerome did occasionally acknowledge minor points of corruption among Hebrew manuscripts. For instance, in his *Comm. Habac.* 2:19 he reveals that some Hebrew manuscripts add the word *omnis* to *spiritus*, while in other manuscripts *spiritus* stands alone. But it does not seem that Jerome perceived in this variation any wider implications about the state of the text.[167] Elsewhere, and more significantly, he considers possible that the Jews falsified their Hebrew texts at Deut. 27:26, where the LXX's *maledictus omnis homo qui non permanserit in omnibus sermonibus Legis huius* ("cursed is every person who does not abide in all the words of this law") provides a reading superior in Jerome's mind to the corresponding text in Hebrew, which lacks *omnis homo* ("every person") and *in omnibus* ("in all"). Three reasons compel Jerome to deem the LXX reading preferable: it makes more sense in context, it agrees with Paul's citation of this verse in Gal. 3:10, and the Samaritan Pentateuch corresponds to the LXX for this verse. He

---

[165] For Jerome's attempts at explaining the LXX readings, see M. Graves, *Jerome's Hebrew Philology* (Leiden, 2007), 55–56, who cites Jerome's comments at Jer. 30:10–11 (= LXX 37:10–11); 27:1 (= LXX 34:1); 28:10 (= LXX 35:10); 17:1. For the hexaplaric readings, see the apparatus in J. Ziegler, *Jeremiah, Baruch, Threni, Epistula Jeremiae*, Septuaginta 15 (Göttingen, 1957).

[166] Similarly, Kamesar, *Jerome*, 57: "But, in the face of the 'trifaria varietas', why did Jerome view the Hexaplaric recension as the correct one? The reason can only be its closer proximity to the Hebrew." However, Kamesar does not address the question as to what extent Jerome may have considered the Origenian recension to represent the original Greek translation. For a persuasive interpretation of Jerome's work on the hexaplaric text as one aspect of his campaign to move the Church toward the Hebrew text, see the wider discussion in Kamesar, *Jerome*, 49–58.

[167] This passage is cited by Graves, *Jerome's Hebrew Philology*, 54 n. 140. For Jerome's general practice of textual criticism, especially in his *Comm. Jer.*, see the entire discussion of Graves on pp. 53–61. See also Williams, *Monk*, 123–128.

speculates that the Jews have changed their text *ne viderentur esse sub maledicto* ("lest they should seem to be under a curse"; *Comm. Gal.* 3:10).[168]

Nevertheless, the confluence of evidence necessary in this case for Jerome to consider the Hebrew corrupt confirms Jerome's fundamental belief in the stability of this text. Moreover, he will later declare laughable any attempt to explain a textual problem by appealing to Jewish falsification: had this happened prior to the NT, then Jesus would surely have condemned the Jews for it (a point Jerome attributes to Origen), and had it happened after the NT, it is incomprehensible how the Jews could have produced through falsification so many messianic prophecies that agree with their fulfillment in the NT (*Comm. Isa.* 6:9). In fact, nearly the same conditions apply to the textual situation for Isa. 6:9 as for Deut. 27:26—Paul's citation of Isa. 6:9 in Acts 28:26–27 agrees with the LXX, which gives a reading much easier to understand than what is found in the Hebrew. However, Jerome's general unwillingness to ascribe error to the Hebrew manuscripts obliges him to find another explanation. Aside from exploring the theology of the passage to make sense of the Hebrew, Jerome offers two explanations for Paul's variant citation of the text in Acts. First, Luke, the author of Acts, routinely used Greek citations rather than Hebrew ones, by which Jerome implies that the historical Paul may have actually used the Hebrew text, while the extant quotation from the LXX is due to Luke.[169] Second, the Epistle to the Hebrews, which Jerome attributes to Paul, attests that this apostle sometimes quoted the variant text of the LXX when he addressed Jews. This is a striking admission from Jerome, who earlier had claimed that Paul never produced testimonies that were not found in Hebrew (*Comm. Gal.* 3:10).

---

[168] On this passage, see Adler, "Jews as Falsifiers," 10–11; Williams, *Monk*, 75–77. Jerome wrote his *Comm. Gal.* in 386. When he later translated the Pentateuch from the Hebrew, he rendered Deut. 26:27 in accordance with the Hebrew as *maledictus qui* [...]. For other occasions when Jerome prefers readings alternative to the Hebrew, see Fürst, *Hieronymus*, 112–114; and S. Rebenich, "Jerome: The 'Vir Trilinguis' and the 'Hebraica Veritas'," *VC* 47 (1993): 50–77 (64 with n. 111 on p. 77). A further example in the *Comm. Gal.* comes at Gal. 3:13 quoting Deut. 21:23, discussed by G. Raspanti, "The Significance of Jerome's *Commentary on Galatians* in his Exegetical Production," in A. Cain and J. Lössl (eds.), *Jerome of Stridon* (Surrey, 2009), 163–171 (169–170).

[169] See Adler, "Jews as Falsifiers," 12; C. Markschies, "Hieronymus und die 'Hebraica Veritas': Ein Beitrag zur Archäologie des protestantischen Schriftverständnisses," in Hengel and Schwemer, *Die Septuaginta*, 131–181 (147 n. 103). A parallel explanation for a variant between a speaker in Acts and the Hebrew text is found in *Qu. hebr. Gen.* 46:26 where Jerome must explain why Stephen in Acts 7:14 said that 75 descendants of Jacob had entered Israel (thus agreeing with the LXX of Gen. 46:27), while the MT of Gen. 46:27 lists the number as 70.

Clearly, Jerome had great faith in the authenticity of the Hebrew text available in his day; not even evidence from NT citations could consistently lead Jerome to emend what he considered the *Hebraica veritas*.[170] On the other hand, Jerome considered the NT to corroborate the stability of the Hebrew text. We have observed the long-standing Christian tradition insisting that the apostolic use of the LXX sanctioned this version for the Church. Jerome agreed that the NT should stand as judge over the correct text of the OT: *perspicuum est illa magis vera esse exemplaria, quae cum novi testamenti auctoritate concordant* ("it is clear that those copies are more true that agree with the authority of the NT"; *Qu. hebr. Gen.* prol.). However, Jerome turned this argument on its head, insisting that the apostles actually quoted from the Hebrew Bible against the LXX in several passages (cf. *Praef. Pent.* 11–19).[171] Jerome argues this point even to the extent of challenging Rufinus to find any passage in the NT quoted from the LXX in disagreement with the Hebrew (*Ruf.* 2.34), a challenge which we have already seen Jerome himself answer.[172] Yet, the argument proved somewhat effective: Augustine comes to see that the apostles quote from both the Hebrew and LXX (*Civ.* 15.14; 18.44; contrast his earlier view at *Epist.* 71.6). Moreover, the passages Jerome uses to establish his point concern messianic prophecies (e.g. Matt. 2:15 quoting Hos. 11:1), the very types of passages which Christians had long

---

[170] Jerome's belief in the stability of the Hebrew text is often emphasized in scholarship; see, e.g., O. Wermelinger, "Le canon des latins au temps de Jérôme et d'Augustin," in J.-D. Kaestli and O. Wermelinger (eds.), *Le Canon de l'Ancien Testament* (Geneva, 1984), 153–196 (187); Graves, *Jerome's Hebrew Philology*, 129; Williams, *Monk*, 127: "He seems unable to imagine that the process of transmission had ever infected the Hebrew textual tradition with multiple readings." On the other hand, Markschies ("Hieronymus und die 'Hebraica Veritas'," 160–161) mistranslates and misinterprets Jerome's statement in *Praef. Paralip. IH* (lines 30–31), *ad Hebraeos igitur revertendum est*, when he suggests that this implies that we should correct the Hebrew text on the basis of the NT quotations; this opinion is accepted by Müller, *First Bible*, 85 and n. 30. For the correct interpretation of this passage in Jerome, see A.S. Jacobs, *Remains of the Jews* (Stanford, Calif., 2004), 80; J. Cameron, "The Rabbinic Vulgate?" in Cain and Lössl, *Jerome of Stridon*, 117–129 (124).

[171] For further references, see A. Fürst, "*Veritas Latina*. Augustins Haltung gegenüber Hieronymus' Bibelübersetzungen," *REAug* 40 (1994): 105–126 (114–115 n. 27). For analysis of how this argument fits in Jerome's presentation of his textual theory, see Schild, *Bibelvorreden*, 34–35; Kamesar, *Jerome*, 63–65; Markschies, "Hieronymus und die 'Hebraica Veritas'," 146–148. For a critique of Jerome on this point, see Benoit, "L'inspiration," 182–183; J.S. Cameron, "The *Vir Tricultus*: An Investigation of the Classical, Jewish and Christian Influences on Jerome's Translation of the Psalter *Iuxta Hebraeos*" (diss.: University of Oxford, 2006), 203–242.

[172] On Rufinus' attempt at an answer to Jerome, see [Hammond] Bammel, "Hexapla," 138–139. Benoit ("L'inspiration," 182 n. 83) characterizes Jerome's challenge as "d'une naïveté qui est presque risible."

accused the Jews of corrupting. Though Jerome does not take the argument beyond vindicating the Hebrew in reference to the NT, it further implies that the current Hebrew text corresponds to the one used by the apostles, which must then be the true and original biblical text. Textual corruption is not a factor.

Thus, though we have noted some exceptions, Jerome generally considered the traditional texts of the Hebrew Bible and LXX current in his day to represent the original forms of those texts. He did not generally explain the differences between them as due to textual corruption. We have seen that Epiphanius held a similar view, but his next step was to deny significant differences between the original and the translation, attributing most perceived differences to translation technique. Jerome, however, recognizes the differences to be true and substantial, so that he arrives at the startling conclusion that the original LXX translation diverges widely and often from the original Hebrew. The only explanation for such a situation is that the LXX translators themselves changed the text. Indeed, Jerome repeatedly makes exactly this point.[173] He even speculates on why the LXX made such changes, often presenting their motives as reasonable but mistaken.[174] On the other hand, Jerome is more disparaging when he adopts the rabbinic tradition about the translators' modifying the text to make it more palatable for the pagan King Ptolemy (cf. *Praef. Pent.* 21–25).[175]

Jerome thus dispelled corruption in transmission as an explanation for the differences between the Greek and Hebrew texts. He saw these differences as true differences, making it necessary to choose one text as opposed to the other. Despite the tradition ascribing prophetic gifts to the Seventy translators, Jerome denied that translation could involve prophesying (*Praef. Pent.* 29–34). Therefore, the changes introduced by the translators, however well-intentioned, were illegitimate and must be rejected. Jerome chose the *Hebraica veritas* as the authentic record of God's revelation, but

---

[173] Cf. *Praef. Isa.* 11–14; *Praef. Ezech.* 9–11. Of course, Jerome knew that the original Seventy translators worked on the Pentateuch alone (cf., e.g., *Qu. hebr. Gen.* prol.; see Hengel, *Septuagint*, 49 n. 78), so the changes that appear in other parts of the canon would be due to other translators, as Jerome hints in *Praef. Dan.* 5–6; cf. *Praef. Ezech.* 9–11 where he wonders whether these are the same translators as elsewhere. At *Qu. hebr. Gen.* prol., he considers the original Seventy translators more accurate than those who later translated the non-Pentateuchal books.

[174] Cf. *Praef. Isa.* 11–14; and see the discussion of altered passages in Jeremiah by Graves, *Jerome's Hebrew Philology*, 56. See also Salvesen, "Convergence," 252–253.

[175] See Kamesar, *Jerome*, 66–67; D. Barthélemy, "Eusèbe, la Septante et 'les autres'," in *La Bible et les Pères* (Paris, 1971), 51–65; repr. in the author's *Études*, 179–193 (187–191).

in this he did not depart from the theory of his predecessors, who also considered the original Hebrew text to be accurate and authoritative. Indeed, Jerome relies on this general acceptance of the authority of the Hebrew text when he repeatedly counsels his opponents to "ask the Hebrews" regarding the accuracy of his translation (cf. *Prol. gal.* 69–73).[176] For, Jerome's translation would be thus vindicated only if his detractors likewise deemed the Hebrew text used by the Jews to be a valid criterion by which to judge any translation. Thus, while Jerome's return to the Hebrew text was completely innovative in practice,[177] he did inherit the theory of an authoritative Hebrew original. It was in his rejection of the LXX as an accurate reflection of the *Hebraica veritas* that Jerome set himself against Christian tradition.

The responses to Jerome's textual work were generally very negative, as may be judged by his prefaces to the translations, which routinely contain defenses against those who were denigrating his work. Even his translations from the LXX and his revision of the Gospels inspired criticisms, but these only increased as he began translating the OT from the Hebrew text.[178] The preface to his translation of Job *iuxta Hebraeos* begins with these words:

> *Cogor per singulos Scripturae divinae libros adversariorum respondere maledictis, qui interpretationem meam reprehensionem Septuaginta interpretum criminantur.*

> I am compelled through individual books of divine Scripture to respond to the curses of adversaries, who accuse my translation of denigrating the Seventy interpreters.

This sentence illustrates that the objections to Jerome's work generally arose from a desire to maintain the LXX and the perception that Jerome posed a threat to this aim. We have seen in this chapter that the typical Christian position involved adherence to the LXX as the best representation

---

[176] See further the quotations compiled by Rebenich, "Jerome," 74 n. 84.

[177] For which see Fürst, *Hieronymus*, 105.

[178] See Schild, *Bibelvorreden*, 19–20. For criticisms of his translations from Greek, see the references collected by Fürst, "*Veritas Latina*," 124 n. 56. On the other hand, Augustine (*Epist.* 28.2) was not displeased with Jerome's translations from the LXX, and he was, indeed, very pleased with Jerome's work on the Gospels (*Epist.* 71.6), on which see H.A.G. Houghton, "Augustine's Adoption of the Vulgate Gospels," *NTS* 54 (2008): 450–464. For Augustine's use of Jerome's versions *iuxta LXX*, see P.-M. Bogaert, "Les bibles d' Augustin," *RTL* 37 (2006): 513–531 (524–525). There were positive evaluations of his work on the Hebrew text: Sophronius rendered some of Jerome's translations into Greek (*Vir. ill.* 134; *Ruf.* 2.24; see Williams, *Monk*, 87–88). For Jerome's impact after his death, see the brief survey by P. Jay, "Jerome (ca. 347–419/420)," in C. Kannengiesser, *Handbook of Patristic Exegesis* (Leiden, 2004), 1094–1133 (1099–1102).

of the original Hebrew Bible, and this probably remained true even for Jerome's detractors. In other words, their opposition to Jerome probably did not entail a rejection of the Hebrew text in theory. At least, Jerome assumed as much. We have just seen that Jerome's insistence that the Jews can vouch for his translation makes sense only if his detractors agreed that the Hebrew text occupied an authoritative position. Rather than rejecting the authority of the Hebrew text, most of Jerome's opponents probably adopted a position that combined adherence to the LXX with a theoretical acknowledgment of the priority and authority of the Hebrew.

For example, some of Jerome's opponents considered him incompetent to translate the Hebrew Bible. In a work no longer extant but summarized in Photius' *Bibliotheca* (cod. 177), Theodore of Mopsuestia disparages Jerome's translation as the product of a man who learned his Hebrew from a second-rate teacher ('Εβραίων τις τῶν χαμαιπετῶν) and thus has no business overturning the translation of the Seventy or anyone else.[179] Though Theodore did not regard the LXX as a perfect translation (see above), he did consider the Seventy translators to be perfectly suited to their task. He describes them as

πρεσβύτεροι τοῦ λαοῦ, ἐπιστήμονες μὲν ἀκριβῶς τῆς γλώττης τῆς οἰκείας, ἐπιστήμονες δὲ καὶ τῶν θείων Γραφῶν, ὑπό τε τοῦ ἱερέως καὶ παντὸς τοῦ Ἰσραηλιτικοῦ
λαοῦ δοκιμασθέντες, ὡς ἂν πάντων μάλιστα πρὸς τὴν ἑρμηνείαν ἄξιοι.

(*Comm. Soph.* 1:4–6)

elders of the people, profoundly learned in their own language, and learned also in the divine Scriptures, approved by both the priest and the entire Israelite people as fit for the task of translation more than anyone else.

The number of translators, their position among the people, their knowledge of Hebrew and scripture, and their selection by Eleazar and the Jewish nation ensure that the LXX translation is reliable; Jerome's qualifications pale in comparison, as does his translation. Rufinus implies a similar criticism of Jerome's translation by saying that the apostles, especially Paul, had the linguistic capacity to check the accuracy of the LXX, but did not care to emend that ancient and revered translation (*Apol. Hier.* 2.37–38).

---

[179] On Theodore's criticisms of Jerome, see Kamesar, *Jerome*, 39–40. For the text of the *Bibliotheca*, see vol. 2 (121b–122a) of R. Henry, *Photius: Bibliothèque*, 9 vols. (Paris, 1959–1991). Photius says that the criticisms concern a man whom Theodore calls 'Αράμ; this must be a nickname for Jerome, apparently based on his (limited) ability to read Aramaic, as suggested by H.B. Swete, *Theodori Episcopi Mopsuesteni in Epistolas B. Pauli Commentarii*, 2 vols. (Cambridge, 1880–1882), 2.332.

A second position advocated by Jerome's detractors can also take Rufinus as its example. Later in his *Apologia adversus Hieronymum*, Rufinus took up again the oft-repeated notion that the Jews altered their text, with the implication that it is this corrupted Hebrew text which Jerome was translating. Rufinus says that Origen's motivation for producing the *Hexapla* derived from discussions with Jews who lied (*mentior*) about passages that were added or subtracted in the LXX. Origen wanted to show that, in fact, it was their texts (*apud illos*) that had suffered additions and deletions. By the Aristarchian signs, Origen did not intend to prescribe new readings to be added or traditional ones deleted (as Jerome interprets the asterisk and obelus; cf., e.g., *Praef. Pent.* 9–11), but rather he wanted to show what had been deleted and added by "other translators" (*alii interpretes*; *Apol. Hier.* 2.40).[180] Rufinus continues the tradition of accusing the Jews of falsifying their texts, which charge entails that the LXX reflects the ancient and authentic text of the Hebrew Bible.

Augustine was perhaps the only contemporary of Jerome who both harbored reservations about the latter's translation enterprise and also took seriously his textual research. Augustine's most mature views on the relationship between the LXX and its Hebrew *Vorlage* are found in his *De civitate dei*, which was written during the years 413–426. The ideas presented in that work developed from earlier and less sophisticated views, as becomes clear through an examination of his correspondence with Jerome.[181] Both of the

---

[180] On Rufinus' criticisms of Jerome's translations, see Rebenich, "Jerome," 63–65; Markschies, "Hieronymus und die 'Hebraica Veritas'," 169–175. My interpretation of Rufinus diverges from that of Cameron, "*Vir Tricultus*," 182–186, who thinks that Rufinus "proceeded upon the belief in the divine inspiration of two separate Old Testaments, one for Jews, and (later) one for Christians, which must be kept separate" (185). On the contrary, Rufinus would not have said that the Hebrew text current among Jews was their version from God, but rather a version corrupted by themselves. This implies that the original, uncorrupted Hebrew text (which Jerome would be incompetent to translate, anyway) is best reflected in the LXX.

[181] The letters most relevant in this context include Augustine's *Epist.* 28.2; 71.3–6; 82.34–35; and Jerome's *Epist.* 112.19–22. On this correspondence, see C. White, *The Correspondence (394–419) between Jerome and Augustine of Hippo* (Lewiston, N.Y., 1990); R. Hennings, *Der Briefwechsel zwischen Augustinus und Hieronymus und ihr Streit um den Kanon des alten Testaments und die Auslegung von Gal. 2,11–14* (Leiden, 1994); A. Fürst, *Augustins Briefwechsel mit Hieronymus* (Münster, 1999); A.-I. Bouton-Touboulic, "Autorité et Tradition. La traduction latine de la Bible selon Saint Jérôme et Saint Augustin," *Aug* 45 (2005): 185–229. Whereas Hennings (pp. 131–217) interpreted Augustine's distress at Jerome's translations as concerning differences of canon, Fürst (140 n. 361) correctly criticizes Hennings for not recognizing that the issue was one of text only. While these two Latin Fathers did advocate different scriptural canons (cf. Jerome, *Prol. gal.*; Augustine, *Doc. chr.* 2.13; and see ch. 2 above), this issue did not arise in their correspondence. For an analysis of Augustine's position

criticisms against Jerome just examined at first characterized Augustine's position, as well. He had at one time doubted Jerome's ability to translate Hebrew, especially if the result diverged from the LXX. Similarly to Theodore and others, Augustine considered the reliability of the LXX to be guaranteed by their number and status, but Augustine also regarded the miraculous agreement among the translators as demonstrating their inspiration.[182] He frankly questions the ability of Jerome or anyone else to find in the original text anything that had eluded so many translators with expertise in Hebrew (*Epist.* 28.2).[183] Moreover, Jerome could surely be wrong on occasion, as confirmed when certain Jews, whether from *inperitia* or *malitia*, declared a part of his translation inaccurate (*Epist.* 71.4–5).[184] His exchange of letters with Jerome led Augustine to concede some utility to a new translation from the Hebrew as a witness to Jewish falsification of their own texts (*Epist.* 82.34; cf. Jerome, *Epist.* 112.20), thus agreeing somewhat with the position of Rufinus. However, Augustine later declares the idea absurd which would posit a general plot by scattered Jews to corrupt their own scriptures

---

highlighting its inconsistencies, see A. Kotzé, "Augustine, Jerome and the Septuagint," in J. Cook (ed.), *Septuagint and Reception* (Leiden, 2009), 244–260.

[182] Cf. *Doctr. chr.* 2.22; *Epist.* 28.2; cf. *Epist.* 71.6. For the different assumptions and misunderstandings Augustine exhibits in *Epist.* 28 and *Epist.* 71, see Fürst, "*Veritas Latina*," which is an innovative analysis as opposed to the more traditional interpretation of, e.g., Markschies, "Hieronymus und die 'Hebraica Veritas'," 163–169. Augustine thought that the LXX should still hold an authoritative position among translations even if the tradition about their miraculous agreement were not true, as Jerome argues (cf. *Praef. Pent.* 25–29). Augustine himself confidently believed the tradition about the separated translators (*Doctr. chr.* 2.22; *Civ.* 18.43: *cum vero tantum in eis signum divinitatis apparuit* [...]).

[183] See J. Lössl, "A Shift in Patristic Exegesis: Hebrew Clarity and Historical Verity in Augustine, Jerome, Julian of Aeclanum and Theodore of Mopsuestia," *AugStud* 32 (2001): 157–175 (157–158). For Jerome's response, cf. his *Epist.* 112.20. Fürst ("*Veritas Latina*," 106–112) maintains that Augustine was unaware at this time of Jerome's translations *iuxta Hebraeos*, in which case Augustine's doubt that anything new could be found in the Hebrew would refer to the hebraized aspect of Jerome's translation of the hexaplaric LXX. However, some evidence suggests that Augustine knew Jerome's translations *iuxta Hebraeos* already in the 390s, though perhaps not as early as his writing *Epist.* 28 (i.e., 394); see H.A.G. Houghton, *Augustine's Text of John* (Oxford, 2008), 10–12.

[184] On this occasion, Jerome's counsel to interrogate Jews for confirmation of his version (see above) backfired. He responds that the Jews in question were either ignorant or having a joke (*Epist.* 112.21–22), thus taking up Augustine's suggestion that these Jews acted out of *inperitia* or *malitia*. Augustine himself apparently later asked Jews to evaluate Jerome's translation, which they did favorably (*Civ.* 18.43). For interaction with Jerome's translations in Jewish writings, see M. Rahmer, *Die hebräischen Traditionen in den Werken des Hieronymus*, vol. 1 (Breslau, 1861), 13, who points out that Talmudic literature shows little knowledge of the Latin Bible, but Jews of the Middle Ages offer criticisms of Jerome's work.

out of spite (*Civ.* 15.13; cf. Jerome, *Comm. Isa.* 6:9).[185] In this way, his later view agrees with that of Jerome that the Hebrew text used by contemporary Jews was an authentic biblical text.

Also like Jerome, Augustine sees the traditional form of the LXX to be essentially identical to the original translation. He does not accept the hexaplaric recension as the authentic LXX; it is useful merely in showing the differences between the true LXX and the text in circulation among the Jews.[186] Augustine does allow for some corruption within the transmission history of the Greek text. His discussion of the ages of the Patriarchs in Gen. 5, which differ in the Hebrew and LXX, includes the suggestion that soon after the original translation mistakes were made in copying that affected all later manuscripts, and someone may have even intentionally changed the numbers in order to promote his own false interpretation of the passage (*Civ.* 15.13). But Augustine admits that this is only a guess at what happened, and he generally does not ascribe error to the Greek manuscript tradition (*Civ.* 15.14).

Thus, Augustine agrees with Jerome that the current Hebrew Bible and traditional LXX reflect accurately the original forms of those texts, and he is more confident in Jerome's abilities as a translator than is Theodore. Augustine knows that the differences between the Hebrew and LXX are significant. This had led Jerome to regard the LXX as a poor translation of the Hebrew, but there is another option open for Augustine, who consistently attributes the prophetic gift to the original translators.[187] Jerome had accused the Seventy translators of erroneously changing the biblical text (*Praef. Pent.* 21–25).[188] Augustine agrees that the Seventy must have changed the biblical text, but as prophets, they did so under the inspiration of the Holy Spirit.

---

[185] Houghton, *Augustine's Text*, 18–21, shows that Augustine generally avoided accusing his opponents of willfully altering the biblical text.

[186] Cf. Augustine's *Epist.* 28.2; 71.3; and see Fürst, "*Veritas Latina,*" 106–112, for Augustine's early misunderstandings regarding the origin and purpose of the critical signs used in Jerome's translations from the hexaplaric LXX.

[187] Cf. *Doctr. chr.* 2.22; *Cons. ev.* 2.128; *Civ.* 15.14; 18.42–44. Augustine does not rely on the argument from the LXX's inspiration in his correspondence with Jerome, though he does laud the translators highly; cf. *Epist.* 28.2; 71.6; and see Fürst, "*Veritas Latina,*" 113–121. For Jerome's denial that a translator can be a prophet, cf. *Praef. Pent.* 29–34, and see discussion above.

[188] Note also that Jerome insists that "truth cannot be diverse" (*Praef. Ezr.* 22–23; and see Bouton-Touboulic, "Autorité," 202–203), while Augustine is able to find room for diversity in truth.

*Merito enim creduntur Septuaginta interpretes accepisse propheticum spiri-*
*tum, ut, si quid eius auctoritate mutarent atque aliter quam erat quod inter-*
*pretabantur dicerent, neque hoc divinitus dictum esse dubitaretur.*

(*Civ.* 15.23)

For rightly are the Seventy translators believed to have received the prophetic
spirit, so that, if they changed anything by its authority and what they were
translating they say in a way different from what it was, neither should this
be doubted to have been said divinely.

Their changes could include additions, subtractions, and alterations in
wording or in meaning (*Civ.* 18.43), and these changes lead the mature Christian reader to contemplate the spiritual significance of the text. Just as the
multiple Hebrew prophets each had a different but true message to deliver
to ancient Israel, so also the Hebrew and Greek texts must be taken together
in order to understand the full revelation from God (*Civ.* 18.43–44).[189]

We thus find in Augustine the first sustained attempt among Christian
authors to divorce the authoritative biblical text from dependence on the
Hebrew. It is significant that in developing this theory Augustine maintains
the importance and even authority of the Hebrew text in its own right.
He may have felt some weight from Christian tradition, or from the arguments of Jerome, in ascribing authority to the Hebrew text, but likely he also
felt compelled to acknowledge the historical utterances of the prophets in
Hebrew as true and inspired (cf. *Civ.* 18.43–44). Nevertheless, Augustine's
textual position as fully developed near the end of his life entails the rejection of the Hebrew criterion for determining the authentic biblical text: the
Church's Bible should not match the original Hebrew text.

---

[189] For other references in Augustine to the ability of the LXX to change the text, see Fürst,
"*Veritas Latina*," 115–116 n. 30. For a recent analysis of Augustine's view of the polysemy of
scripture, see Bouton-Touboulic, "Autorité," 209–226, and contrast Jerome's view (previous
note); see also Williams, *Monk*, 117–118, 127–128, 222–223; and A.-M. La Bonnardière, "Did
Augustine Use Jerome's Vulgate?" in P. Bright (ed.), *Augustine and the Bible* (Notre Dame,
Ind., 1999), 42–51, who points to eighteen passages in Augustine's *Quaest. in Hept.* and six
more in his *Civ.* where he juxtaposes Jerome's version from the Hebrew to that of the LXX.
Each example shows that Augustine either harmonizes the LXX and Hebrew to show that
they really say the same thing, or he uses both readings to arrive at a deeper, spiritual sense.
The present analysis thus sees Augustine's (especially later) textual theory to entail a more
positive view of the Hebrew text than is allowed by Lössl, "Shift," 159–163, though it does
not go so far as Williams (*Monk*, 199) in saying that Augustine "became a firm advocate
of Jerome's translations." See Wermelinger, "Le canon des Latins": "Tout en affirmant avec
la même insistance l'autorité apostolique de la LXX dans l'Église, il prend de plus en plus
conscience de l'importance du texte hébraïque et finit par accepter l'inspiration divine du
texte de la Bible hébraïque" (184); see also M. Moreau, I. Bochet, and G. Madec, *La doctrine
chrétienne*, Bibliothèque augustinienne, Oeuvres de saint Augustin 11/2 (Paris, 1997), 514–523.

CONCLUSION

This chapter has surveyed the ways in which Jews and Christians treated and conceived of the differences among the various biblical texts existing in antiquity. We have found that, without exception, Jews regarded the Hebrew text of the Bible as authoritative. This includes even Jews such as Philo who treated the LXX (i.e., the Greek Pentateuch) as if it were the original text on the assumption that it was the perfect counterpart to the Hebrew. For the most part, Christians took up this notion that the LXX, now expanded to include all Greek Jewish scripture, reflected the original Hebrew text accurately. Where differences existed between the current Hebrew text and current LXX, these should be explained as a result of corruption in the manuscript tradition of one of the two texts.

The three greatest and most influential Christian authors in the classical patristic period did not believe that the LXX always accurately reflected the original Hebrew text, and yet they all three still held the original text in very high esteem. Origen did not develop a general theory based on his perception of the genuine differences in the texts, and he was usually content to rely on textual corruption as an explanation. Jerome and Augustine became convinced that very few of the divergences between the LXX and Hebrew text could be explained through textual corruption; rather, they must be due to the work of the LXX translators themselves. The two great Latin Fathers interpreted this situation in different and innovative ways. Jerome was willing to advocate the authority of the Hebrew Bible over against the LXX, a move that inspired a great deal of resistance among those Christians who were still convinced that the LXX provided the best means of accessing the original Hebrew text. On the other hand, Augustine developed a theological approach to textual diversity that allowed for variant readings to contribute mutually to a deeper understanding of God's word. It is only with this position of Augustine's that the Hebrew criterion becomes ineffective for determining the correct biblical text.

# BIBLIOGRAPHY

Aaron, David H. "Judaism's Holy Language." Pages 49–107 in *Approaches to Ancient Judaism, New Series*. Vol. 16. Edited by Jacob Neusner. Atlanta: Scholars Press, 1999.

Adler, William. "The Jews as Falsifiers: Charges of Tendentious Emendation in Anti-Jewish Christian Polemic." Pages 1–27 in *Translation of Scripture: Proceedings of a Conference at the Annenberg Research Institute, May 15–16, 1989*. Jewish Quarterly Review Supplement. Philadelphia: Annenburg Research Institute, 1990.

———. "The Pseudepigrapha in the Early Church." Pages 211–228 in *The Canon Debate*. Edited by Lee Martin McDonald and James A. Sanders. Peabody, Mass.: Hendrickson, 2002.

———. "Sextus Julius Africanus and the Roman Near East in the Third Century." *Journal of Theological Studies* n.s. 55 (2004): 520–550.

———. " 'What the Hebrews Say': Translation, Authority, and the Story of Susanna and the Elders." Pages 19–39 in *Biblical Translation in Context*. Edited by Frederick W. Knobloch. Bethesda, Md.: University Press of Maryland, 2002.

Aitken, James K. "Hebrew Study in Ben Sira's *Beth Midrash*." Pages 27–37 in *Hebrew Study from Ezra to Ben Yehuda*. Edited by William Horbury. Edinburgh: T&T Clark, 1999.

———. "Jewish Use of Greek Proverbs." Pages 53–77 in *Jewish Reception of Greek Bible Versions: Studies in Their Use in Late Antiquity and the Middle Ages*. Edited by Nicholas de Lange, Julia G. Krivoruchko, and Cameron Boyd-Taylor. Tübingen: Mohr (Siebeck), 2009.

———. "The Literary Attainment of the Translator of Greek Sirach." Pages 95–126 in *The Texts and Versions of the Book of Ben Sira: Transmission and Interpretation*. Edited by Jean-Sébastien Rey and Jan Joosten. Supplements to the Journal for the Study of Judaism 150. Leiden: Brill, 2011.

Albright, William Foxwell. "A Biblical Fragment from the Maccabaean Age: The Nash Papyrus." *Journal of Biblical Literature* 56 (1937): 145–176.

Alexander, Philip S. "The Cultural History of the Ancient Bible Versions: The Case of Lamentations." Pages 78–102 in *Jewish Reception of Greek Bible Versions: Studies in Their Use in Late Antiquity and the Middle Ages*. Edited by Nicholas de Lange, Julia G. Krivoruchko, and Cameron Boyd-Taylor. Tübingen: Mohr (Siebeck), 2009.

———. "How Did the Rabbis Learn Hebrew?" Pages 71–89 in *Hebrew Study from Ezra to Ben-Yehuda*. Edited by William Horbury. Edinburgh: T&T Clark, 1999.

———. *The Targum of Canticles*. Aramaic Bible 17A. Collegeville, Minn.: Liturgical Press, 2003.

———. "Why no Textual Criticism in Rabbinic Midrash? Reflections on the Textual Culture of the Rabbis." Pages 75–90 in *Jewish Ways of Reading the Bible*. Edited by George J. Brooke. Oxford: Oxford University Press, 2000.

Allen, Willoughby C. *A Critical and Exegetical Commentary on the Gospel Accord-*

*ing to S. Matthew*. International Critical Commentary. Edinburgh: T&T Clark, 1907.

Aly, Zaki, and Ludwig Koenen, eds. *Three Rolls of the Early Septuagint: Genesis and Deuteronomy*. Bonn: Habelt, 1980.

Ameling, Walter, ed. *Inscriptiones Judaicae Orientis*. Vol. 2: *Kleinasien*. Texts and Studies in Ancient Judaism 99. Tübingen: Mohr (Siebeck), 2004.

Anderson, G.W. "Canonical and Non-Canonical." Pages 113–159 in *The Cambridge History of the Bible*. Vol. 1: *From the Beginnings to Jerome*. Edited by P.R. Ackroyd and C.F. Evans. Cambridge: Cambridge University Press, 1970.

Audet, Jean-Paul. "A Hebrew-Aramaic List of Books of the Old Testament in Greek Transcription," *Journal of Theological Studies* n.s. 1 (1950): 135–154. Repr. pages 52–71 in *The Canon and Masorah of the Hebrew Bible: An Introductory Reader*. Edited by Sid Z. Leiman. New York: Ktav, 1974.

Aune, David E. *Prophecy in Early Christianity and the Ancient Mediterranean World*. Grand Rapids: Eerdmans, 1983.

———. "The Use of ΠΡΟΦΗΤΗΣ in Josephus." *Journal of Biblical Literature* 101 (1982): 419–421.

Auwers, J.-M., and H.J. de Jonge, eds. *The Biblical Canons*. Bibliotheca Ephemeridum Theologicarum Lovaniensium 163. Leuven: Leuven University Press, 2003.

Ball, C.J. "The History of Susanna." Pages 323–343 in vol. 2 of *The Holy Bible, according to the Authorized Version (A.D. 1611), with an Explanatory and Critical Commentary and a Revision of the Translation: Apocrypha*. Speaker's Commentary. Edited by Henry Wace. 2 vols. London: John Murray, 1888.

Bandt, Cordula. *Der Traktat "Vom Mysterium der Buchstaben": Kritischer Text mit Einführung, Übersetzung und Anmerkungen*. Texte und Untersuchungen 162. Berlin: de Gruyter, 2007.

Barag, Dan. "Samaritan Writing and Writings." Pages 303–323 in *From Hellenism to Islam: Cultural and Linguistic Change in the Roman Near East*. Edited by Hannah M. Cotton, Robert G. Hoyland, Jonathan J. Price, and David J. Wasserstein. Cambridge: Cambridge University Press, 2009.

Barclay, John M.G. *Against Apion*. Vol. 10 of *Flavius Josephus: Translation and Commentary*. Edited by Steve Mason. Leiden: Brill, 2007.

Bardy, Gustave, and Maurice Lefèvre, eds. *Hippolyte. Commentaire sur Daniel*. Sources chrétiennes 14. Paris: Cerf, 1947.

Barr, James. "Hebrew, Aramaic and Greek in the Hellenistic Age." Pages 79–114 in *The Cambridge History of Judaism*. Vol. 2: *The Hellenistic Age*. Edited by W.D. Davies and Louis Finkelstein. Cambridge: Cambridge University Press, 1989.

Barrett, C.K. *A Critical and Exegetical Commentary on the Acts of the Apostles*. 2 vols. International Critical Commentary. Edinburgh: T&T Clark, 1994–1998.

Barthélemy, Dominique. "Eusèbe, la Septante et 'les autres'." Pages 51–65 in *La Bible et les Pères, colloque de Strasbourg*. Paris: University Presses of France, 1971. Repr. pages 179–193 in *Études d'histoire du texte de l'Ancien Testament*. Göttingen: Vandenhoeck & Ruprecht, 1978.

———. *Les devanciers d'Aquila: première publication intégrale du texte des fragments du Dodécaprophéton*. Leiden: Brill, 1963.

———. "L'État de la Bible juive depuis le début de notre ère jusqu'à la deuxième révolte contre Rome (131–135)." Pages 9–45 in *Le Canon de l'Ancien Testament:*

*Sa formation et son histoire*. Edited by Jean-Daniel Kaestli and Otto Wermelinger. Geneva: Labor et Fides, 1984.

——. "Origène et le texte de l'Ancien Testament." Pages 247–261 in *Epektasis: mélanges patristiques offerts au cardinal Jean Danielou*. Edited by Jacques Fontains and Charles Kannengiesser. Paris: Beauchesne, 1972. Repr. pages 203–217 in *Études d'histoire du texte de l'Ancien Testament*. Göttingen: Vandenhoeck & Ruprecht, 1978.

——. "La place de la Septante dans l'Église." Pages 13–28 in *Aux grands carrefours de la révélation et de l'exégèse de l'Ancien Testament*. Paris: Desclée de Brouwer, 1967. Repr. pages 111–126 in *Études d'histoire du texte de l'Ancien Testament*. Göttingen: Vandenhoeck & Ruprecht, 1978.

——. "Pourquoi la Torah a-t-elle été traduite en grec?" Pages 23–41 in *On Language, Culture, and Religion: In Honor of Eugene A. Nida*. Edited by Matthew Black and William A. Smalley. The Hague: Mouton, 1974. Repr. pages 322–340 in *Études d'histoire du texte de l'Ancien Testament*. Göttingen: Vandenhoeck & Ruprecht, 1978.

——. Review of Kevin G. O'Connell, *The Theodotionic Revision of the Book of Exodus*. *Biblica* 55 (1974): 91–93. Repr. pages 304–306 in *Études d'histoire du texte de l'Ancien Testament*. Göttingen: Vandenhoeck & Ruprecht, 1978.

Bartholomew, Craig G., Scott Hahn, Robin Parry, Christopher Seitz, and Al Wolters, eds. *Canon and Biblical Interpretation*. Grand Rapids: Zondervan, 2006.

Barton, John. "Canons of the Old Testament." Pages 200–222 in *Text in Context: Essays by Members of the Society for Old Testament Study*. Edited by John Day. Oxford: Oxford University Press, 2000.

——. *Holy Writings, Sacred Text: The Canon in Early Christianity*. Louisville: Westminster John Knox, 1997.

——. *Oracles of God: Perceptions of Ancient Prophecy in Israel after the Exile*. London: Darton, Longman and Todd, 1986. Repr., Oxford: Oxford University Press, 2007.

Bauckham, Richard. *The Fate of the Dead: Studies on the Jewish and Christian Apocalypses*. Leiden: Brill, 1998.

——. *Jude and the Relatives of Jesus in the Early Church*. Edinburgh: T&T Clark, 1990.

Baumgarten, Albert I. "Bilingual Jews and the Greek Bible." Pages 13–30 in *Shem in the Tents of Japhet: Essays on the Encounter of Judaism and Hellenism*. Edited by James L. Kugel. Leiden: Brill, 2002.

Beattie, D.R.G., and Philip R. Davies. "What Does Hebrew Mean?" *Journal of Semitic Studies* 56 (2011): 71–83.

Beckwith, Roger T. *The Old Testament Canon of the New Testament Church and Its Background in Early Judaism*. Grand Rapids: Eerdmans, 1985.

Benoit, Pierre. "L'inspiration des Septante d'après les Pères." Pages 169–187 in vol. 1 of *L'homme devant Dieu: mélanges offerts au père Henri de Lubac*. 3 vols. Théologie 56–58. Paris: Aubier, 1963–1964.

Bettiolo, Paolo, Alda Giambelluca Kossova, Claudio Leonardi, Enrico Norelli, and Lorenzo Perrone, eds. *Ascensio Isaiae: Textus*. Corpus Christianorum: Series apocryphorum 7. Turnhout: Brepols, 1995.

Birnbaum, Salomo A. *The Hebrew Scripts*. Leiden: Brill, 1971.

214 BIBLIOGRAPHY

Blenkinsopp, Joseph. *Opening the Sealed Book: Interpretations of the Book of Isaiah in Late Antiquity*. Grand Rapids: Eerdmans, 2006.

Bogaert, Pierre-Maurice. "Les bibles d'Augustin." *Revue théologique de Louvain* 37 (2006): 513–531.

———. *Judith*. Vetus Latina 7/2. Fascicle 1. Freiburg: Herder, 2001.

———. "Aux origines de la fixation du canon: Scriptoria, listes et titres. Le *Vaticanus* et la stichométrie de Mommsen." Pages 153–176 in *The Biblical Canons*. Edited by J.-M. Auwers and H.J. de Jonge. Bibliotheca Ephemeridum Theologicarum Lovaniensium 163. Leuven: Leuven University Press, 2003.

Boitani, Piero. "Susanna in Excelsis." Pages 7–19 in *The Judgment of Susanna: Authority and Witness*. Edited by Ellen Spolsky. Atlanta: Scholars Press, 1996.

Bouton-Touboulic, Anne-Isabelle. "Autorité et Tradition. La traduction latine de la Bible selon Saint Jérôme et Saint Augustin." *Augustinianum* 45 (2005): 185–229.

Brakke, David. "A New Fragment of Athanasius's 39th *Festal Letter*: Heresy, Apocrypha, and the Canon." *Harvard Theological Review* 103 (2010): 47–66.

Braverman, Jay. *Jerome's Commentary on Daniel: A Study of Comparative Jewish and Christian Interpretations of the Hebrew Bible*. Washington, D.C.: The Catholic Biblical Association of America, 1978.

Brock, Sebastian P. "Aspects of Translation Technique in Antiquity." *Greek, Roman, and Byzantine Studies* 20 (1979): 69–87.

———. "Origen's Aims as a Textual Critic of the Old Testament." *Studia Patristica* 10. Texte und Untersuchungen 107 (1970): 215–218.

———. "The Phenomenon of Biblical Translation in Antiquity." *Alta* II 8 (1969): 96–102. Repr. pages 541–571 in *Studies in the Septuagint: Origins, Recensions, and Interpretations*. Edited by Sidney Jellicoe. New York: Ktav, 1974.

———. "To Revise or Not to Revise: Attitudes to Jewish Biblical Translation." Pages 301–338 in *Septuagint, Scrolls, and Cognate Writings: Papers Presented to the International Symposium on the Septuagint and Its Relation to the Dead Sea Scrolls and Other Writings*. Edited by George J. Brooke and Barnabas Lindars. Atlanta: Scholars Press, 1992.

Brooks, E.C. "The Translation Techniques of Rufinus of Aquileia (343–411)." *Studia Patristica* 17/1 (1982): 357–364.

Brown, Dennis. *Vir Trilinguis: A Study in the Biblical Exegesis of Saint Jerome*. Kampen: Kok Pharos, 1992.

Bruns, Peter. "Polychronius von Apamea—Der Exeget und Theologe." *Studia Patristica* 37 (2001): 404–412.

Burkitt, F. Crawford. *Fragments of the Books of Kings according to the Translation of Aquila*. Cambridge: Cambridge University Press, 1897.

Burns, Joshua Ezra. "The Special Purim and the Reception of the Book of Esther in the Hellenistic and Early Roman Eras." *Journal for the Study of Judaism* 37 (2006): 1–35.

Cain, Andrew. "In Ambrosiaster's Shadow: A Critical Re-Evaluation of the Last Surviving Letter Exchange between Pope Damasus and Jerome." *Revue d'études augustiniennes et patristiques* 51 (2005): 257–277.

Cameron, John [S]. "The Rabbinic Vulgate?" Pages 117–129 in *Jerome of Stridon: His Life, Writings and Legacy*. Edited by Andrew Cain and Josef Lössl. Surrey: Ashgate, 2009.

————. "The *Vir Tricultus*: An Investigation of the Classical, Jewish and Christian Influences on Jerome's Translation of the Psalter *Iuxta Hebraeos*." Dissertation, University of Oxford, 2006.

Cappelletti, Silvia. "Biblical Quotations in the Greek Jewish Inscriptions of the Diaspora." Pages 128–141 in *Jewish Reception of Greek Bible Versions: Studies in Their Use in Late Antiquity and the Middle Ages*. Edited by Nicholas de Lange, Julia G. Krivoruchko, and Cameron Boyd-Taylor. Tübingen: Mohr (Siebeck), 2009.

————. *The Jewish Community of Rome: From the Second Century B.C. to the Third Century C.E.* Leiden: Brill, 2006.

Carleton Paget, J.N.B. "The Christian Exegesis of the Old Testament in the Alexandrian Tradition." Pages 478–542 in *Hebrew Bible/Old Testament: The History of Its Interpretation*. Vol. 1: *From the Beginnings to the Middle Ages (until 1300). Part 1: Antiquity*. Edited by Magne Saebø. Göttingen: Vandenhoeck & Ruprecht, 1996.

Carr, David M. "Canonization in the Context of Community: An Outline of the Formation of the Tanakh and the Christian Bible." Pages 22–64 in *A Gift of God in Due Season: Essays on Scripture and Community in Honor of James A. Sanders*. Edited by Richard D. Weis and David M. Carr. Sheffield: Sheffield Academic, 1996.

————. *The Formation of the Hebrew Bible: A New Reconstruction*. Oxford: Oxford University Press, 2011.

————. *Writing on the Tablet of the Heart: Origins of Scripture and Learning*. Oxford: Oxford University Press, 2005.

Casey, P.M. "Porphyry and the Origin of the Book of Daniel." *Journal of Theological Studies* n.s. 27 (1976): 15–33.

Cavallera, Ferdinand. *Saint Jérôme: sa vie et son oeuvre*. 2 vols. Paris: Champion, 1922.

Chapman, Stephen B. "The Canon Debate: What It Is and Why It Matters." *Journal of Theological Interpretation* 4 (2010): 273–294.

————. *The Law and the Prophets. A Study in Old Testament Canon Formation*. Tübingen: Mohr (Siebeck), 2000.

Chiesa, Bruno. "Textual History and Textual Criticism of the Hebrew Old Testament." Pages 257–272 in vol. 2 of *The Madrid Qumran Congress: Proceedings of the International Congress on the Dead Sea Scrolls, Madrid, 18–21 March 1991*. 2 vols. Edited by Julio Trebolle Barrera and Luis Vegas Montaner. Leiden: Brill, 1992.

Charles, R.H. *The Ascension of Isaiah*. London: Adam and Charles Black, 1900.

————. *The Book of Jubilees or the Little Genesis*. London: Adam and Charles Black, 1902.

Charlesworth, James H. *The Pesharim and Qumran History: Chaos or Consensus?* Grand Rapids: Eerdmans, 2002.

Childs, Brevard S. *Introduction to the Old Testament as Scripture*. Philadelphia: Fortress, 1979.

Clements, Ruth. "Origen's *Hexapla* and Christian-Jewish Encounter in the Second and Third Centuries." Pages 303–329 in *Religious Rivalries and the Struggle for Success in Caesarea Maritima*. Edited by Terence L. Donaldson. Waterloo, Ont.: Wilfred Laurier University Press, 2000.

Cohen, Shaye J.D. *The Beginnings of Jewishness: Boundaries, Varieties, Uncertainties*. Berkeley: University of California Press, 1999.

————. *From the Maccabees to the Mishnah*. 2d ed. Louisville: Westminster John Knox, 2006.

Cohick, Lynn H. *The Peri Pascha Attributed to Melito of Sardis: Setting, Purpose, and Sources.* Brown Judaic Studies 327. Providence, R.I.: Brown Judaic Studies, 2000.

Collins, John J., and Gregory E. Sterling, eds. *Hellenism in the Land of Israel.* Notre Dame, Ind.: University of Notre Dame Press, 2001.

Conybeare, F.C., ed. *The Dialogues of Athanasius and Zacchaeus and of Timothy and Aquila.* Oxford: Oxford University Press, 1898.

Cook, John Granger. *The Interpretation of the Old Testament in Greco-Roman Paganism.* Tübingen: Mohr (Siebeck), 2004.

Cook, L. Stephen. *On the Question of the "Cessation of Prophecy" in Ancient Judaism.* Texts and Studies in Ancient Judaism 145. Tübingen: Mohr Siebeck, 2011.

Costello, Charles Joseph. *St. Augustine's Doctrine on the Inspiration and Canonicity of Scripture.* Washington, D.C.: The Catholic University of America, 1930.

Cotton, Hannah M. "The Bar Kokhba Revolt and the Documents from the Judaean Desert: Nabataean Participation in the Revolt (*P. Yadin* 52)." Pages 133–152 in *The Bar Kokhba War Reconsidered: New Perspectives on the Second Jewish Revolt against Rome.* Edited by Peter Schäfer. Texts and Studies in Ancient Judaism 100. Tübingen: Mohr (Siebeck), 2003.

——. "The Languages of the Legal and Administrative Documents from the Judaean Desert." *Zeitschrift für Papyrologie und Epigraphik* 125 (1999): 219–231.

Cotton, Hannah M., and Joseph Geiger, eds. *Masada: The Yigael Yadin Excavations 1963–1965: Final Reports.* Vol. 2: *The Latin and Greek Documents.* Jerusalem: Israel Exploration Society, 1989.

Cotton, Hannah M., Leah di Segni, Werner Eck, Benjamin Isaac, Alla Kushnir-Stein, Haggai Misgav, Jonathan Price, Israel Rolle, and Ada Yardeni, eds. *Corpus inscriptionum Iudaeae/Palestinae.* Vol. 1: *Jerusalem.* Part 1: *1–704.* Berlin: de Gruyter, 2010.

Cross, Frank Moore. *The Ancient Library of Qumran.* 3d ed. Sheffield: Sheffield Academic, 1995.

——. "The Development of the Jewish Scripts." Pages 133–202 in *The Bible and the Ancient Near East: Essays in Honor of William Foxwell Albright.* Edited by George Ernest Wright. Garden City, N.Y.: Doubleday, 1961. Repr. Winona Lake, Ind.: Eisenbrauns, 1979.

——. "The Evolution of a Theory of Local Texts." Pages 306–320 in *Qumran and the History of the Biblical Text.* Edited by Frank Moore Cross and Shemaryahu Talmon. Cambridge, Mass.: Harvard University Press, 1975.

——. *From Epic to Canon: History and Literature in Ancient Israel.* Baltimore: Johns Hopkins University Press, 1998.

——. "The Hebrew Inscriptions from Sardis." *Harvard Theological Review* 95 (2002): 3–19.

——. "The History of the Biblical Text in the Light of Discoveries in the Judaean Desert." *Harvard Theological Review* 57 (1964): 281–299. Repr. pages 177–195 in *Qumran and the History of the Biblical Text.* Edited by Frank Moore Cross and Shemaryahu Talmon. Cambridge, Mass.: Harvard University Press, 1975.

Cross, Frank Moore, and Shemaryahu Talmon, eds. *Qumran and the History of the Biblical Text.* Cambridge, Mass.: Harvard University Press, 1975.

Dalman, Gustaf. *Grammatik des jüdisch-palästinischen Aramäisch nach den Idiomen das palästinischen Talmud des Onkelostargum und Prophetentargum und der jerusalemischen Targume.* 2d ed. Leipzig: Hinrichs, 1905.

Davies, Philip R. *Scribes and Schools: The Canonization of the Hebrew Scriptures.* Louisville: Westminster John Knox, 1998.

Davila, James R. *The Provenance of the Pseudepigrapha: Jewish, Christian, or Other?* Leiden: Brill, 2005.

De Bruyne, D. "Le prologue, le titre et la finale de l' Ecclésiastique." *Zeitschrift für die alttestamentliche Wissenschaft* 47 (1929): 257–263.

De Crom, Dries. "Translation Equivalence in the Prologue to Greek Ben Sirach." Pages 99–111 in *XIII Congress of the International Organization for Septuagint and Cognate Studies, Ljubljana, 2007.* Edited by Melvin K.H. Peters. Atlanta: Scholars Press, 2008.

De Lange, N.R.M. "Introduction." Pages 1–6 in *Jewish Reception of Greek Bible Versions: Studies in Their Use in Late Antiquity and the Middle Ages.* Edited by Nicholas de Lange, Julia G. Krivoruchko, and Cameron Boyd-Taylor. Tübingen: Mohr (Siebeck), 2009.

———. "Jews in the Age of Justinian." Pages 401–426 in *The Cambridge Companion to the Age of Justinian.* Edited by Michael Maas. Cambridge: Cambridge University Press, 2005.

———. "The Letter to Africanus: Origen's Recantation?" *Studia Patristica* 16.2. Textc und Untersuchungen 129 (1985): 242–247.

———. *Origen and the Jews: Studies in Jewish-Christian Relations in Third-Century Palestine.* Cambridge: Cambridge University Press, 1976.

———, ed. *Origène, La Lettre à Africanus sur l'histoire de Suzanne.* Pages 469–578 in Origène, *Philocalie, 1–20: Sur les Écritures.* Edited by Marguerite Harl. Sources chrétiennes 302. Paris: Cerf, 1983.

———. "The Revival of the Hebrew Language in the Third Century CE." *Jewish Studies Quarterly* 3 (1996): 342–358.

———. "A Thousand Years of Hebrew in Byzantium." Pages 147–161 in *Hebrew Study from Ezra to Ben-Yehuda.* Edited by William Horbury. Edinburgh: T&T Clark, 1999.

De Lange, Nicholas, Julia G. Krivoruchko, and Cameron Boyd-Taylor, eds. *Jewish Reception of Greek Bible Versions: Studies in Their Use in Late Antiquity and the Middle Ages.* Tübingen: Mohr (Siebeck), 2009.

Dean, James E. *Epiphanius' Treatise on Weights and Measures: The Syriac Version.* Chicago: University of Chicago Press, 1935.

Decock, Paul B. "Jerome's Turn to the Hebraica Veritas and His Rejection of the Traditional View of the Septuagint." *Neotestamentica* 42 (2008): 205–222.

Denzinger, Heinrich, and Peter Hünermann. *Enchiridion symbolorum definitionum et declarationum de rebus fidei et morum.* 39th ed. Freiburg: Herder, 2001.

Digeser, Elizabeth DePalma. "Porphyry, Julian, or Hierocles? The Anonymous Hellene in Makarios Magnēs' Apokritikos." *Journal of Theological Studies* n.s. 53 (2002): 466–502.

Diringer, D. "Early Hebrew Script versus Square Script." Pages 35–49 in *Essays and Studies Presented to Stanley Arthur Cook.* Edited by D. Winton Thomas. London: Taylor's Foreign Press, 1950.

Dorival, Gilles. "L' apport des Pères de l' Église à la question de la clôture du canon de l' Ancien Testament." Pages 81–110 in *The Biblical Canons.* Edited by J.-M. Auwers and H.J. de Jonge. Bibliotheca Ephemeridum Theologicarum Lovaniensium 163. Leuven: Leuven University Press, 2003.

———. "La formation du canon biblique de l'Ancien Testament: Position actuelle et problèmes." Pages 83–112 in *Recueils normatifs et canons dans l'Antiquité: Perspectives nouvelles sur la formation des canons juif et chrétien dans leur contexte culturel*. Edited by Enrico Norelli. Prahins: Éditions du Zèbre, 2004.

———. "Has the Category of 'Deuterocanonical Books' a Jewish Origin?" Pages 1–10 in *The Books of the Maccabees: History, Ideology, Theology. Papers of the Second International Conference on the Deuterocanonical Books, Pápa, Hungary, 9–11 June, 2005*. Edited by Géza G. Xeravits and József Zsengellér. Leiden: Brill, 2007.

———. "Origène, témoin des textes de l'Anicen Testament." Pages 351–366 in *Lectures et relectures de la Bible: festschrift P.-M. Bogaert*. Edited by J.-M. Auwers and A. Wénin. Leuven: Peeters, 1999.

Dorival, Gilles, Marguerite Harl, and Olivier Munnich. *La Bible grecque des Septante: Du judaïsme hellénistique au christianisme ancien*. Paris: Cerf, 1988.

Drost-Abgarjan, Armenuhi. "Ein neuer Fund zur armenischen Version der Eusebios-Chronik." Pages 255–262 in *Julius Africanus und die christliche Weltchronistik*. Edited by Martin Wallraff. Berlin: de Gruyter, 2006.

Dummer, Jürgen. "Die Sprachkenntnisse des Epiphanius." Pages 392–435 in part 1 of vol. 5 of *Die Araber in der alten Welt*. Edited by Franz Altheim and Ruth Stiehl. Berlin: de Gruyter, 1968. Repr. pages 29–72 in *Philologia Sacra et Profana: ausgewählte Beiträge zur Antike und zu ihrer Wirkungsgeschichte*. Stuttgart: Steiner, 2006.

Eco, Umberto. *The Search for the Perfect Language*. Translated by James Fentress. Oxford: Blackwell, 1995.

Edrei, Arye, and Doron Mendels. "A Split Jewish Diaspora: Its Dramatic Consequences." *Journal for the Study of the Pseudepigrapha* 16 (2007): 91–137; 17 (2008): 163–187.

———. *Zweierlei Diaspora: Zur Spaltung der antiken jüdischen Welt*. Göttingen: Vandenhoeck & Ruprecht, 2010.

Edwards, James R. *The Hebrew Gospel and the Development of the Synoptic Tradition*. Grand Rapids: Eerdmans, 2009.

Edwards, M.J. "Precursors of Origen's Hermeneutic Theory." *Studia Patristica* 29 (1996): 232–237.

Eilberg-Schwartz, Howard. "Who's Kidding Whom? A Serious Reading of Rabbinic Word Plays." *Journal of the American Academy of Religion* 55 (1987): 765–788.

Ellingworth, Paul. "Hebrew or Aramaic?" *Bible Translator* 37 (1986): 338–341.

Elliott, C.J. "Hebrew Learning among the Fathers." Pages 851–872 in vol. 2 of *Dictionary of Christian Biography*. 4 vols. Edited by William Smith and Henry Wace. London: John Murray, 1877–1887.

Ellis, E. Earle. *The Old Testament in Early Christianity: Canon and Interpretation in the Light of Modern Research*. Tübingen: Mohr (Siebeck), 1991.

Engel, Helmut. *Das Susanna-Erzählung: Einleitung, Übersetzung und Kommentar zum Septuaginta-Text und zur Theodotion-Bearbeitung*. Orbis biblicus et orientalis 61. Göttingen: Vandenhoeck & Ruprecht, 1985.

Eshel, Hanan. "Documents of the First Jewish Revolt from the Judean Desert." Pages 157–163 in *The First Jewish Revolt: Archaeology, History, and Ideology*. Edited by Andrea M. Berlin and J. Andrew Overman. New York: Routledge, 2002.

Evans, Craig A. "The Jewish Christian Gospel Tradition." Pages 241–277 in *Jewish Believers in Jesus: The Early Centuries*. Edited by Oskar Skarsaune and Reidar Hvalvik. Peabody, Mass.: Hendrickson, 2007.

Evans, C.A., and E. Tov, eds. *Exploring the Origins of the Bible: Canon Formation in Historical, Literary, and Theological Perspective*. Grand Rapids: Baker, 2008.

Everson, David L. "An Examination of Synoptic Portions within the Vulgate." *Vetus Testamentum* 58 (2008): 178–190.

Fairweather, E.R. "St. Augustine's Interpretation of Infant Baptism." Pages 897–903 in vol. 2 of *Augustinus Magister. Congrès International Augustinien, Paris, 21–24 September 1954*. 3 vols. Paris: Études augustiniennes, 1954.

Fellman, Jack. "The Linguistic Status of Mishnaic Hebrew." *Journal of Northwest Semitic Languages* 5 (1977): 21–22.

Fernández Marcos, Natalio. "*Non placet Septuaginta*: Revisions and New Greek Versions of the Bible in Byzantium." Pages 39–50 in *Jewish Reception of Greek Bible Versions: Studies in Their Use in Late Antiquity and the Middle Ages*. Edited by Nicholas de Lange, Julia G. Krivoruchko, and Cameron Boyd-Taylor. Tübingen: Mohr (Siebeck), 2009.

———. *Scribes and Translators: Septuagint and Old Latin in the Books of Kings*. Leiden: Brill, 1994.

———. *The Septuagint in Context: Introduction to the Greek Versions of the Bible*. Translated by Wilfred G.E. Watson. Leiden: Brill, 2000.

———. "Some Reflections on the Antiochian Text of the Septuagint." Pages 219–229 in *Studien zur Septuaginta—Robert Hanhart zu Ehren: aus Anlass seines 65. Geburtstages*. Edited by Detlef Fraenkel, Udo Quast, and John Wm Wevers. Göttingen: Vandenhoeck & Ruprecht, 1990.

Fisch, Harold. "Susanna as Parable: A Response to Piero Boitani." Pages 35–41 in *The Judgment of Susanna: Authority and Witness*. Edited by Ellen Spolsky. Atlanta: Scholars Press, 1996.

Fitzgerald, Allan D., ed. *Augustine through the Ages: An Encyclopedia*. Grand Rapids: Eerdmans, 1999.

Fitzmyer, Joseph A. "The Languages of Palestine in the First Century A.D." *Catholic Biblical Quarterly* 32 (1970): 501–531.

———. *A Wandering Aramean: Collected Aramaic Essays*. Missoula, Mont.: Society of Biblical Literature, 1979.

Forte, Anthony J. "The Old Latin Version of Sirach: Editio Critica and Textual Problems." Pages 199–214 in *The Texts and Versions of the Book of Ben Sira: Transmission and Interpretation*. Edited by Jean-Sébastien Rey and Jan Joosten. Leiden: Brill, 2011.

Fraade, Steven D. "Rabbinic Views on the Practice of Targum, and Multilingualism in the Jewish Galilee of the Third-Sixth Centuries." Pages 253–286 in *The Galilee in Latin Antiquity*. Edited by Lee I. Levine. New York: Jewish Theological Seminary of America, 1992.

Frede, Hermann Josef. *Ad Thessalonicenses, Timotheum*. Vetus Latina 25/1. Fasc. 10. Freiburg: Herder, 1982.

Freedman, David Noel. "Canon of the OT." Pages 130–136 in *Interpreter's Dictionary of the Bible, Supplement*. Edited by K.R. Crim. Nashville: Abingdon, 1976.

Frey, Jean-Baptiste, ed. *Corpus Inscriptionum Judaicarum*. Vol. 1: *Europe*. Vol. 2: *Asie-Afrique*. Rome: Pontificio istituto di archeologia cristiana, 1936–1952. Vol. 1 repr. with prolegomena by Baruch Lifshitz. New York: Ktav, 1975.

Funk, Franciscus Xaverius. *Didascalia et Constitutiones Apostolorum*. 2 vols. Paderborn: Ferdinand Schoeningh, 1905.

Fürst, Alfons. *Augustins Briefwechsel mit Hieronymus*. Münster: Aschendorff, 1999.

———. *Hieronymus: Askese und Wissenschaft in der Spätantike*. Freiburg: Herder, 2003.

———. "*Veritas Latina*. Augustins Haltung gegenüber Hieronymus' Bibelübersetzungen." *Revue des études augustiniennes* 40 (1994): 105–126.

Gallagher, Edmon L. "The Old Testament 'Apocrypha' in Jerome's Canonical Theory." *Journal of Early Christian Studies* 20.2 (forthcoming, 2012).

———. "The Religious Provenance of the Aquila Manuscripts from the Cairo Genizah." *Journal of Jewish Studies* (forthcoming).

———. "The Septuagint's Fidelity to Its *Vorlage* in Greek Patristic Thought." In *XIV Congress of the International Organization for Septuagint and Cognate Studies: Helsinki, 2010*. Edited by Melvin K.H. Peters. Atlanta: Society of Biblical Literature, forthcoming (2012).

Geiger, Abraham. *Lehr- und Lesebuch zur Sprache der Mischnah*. Breslau: Leuckart, 1845.

Gentry, Peter J. *The Asterisked Materials in the Greek Job*. Atlanta: Scholars Press, 1995.

———. "The Place of Theodotion-Job in the Textual History of the Septuagint." Pages 199–229 in *Origen's Hexapla and Fragments: Papers Presented at the Rich Seminar on the Hexapla, Oxford Centre for Hebrew and Jewish Studies, 25th–3rd August 1994*. Edited by Alison Salvesen. Tübingen: Mohr (Siebeck), 1998.

———. "The Septuagint and the Text of the Old Testament." *Bulletin for Biblical Research* 16 (2006): 193–218.

Ginzberg, Louis. *The Legends of the Jews*. 7 vols. Philadelphia: Jewish Publication Society, 1909–1938.

Glorie, Franciscus. *S. Hieronymi Presbyteri Commentariorum in Danielem libri III <IV>*. Corpus Christianorum: Series latina 75A. Turnhout: Brepols, 1964.

Goldstein, Jonathan A. *1 Maccabees*. Anchor Bible 41. Garden City, N.Y.: Doubleday, 1976.

Goodblatt, David. *Elements of Ancient Jewish Nationalism*. Cambridge: Cambridge University Press, 2006.

Gooding, D.W. *Recensions of the Septuagint Pentateuch*. London: Tyndale, 1955.

Goshen Gottstein, Alon. "Ben Sira's Praise of the Fathers: A Canon-Conscious Reading." Pages 235–267 in *Ben Sira's God: Proceedings of the International Ben Sira Conference, Durham—Ushaw College, 2001*. Edited by Renate Egger-Wenzel. Berlin: de Gruyter, 2002.

Goulet, Richard. *Études sur les Vies de philosophes de l'Antiquité tardive: Diogène Laërce, Porphyre de Tyr, Eunape de Sardes*. Paris: J. Vrin, 2001.

———. "Hypothèses récentes sur le traité de Porphyre Contre les chrétiens." Pages 61–109 in *Hellénisme et christianisme*. Edited by Michel Narcy and Éric Rebillard. Villeneuve d'Ascq: Presses universitaires du Septentrion, 2004.

———. *Macarios de Magnésie: Le monogénès*. 2 vols. Paris: J. Vrin, 2003.

————. "Porphyre et la datation de Moïse." *Revue de l'histoire des religions* 4 (1977): 137–164. Repr. pages 245–266 in *Études sur les Vies de philosophes de l'Antiquité tardive: Diogène Laërce, Porphyre de Tyr, Eunape de Sardes*. Paris: J. Vrin, 2001.

————. "Porphyre et Macaire de Magnésie." *Studia Patristica* 15. Texte und Untersuchungen 128 (1984): 448–452. Repr. pages 295–299 in *Études sur les Vies de philosophes de l'Antiquité tardive: Diogène Laërce, Porphyre de Tyr, Eunape de Sardes*. Paris: J. Vrin, 2001.

Govaars, Marylinda, Marie Spiro, and L. Michael White. *Field O: The "Synagogue" Site*. The Joint Expedition to Caesarea Maritima Excavation Reports 9. Boston: American Schools of Oriental Research, 2009.

Grabbe, Lester L. *Etymology in Early Jewish Interpretation: The Hebrew Names in Philo*. Atlanta: Scholars Press, 1988.

Grafton, Anthony, and Megan Williams. *Christianity and the Transformation of the Book: Origen, Eusebius, and the Library of Caesarea*. Cambridge, Mass.: Belknap, 2006.

Grant, Robert M. "Historical Criticism in the Ancient Church." *Journal of Religion* 25 (1945): 183–196.

————. "The *Stromateis* of Origen." Pages 285–292 in *Épektasis: mélanges patristiques offerts au cardinal Jean Daniélou*. Edited by Jacques Fontaine and Charles Kannengiesser. Paris: Beauchesne, 1972.

Graves, Michael. *Jerome's Hebrew Philology: A Study Based on His Commentary on Jeremiah*. Leiden: Brill, 2007.

————. "'Judaizing' Christian Interpretations of the Prophets as Seen by Saint Jerome." *Vigiliae Christianae* 61 (2007): 142–156.

Gray, Rebecca. *Prophetic Figures in Late Second Temple Jewish Palestine: The Evidence from Josephus*. Oxford: Oxford University Press, 1993.

Green, Gene L. "'As for Prophecies, They Will Come to an End': 2 Peter, Paul and Plutarch on 'The Obsolescence of Oracles'." *Journal for the Study of the New Testament* 82 (2001): 107–122.

Greenspahn, Frederick E. "Why Prophecy Ceased." *Journal of Biblical Literature* 108 (1989): 37–49.

Greenspoon, Leonard J. "The *Kaige* Recension: The Life, Death, and Postmortem Existence of a Modern—and Ancient—Phenomenon." Pages 5–16 in *XII Congress of the International Organization for Septuagint and Cognate Studies, Leiden, 2004*. Edited by Melvin K.H. Peters. Atlanta: Society of Biblical Literature, 2006.

Gruber, Mayer. "Language(s) in Judaism." Pages 783–797 in vol. 2 of *The Encyclopaedia of Judaism*. Edited by Jacob Neusner, Alan J. Avery-Peck, and William Scott Green. 3 vols. Leiden: Brill, 2000.

Guinot, Jean-Noel. "La fortune des *Hexaples* d' Origène aux IV$^e$ et V$^e$ siècles en milieu antiochien." Pages 215–225 in *Origeniana Sexta: Origène et la Bible/Origen and the Bible*. Edited by Gilles Dorival and Alain Le Boulluec. Leuven: Peeters, 1995.

————. "Théodoret de Cyr: une lecture critique de la Septante." Pages 393–407 in Κατα τους ο'—*Selon les Septante: trente études sur la Bible grecque des Septante en hommage à Marguerite Harl*. Edited by Gilles Dorival and Olivier Munnich. Paris: Cerf, 1995.

Haar Romeny, R.B. ter. *A Syrian in Greek Dress: The Use of Greek, Hebrew, and Syriac*

*Biblical Texts in Eusebius of Emesa's Commentary on Genesis*. Leuven: Peeters, 1997.

Haas, Christopher. *Alexandria in Late Antiquity: Topography and Social Conflict*. Baltimore: Johns Hopkins University Press, 1997.

Haase, Wolfgang, ed. *Aufstieg und Niedergang der römischen Welt: Geschichte und Kultur Roms im Spiegel der neueren Forschung*. Part 2: *Principat*, 20.1. New York: de Gruyter, 1987.

Hahneman, Geoffrey Mark. *The Muratorian Fragment and the Development of the Canon*. Oxford: Oxford University Press, 1992.

Hallermayer, Michaela. *Text und Überlieferung des Buches Tobit*. Berlin: de Gruyter, 2008.

[Hammond] Bammel, Caroline P. "Die Hexapla des Origenes: Die Hebraica Veritas im Streit der Meinungen." *Augustinianum* 28 (1988): 125–149.

Handmann, Rudolf. *Das Hebräer-Evangelium*. Marburg: n.p., 1888.

Hanson, Richard S. "Paleo-Hebrew Scripts in the Hasmonean Age." *Bulletin of the American Schools of Oriental Research* 175 (1964): 26–42.

Hanson, R.P.C. *Allegory and Event: A Study of the Sources and Significance of Origen's Interpretation of Scripture*. Richmond: John Knox, 1959.

———. *Origen's Doctrine of Tradition*. London: SPCK, 1954.

Hardwick, Michael E. *Josephus as an Historical Source in Patristic Literature through Eusebius*. Brown Judaic Studies 128. Atlanta: Scholars Press, 1989.

Harl, Marguerite, ed. *Origène, Philocalie 1–20 Sur les Écritures*. Sources chrétiennes 302. Paris: Cerf, 1983.

Harnack, Adolf. *Bible Reading in the Early Church*. Translated by J.R. Wilkinson. New York: Putnam, 1912.

Haslam, Michael. "Homeric Papyri and Transmission of the Text." Pages 55–100 in *A New Companion to Homer*. Edited by Ian Morris and Barry Powell. Leiden: Brill, 1997.

Hay, David M. "Philo's View of Himself as an Exegete: Inspired, but not Authoritative." *Studia Philonica Annual* 3 (1991): 40–52.

Hayward, C.T.R. *Saint Jerome's Hebrew Questions on Genesis*. Oxford: Oxford University Press, 1995.

Heine, Ronald E. *Gregory of Nyssa's Treatise on the Inscriptions of the Psalms: Introduction, Translation and Notes*. Oxford: Oxford University Press, 1995.

Hengel, Martin. *Judaism and Hellenism: Studies in Their Encounter in Palestine during the Early Hellenistic Period*. Translated by John Bowden. 2 vols. Philadelphia: Fortress, 1974.

———. *The Septuagint as Christian Scripture: Its Prehistory and the Problem of Its Canon*. Grand Rapids: Baker, 2002.

Hennings, Ralph. *Der Briefwechsel zwischen Augustinus und Hieronymus und Ihr Streit um den Kanon des Alten Testaments und die Auslegung von Gal. 2,11–14*. Leiden: Brill, 1994.

Henry, René. *Photius: Bibliothèque*. 9 vols. Collection byzantine (vols. 1–8), Collection des universités de France (vol. 9). Paris: Société d' édition Les Belles lettres, 1959–1991.

Hezser, Catherine. *Jewish Literacy in Roman Palestine*. Texts and Studies in Ancient Judaism 81. Tübingen: Mohr (Siebeck), 2001.

———. "The Mishnah and Ancient Book Production." Pages 167–192 in *The Mishnah in Contemporary Perspective*. Edited by Alan J. Avery-Peck and Jacob Neusner. Leiden: Brill, 2002.

Hilhorst, Anthony. "The Prestige of Hebrew in the Christian World of Late Antiquity and Middle Ages." Pages 777–802 in *Flores Florentino: Dead Sea Scrolls and Other Early Jewish Studies in Honour of Florentino García Martínez*. Edited by Anthony Hilhorst, Émil Puech, and Eibert Tigchelaar. Leiden: Brill, 2007.

Hill, Robert C. *Theodoret of Cyrus: Commentary on Daniel*. Atlanta: Scholars Press, 2006.

Holl, Karl, ed. *Epiphanius I: Ancoratus und Panarion haer. 1–33*. Die griechischen christlichen Schriftsteller der ersten drei Jahrhunderte 25. Leipzig: Hinrichs, 1915.

Holladay, Carl R. *Fragments from Hellenistic Jewish Authors*. Vol. 1: *Historians*; vol. 2: *Poets*; vol. 3: *Aristobulus*; vol. 4: *Orphica*. Atlanta: Scholars Press, 1983–1996.

Holmes, Michael W. "The Biblical Canon." Pages 406–426 in *The Oxford Handbook of Early Christian Studies*. Edited by Susan Ashbrook Harvey and David G. Hunter. Oxford: Oxford University Press, 2008.

Honigman, Sylvie. *The Septuagint and Homeric Scholarship in Alexandria: A Study in the Narrative of the Letter of Aristeas*. New York: Routledge, 2003.

Horbury, William. "The Christian Use and the Jewish Origins of the Wisdom of Solomon." Pages 182–196 in *Wisdom in Ancient Israel: Essays in Honour of J.A. Emerton*. Edited by John Day, Robert P. Gordon, and H.G.M. Williamson. Cambridge: Cambridge University Press, 1995.

———, ed. *Hebrew Study from Ezra to Ben-Yehuda*. Edinburgh: T&T Clark, 1999.

———. "The Wisdom of Solomon in the Muratorian Fragment." *Journal of Theological Studies* n.s. 45 (1994): 149–159.

Horbury, William, and David Noy, eds. *Jewish Inscriptions of Graeco-Roman Egypt*. Cambridge: Cambridge University Press, 1992.

Horst, Pieter W. van der. *Ancient Jewish Epitaphs: An Introductory Survey of a Millennium of Jewish Funerary Epigraphy (300 BCE–700 CE)*. Kampen: Kok Pharos, 1991.

———. "Greek in Jewish Palestine in Light of Jewish Epigraphy." Pages 154–174 in *Hellenism in the Land of Israel*. Edited by John J. Collins and Gregory E. Sterling. Notre Dame, Ind.: University of Notre Dame Press, 2001.

———. "*Inscriptiones Judaicae Orientis*: A Review Article." *Journal for the Study of Judaism* 3 (2005): 65–83.

Houghton, H.A.G. "Augustine's Adoption of the Vulgate Gospels." *New Testament Studies* 54 (2008): 450–464.

———. *Augustine's Text of John: Patristic Citations and Latin Gospel Manuscripts*. Oxford: Oxford University Press, 2008.

Howard, George. "The Tetragram and the New Testament." *Journal of Biblical Literature* 96 (1977): 63–83.

Howorth, H.H. "The Influence of St. Jerome on the Canon of Western Christianity." *Journal of Theological Studies* 10 (1908–1909): 481–496; 11 (1909–1910): 321–347; 13 (1911–1912): 1–18.

Humphries, Mark. "Rufinus' Eusebius: Translation, Continuation, and Edition in the Latin *Ecclesiastical History*." *Journal of Early Christian Studies* 16 (2008): 143–164.

Hurvitz, Avi. "Was QH a 'Spoken' Language? On Some Recent Views and Positions: Comments." Pages 110–114 in *Diggers at the Well: Proceedings of a Third*

*International Symposium on the Hebrew of the Dead Sea Scrolls and Ben Sira.* Edited by T. Muraoka and John F. Elwolde. Studies on the Texts of the Desert of Judah 36. Leiden: Brill, 2000.

Inowlocki, Sabrina. "'Neither Adding nor Omitting Anything': Josephus' Promise not to Modify the Scriptures in Greek and Latin Context." *Journal of Jewish Studies* 56 (2005): 48–65.

Jacobs, Andrew S. *Remains of the Jews: The Holy Land and Christian Empire in Late Antiquity.* Stanford, Calif.: Stanford University Press, 2004.

Jacobs, Louis. *Structure and Form in the Babylonian Talmud.* Cambridge: Cambridge University Press, 1991.

Jacobson, Howard. *The Exagoge of Ezekiel.* Cambridge: Cambridge University Press, 1983.

Jaeger, Werner, ed. *Contra Eunomium Libri I et II.* Gregorii Nysseni Opera 1. Leiden: Brill 1960.

Janowitz, Naomi. "Theories of Divine Names in Origen and Pseudo-Dionysius." *History of Religions* 30 (1991): 359–372.

Jay, Pierre. *L'exégèse de saint Jérôme d'après son 'Commentaire sur Isaïe'.* Paris: Études augustiniennes, 1985.

———. "Jerome (ca. 347–419/420)." Pages 1094–1133 in *Handbook of Patristic Exegesis: The Bible in Ancient Christianity*, by Charles Kannengiesser. Leiden: Brill, 2004.

Jellicoe, Sidney. *The Septuagint and Modern Study.* Oxford: Oxford University Press, 1968.

Jenkins, R.G. "The First Column of the Hexapla: The Evidence of the Milan Codex (Rahlfs 1098) and the Cairo Genizah Fragment (Rahlfs 2005)." Pages 88–102 in *Origen's Hexapla and Fragments: Papers Presented at the Rich Seminar on the Hexapla, Oxford Centre for Hebrew and Jewish Studies, 25th–3rd August 1994.* Edited by Alison Salvesen. Tübingen: Mohr (Siebeck), 1998.

Joannou, Périclès-Pierre. *Discipline générale antique.* 2 vols. Fonti codificazione canonica orientale 9. Grottaferrata (Rome): Tip. Italo-Orientale "S. Nilo", 1961–1964.

Joisten-Pruschke, Anke. *Das religiöse Leben der Juden von Elephantine in der Achämenidenzeit.* Wiesbaden: Harrasowitz, 2008.

Julius, Caspar. *Die griechischen Danielzusätze und ihre kanonische Geltung.* Biblische Studien 6.3–4. Freiburg: Herder, 1901.

Junod, Éric. "La formation et la composition de l'Ancien Testament dans l'Église grecque des quatre premiers siècles." Pages 105–134 in *Le Canon de l'Ancien Testament: Sa formation et son histoire.* Edited by Jean-Daniel Kaestli and Otto Wermelinger. Geneva: Labor et Fides, 1984.

Kadman, Leo. *The Coins of the Jewish War of 66–73 C.E.* Tel Aviv: Schocken, 1960.

Kaestli, Jean-Daniel. "Le récit de IV Esdras 14 et sa valeur pour l'histoire du canon de l'Ancien Testament." Pages 71–97 in *Le Canon de l'Ancien Testament: Sa formation et son histoire.* Edited by Jean-Daniel Kaestli and Otto Wermelinger. Geneva: Labor et Fides, 1984.

Kaestli, Jean-Daniel, and Otto Wermelinger, eds. *Le Canon de l'Ancien Testament: Sa formation et son histoire.* Geneva: Labor et Fides, 1984.

Kalmin, Richard. "The Miracle of the Septuagint in Ancient Rabbinic and Christian Literature." Pages 241–253 in *"Follow the Wise": Studies in Jewish History and*

*Culture in Honor of Lee I. Levine.* Edited by Zeev Weiss, Oded Irshai, Jodi Magness, and Seth Schwartz. Winona Lake, Ind.: Eisenbrauns, 2010.

Kamesar, Adam. "Biblical Interpretation in Philo." Pages 65–91 in *The Cambridge Companion to Philo.* Edited by Adam Kamesar. Cambridge: Cambridge University Press, 2009.

———. "Hilary of Poitiers, Judeo-Christianity, and the Origins of the LXX: A Translation of Tractatus super Psalmos 2.2–3 with Introduction and Commentary." *Vigiliae Christianae* 59 (2005): 264–285.

———. *Jerome, Greek Scholarship, and the Hebrew Bible: A Study of the Quaestiones Hebraicae in Genesim.* Oxford: Oxford University Press, 1993.

———. "San Basilio, Filone, e la tradizione ebraica." *Henoch* 17 (1995): 129–140.

———. "The Virgin of Isaiah 7:14: The Philological Argument from the Second to the Fifth Century." *Journal of Theological Studies* n.s. 41 (1990): 51–75.

Kannengiesser, Charles, and William L. Petersen, eds. *Origen of Alexandria: His World and His Legacy.* Notre Dame, Ind.: University of Notre Dame Press, 1988.

Karpp, Heinrich. "'Prophet' oder 'Dolmetscher'? Die Geltung der Septuaginta in der Alten Kirche." Pages 103–117 in *Festschrift für Günther Dehn: zum 75. Geburtstag am 18. April 1957 dargebracht von der Evangelisch-Theologischen Fakultät der Rheinischen Friedrich Wilhelms-Universität zu Bonn.* Edited by Wilhelm Schneemelcher. Neukirchen: Kreis Moers, 1957. Repr. pages 128–150 in *Vom Umgang der Kirche mit der Heiligen Schrift: Gesammelte Aufsätze.* Cologne: Böhlau, 1983.

Karst, Josef, ed. *Eusebius Werke V: Die Chronik, aus dem Armenischen übersetzt.* Die griechischen christlichen Schriftsteller der ersten drei Jahrhunderte 20. Leipzig: Hinrichs, 1911.

Katz, Peter. "The Old Testament Canon in Palestine and Alexandria." *Zeitschrift für die neutestamentliche Wissenschaft und die Kunde der älteren Kirche* 47 (1956): 191–217. Repr. pages 72–98 in *The Canon and Masorah of the Hebrew Bible: An Introductory Reader.* Edited by Sid Z. Leiman. New York: Ktav, 1974.

Kay, D.M. "Susanna." Pages 638–651 in vol. 1 of *The Apocrypha and Pseudepigrapha of the Old Testament in English.* 2 vols. Edited by R.H. Charles. Oxford: Oxford University Press, 1913.

Kelly, J.N.D. *Jerome: His Life, Writings, and Controversies.* New York: Duckworth, 1975.

———, trans. *Rufinus: A Commentary on the Apostle's Creed.* Ancient Christian Writers 20. New York: Paulist, 1955.

King, Daniel. "*Vir Quadrilinguis*? Syriac in Jerome and Jerome in Syriac." Pages 209–224 in *Jerome of Stridon: His Life, Writings and Legacy.* Edited by Andrew Cain and Josef Lössl. Surrey: Ashgate, 2009.

Kittel, Gerhard, and Gerhard Friederich, eds. *Theological Dictionary of the New Testament.* Translated by Geoffrey W. Bromiley. 10 vols. Grand Rapids: Eerdmans, 1964–1976.

Klein-Franke, Felix. "A Hebrew Lamentation from Roman Egypt." *Zeitschrift für Papyrologie und Epigraphik* 51 (1983): 80–84.

Klijn, A.F.J. "The Letter of Aristeas and the Greek Translation of the Pentateuch in Egypt." *New Testament Studies* 11 (1965): 154–158.

Klostermann, Erich, ed. *Origenes Werke III: Jeremiahomilien. Klageliederkommentar. Erklärung der Samuel- und Königsbücher.* Die griechischen christlichen Schriftsteller der ersten drei Jahrhunderte 6. Leipzig: Hinrichs, 1901.

Knibb, Michael A. "Martyrdom and Ascension of Isaiah." Pages 143–176 in vol. 2 of *The Old Testament Pseudepigrapha*. Edited by James H. Charlesworth. 2 vols. Garden City, N.Y.: Doubleday, 1983–1985.

———. "Isaianic Traditions in the Apocrypha and Pseudepigrapha." Pages 633–650 in vol. 2 of *Writing and Reading the Scroll of Isaiah: Studies of an Interpretive Tradition*. Edited by Craig C. Broyles and Craig A. Evans. 2 vols. Leiden: Brill, 1997.

Kofsky, Aryeh. *Eusebius of Caesarea Against Paganism*. Leiden: Brill, 2000.

Kooij, Arie van der. "Canonization of Ancient Hebrew Books and Hasmonean Politics." Pages 27–38 in *The Biblical Canons*. Edited by J.-M. Auwers and H.J. de Jonge. Bibliotheca Ephemeridum Theologicarum Lovaniensium 163. Leuven: Leuven University Press, 2003.

Kottsieper, Ingo. "'And They Did Not Care to Speak Yehudit': On Linguistic Change in Judah during the Late Persian Era." Pages 95–124 in *Judah and the Judeans in the Fourth Century B.C.E.* Edited by Oded Lipschits, Gary N. Knoppers, and Rainer Albertz. Winona Lake, Ind.: Eisenbrauns, 2007.

Kotzé, Annemaré. "Augustine, Jerome and the Septuagint." Pages 245–260 in *Septuagint and Reception: Essays Prepared for the Association for the Study of the Septuagint in South Africa*. Edited by Johann Cook. Leiden: Brill, 2009.

Kraabel, A.T. "Melito the Bishop and the Synagogue at Sardis: Text and Context." Pages 72–85 in *Studies Presented to George M.A. Hanfmann*. Edited by David Gordon Mitten, John Griffiths Pedley, and Jane Ayer Scott. Cambridge, Mass.: Fogg Art Museum, 1971. Repr. pages 197–208 in *Diaspora Jews and Judaism: Essays in Honor of, and in Dialogue with, A. Thomas Kraabel*. Edited by J. Andrew Overman and Robert S. MacLennan. Atlanta: Scholars Press, 1992.

Kraft, Robert A. *Exploring the Scripturesque: Jewish Texts and Their Christian Contexts*. Leiden: Brill, 2009.

———. "Philo's Bible Revisited: the 'Aberrant Texts' and Their Quotations of Moses." Pages 237–253 in *Interpreting Translation: Studies on the LXX and Ezekiel in Honour of Johan Lust*. Edited by F. García Martínez and M. Vervenne with the collaboration of B. Doyle. Leuven: Peeters, 2005.

———. "The 'Textual Mechanics' of Early Jewish LXX/OG Papyri and Fragments." Pages 51–72 in *The Bible as Book: The Transmission of the Greek Text*. Edited by Scot McKendrick and Orlaith A. O'Sullivan. New Castle, Del.: Oak Knoll, 2003.

Kreuzer, Siegfried. "From 'Old Greek' to the Recensions: Who and What Caused the Change of the Hebrew Reference Text of the Septuagint." Pages 225–237 in *Septuagint Research: Issues and Challenges in the Study of the Greek Jewish Scriptures*. Edited by Wolfgang Kraus and R. Glenn Wooden. Atlanta: Society of Biblical Literature, 2006.

Kroll, John H. "The Greek Inscriptions of the Sardis Synagogue." *Harvard Theological Review* 94 (2001): 5–55.

La Bonnardière, A.-M. *Biblia Augustiniana, A.T.* (vol. 4): *Le Livre de la Sagesse*. Paris: Études augustiniennes, 1970.

———. "The Canon of Sacred Scripture." Pages 26–41 in *Augustine and the Bible*. Edited by Pamela Bright. Notre Dame, Ind.: University of Notre Dame Press, 1999.

———. "Did Augustine Use Jerome's Vulgate?" Pages 42–51 in *Augustine and the Bible*. Edited by Pamela Bright. Notre Dame, Ind.: University of Notre Dame Press, 1999.

La Matina, Marcello. "Philosophy of Language." Pages 604–611 in *Brill's Dictionary of Gregory of Nyssa*. Edited by Lucas Francisco Mateo-Seco and Giulio Maspero. Translated by Seth Cherney. Supplements to Vigiliae Christianae 99. Leiden: Brill, 2009.

Labendz, Jenny R. "Aquila's Bible Translation in Late Antiquity: Jewish and Christian Perspectives." *Harvard Theological Review* 102 (2009): 353–388.

Lagarde, Paul de, ed. *Onomastica Sacra*. Göttingen: Adalbert, 1870.

Lahey, Lawrence. "Hebrew and Aramaic in the *Dialogue of Timothy and Aquila*." Pages 106–121 in *Hebrew Study from Ezra to Ben-Yehuda*. Edited by William Horbury. Edinburgh: T&T Clark, 1999.

Lake, Kirsopp, trans. *Eusebius: The Ecclesiastical History*. Vol. 1. Loeb Classical Library. Cambridge, Mass.: Harvard University Press, 1926.

Lampe, G.W.H., ed. *A Patristic Greek Lexicon*. Oxford: Oxford University Press, 1961.

Lange, Armin. *Handbuch der Textfunde vom Toten Meer*. Vol. 1: *Die Handschriften biblischer Bücher von Qumran und den anderen Fundorten*. Tübingen: Mohr (Siebeck), 2009.

———. "Kriterien essenischer Texte." Pages 59–69 in *Qumran Kontrovers: Beiträge zu den Textfunden vom Toten Meer*. Edited by Jörg Frey and Hartmut Stegemann. Paderborn: Bonifatius, 2003.

———. "'They Confirmed the Reading' (*y. Ta'an.* 4.68a): The Textual Standardization of Jewish Scriptures in the Second Temple Period." Pages 29–80 in *From Qumran to Aleppo: A Discussion with Emanuel Tov about the Textual History of Jewish Scriptures in Honor of his 65th Birthday*. Edited by Armin Lange, Matthias Weigold, and József Zsengellér. Göttingen: Vandenhoeck & Ruprecht, 2009.

Langer, Ruth. "Revisiting Early Rabbinic Liturgy: The Recent Contributions of Ezra Fleischer." *Prooftexts* 19 (1999): 179–204.

———. *To Worship God Properly: Tensions between Liturgical Custom and Halakhah in Judaism*. Cincinnati: Hebrew Union College Press, 1998.

Langerbeck, Hermann, ed. *In Canticum Canticorum*. Gregorii Nysseni Opera 6. Leiden: Brill, 1960.

Lapin, Hayim. "Palm Fronds and Citrons: Notes on Two Letters from Bar Kosiba's Administration." *Hebrew Union College Annual* 64 (1993): 111–135.

Larcher, C. *Études sur le Livre de la Sagesse*. Paris: J. Gabalda, 1969.

Lardet, Pierre. *Apologie contre Rufin*. Sources chrétiennes 303. Paris: Cerf, 1983.

———. *L'Apologie de Jérôme contre Rufin: un commentaire*. Leiden: Brill, 1993.

Lauchert, Friedrich. *Die Kanones der wichtigsten altkirchlichen Concilien nebst den Apostolischen Kanones*. 1896. Repr. Frankfurt: Minerva, 1961.

Law, T.M. "Origen's Parallel Bible: Textual Criticism, Apologetics, or Exegesis?" *Journal of Theological Studies* n.s. 59 (2008): 1–21.

Lawson, R.P. *Origen: The Song of Songs, Commentary and Homilies*. Ancient Christian Writers 26. Westminster, Md.: Newman, 1957.

Lee, Samuel, ed. *Eusebius, Bishop of Caesarea, on the Theophania or Divine Manifestation of Our Lord and Saviour Jesus Christ: a Syriac version edited from an ancient manuscript recently discovered*. London: Society for the Publication of Oriental Texts, 1842.

———, trans. *Eusebius, Bishop of Caesarea, on the Theophania or Divine Manifes-*

*tation of Our Lord and Savior Jesus Christ: Translated into English.* Cambridge: Cambridge University Press, 1843.

Leemans, Johan. "Athanasius and the Book of Wisdom." *Ephemerides theologicae lovanienses* 73 (1997): 349–369.

———. "Canon and Quotation: Athanasius' Use of Jesus Sirach." Pages 265–277 in *The Biblical Canons.* Edited by J.-M. Auwers and H.J. de Jonge. Bibliotheca Ephemeridum Theologicarum Lovaniensium 163. Leuven: Leuven University Press, 2003.

Legrand, Thierry. "La version latine de Ben Sira: état de la question, essai classement thématique des 'additions'." Pages 215–234 in *The Texts and Versions of the Book of Ben Sira: Transmission and Interpretation.* Edited by Jean-Sébastien Rey and Jan Joosten. Leiden: Brill, 2011.

Leiman, Sid Z., ed. *The Canon and Masora of the Hebrew Bible: An Introductory Reader.* New York: Ktav, 1974.

———. *The Canonization of Hebrew Scripture: The Talmudic and Midrashic Evidence.* Hamden, Conn.: Archon Books, 1976.

———. "Inspiration and Canonicity: Reflections on the Formation of the Biblical Canon." Pages 56–63 in *Jewish and Christian Self-Definition.* Vol. 2: *Aspects of Judaism in the Graeco-Roman Period.* Edited by E.P. Sanders. Philadelphia: Fortress, 1981.

———. "Josephus and the Canon of the Bible." Pages 50–58 in *Josephus, the Bible, and History.* Edited by Louis H. Feldman and Gohei Hata. Detroit: Wayne State University Press, 1989.

Leisering, Christina. *Susanna und der Sündenfall der Ältesten: Eine vergleichende Studie zu den Geschlechterkonstruktionen der Septuaginta- und Theodotion-fassung von Dan 13 und ihren intertextuellen Bezügen.* Berlin: Lit, 2008.

Leon, Harry J. *The Jews of Ancient Rome.* Philadelphia: Jewish Publication Society, 1960.

Levine, Lee I. "The Sages and the Synagogue in Late Antiquity." Pages 201–222 in *The Galilee in Latin Antiquity.* Edited by Lee I. Levine. New York: Jewish Theological Seminary of America, 1992.

Lewis, Naphtali. *The Documents from the Bar Kokhba Period in the Cave of Letters: Greek Papyri.* Jerusalem: Israel Exploration Society, 1989.

Lieberman, Saul. *Greek in Jewish Palestine: Studies in the Life and Manners of Jewish Palestine in the II–IV Centuries C. E.* New York: Jewish Theological Seminary of America, 1942.

———. *Hellenism in Jewish Palestine: Studies in the Literary Transmission, Beliefs and Manners of Palestine in the I Century B.C.E.–IV century C.E.* 2d ed. New York: Jewish Theological Seminary of America, 1962.

Lightstone, Jack N. "The Rabbis' Bible: The Canon of the Hebrew Bible and the Early Rabbinic Guild." Pages 163–184 in *The Canon Debate.* Edited by Lee Martin McDonald and James A. Sanders. Peabody, Mass.: Hendrickson, 2002.

Lim, Timothy H. "The Defilement of the Hands as a Principle Determining the Holiness of Scriptures." *Journal of Theological Studies* 61 (2010): 501–515.

Lincicum, D. "The Epigraphic Habit and the Biblical Text: Inscriptions as a Source for the Study of the Greek Bible." *Bulletin of the International Organization for Septuagint and Cognate Studies* 41 (2008): 84–92.

Linder, Amnon. *The Jews in Roman Imperial Legislation*. Detroit: Wayne State University Press, 1987.

Lössl, Josef. "A Shift in Patristic Exegesis: Hebrew Clarity and Historical Verity in Augustine, Jerome, Julian of Aeclanum and Theodore of Mopsuestia." *Augustinian Studies* 32 (2001): 157–175.

Louth, Andrew. *The Origins of the Christian Mystical Tradition: From Plato to Denys*. 2d ed. Oxford: Oxford University Press, 1981.

Lubac, Henri de. *Medieval Exegesis*. 2 vols. Translated by Mark Sebanc. Grand Rapids: Eerdmans, 1998. Translation of *Exégèse Médiévale: les quatres sens de l'écriture*. 2 vols. Paris: Aubier, 1959–1964.

Lütcke, Karl-Heinrich. "Auctoritas." Pages 498–510 in *Augustinus-Lexikon*. Edited by Cornelius Mayer. Vol. 1. Basel: Schwabe, 1986–1994.

Magness, Jodi. "The Date of the Sardis Synagogue in Light of the Numismatic Evidence." *American Journal of Archaeology* 109 (2005): 443–475.

Malcom, Noel. *Aspects of Hobbes*. Oxford: Oxford University Press, 2002.

Markschies, Christoph. "Hieronymus und die 'Hebraica Veritas': Ein Beitrag zur Archäologie des protestantischen Schriftverständnisses." Pages 131–181 in *Die Septuaginta zwischen Judentum und Christentum*. Edited by Martin Hengel and Anna Maria Schwemer. Tübingen: Mohr (Siebeck), 1994.

Martin, Matthew J. "Origen's Theory of Language and the First Two Columns of the Hexapla." *Harvard Theological Review* 97 (2004): 99–106.

———. "Writing Divine Speech: Greek Transliterations of Near Eastern Languages in the Hellenistic East." Pages 251–273 in *Politics of Orality*. Edited by Craig Cooper. Leiden: Brill, 2007.

Mason, Steve. "Josephus and His Twenty-Two Book Canon." Pages 110–127 in *The Canon Debate*. Edited by Lee Martin McDonald and James A. Sanders. Peabody, Mass.: Hendrickson, 2002.

———. "Josephus on Canon and Scripture." Pages 217–235 in *Hebrew Bible/Old Testament: The History of Its Interpretation*. Vol. 1: *From the Beginnings to the Middle Ages (until 1300)*. Part 1: *Antiquity*. Edited by Magne Saebø. Göttingen: Vandenhoeck & Ruprecht, 1996.

Matthews, K.A. "The Background of the Paleo-Hebrew Texts at Qumran." Pages 549–568 in *The Word of the Lord Shall Go Forth: Essays in Honor of David Noel Freedman in Celebration of His Sixtieth Birthday*. Edited by Carol L. Meyers and M. O'Connor. Winona Lake, Ind: Eisenbrauns, 1983.

McDonald, Lee Martin. *The Biblical Canon: Its Origin, Transmission, and Authority*. Peabody, Mass.: Hendrickson, 2007.

McDonald, Lee Martin, and James A. Sanders, eds. *The Canon Debate*. Peabody, Mass.: Hendrickson, 2002.

McDonough, Jacob, and Paul Alexander, eds. *In inscriptiones Psalmorum, In sextum Psalmum, In ecclesiasten homiliae*. Gregorii Nysseni Opera 5. Leiden: Brill, 1962.

McLay, [R.] Tim[othy]. *The OG and Th Versions of Daniel*. Atlanta: Scholars Press, 1996.

———. *The Use of the Septuagint in New Testament Research*. Grand Rapids: Eerdmans, 2003.

Merk, Augustin. "Origenes und der Kanon des Alten Testaments." *Biblica* 6 (1925): 200–205.

Meshorer, Ya'akov. *A Treasury of Jewish Coins: From the Persian Period to Bar Kokhba*. Translated by Robert Amoils. Jerusalem: Yad Ben-Zvi, 2001.

Metzger, Bruce M. *Manuscripts of the Greek Bible: An Introduction to Greek Palaeography*. Oxford: Oxford University Press, 1981.

Meyer, Arnold. *Jesu Muttersprache: Das galiläische Aramaisch in seiner Bedeutung für die Erklärung der Reden Jesu und der Evangelien überhaupt*. Leipzig: Mohr (Siebeck), 1896.

Mildenberg, Leo. *The Coinage of the Bar Kokhba War*. Aarau: Sauerländer, 1984.

Milik, J.T. *Ten Years of Discovery in the Wilderness of Judaea*. Translated by J. Strugnell. Naperville, Ill.: Allenson, 1959.

Millar, Fergus. "Christian Emperors, Christian Church and the Jews of the Diaspora in the Greek East, CE 379–450." *Journal of Jewish Studies* 55 (2004): 1–25.

———. "The Many Worlds of the Late Antique Diaspora: Supplements to the 'Cambridge History of Judaism' vol. IV." *Journal of Jewish Studies* 59 (2008): 120–138.

———. "A Rural Jewish Community in Late Roman Mesopotamia, and the Question of a 'Split' Jewish Diaspora." *Journal for the Study of Judaism* 42 (2011): 351–374.

Moll, Sebastian. *The Arch-Heretic Marcion*. Wissenschaftliche Untersuchungen zum Neuen Testament 250. Tübingen: Mohr Siebeck, 2010.

Mondésert, Claude, ed. *Le monde grec ancien et la Bible*. Bible de tous les temps 1. Paris: Beauchesne, 1984.

Moore, Carey A. *Daniel, Esther and Jeremiah: The Additions*. Anchor Bible 44. New York: Doubleday, 1977.

———. *Judith*. Anchor Bible 40. Garden City, N.Y.: Doubleday, 1985.

Moreau, Madeleine, Isabelle Bochet, and Goulven Madec. *La doctrine chrétienne*. Bibliothèque augustinienne, Oeuvres de saint Augustin 11/2. Paris: Institut d'Études Augustiniennes, 1997.

Moutsoula, Elia D. "Τὸ Περὶ μέτρων καὶ σταθμῶν' ἔργον Ἐπιφανίου τοῦ Σαλαμῖνος." *Theologia* 44 (1973): 157–200.

Müller, Mogens. *The First Bible of the Church: A Plea for the Septuagint*. Journal for the Study of the Old Testament: Supplement Series 206. Sheffield: Sheffield Academic, 1996.

Munier, C. *Concilia Africae a. 345–525*. Corpus Christianorum: Series latina 149. Turnhout: Brepols, 1974.

———. "La tradition manuscrite de l'Abrégé d'Hippone et le Canon des Écritures des églises africaines." *Sacris Erudiri* 21 (1972–1973): 43–55.

Munnich, Olivier. "Contribution à l'étude de la première révision de la Septante." *ANRW* 20.1:190–220. Part 2, *Principat*, 20.1. Edited by Wolfgang Haase. New York: de Gruyter, 1987.

———. "Le texte du Pentateuque grec et son histoire." Pages 51–59 in *Le Pentateuque d'Alexandrie: texte grec et traduction*. Edited by Cécile Dogniez and Marguerite Harl. Paris: Cerf, 2001.

Myers, Jacob M. *Ezra, Nehemiah*. Anchor Bible 14. Garden City, N.Y.: Doubleday, 1965.

Nautin, Pierre. *Origène: Sa vie et son oeuvre*. Paris: Beuchesne, 1977.

Naveh, Joseph. *Early History of the Alphabet: An Introduction to West Semitic Epigraphy and Palaeography*. 2d ed. Jerusalem: Magnes, 1987.

————. "Hebrew Texts in Aramaic Script in the Persian Period?" *Bulletin of the American Schools of Oriental Research* 203 (1971): 27–32.

————. "Scripts and Inscriptions in Ancient Samaria." *Israel Exploration Journal* 48 (1998): 91–100.

Neuschäfer, Bernhard. *Origenes als Philologe.* 2 vols. Schweizerische Beiträge zur Altertumswissenschaft 18. Basel: Reinhardt, 1987.

Neusner, Jacob, trans. *The Tosefta: Translated from the Hebrew with a New Introduction.* 2 vols. Peabody, Mass.: Hendrickson, 2002.

Newman, Hillel I. "How Should We Measure Jerome's Hebrew Competence?" Pages 131–140 in *Jerome of Stridon: His Life, Writings and Legacy.* Edited by Andrew Cain and Josef Lössl. Surrey: Ashgate, 2009.

Nickelsburg, George W.E. *1 Enoch 1: A Commentary on the Book of 1 Enoch, Chapters 1–36; 81–108.* Hermeneia. Minneapolis: Fortress, 2001.

Niehoff, Maren R. *Jewish Exegesis and Homeric Scholarship in Alexandria.* Cambridge: Cambridge University Press, 2011.

Nogalski, James. *Literary Precursors to the Book of the Twelve.* Beihefte zu Zeitschrift für die alttestamentliche Wissenschaft 217. Berlin: de Gruyter, 1993.

Norelli, Enrico. "Ascension d' Isaïc." Pages 499–545 in *Écrits apocryphes chrétiens I.* Edited by François Bovon and Pierre Geoltrain. Paris: Gallimard, 1997.

————. "The Political Issue of the *Ascension of Isaiah*: Some Remarks on Jonathan Knight's Thesis, and Some Methodological Problems." Pages 267–279 in *Early Christian Voices in Texts, Traditions, and Symbols: Essays in Honor of François Bovon.* Edited by David H. Warren, Anne Graham Brock, and David W. Pao. Leiden: Brill, 2003.

————. *Ascensio Isaiae: Commentarius.* Corpus Christianorum: Series apocryphorum 8. Turnhout: Brepols, 1995. [For the volume of *Textus*, see above under Bettiolo.]

Norris, Richard A. "The Soul Takes Flight: Gregory of Nyssa and the Song of Songs." *Anglican Theological Review* 80 (1998): 517–532.

Norton, Gerald J. "Observations on the First Two Columns of the Hexapla." Pages 103–124 in *Origen's Hexapla and Fragments: Papers Presented at the Rich Seminar on the Hexapla, Oxford Centre for Hebrew and Jewish Studies, 25th–3rd August 1994.* Edited by Alison Salvesen. Tübingen: Mohr (Siebeck), 1998.

Noy, David, ed. *Jewish Inscriptions of Western Europe.* 2 vols. Cambridge: Cambridge University Press, 1993–1995.

————. "'Peace upon Israel': Hebrew Formulae and Names in Jewish Inscriptions from the Western Roman Empire." Pages 135–146 in *Hebrew Study from Ezra to Ben Yehuda.* Edited by William Horbury. Edinburgh: T&T Clark, 1999.

————. "Writing in Tongues: The Use of Greek, Latin and Hebrew in Jewish Inscriptions from Roman Italy." *Journal of Jewish Studies* 48 (1997): 300–311.

Noy, David, Alexander Panayotov, and Hanswulf Bloedhorn, eds. *Inscriptiones Judaicae Orientis.* Vol. 1: *Eastern Europe.* Texts and Studies in Ancient Judaism 101. Tübingen: Mohr (Siebeck), 2004.

Noy, David, and Hanswulf Bloedhorn, eds. *Inscriptiones Judaicae Orientis.* Vol. 3: *Syria and Cyprus.* Texts and Studies in Ancient Judaism 102. Tübingen: Mohr (Siebeck), 2004.

Obbink, Dirk. "Bilingual Literacy and Syrian Greek." *Bulletin of the American Society of Papyrologists* 28 (1991): 51–57.

O'Connell, Kevin G. *The Theodotionic Revision of the Book of Exodus: A Contribution to the Study of the Early History of the Transmission of the Old Testament in Greek.* Harvard Semitic Monographs 3. Cambridge, Mass.: Harvard University Press, 1972.

Ohlig, Karl-Heinz. "Canon scripturarum." Pages 713–724 in *Augustinus-Lexikon.* Edited by Cornelius Mayer. Vol. 1. Basel: Schwabe, 1986–1994.

Orlinsky, Harry M. "The Septuagint as Holy Writ and the Philosophy of the Translators." *Hebrew Union College Annual* 46 (1975): 89–114.

Overman, J. Andrew. "The Diaspora in the Modern Study of Ancient Judaism." Pages 63–78 in *Diaspora Jews and Judaism: Essays in Honor of, and in Dialogue with, A. Thomas Kraabel.* Edited by J. Andrew Overman and Robert S. MacLennan. Atlanta, 1992.

Overman, J. Andrew and Robert S. MacLennan, eds. *Diaspora Jews and Judaism: Essays in Honor of, and in Dialogue with, A. Thomas Kraabel.* Atlanta: Scholars Press, 1992.

Pastis, Jacqueline Z. "Dating the *Dialogue of Timothy and Aquila*: Revisiting the Earlier *Vorlage* Hypothesis." *Harvard Theological Review* 95 (2002): 169–195.

Paul, André. "La Bible grecque d'Aquila et l'idéologie du judaïsme ancien." *ANRW* 20.1:221–245. Part 2, *Principat*, 20.1. Edited by Wolfgang Haase. New York: de Gruyter, 1987.

Pelletier, André. *Flavius Josèphe adaptateur de la Lettre d'Aristée: une reaction atticisante contre la Koiné.* Paris: Librairie C. Klincksieck, 1962.

Penner, Ken. "What Language Did Paul Speak in Acts 21–22? Ancient Names for Hebrew and Aramaic." Paper presented at the annual meeting of the Canadian Society of Biblical Studies. Halifax, 2003. Available online at http://ocp.acadiau .ca/kpenner/papers/hebrais/.

Perrot, Charles. "L'inspiration des Septante et le pouvoir scripturaire." Pages 169–183 in Κατα τους ο'—*Selon les Septante: trente études sur la Bible grecque des Septante en hommage à Marguerite Harl.* Edited by Gilles Dorival and Olivier Munnich. Paris: Cerf, 1995.

Petersen, Nicholas. "An Analysis of Two Early LXX Manuscripts from Qumran: 4QLXXNum and 4QLXXLevᵃ in the Light of Previous Studies." *Bulletin for Biblical Research* 19 (2009): 481–510.

Pfeiffer, Robert H. *History of New Testament Times with an Introduction to the Apocrypha.* New York: Harper, 1949.

Pfeiffer, Rudolf. *History of Classical Scholarship: From the Beginnings to the End of the Hellenistic Age.* Oxford: Oxford University Press, 1968.

*Philo.* Translated by F.H. Colson et al. 12 vols. Loeb Classical Library. Cambridge: Harvard University Press, 1929–1953.

Pietersma, Albert. "Kyrios or Tetragram: A Renewed Quest for the Original LXX." Pages 85–101 in *De Septuaginta: Studies in Honour of John William Wevers on His Sixty-fifth Birthday.* Edited by Albert Pietersma and Claude Cox. Mississauga, Ont.: Benben, 1984.

Pizzolato, Luigi F., and Chiara Somenzi. *I sette fratelli Macabei nella chiesa antica d'Occidente.* Milan: Vita e Pensiero, 2005.

Poirier, John C. "4Q464: Not Eschatological." *Revue de Qumran* 20 (2002): 583–587.
———. "The Linguistic Situation in Jewish Palestine in Late Antiquity." *Journal of Greco-Roman Christianity and Judaism* 4 (2007): 55–134, available online at http://www.jgrchj.net/volume4/JGRChJ4-3_Poirer.pdf.
Polak, Frank H. "Sociolinguistics and the Judean Speech Community in the Achaemenid Empire." Pages 589–628 in *Judah and the Judeans in the Persian Period.* Edited by Oded Lipschits and Manfred Oeming. Winona Lake, Ind.: Eisenbrauns, 2006.
Polman, Andries Derk Rietema. *The Word of God According to St. Augustine.* Translated by A.J. Pomerans. Grand Rapids: Eerdmans, 1961.
Porton, Gary G. "Isaiah and the Kings: The Rabbis on the Prophet Isaiah." Pages 693–716 in vol. 2 of *Writing and Reading the Scroll of Isaiah: Studies of an Interpretive Tradition.* Edited by Craig C. Broyles and Craig A. Evans. 2 vols. Leiden: Brill, 1997.
Preuschen, Erwin, ed. *Origenes Werke IV: Der Johanneskommentar.* Die griechischen christlichen Schriftsteller der ersten drei Jahrhunderte 10. Leipzig: Hinrichs, 1903.
Price, Jonathan J., and Shlomo Naeh. "On the Margins of Culture: The Practice of Transcription in the Ancient World." Pages 257–288 in *From Hellenism to Islam: Cultural and Linguistic Change in the Roman Near East.* Edited by Hannah M. Cotton, Robert G. Hoyland, Jonathan J. Price, and David J. Wasserstein. Cambridge: Cambridge University Press, 2009.
Pummer, Reinhard. "The Samareitikon Revisited." Pages 381–451 in *Essays in Honour of G.D. Sixdenier: New Samaritan Studies of the Société d'études samaritaines.* Vols. 3 and 4. Edited by Alan D. Crown and Lucy Davey. Sydney: Mandelbaum, 1995.
———. "The Samaritans and Their Pentateuch." Pages 237–269 in *The Pentateuch as Torah: New Models for Understanding Its Promulgation and Acceptance.* Edited by Gary N. Knoppers and Bernard M. Levinson. Winona Lake, Ind.: Eisenbrauns, 2007.
Qimron, Elisha. "The Nature of DSS Hebrew and Its Relation to BH and MH." Pages 232–244 in *Diggers at the Well: Proceedings of a Third International Symposium on the Hebrew of the Dead Sea Scrolls and Ben Sira.* Edited by T. Muraoka and John F. Elwolde. Studies on the Texts of the Desert of Judah 36. Leiden: Brill, 2000.
———. "Observations on the History of Early Hebrew (1000 BCE–200 CE) in the Light of the Dead Sea Documents." Pages 349–361 in *The Dead Sea Scrolls: Forty Years of Research.* Edited by Devorah Dimant and Uriel Rappaport. Leiden: Brill, 1992.
Quasten, Johannes. *Patrology.* 4 vols. Westminster, Md.: Newman, 1950–1986.
Rabin, Chaim. "The Historical Background of Qumran Hebrew." Pages 144–161 in *Aspects of the Dead Sea Scrolls.* Edited by Chaim Rabin and Yigael Yadin. Scripta Hierosolymitana 4. Jerusalem: Magnes, 1958.
Rahlfs, Alfred, ed. *Psalmi cum Odis.* Septuaginta 10. Göttingen: Vandenhoeck & Ruprecht, 1931.
Rahlfs, Alfred, and Detlef Fraenkel. *Verzeichnis der griechischen Handschriften des Alten Testaments.* Volume I,1: *Die Überlieferung bis zum VIII. Jahrhundert.* Göttingen: Vandenhoeck & Ruprecht, 2004.
Rahmer, Moritz. *Die hebräischen Traditionen in den Werken des Hieronymus,* vol. 1: *Die "Quaestiones in Genesin".* Breslau: Schletter, 1861.

Rajak, Tessa. *Josephus: The Historian and His Society*. 2d ed. London: Duckworth, 2002.

——. *Translation and Survival: The Greek Bible of the Ancient Jewish Diaspora*. Oxford: Oxford University Press, 2009.

Raspanti, Giacomo. "The Significance of Jerome's *Commentary on Galatians* in his Exegetical Production." Pages 163–171 in *Jerome of Stridon: His Life, Writings and Legacy*. Edited by Andrew Cain and Josef Lössl. Surrey: Ashgate, 2009.

Reale, Giovanni. *A History of Ancient Philosophy*. Vol. 3: *The Systems of the Hellenistic Age*. Translated by John R. Catan. Albany: State University of New York Press, 1985.

Rebenich, Stefan. *Jerome*. London: Routledge, 2002.

——. "Jerome: The 'Vir Trilinguis' and the 'Hebraica Veritas'." *Vigiliae Christianae* 47 (1993): 50–77.

Reed, Annette Yoshiko. "Job as Jobab: The Interpretation of Job in LXX Job 42:17b–e." *Journal of Biblical Literature* 120 (2001): 31–55.

Reichardt, Walther. *Die Briefe des Sextus Julius Africanus an Aristides und Origenes*. Texte und Untersuchungen 34.3. Leipzig: Hinrichs, 1909.

Reider, Joseph. *Prolegomena to a Greek-Hebrew and Hebrew-Greek Index to Aquila*. Philadelphia: Dropsie College, 1916.

Reider, Joseph, and Nigel Turner. *An Index to Aquila: Greek-Hebrew; Hebrew-Greek; Latin-Hebrew, with the Syriac and Armenian Evidence*. Leiden: Brill, 1966.

Reif, Stefan C. *A Jewish Archive from Old Cairo: The History of Cambridge University's Genizah Collection*. Surrey: Curzon, 2000.

Resnick, Irven M. "The Falsification of Scripture and Medieval Christian and Jewish Polemics." *Medieval Encounters* 2 (1996): 344–380.

Richard, Marcel, ed. *Hippolytus Werke I. Kommentar zu Daniel*, Die griechischen christlichen Schriftsteller der ersten drei Jahrhunderte, Neue Folge 7. Berlin: Akademie Verlag, 2000.

Rinaldi, Giancarlo. *Biblia Gentium: A First Contribution Towards an Index of Biblical Quotations, References and Allusions Made by Greek and Latin Heathen Writers of the Roman Imperial Times*. Rome: Libreria Sacre Scritture, 1989.

Roitman, Adolfo D. "'This People Are Descendants of Chaldeans' (Judith 5:6): Its Literary Form and Historical Setting." *Journal of Biblical Literature* 113 (1994): 245–263.

Rösel, Martin. "The Reading and Translation of the Divine Name in the Masoretic Tradition and the Greek Pentateuch." *Journal for the Study of the Old Testament* 31 (2007): 411–428.

Rosén, Haiim B. *Hebrew at the Crossroads of Cultures: From Outgoing Antiquity to the Middle Ages*. Leuven: Peeters, 1995.

Rubin, Milka. "The Language of Creation or the Primordial Language: A Case of Cultural Polemics in Antiquity." *Journal of Jewish Studies* 49 (1998): 306–333.

Rüger, Hans-Peter. "Apokryphen." Pages 289–316 in vol. 3 of *Theologische Realenzyklopädie*. Berlin: de Gruyter, 1978.

——. "Le Siracide: un livre à la frontière du canon." Pages 47–69 in *Le Canon de l'Ancien Testament: Sa formation et son histoire*. Edited by Jean-Daniel Kaestli and Otto Wermelinger. Geneva: Labor et Fides, 1984.

Runia, David T. *Philo in Early Christian Literature: A Survey*. Compendia rerum iudaicarum ad Novum Testamentum 3.3. Assen: Van Gorcum, 1993.

Rutgers, L[eonard] V. *The Hidden Heritage of Diaspora Judaism.* Leuven: Peeters, 1998.

———. *The Jews in Late Ancient Rome.* Leiden: Brill, 1995.

———. "Justinian's Novella 146 between Jews and Christians." Pages 385–406 in *Jewish Culture and Society under the Christian Roman Empire.* Edited by Richard Kalmin and Seth Schwartz. Leuven: Peeters, 2003. Repr. pages 49–77 in *Making Myths: Jews in Early Christian Identity Formation.* Leuven: Peeters, 2009.

Ruwet, Jean. "Duo Textus Origenis de Canone Antiqui Testamenti." *Biblica* 2 (1921): 57–60.

———. "Le canon alexandrin des Écritures. Saint Athanase." *Biblica* 33 (1952): 1–29.

———. "Les 'Antilegomena' dans les œuvres d' Origène: les antilegomena de l' Ancien Testament." *Biblica* 24 (1943): 18–58.

———. "Les apocryphes dans les œuvres d' Origène." *Biblica* 25 (1944): 143–166, 311–334.

Ryle, Herbert Edward. *The Canon of the Old Testament: An Essay on the Gradual Growth and Formation of the Hebrew Canon of Scripture.* London: Macmillan, 1892.

Saebø, Magne, ed. *Hebrew Bible/Old Testament: The History of Its Interpretation.* Vol. 1: *From the Beginnings to the Middle Ages (until 1300).* Part 1: *Antiquity.* Göttingen: Vandenhoeck & Ruprecht, 1996.

Sáenz-Badillos, Angel. *A History of the Hebrew Language.* Translated by John Elwolde. Cambridge: Cambridge University Press, 1993.

Salmon, [George]. "The Apocrypha: General Introduction." Pages ix–xlvi in vol. 1 of *The Holy Bible, according to the Authorized Version (A.D. 1611), with an Explanatory and Critical Commentary and a Revision of the Translation: Apocrypha.* Speaker's Commentary. Edited by Henry Wace. 2 vols. London: John Murray, 1888.

Salvesen, Alison. "A Convergence of the Ways? The Judaizing of Christian Scripture by Origen and Jerome." Pages 233–258 in *The Ways that Never Parted: Jews and Christians in Late Antiquity and the Early Middle Ages.* Edited by Adam H. Becker and Annette Yoshiko Reed. Texts and Studies in Ancient Judaism 95. Tübingen: Mohr (Siebeck), 2003.

———, ed. *Origen's Hexapla and Fragments: Papers Presented at the Rich Seminar on the Hexapla, Oxford Centre for Hebrew and Jewish Studies, 25th–3rd August 1994.* Tübingen: Mohr (Siebeck), 1998.

———. "Psalm 135(136):25 in a Jewish Greek Inscription from Nicaea." Pages 212–221 in *Semitic Studies in Honour of Edward Ullendorff.* Edited by Geoffrey Khan. Leiden: Brill, 2005.

———. *Symmachus in the Pentateuch.* Manchester: University of Manchester, 1991.

Sanders, James A. "Canon: Hebrew Bible." Pages 837–852 in vol. 1 of *The Anchor Bible Dictionary.* Edited by David Noel Freedman. 6 vols. New York: Doubleday, 1992.

Sandmel, Samuel. *Judaism and Christian Beginnings.* New York: Oxford University Press, 1978.

Sarason, Richard S. Introduction to the reprint of *Literature of the Synagogue,* by Joseph Heinemann and Jakob J. Petuchowski (1975). Repr. Piscataway, N.J.: Gorgias, 2006.

Satran, David. *Biblical Prophets in Byzantine Palestine: Reassessing the Lives of the Prophets.* Leiden: Brill, 1995.

Sawyer, John F.A. *Sacred Languages and Sacred Texts*. London: Routledge, 1999.

Schade, Ludwig. *Die Inspirationslehre des heiligen Hieronymus: Eine biblisch-geschichtliche Studie*. Biblische Studien 15.4–5. Freiburg: Herder, 1910.

Schäfer, Peter. *Die Vorstellung vom heiligen Geist in der rabbinischen Literatur*. Munich: Kösel, 1972.

Schaper, Joachim. "The Origin and Purpose of the Fifth Column of the Hexapla." Pages 3–15 in *Origen's Hexapla and Fragments: Papers Presented at the Rich Seminar on the Hexapla, Oxford Centre for Hebrew and Jewish Studies, 25th–3rd August 1994*. Edited by Alison Salvesen. Tübingen: Mohr (Siebeck), 1998.

Schäublin, Christoph. *Untersuchungen zu Methode und Herkunft der antiochenischen Exegese*. Cologne: P. Hanstein, 1974.

Scheindler, Augustin. *Nonni Panopolitani Paraphrasis S. Evangelii Ioannei*. Leipzig: Teubner, 1881.

Schild, Maurice E. *Abendländische Bibelvorreden bis zur Lutherbibel*. Heidelberg: Gütersloher Verlagshaus, 1970.

Schniedewind, William M. *How the Bible Became a Book: The Textualization of Ancient Israel*. Cambridge: Cambridge University Press, 2004.

———. "Linguistic Ideology in Qumran Hebrew." Pages 245–255 in *Diggers at the Well: Proceedings of a Third International Symposium on the Hebrew of the Dead Sea Scrolls and Ben Sira*. Edited by T. Muraoka and John F. Elwolde. Studies on the Texts of the Desert of Judah 36. Leiden: Brill, 2000.

———. "Prolegomena for the Sociolinguistics of Classical Hebrew." *Journal of Hebrew Scriptures* 5 (2004): article 6, available online at http://www.arts.ualberta.ca/JHS/Articles/article_36.pdf.

———. "Qumran Hebrew as an Antilanguage." *Journal of Biblical Literature* 118 (1999): 235–252.

Schramm, Gene. "Languages (Hebrew): Hebrew as a Language Name." Pages 203–204 in vol. 4 of *Anchor Bible Dictionary*. Edited by David Noel Freedman. 6 vols. New York: Doubleday, 1992.

Schreckenberg, Heinz. *Die Flavius-Josephus-Tradition in Antike und Mittelalter*. Leiden: Brill, 1972.

———. "The Works of Josephus and the Early Christian Church." Pages 315–324 in *Josephus, Judaism, and Christianity*. Edited by Louis H. Feldman and Gohei Hata. Detroit: Wayne State University Press, 1987.

Schreckenberg, Heinz, and Kurt Schubert. *Jewish Historiography and Iconography in Early and Medieval Christianity*. Compendia rerum iudaicarum ad Novum Testamentum 3.2. Minneapolis: Fortress, 1992.

Schürer, Emil. *A History of the Jewish People in the Time of Jesus Christ*. 5 vols. Translated by John Macpherson. New York: Scribners, 1885–1891.

———. *The History of the Jewish People in the Age of Jesus Christ (175 BC–AD 135)*. Revised by Geza Vermes, Fergus Millar, and Matthew Black. 3 vols. in 4. Edinburgh: T&T Clark, 1973–1985.

Schwartz, Daniel R. *2 Maccabees*. Commentaries on Early Jewish Literature. Berlin: de Gruyter, 2008.

Schwartz, Seth. "Language, Power and Identity in Ancient Palestine." *Past & Present* 148 (1995): 3–47.

Schwarz, W. *Principles and Problems of Biblical Translation: Some Reformation*

*Controversies and Their Background*. Cambridge: Cambridge University Press, 1955.

Segal, Michael. *The Book of Jubilees: Rewritten Bible, Redaction, Ideology, and Theology*. Leiden: Brill, 2007.

Segal, M.H. *A Grammar of Mishnaic Hebrew*. Oxford: Oxford University Press, 1927.

Sevenster, J.N. *Do You Know Greek? How Much Greek Could the First Jewish Christian Have Known?* Supplements to Novum Testamentum 19. Leiden: Brill, 1968.

Shepardson, Christine. "Paschal Politics: Deploying the Temple's Destruction against Fourth-Century Judaizers." *Vigiliae Christianae* 62 (2008): 233–260.

Simon-Shoshan, Moshe. "The Tasks of the Translators: The Rabbis, the Septuagint, and the Cultural Politics of Translation." *Prooftexts* 27 (2007): 1–39.

Simonsohn, Shlomo. "The Hebrew Revival among Early Medieval European Jews." Pages 831–858 in vol. 2 of *Salo Wittmayer Baron Jubilee Volume on the Occasion of His Eightieth Birthday*. Edited by Saul Lieberman. 3 vols. Jerusalem: American Academy for Jewish Research, 1974.

Skarsaune, O. "Evidence for Jewish Believers in Greek and Latin Patristic Literature." Pages 505–567 in *Jewish Believers in Jesus: The Early Centuries*. Edited by Oskar Skarsaune and Reidar Hvalvik. Peabody, Mass.: Hendrickson, 2007.

———. "The Question of Old Testament Canon and Text in the Early Greek Church." Pages 443–450 in *Hebrew Bible/Old Testament: The History of Its Interpretation*. Vol. 1: *From the Beginnings to the Middle Ages (until 1300)*. Part 1: *Antiquity*. Edited by Magne Saebø. Göttingen: Vandenhoeck & Ruprecht, 1996.

Skehan, Patrick W. "The Divine Name at Qumran, in the Masada Scroll, and in the Septuagint." *Bulletin of the International Organization for Septuagint and Cognate Studies* 13 (1980): 14–44.

———. "St. Jerome and the Canon of the Holy Scriptures." Pages 257–287 in *A Monument to St. Jerome: Essays on Some Aspects of His Life, Works, and Influence*. Edited by Francis X. Murphy. New York: Sheed & Ward, 1952.

Skemp, Vincent T.M. "Jerome's Tobit: A Reluctant Contribution to the Genre Rewritten Bible." *Revue bénédictine* 112 (2002): 5–35.

———. *The Vulgate of Tobit Compared with Other Ancient Versions*. Atlanta: Scholars Press, 2000.

Smelik, Willem [F]. "Code-switching: The Public Reading of the Bible in Hebrew, Aramaic and Greek." Pages 123–151 in *Was ist ein Text? Alttestamentliche, ägyptologische und altorientalistische Perspektiven*. Edited by Ludwig Morenz and Stefan Schorch. Berlin: de Gruyter, 2007.

———. 'Justinian's Novella 146 and Contemporary Judaism.' In *The Greek Scriptures and the Rabbis: Studies from the European Association of Jewish Studies Seminar, 2010*. Edited by T.M. Law and A.G. Salvesen. Contributions to Biblical Exegesis and Theology. Leuven: Peeters, *forthcoming*.

———. "Language, Locus, and Translation between the Talmudim." *Journal for the Aramaic Bible* 3 (2001): 199–224.

———. "Language Selection and the Holy Tongue in Early Rabbinic Literature." Pages 91–151 in *Interpretation, Religion and Culture in Midrash and Beyond: Proceedings of the 2006 and 2007 SBL Midrash Sessions*. Edited by Lieve Teugels and Rivka Ulmer. Judaism in Context 6. Piscataway, N.J.: Gorgias, 2008.

———. "The Languages of Roman Palestine." Pages 122–141 in *The Oxford Handbook of Jewish Daily Life in Roman Palestine*. Edited by Catherine Hezser. Oxford: Oxford University Press, 2010.

———. *The Targum of Judges*. Leiden: Brill, 1995.

Sokoloff, Michael, and Joseph Yahalom. "Christian Palimpsests from the Cairo Geniza." *Revue d'Histoire des Textes* 8 (1978): 109–132.

Sommer, Benjamin D. "Did Prophecy Cease? Evaluating a Reevaluation." *Journal of Biblical Literature* 115 (1996): 31–47.

Southwood, Katherine E. "'And They Could Not Understand Jewish Speech': Language, Ethnicity, and Nehemiah's Intermarriage Crisis." *Journal of Theological Studies* 62 (2011): 1–19.

Spolsky, Bernard. "Jewish Multilingualism in the First Century: An Essay in Historical Sociolinguistics." Pages 35–50 in *Readings in the Sociology of Jewish Languages*. Edited by Joshua A. Fishman. Leiden: Brill, 1985.

Sperber, Daniel. "Rabbinic Knowledge of Greek." Pages 627–640 in *The Literature of the Sages. Second Part: Midrash and Targum, Liturgy, Poetry, Mysticism, Contracts, Inscriptions, Ancient Science, and the Languages of Rabbinic Literature*. Edited by Shmuel Safrai, Zeev Safrai, Joshua Schwartz, and Peter J. Tomson. Compendia rerum iudaicarum ad Novum Testamentum 2.3b. Minneapolis: Fortress, 2006.

Stein, Edmund. *Alttestamentliche Bibelkritik in der späthellenistischen Literatur*. Lwow: n.p., 1935.

Steinmann, Andrew E. *The Oracles of God: The Old Testament Canon*. St. Louis: Concordia Academic, 1999.

Stenzel, Meinrad. "Der Bibelkanon des Rufin von Aquileja." *Biblica* 23 (1942): 43–61.

Stone, Michael E. "Armenian Canon Lists V—Anonymous Texts." *Harvard Theological Review* 83 (1990): 141–161.

———. *Fourth Ezra: A Commentary on the Book of Fourth Ezra*. Hermeneia. Minneapolis: Augsburg Fortress, 1990.

Strack, Hermann L., and Paul Billerbeck. *Kommentar zum Neuen Testament aus Talmud und Midrasch*. 6 vols. Munich: C.H. Beck 1922–1961.

Stuhlhofer, Franz. *Der Gebrauch der Bibel von Jesus bis Euseb: eine statistische Untersuchung zur Kanonsgeschichte*. Wuppertal: R. Brockhaus, 1988.

Sundberg, Albert C. "Canon Muratori: A Fourth Century List." *Harvard Theological Review* 66 (1973): 1–41.

———. *The Old Testament of the Early Church*. Harvard Theological Studies 20. Cambridge, Mass.: Harvard University Press, 1964.

Swete, Henry Barclay. *An Introduction to the Old Testament in Greek*. Revised by Richard Rusden Ottley. Cambridge: Cambridge University Press, 1914.

———. *Theodori Episcopi Mopsuesteni in Epistolas B. Pauli Commentarii*. 2 vols. Cambridge: Cambridge University Press, 1880–1882.

Taylor, C. *Hebrew-Greek Cairo Genizah Palimpsests from the Taylor-Schechter Collection: Including a Fragment of the Twenty-second Psalm according to Origen's Hexapla*. Cambridge: Cambridge University Press, 1900.

Taylor, Finian D. "Augustine of Hippo's Notion and Use of the Apocrypha." Dissertation, University of Notre Dame, 1978.

Tcherikover, Victor A., and Alexander Fuks, eds. *Corpus Papyrorum Judaicarum*. 3 vols. Cambridge, Mass.: Harvard University Press, 1957–1964.

Tchernetska, Natalie. "Greek-Oriental Palimpsests in Cambridge: Problems and Prospects." Pages 243–256 in *Literacy, Education and Manuscript Transmission in Byzantium and Beyond*. Edited by Catherine Holmes and Judith Waring. Leiden: Brill, 2002.

Thomson, Francis J. "SS. Cyril and Methodius and a Mythical Western Heresy: Trilinguism. A Contribution to the Study of Patristic and Mediaeval Theories of Sacred Languages." *Analecta Bollandiana* 110 (1992): 67–122.

Toorn, Karl van der. *Scribal Culture and the Making of the Hebrew Bible*. Cambridge, Mass., Harvard University Press, 2007.

Tov, Emanuel. "The Biblical Texts from the Judaean Desert—An Overview and Analysis of the Published Texts." Pages 139–166 in *The Bible As Book: The Hebrew Bible and the Judaean Desert Discoveries*. Edited by Edward D. Herbert and Emanuel Tov. New Castle, Del.: Oak Knoll, 2002.

———. "The Evaluation of the Greek Scripture Translations in Rabbinic Sources." Pages 385–399 in *Interpreting Translation: Studies on the LXX and Ezekiel in Honour of Johan Lust*. Edited by F. García Martínez and M. Vervenne. Leuven: Peeters, 2005. Repr. pages 365–377 in *Hebrew Bible, Greek Bible, and Qumran: Collected Essays*. Tübingen: Mohr (Siebeck), 2008.

———. "The Greek Biblical Texts from the Judean Desert." Pages 97–122 in *The Bible as Book: The Transmission of the Greek Text*. Edited by Scot McKendrick and Orlaith A. O'Sullivan. New Castle, Del.: Oak Knoll, 2003.

———. "The Rabbinic Tradition concerning the 'Alterations' Inserted into the Greek Translation of the Torah and Their Relation to the Original Text of the Septuagint." *Journal for the Study of Judaism* 15 (1984): 65–89. Repr. pages 1–20 in *The Greek and Hebrew Bible: Collected Essays on the Septuagint*. Leiden: Brill, 1999.

———. Review of Kevin G. O'Connell, *The Theodotionic Revision of the Book of Exodus*. *Journal of Biblical Literature* 93 (1974): 114–115.

———. *Scribal Practices and Approaches Reflected in the Texts Found in the Judean Desert*. Leiden: Brill, 2004.

———. *The Text-Critical Use of the Septuagint in Biblical Research*. 2d ed. Jerusalem: Simor, 1997.

———, ed. *The Texts from the Judaean Desert: Indices and an Introduction to the Discoveries in the Judaean Desert Series*. Discoveries in the Judaean Desert 39. Oxford: Oxford University Press, 2002.

———. *Textual Criticism of the Hebrew Bible*. 3d ed. Minneapolis: Fortress, 2012.

Trebilco, Paul. *Jewish Communities in Asia Minor*. Cambridge: Cambridge University Press, 1991.

Tregelles, Samuel Prideaux. *Canon Muratorianus: The Earliest Catalogue of the Books of the New Testament*. Oxford: Oxford University Press, 1867.

Trigg, Joseph W. *Biblical Interpretation*. Wilmington, Del.: Glazier, 1988.

Ulrich, Eugene. "The Canonical Process, Textual Criticism, and Latter Stages in the Composition of the Bible." Pages 267–291 in *Sha'arei Talmon: Studies in the Bible, Qumran, and the Ancient Near East presented to Shemaryahu Talmon*. Edited by Michael Fishbane and Emanuel Tov. Winona Lake, Ind.: Eisenbrauns, 1992. Repr. pages 51–78 in *The Dead Sea Scrolls and the Origins of the Bible*. Grand Rapids: Eerdmans, 1999.

———. *The Dead Sea Scrolls and the Origins of the Bible*. Grand Rapids: Eerdmans, 1999.

———. "Horizons of Old Testament Textual Research at the Thirtieth Anniversary of Qumran Cave 4." *Catholic Biblical Quarterly* 46 (1984): 613–636.

———. "Josephus's Biblical Text for the Books of Samuel." Pages 81–96 in *Josephus, the Bible, and History*. Edited by Louis H. Feldman and Gohei Hata. Detroit: Wayne State University Press, 1989. Repr. pages 184–201 in *The Dead Sea Scrolls and the Origins of the Bible*. Grand Rapids: Eerdmans, 1999.

———. "The Notion and Definition of Canon." Pages 21–35 in *The Canon Debate*. Edited by Lee Martin McDonald and James A. Sanders. Peabody, Mass.: Hendrickson, 2002.

———. "The Palaeo-Hebrew Biblical Manuscripts from Qumran Cave 4." Pages 103–129 in *Time to Prepare the Way in the Wilderness: Papers on the Qumran Scrolls*. Edited by Devorah Dimant and Lawrence H. Schiffman. Leiden: Brill, 1995. Repr. pages 121–147 in *The Dead Sea Scrolls and the Origins of the Bible*. Grand Rapids: Eerdmans, 1999.

———. *The Qumran Text of Samuel and Josephus*. Missoula, Mont.: Scholars Press, 1978.

———. "The Septuagint Manuscripts from Qumran: A Reappraisal of Their Value." Pages 49–80 in *Septuagint, Scrolls and Cognate Writings: Papers Presented to the International Symposium on the Septuagint and Its Relations to the Dead Sea Scrolls and Other Writings*. Atlanta: Scholars Press, 1992. Repr. pages 165–183 in *The Dead Sea Scrolls and the Origins of the Bible*. Grand Rapids: Eerdmans, 1999.

Van Henten, Jan Willem. "The Ancestral Language of the Jews in 2 Maccabees." Pages 53–68 in *Hebrew Study from Ezra to Ben Yehuda*. Edited by William Horbury. Edinburgh: T&T Clark, 1999.

VanderKam, James C. "1 Enoch, Enochic Motifs, and Enoch in Early Christian Literature." Pages 33–101 in *The Jewish Apocalyptic Heritage in Early Christianity*. Edited by James C. VanderKam and William Adler. Compendia rerum iudaicarum ad Novum Testamentum 3.4. Minneapolis, 1996.

———. *The Book of Jubilees*. 2 vols. Corpus Scriptorum Christianorum Orientalium 510–511. Leuven: Peeters, 1989.

———. "Genesis 1 in Jubilees 2." *Dead Sea Discoveries* 1 (1994): 300–321.

———. *From Revelation to Canon: Studies in the Hebrew Bible and Second Temple Literature*. Leiden: Brill, 2000.

———. "Jubilees, Book of." Pages 434–438 in vol. 2 of *Encyclopedia of the Dead Sea Scrolls*. Edited by Lawrence H. Schiffman and James C. VanderKam. 2 vols. Oxford: Oxford University Press, 2000.

VanderKam, James, and Peter Flint. *The Meaning of the Dead Sea Scrolls: Their Significance for Understanding the Bible, Judaism, Jesus, and Christianity*. New York: HarperCollins, 2002.

Veltri, Giuseppe. *Eine Tora für den König Talmai: Untersuchungen zum Übersetzungsverständnis in der jüdisch-hellenistischen und rabbinischen Literatur*. Texts and Studies in Ancient Judaism 41. Tübingen: Mohr (Siebeck), 1994.

———. "Der griechische Targum Aquilas: Ein Beitrag zum rabbinischen Übersetzungsverständnis." Pages 92–115 in *Die Septuaginta zwischen Judentum und Christentum*. Edited by Martin Hengel and Anna Maria Schwemer. Wissenschaftliche

Untersuchungen zum Neuen Testament 72. Tübingen: Mohr (Siebeck), 1994. Repr. pages 75–103 in *Gegenwart der Tradition: Studien zur jüdischen Literatur und Kulturgeschichte*. Supplements to the Journal for the Study of Judaism 69. Leiden: Brill, 2002.

———. *Libraries, Translations, and 'Canonic' Texts: The Septuagint, Aquila, and Ben Sira in the Jewish and Christian Traditions*. Supplements to the Journal for the Study of Judaism 109. Leiden: Brill, 2006.

———. "Die Novelle 146 περὶ Ἑβραίων: Das Verbot des Targumvortrags in Justinians Politik." Pages 116–130 in *Die Septuaginta zwischen Judentum und Christentum*. Edited by Martin Hengel and Anna Maria Schwemer. Tübingen: Mohr (Siebeck), 1994.

———. "The Septuagint in Disgrace: Some Notes on the Stories on Ptolemy in Rabbinic and Medieval Judaism." Pages 142–154 in *Jewish Reception of Greek Bible Versions: Studies in Their Use in Late Antiquity and the Middle Ages*. Edited by Nicholas de Lange, Julia G. Krivoruchko, and Cameron Boyd-Taylor. Tübingen: Mohr (Siebeck), 2009.

Verheyden, Joseph. "The Canon Muratori: A Matter of Dispute." Pages 487–556 in *The Biblical Canons*. Edited by J.-M. Auwers and H.J. de Jonge. Bibliotheca Ephemeridum Theologicarum Lovaniensium 163. Leuven: Leuven University Press, 2003.

Vermes, Geza. *Discovery in the Judean Desert*. New York: Desclee Company, 1956.

Wacholder, Ben Zion. "The Ancient Judaeo-Aramaic Literature (500–164 BCE): A Classification of Pre-Qumranic Texts." Pages 257–281 in *Archaeology and History in the Dead Sea Scrolls: The New York University Conference in Memory of Yigael Yadin*. Edited by Lawrence H. Schiffman. Sheffield: JSOT Press, 1990.

Wallraff, Martin, ed. *Iulius Africanus Chronographiae: The Extant Fragments*. Translated by William Adler. Die griechischen christlichen Schriftsteller der ersten drei Jahrhunderte, Neue Folge 15. Berlin: de Gruyter, 2007.

Walter, Nikolaus. *Der Thoraausleger Aristobulos: Untersuchungen zu seinen Fragmenten und zu pseudepigraphischen Resten der jüdisch hellenistischen Literatur*. Berlin: Akademie-Verlag, 1964.

Wasserstein, Abraham and David J. Wasserstein. *The Legend of the Septuagint: From Classical Antiquity to Today*. Cambridge: Cambridge University Press, 2006.

Weber, Robert and Roger Gryson, eds. *Biblia Sacra iuxta vulgatam versionem*. 4th ed. Stuttgart: Deutsche Bibelgesellschaft, 1994.

Weitzman, Steve. "Why Did the Qumran Community Write in Hebrew?" *Journal of the American Oriental Society* 119 (1999): 35–45.

Wendland, Paul, ed. *Aristeae ad Philocratem Epistula cum ceteris de origine versionis LXX interpretum testimoniis*. Leipzig: Teubner, 1900.

Wermelinger, Otto. "Le canon des latins au temps de Jérôme et d'Augustin." Pages 153–196 in *Le Canon de l'Ancien Testament: Sa formation et son histoire*. Edited by Jean-Daniel Kaestli and Otto Wermelinger. Geneva: Labor et Fides, 1984.

Werner, Eric. "Melito of Sardis, the First Poet of Deicide." *Hebrew Union College Annual* 37 (1966): 191–210.

Wevers, John William. "The Dead Sea Scrolls and the Septuagint." *Bulletin of the International Organization of the Septuagint and Cognate Studies* 38 (2005): 1–24.

———. "The Earliest Witness to the LXX Deuteronomy." *Catholic Biblical Quarterly* 39 (1977): 240–244.

———, ed. *Exodus*. Septuaginta 2.1. Göttingen: Vandenhoeck & Ruprecht, 1991.

———. "The Interpretive Character and Significance of the LXX." Pages 84–107 in *Hebrew Bible/Old Testament: The History of Its Interpretation*. Vol. 1: *From the Beginnings to the Middle Ages (until 1300)*. Part 1: *Antiquity*. Edited by Magne Saebø. Göttingen: Vandenhoeck & Ruprecht, 1996.

———. "Die Methode." Pages 12–19 in *Das Göttinger Septuaginta-Unternehmen*. Edited by Robert Hanhart and John William Wevers. Göttingen: Vandenhoeck & Ruprecht, 1977.

———. "PreOrigen Recensional Activity in the Greek Exodus." Pages 121–139 in *Studien zur Septuaginta—Robert Hanhart zu Ehren: aus Anlass seines 65. Geburtstages*. Edited by Detlef Fraenkel, Udo Quast, and John Wm Wevers. Göttingen: Vandenhoeck & Ruprecht, 1990.

———. *Text History of the Greek Deuteronomy*. Göttingen, 1978.

———. *Text History of the Greek Exodus*. Göttingen, 1992.

White, Carolinne. *The Correspondence (394–419) between Jerome and Augustine of Hippo*. Lewiston, N.Y.: Mellen, 1990.

Wiles, Maurice F. *The Divine Apostle: The Interpretation of St. Paul's Epistles in the Early Church*. Cambridge: Cambridge University Press, 1967.

Williams, Margaret. *The Jews among the Greeks and Romans: A Diasporan Sourcebook*. Baltimore: Johns Hopkins University Press, 1998.

Williams, Megan Hale. *The Monk and the Book: Jerome and the Making of Christian Scholarship*. Chicago: University of Chicago Press, 2006.

Williamson, H.G.M. *Ezra, Nehemiah*. Word Biblical Commentary 16. Waco, Tex., 1982.

Winston, David. "Aspects of Philo's Linguistic Theory." *Studia Philonica Annual* 3 (1991): 109–125.

Wise, Michael Owen. "Accidents and Accidence: A Scribal View of Linguistic Dating of the Aramaic Scrolls from Qumran." Pages 123–166 in *Studies in Qumran Aramaic*. Edited by T. Muraoka. Abr-Nahrain: Supplement Series 3. Leuven: Peeters, 1992. Repr. pages 103–151 in *Thunder in Gemini: and Other Essays on the History, Language and Literature of Second Temple Palestine*. Sheffield: Sheffield Academic, 1994.

Wong, Chan-Kok. "Philo's Use of *Chaldaioi*." *Studia Philonica Annual* 4 (1992): 1–14.

Wooden, R. Glenn. "The Role of 'the Septuagint' in the Formation of the Biblical Canons." Pages 129–146 in *Exploring the Origins of the Bible: Canon Formation in Historical, Literary, and Theological Perspective*. Edited by Craig A. Evans and Emanuel Tov. Grand Rapids: Baker, 2008.

Wright, Benjamin G., III. "Access to the source: Cicero, Ben Sira, the Septuagint and their Audience." *Journal for the Study of Judaism* 34 (2003): 1–27.

———. "Translation as Scripture: The Septuagint in Aristeas and Philo." Pages 47–61 in *Septuagint Research: Issues and Challenges in the Study of the Greek Jewish Scriptures*. Edited by Wolfgang Kraus and R. Glenn Wooden. Atlanta: Society of Biblical Literature, 2006.

———. "Translation Greek in Sirach in Light of the Grandson's Prologue." Pages 75–94 in *The Texts and Versions of the Book of Ben Sira: Transmission and Interpreta-*

*tion.* Edited by Jean-Sébastien Rey and Jan Joosten. Supplements to the Journal for the Study of Judaism 150. Leiden: Brill, 2011.

———. "Why a Prologue? Ben Sira's Grandson and His Greek Translation." Pages 633–644 in *Emanuel: Studies in the Hebrew Bible, Septuagint, and Dead Sea Scrolls in Honor of Emanuel Tov.* Edited by Shalom M. Paul, Robert A. Kraft, Lawrence H. Schiffman, and Weston W. Fields. Supplements to Vetus Testamentum 94. Leiden: Brill, 2003.

Wright, John "Origen in the Scholar's Den: A Rationale for the Hexapla." Pages 48–62 in *Origen of Alexandria: His World and His Legacy.* Edited by Charles Kannengiesser and William L. Petersen. Notre Dame, Ind.: University of Notre Dame Press, 1988.

Yadin, Yigael. "Expedition D." *Israel Exploration Journal* 11 (1961): 36–52.

———. "Expedition D—The Cave of Letters." *Israel Exploration Journal* 12 (1962): 227–257.

Yadin, Yigael, Jonas C. Greenfield, Baruch A. Levine, and Ada Yardeni, eds. *The Documents from the Bar Kokhba Period in the Cave of Letters: Hebrew, Aramaic, and Nabatean-Aramaic Papyri.* 2 vols. Judean Desert Studies. Jerusalem: Israel Exploration Society, 2002.

Yadin, Yigael, and Joseph Naveh, eds. *Masada: The Yigael Yadin Excavations 1963–1965: Final Reports.* Vol. 1: *The Aramaic and Hebrew Ostraca and Jar Inscriptions.* Jerusalem: Israel Exploration Society, 1989.

Yahalom, Joseph. "Angels Do Not Understand Aramaic: On the Literary Use of Jewish Palestinian Aramaic in Late Antiquity." *Journal of Jewish Studies* 47 (1996): 33–44.

Yardeni, Ada. *The Book of Hebrew Script: History, Palaeography, Script Styles, Calligraphy & Design.* London: Oak Knoll, 2002.

Zahn, Theodor. *Geschichte des neutestamentlichen Kanons.* 2 vols. Erlangen: A. Deichert, 1888–1892. Repr. New York: Georg Olms, 1975.

Zeitlin, Solomon. "An Historical Study of the Canonization of the Hebrew Scriptures." *Proceedings of the American Academy of Jewish Research* 3 (1931–1932): 121–158. Repr. pages 164–201 in *The Canon and Masorah of the Hebrew Bible: An Introductory Reader.* Edited by Sid Z. Leiman. New York: Ktav, 1974.

———. "Jewish Apocryphal Literature." *Jewish Quarterly Review* 40 (1950): 223–250.

Ziadé, Raphaëlle. *Les martyrs Maccabées: de l'histoire juive au culte chrétien. Les homélies de Grégoire de Nazianze et de Jean Chrysostome.* Leiden: Brill, 2007.

Ziegler, Joseph, ed. *Jeremiah, Baruch, Threni, Epistula Jeremiae.* Septuaginta 15. Göttingen: Vandenhoeck & Ruprecht, 1957.

———. *Sapientia Iesu Filii Sirach.* 2d ed. Septuaginta 12.2. Göttingen: Vandenhoeck & Ruprecht, 1980.

Ziegler, Joseph, Olivier Munnich, and Detlef Fraenkel, eds. *Susanna, Daniel, Bel et Draco.* 2d ed. Septuaginta Gottingensis 16.2. Göttingen: Vandenhoeck & Ruprecht, 1999.

# INDEX OF ANCIENT SOURCES

## 1. BIBLE